W9-BRF-908

JEWISH CEMETERY ▲ 191 | CASTLE ▲ 201 | STRAHOV MONASTERY ▲ 237

↑
VELETRŽNÍ
PALACE

HLÁVKŮV MOST

OSTROV ŠTVANICE

KARLÍN

EŠE

ŠVERMŮV MOST

VLTAVA→

FRANTIŠKU

POBŘEŽNÍ

SOKOLOVSKÁ

KLÁSTER
SV. ANEŽKY

KLIMENTSKÁ

REVOLUČNÍ

KŘIŽÍKOVA

JOSEFOV

PETRSKÁ

WILSONOVA

ŽIŽKOV

NA PORÍČÍ

TOWN
UARE
✪

ŽEL. ST. PRAHA
MASARYKOVO
NÁDRAŽÍ

HUSITSKÁ

HUSITSKÁ

KAROLINUM

OBCENI DŮM

HYBERNSKÁ

ARÉ MĚSTO

SEIFERTOVA

JINDŘIŠSKÁ

VÁCLAVSKÉ NÁMĚSTÍ

ŽEL. ST. PRAHA
HLAVNÍ
NÁDRAŽÍ

VLKOVA

KUBELÍKOVA

VODIČKOVA

VOZOVÁ

STÁTNÍ
OPERA

RIEGROVY
SADY

MĚST.
NÍCE

NÁRODNÍ
MUZEUM

VINOHRADY

VINOHRADSKÁ

POLSKÁ

ŽITNÁ

SLEZSKÁ

JEČNÁ

KORUNNÍ

CAFÉ SLAVIA ▲ 298 | MASARYK QUAY ▲ 301 | VYŠEHRAD ▲ 325

monastery boasts two magnificent Baroque libraries and a fine picture gallery.

MALÁ STRANA
With its Renaissance and Baroque houses, this district is one of the most atmospheric in Prague.

ST NICHOLAS' CHURCH
This Baroque church in Malá Strana is encrusted with guilding, stucco and trompe l'œil painting.

KAMPA ISLAND
The island's mills, park and lawns make it a haven of peace.

CAFÉ SLAVIA
Favorite haunt of the Czech intelligentsia, this café is imbued with the memories and atmosphere of days gone by.

MASARYK QUAY
The neo-Renaissance, neo-Baroque and Art-

Nouveau façades that line the quay make it a superb architectural ensemble.

VYŠEHRAD
This hill, the legendary birthplace of the princes of Bohemia, commands fine views over Prague.

PRAGUE

● Encyclopedia section

■ **NATURE** The natural heritage: species and habitats characteristic to the area covered by the guide, annotated and illustrated by naturalist authors and artists.

HISTORY OF PRAGUE The impact of international history on local events, from the arrival of the first inhabitants, with key dates appearing alongside the text.

ARTS AND TRADITIONS Customs and traditions in Prague and their continuing role in contemporary life.

ARCHITECTURE The architectural heritage, focusing on style and topology; a look at urban buildings and major civil, religious and military monuments.

AS SEEN BY PAINTERS A selection of paintings by artists from different periods and countries, arranged thematically.

AS SEEN BY WRITERS An anthology of texts, extracts taken from different periods and countries, arranged thematically.

▲ Itineraries in Prague

Each itinerary begins with a map of the area to be explored.

✪ **NOT TO BE MISSED** These sites, highlighted in gray boxes, should be seen at all costs.

★ **EDITOR'S CHOICE** Sites singled out by the editor for special attention.

INSETS On richly illustrated double pages, these insets turn the spotlight on subjects deserving more in-depth treatment.

◆ Practical information

All the travel information you will need before you go and when you get there.

USEFUL ADDRESSES A selection of hotels, restaurants and brasseries.

PLACES TO VISIT A handy table of addresses and opening hours.

APPENDICES Bibliography, list of illustrations and general index.

MAP SECTION Maps of all the areas covered by the guide and a street index; these maps are marked out with letters and figures making it easy for the reader to pinpoint a region or site. A plan of local transport.

◆ OLD TOWN SQUARE, JOSEFOV

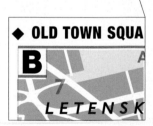

◆ OLD TOWN SQUA

Each map in the section is designated by a letter. In the practical information section, all the sites of interest are given a map reference (for example: ◆ **B** C4).

The mini-map pinpoints the itinerary within the wider area covered by the guide

★ The star symbol indicates sites singled out by the editor for special attention.

The itinerary map shows the main sites and the places not to be missed.

▲ FROM OLD TOWN SQUARE TO CHARLES BRIDGE

1. CLEMENTINUM ● 2. SMETANA MUSEUM ▲ 3. CHURCH OF ST FRANCIS ▲ 4. ST GILES ▲ 5. CHURCH OF ST SAVIOR ▲ 6. VIA ... ▲ 7. "AT MINUTE" HOUSE ▲ 8. CELETNÁ STREET ▲ 9. KINSKÝ PALACE ▲ 10. TOWN HALL ▲ 11. GALLAS PALACE ▲ 12. KAROLINUM ▲ 13. TÝN COURTYARD ▲ 14. CHURCH OF ST NICHOLAS ▲ 15. OLD TOWN SQUARE ● 16. "OUR LADY" ... ▲ 17. CHURCH OF OUR LADY ▲

OLD TOWN SQUARE ★ ▲ 138

The histories of Old Town (Staré Město) and its Square (Staroměstské náměstí) are closely inter-related. Much of our knowledge of the city in its earliest days is based

◻ One day
◆ B A4-B4-C4

OLD TOWN SQUARE, THE HEART OF PRAGUE ❖ Old Town Square, an open space in the midst of narrow streets, is dominated by the soaring spires of the Church of Our Lady of Týn, Golz-Kinský Palace and the statue of Jan Hus. It is worth climbing the clocktower of the Old Town Hall for the 360° view over Prague that it offers. From ground level, the performance of the Apostles in the astronomical clock is an entertaining spectacle. For a drink afterwards, avoid the cosmopolitan café terraces in the square in favor of the quieter ones to be found in Týn Courtyard.

on a document written by an emissary of the Caliph of Cordoba, the diplomat and merchant Ibrahim Ibn Jacob. His stay from 965 to 966 inspired him to write of his journey, during which he came to realize that the city was an important center of commercial exchange. The opening of the city to the west and the development of commerce encouraged Soběslav I (1125–40) to play a more active role in the commercial Týn Courtyard (Ungelt) ▲ 160 behind the Church of Our Lady. This was the start of Prague's role as an important commercial center.

NEWCOMERS. New communities from Piedmont, Burgundy, Germany and Flanders settled in Prague during the 12th century, and their arrival increased the amount of business transactions, already stimulated by the needs of the Royal Court. At this time, the Germans occupied an area that was to become Old Town Square; there, they founded a church dedicated to St Nicholas ▲ 145, the patron saint of merchants, and they also built a hospital, houses and shops. The square began to look a little as it does today: the houses on the north, east and south sides, including Kinský Palace, are aligned on axes already determined in the 12th and 13th centuries.

AIMING FOR MUNICIPAL STATUS. In 1230, Old Town acquired the status of a town, but it was not entitled to have a Town Hall, the decisive symbol in the Middle Ages of city freedom. It was not for another hundred years, in 1338, that John of Luxemburg granted the right to erect a Town Hall in Old Town Square. With political and judiciary power now hand in hand, the bourgeoisie sought to install a prison inside the Town Hall and stocks in the square. As the town's political center, the square established itself as the economic and social epicenter, and it was inhabited by the wealthiest families. Apart from commercial activities, the square also hosted festive occasions, including tourneys.

HISTORIC EVENTS. Down through the centuries, Old Town Square has been the scene of momentous and bloody events: after his victory at White Mountain on November 8, 1620 ● 34, Ferdinand II sent twenty-seven noble and bourgeois rebels to the scaffold (the deed is today marked by a rectangle of black stones); then, twelve heads were hung on the tower on Charles Bridge for ten long years, and were not buried until 1631, the Lutheran Saxons occupying Prague. On May 8–9, 1945, the partisans fought a ferocious battle here to liberate the city from the Nazis, and then on February 21, 1948, Klement Gottwald proclaimed the victory of Soviet Communism ● 39 from the balcony of Kinský Palace ▲ 139. In a previous age, the Palace had housed the German-language Imperial High School attended by the German-speaking intelligentsia, notably Max Brod and Kafka ▲ 110; and by 1968, the square had come to be known as "Hyde Park" and was soon the favorite venue for student meetings. Today, more people meet up and go for walks here than in Wenceslas Square or any other square in Prague.

Above: an old engraving showing the execution of rebel leaders in 1621. Below: scenes of the liberation of Prague in Old Town Square, May 1945.

136

137

At the beginning of each itinerary, the distance, the suggested mode of travel and the time it will take to cover the area are indicated beneath the maps.
🚶 On foot

❖ This symbol indicates places not to be missed.

● ■ ▲ ◆
The above symbols within the text provide cross-references to a place or a theme discussed elsewhere in the guide.

03

● Encyclopedia section

▲ Itineraries in Prague

◆ Practical information

FROM OLD TOWN SQUARE TO CHARLES BRIDGE ▲ 135
From this square, the heart of the city and the embodiment of its architectural riches, a maze of cobbled lanes lined with Renaissance palaces and Baroque churches leads to the famous Charles Bridge, blackened by the grime of ages. Of special interest is Malé Náměstí (Little Square), where historic Rott House is to be found.

AROUND WENCESLAS SQUARE ▲ 157
Celetná Street leads from the Old Town to Powder Tower. Further on, around Wenceslas Square, focal point of the Velvet Revolution, stretches the New Town, an administrative and banking district where smart hotels and shopping centers, the result of the introduction of a market economy, are also to be found.

FROM THE NA FRANTIŠKU QUARTER TO JOSEFOV ▲ 179
It was in this quarter of the Old Town that Secessionist and Art Nouveau architecture developed in the late 19th century, exemplified by Paris Avenue, with prestigious shops and restaurants. Vestiges of the former Ghetto, which was razed for health reasons, include several synagogues and one of Europe's oldest Jewish cemeteries.

PRAGUE CASTLE ▲ 199
This extensive complex, ancient seat of Czech spiritual and political power, consists of a harmonious group of buildings, including a palace, churches, a convent, museums and gardens overlooking the city. St Vitus' Cathedral, monumental and richly endowed, and Golden Lane, haunt of alchemists, are unmissable features.

FROM HRADČANY TO MALÁ STRANA ▲ 225
The appeal of the Castle district is due in large measure to the peaceful atmosphere that envelops its many palaces and churches, convents and monasteries. Here is the Church of Our Lady of Loreto and Strahov Monastery, which is surrounded by greenery and boasts an outstanding library.

MALÁ STRANA 1: AT THE FOOT OF THE CASTLE ▲ 245
The appealing and atmospheric "Little Town", is laid out around Malostranské Square, over which towers the dazzling St Nicholas' Church. Baroque palaces, parks and courtyards hidden behind the gateways of ancient houses with magical names invite exploration.

MALÁ STRANA 2: FROM KAMPA TO PETŘÍN HILL ▲ 265
From Kampa Island to the top of Petřín Hill, where a belvedere offers a unique panorama over Prague, this itinerary takes in buildings raised by the Knights of Malta, including Our Lady Under the Chain, the oldest church in Malá Strana, and countless burghers' houses.

FROM THE CAROLINUM TO THE NATIONAL THEATER ▲ 277
Starting at the administrative center of the University of Prague and taking in the Estates Theater, Bethlehem Square and the Rotunda of the Holy Cross, this itinerary leads to Národní Avenue with its Art Nouveau façades and the National Theater, symbol of Czech culture. This district also buzzes with student cafés and trendy restaurants.

AROUND CHARLES SQUARE ▲ 299
The area around Charles Square offers much of interest over a wide area. There are many churches and striking Cubist houses, the splendid neo-Baroque and Secessionist façades of Masaryk Quay and the architectural ensemble of Charles Square. Here also are the devilish Faustus House and Villa Amerika, now the Dvořák Museum.

THE OUTSKIRTS ▲ 315
No visit to Prague would be complete without a visit to the Museum of Modern Art, to Troja Castle, in its bucolic setting, and to Zbraslav Convent and the opulent Villa Bertramka. Finally, climb the hill to Vyšehrad Castle, birthplace of Prague and ancient rival to its castle, to take in a sublime panorama of the city.

**NUMEROUS SPECIALISTS AND ACADEMICS
HAVE CONTRIBUTED TO THIS GUIDE**

● Encyclopedia section

NATURE
Philippe Dubois, Karel Štastný
HISTORY OF PRAGUE
Marie-Elisabeth Ducreux,
Antoine Marès, Zdeněk Hojda
LANGUAGE
Dagmar Hobzova
ARTS AND TRADITIONS
Guy Erismann, Daniela Langer,
Danièle Montmarte, Sylvie Clopet,
Gérard-Georges Lemaire,
Petra Jarošová
ARCHITECTURE
Nathalie Vaillant, Jean-Pierre Lange,
Marie-Élisabeth Ducreux, Aleš Vošahlík,
Bruno Queysanne
PRAGUE AS SEEN BY PAINTERS
Gérard-Georges Lemaire
CZECH ART IN THE EARLY 20TH-CENTURY
Gérard-Georges Lemaire
PRAGUE AS SEEN BY WRITERS
Sylvie Germain
FRANZ KAFKA
Patrizia Runfola

▲ Itineraries in Prague

Patrick Jusseaux, Serge Guilbert,
Guy Erismann, Marie-Elisabeth Ducreux,
Zdeněk Hojda, Gérard-Georges Lemaire,
Françoise de Bonnières,
Catherine Monroy, Dagmar Hobzova,
Milena Braud, Olga Bašeová

◆ Practical information

Grégory Pinson, Iveta Kucerová, and
Robert Anderson of the *Financial Times*
for hotels and restaurants

This is a Borzoi Book
published by Alfred A. Knopf

Completely revised and updated in 2003

Copyright © 1994 Alfred A. Knopf, New York.
All rights reserved under International and
Pan-American Copyright Conventions.
Published in the United States by Alfred
A. Knopf, a division of Random House, Inc.,
New York, and simultaneously in Canada by
Random House of Canada Limited, Toronto.
Distributed by Random House, Inc., New York.

Knopf, Borzoi Books, and the colophon are
registered trademarks of Random House, Inc

www.aaknopf.com

Library of Congress
Cataloging-in-Publication Data

Prague. English
Prague/ [Gallimard editions].
p. cm.– (Knopf guides)
Includes bibliographical references and index.
ISBN 0-679-75437-7 : $25.00
1. Prague (Czech Republic) – Guidebooks.
I. Gallimard (Firm) . II. Title. III. Series
DB2607.P735   1994
914.47'12 – dc20
CIP 94-5867

Originally published in France by Nouveaux-
Loisirs, a subsidiary of Editions Gallimard,
Paris, 1994. Copyright © 1994 by Editions
Nouveaux-Loisirs

Translated by
Michael Cunningham and
Dafydd Rees-Roberts

Edited and typeset by
Book Creation Services, London

Printed and bound in Italy by
Editoriale Lloyd

PRAGUE
EDITORS
Julie Wood, Sophie Mastelinck, Anne-J. Magniant,
Claire Burgot (architecture), Alpha Presse (Macha
Séry), Michèle Grinstein, Gonzague de Bouville
(Practical information) Virginia Rigot-Müller
UPDATING
Anne-Sophie Baumann, Philippe Bénet, Nicolas
Christitch, Fanny Labbé, Florence Picquot,
Grégory Pinson, Odile Simon
LAYOUT
Riccardo Tremori, Nicolas Christitch (Practical
information)
PICTURE RESEARCH
William Fischer, Véronique Legrand
TRANSLATION
Claudia Ancelot, Marie-Élisabeth Ducreux,
Milena Braud, Radim Brabec, Émilie Djiboghlian
MAP SECTION
Édigraphie

ILLUSTRATIONS
Nature: Jean Chevallier, François Desbordes,
Claire Felloni, Catherine Lachaud
Architecture: Bruno Lenormand, Maurice
Pommier, Amato Sorro, François Pichon, Jean-
Marie Guillou, Claude Quiec, Jean-Claude Séné,
Philippe Candé
Itineraries: Maurice Pommier, Philippe Candé,
Jean-Michel Kacédan, Laure Massin
Maps: Éric Gillion, Isabelle-Anne Chatelard,
Patrick Merienne
Computer graphics: Édigraphie,
Paul Coulbois, Antoine Fumet

PHOTOGRAPHY
Serge Guibert, Danièle Rolland, Renata
Holzbachová, Philippe Bénet

SPECIAL THANKS TO
Hélène Bourgois, Jean-Pierre Azvazadourian,
Léopold Chappe (Chambre Française du
Commerce Franco-Tchèque, Paris)
and, especially, Marie-Élisabeth Ducreux

Encylopedia section

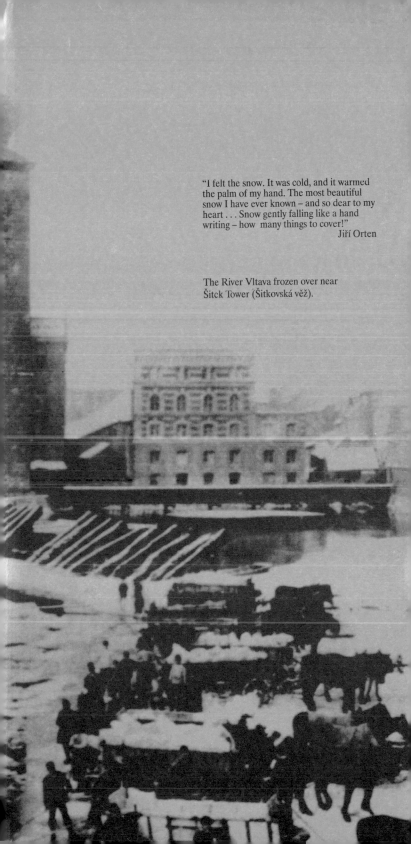

"1 felt the snow. It was cold, and it warmed the palm of my hand. The most beautiful snow I have ever known – and so dear to my heart . . . Snow gently falling like a hand writing – how many things to cover!"
Jiří Orten

The River Vltava frozen over near Šitck Tower (Šitkovská věž).

"Ah! The good old days
when the whole town resembled a thimble, a fan
and a bird's song or a shellfish on the beach!
– farewell, farewell, you beautiful women
whom we met today
and will never see again."
Jaroslav Seifert

A bus tour of Prague at the beginning of the 20th century.

Nature

THE RIVER VLTAVA

GRASS SNAKE
This snake lives on river banks, and hunts amphibians and small rodents.

The River Vltava (pronounced "Valtava"), which is still called the Moldau in German, rises in the Šumava mountains which run along the German border in the southwest of the Czech Republic. It then crosses Prague along a steep-sided valley before joining the River Labe, or the Elbe as it is known in Germany. The Vltava twists and turns through Prague, making any number of winter refuges for water birds forced off the lakes when they ice over. Every year, the river attracts almost five thousand over-wintering birds. Despite a high degree of pollution (salmon disappeared as many as thirty or forty years ago), people still go fishing from boats in the center of the city.

Young

Adult

WHITE WILLOW
The white willow grows abundantly on river banks, and often close to poplars.

MUTE SWAN
This swan has been known to venture into the very center of Prague, but usually breeds on quiet islands and river banks.

Summer

Winter

LITTLE GREBE
The little grebe gathers in large groups during the winter, but can be difficult to spot when mingling with ducks and larger coots.

The construction of dams upstream from Prague has affected the flow of water, and has enabled the population of certain fish to increase in number.

Male Female Male Female

MALLARD
This bird nests in Prague throughout the year. Many have interbred with domestic ducks.

POCHARD
In early autumn, this duck returns to the Vltava where several hundred birds seek refuge, particularly opposite the zoo in Prague.

Male

Female

COOT
The coot feeds on aquatic vegetation, and accounts for the majority of over-wintering birds.

TUFTED DUCK
This kind of duck is extremely common in the Czech Republic. It frequently over-winters with the mallard and the pochard.

Summer Winter

CORMORANT
The population of this bird is increasing in Europe. It usually over-winters close to the river, and in the evenings forms large roosting flocks.

BLACK-HEADED GULL
This bird stays in Prague throughout the year. In winter, the black-headed gull is often found scavenging for food thrown by people walking along the quays and over the bridges.

◼ Petřín Hill

Leaf of oak
Leaf of plane
Leaf of horse-chestnut

Petřín Hill has long been wooded, and even now there are signs of the forests of hornbeam, beech, oak, maple and chestnut that once surrounded the city. Almost 250 species of plants and 600 kinds of fungi have been identified on the mountain's slopes; there are also many rare kinds of wild woodland animals. A tower at the summit of Petřín Hill commands a splendid view of Prague.

Where once there were vineyards, beautifully kept orchards now spread out at the foot of Petřín Hill. Plum, pear and apple trees are the dominant varieties. In spring, the beauty of the area is furthered enhanced by white and pink blossom.

TAWNY OWL
A few pairs still nest in the more densely wooded parts of Petřín Hill.

SPARROWHAWK
There are said to be as many a hundred pairs of this magnificent bird of prey in central Prague.

WOODPIGEON
Over the last five to seven years, the woodpigeon has started living in the city.

GREEN WOODPECKER
This large woodpecker feeds mainly on wood-eating insects and ants.

GREAT SPOTTED WOODPECKER
This type of woodpecker is frequently found in wooded areas. It begins its woodpecking activities in early March.

NUTHATCH
The nuthatch searches tree trunks for grubs and insects.

SPOTTED FLYCATCHER
The color of its plumage helps it to merge into the background.

NOCTULE BAT
Has only recently begun hibernating in Prague. It lives in ventilation ducts.

WOOD ANEMONE
This plant flowers in April, covering the slopes of Petřín Hill in white.

WOLF'S-BANE
The flowers are usually violet, or more rarely yellow. They grow in damp, shaded areas.

This park, laid out on what had once been riverside forest and fields, dates from 1268, when Otakar II turned it into a royal hunting reserve. Stromovka ("Orchard") was turned into a park in 1803 after being almost completely destroyed in the course of the wars that ravaged the region in the 18th century. Today, this 250-acre park contains oak trees over a hundred years old and a remarkable range of original and introduced species. There is also a rose garden, and a number of artificial ponds inhabited by a variety of animals.

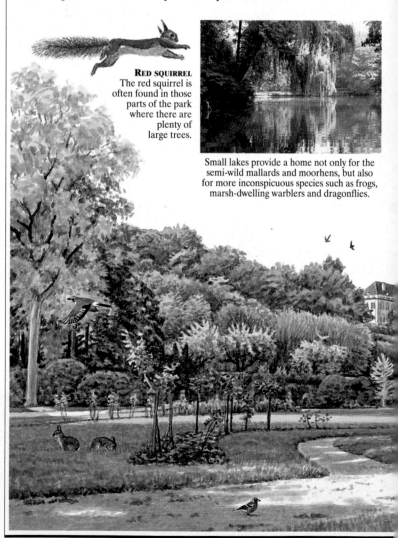

RED SQUIRREL
The red squirrel is often found in those parts of the park where there are plenty of large trees.

Small lakes provide a home not only for the semi-wild mallards and moorhens, but also for more inconspicuous species such as frogs, marsh-dwelling warblers and dragonflies.

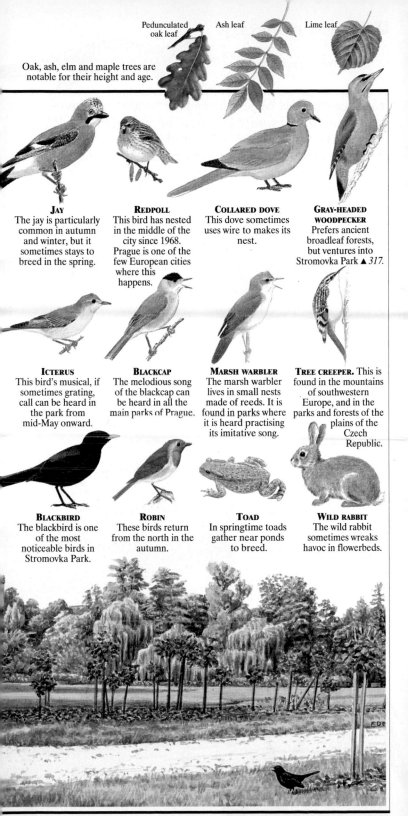

Pedunculated oak leaf

Ash leaf

Lime leaf

Oak, ash, elm and maple trees are notable for their height and age.

JAY
The jay is particularly common in autumn and winter, but it sometimes stays to breed in the spring.

REDPOLL
This bird has nested in the middle of the city since 1968. Prague is one of the few European cities where this happens.

COLLARED DOVE
This dove sometimes uses wire to makes its nest.

GRAY-HEADED WOODPECKER
Prefers ancient broadleaf forests, but ventures into Stromovka Park ▲ *317*.

ICTERUS
This bird's musical, if sometimes grating, call can be heard in the park from mid-May onward.

BLACKCAP
The melodious song of the blackcap can be heard in all the main parks of Prague.

MARSH WARBLER
The marsh warbler lives in small nests made of reeds. It is found in parks where it is heard practising its imitative song.

TREE CREEPER. This is found in the mountains of southwestern Europe, and in the parks and forests of the plains of the Czech Republic.

BLACKBIRD
The blackbird is one of the most noticeable birds in Stromovka Park.

ROBIN
These birds return from the north in the autumn.

TOAD
In springtime toads gather near ponds to breed.

WILD RABBIT
The wild rabbit sometimes wreaks havoc in flowerbeds.

WILDLIFE IN THE CITY

STONE MARTEN
The stone marten lives in the attics and lofts of Prague, and only emerges at night.

Parks, gardens, old cemeteries and the wooded sections of Petřín Hill are all favorite haunts of the birds of Prague. The countryside is not far away and provides a splendid habitat for the wide variety of local fauna. Prague Castle is home to a small colony of kestrels that spend much of their time hunting pigeons.

Kestrels are increasingly settling in large European cities where they can easily find food.

HOUSE SPARROW
House sparrows can be seen everywhere in Prague, but for some reason their numbers are decreasing.

ROCK PIGEON
About 140,000 rock pigeons inhabit Prague. Wounded individuals are easy prey for kestrels and stone martens.

SWIFT
Large numbers of swifts nest under the gutters and eaves of Prague Castle.

HOUSE MARTIN
The house martin often nests in colonies on the tall buildings of Prague.

KESTREL
About ten pairs nest on various buildings in the castle.

BLACK REDSTART
The black redstart is often heard singing from the tops of chimney stacks and television aerials.

MAGPIE
The magpie population is rapidly increasing in cities; it is able to build its nest almost anywhere.

22

History of Prague

FROM THE 9TH TO THE 13TH CENTURIES

7TH CENTURY
Legendary birth of the Přemyslid dynasty (prophecies of Libussa and the ploughman, opposite, right) which was to reign until 1306.

880
The Czech Duke Bořivoj is baptized by Bishop Methodius.

929 or 935
Václav (Wenceslas I) is murdered by his brother, Boleslav. Wenceslas later became the country's patron saint.

995
The ruling Přemyslid kings capture Libice Castle, and thereby succeed in unifying Bohemia.

1039
Břetislav I (1034–55) forces his subjects to obey the fundamental laws of Christianity.

Vyšehrad Codex.

1085
Vratislav II ● 30 is crown first king of Bohemia.

1251–78
The Czech State expands into Austria under Přemysl King Otakar II, known as the "the king of iron and gold".

THE CITY'S ORIGINS. Slav tribes built the first villages near modern Prague as early as the second half of the 6th century, but, seeking protection, moved up into the surrounding hills in the 7th century. Around 880, the dukes who commanded the Czech tribe founded Prague Castle on a promontory overlooking the Vltava, and later, in 900, built the Castle of Chrasten-Vyšehrad. For the most part, people inhabited the area that ran between the two fortresses, but the most important of the colonies was established at the foot of the Castle walls where Malá Strana now stands.

THE BEGINNINGS OF A CHRISTIAN CAPITAL. Around 885, Duke Bořivoj (died 895) built a wooden church within the confines of the Castle; it was dedicated to the Virgin Mary and is the oldest church in Prague. St George's Basilica was built later in 915–21, and this was followed by the Rotunda of St Vitus in 925, after an arm allegedly belonging to that saint was acquired by the Emperor Henry I. The foundation of the first monastery in Bohemia around 970, and the establishment of the Archbishopric of Prague in 973, confirmed the Castle as the center of the ecclesiastical activities of the Czech State as it moved slowly toward unity. After 1070, the Czech monarchy took a new interest in Vyšehrad, and a chapter was founded there; it became the residence of Vratislav II (1061–92), and later Soběslav I (1125–40).

ROMANESQUE TOWN AT THE FOOT OF THE CASTLE WALLS. Writing in 1091, Kosmas, the first Czech chronicler, refers to groups of Jewish merchants settling on the hillside below the Castle and along the road to Vyšehrad. After 1100, there was also a market on the right bank of the Vltava where Old Town Square now stands. An early church dedicated to the Virgin Mary was built there before 1135, and the Týn Courtyard (Ungelt) ▲ *160* was attached to it after 1250. The first stone bridge, Judith Bridge, was begun around 1157 and connected the two banks of the Vltava just a short distance upstream from present-day Charles Bridge. The right bank developed rapidly from the middle of the 12th century onward, and by 1230 a group of stone houses and no fewer than twenty-three Romanesque churches had sprung up.

Fresco depicting Charles IV in the chapel of Our Lady of Karlštejn.

13TH TO 14TH CENTURIES: A MEDIEVAL METROPOLIS

A RESIDENCE FIT FOR KINGS AND EMPERORS. In 1231, King Wenceslas I (1230–53) began the fortification of 346 acres of Old Town (Staré Město). Then, after 1257, the Přemyslid King Otakar II (1253–78) brought together the dispersed settlements of inhabitants within a fortified enclosure called the "New Town", a name that derived in part from the "Little City" (Malá Strana). It was not until 1287 that the territory occupied by Old Town, which was already acknowledged as the capital by the other towns of the kingdom, was legally unified; the Jewish town was not, however, included. It was then decided to raise the level of the town by 7–10 feet so as to protect it from flooding. Numerous religious houses were also constructed, including the Convent of St Agnes ▲ *182* and Na Františku founded on the banks of the Vltava around 1294 by Anežka Přemyslovna, the sister of King Wenceslas I, and shared by the Poor Clares and the Franciscans. A form of administration governing the town is documented in texts dated 1258; Old Town had its own Chancellery in 1229 and a Town Hall was built in 1338. The growing power of the nobility was demonstrated when, in 1306, they attempted to seize power after the death of the last of the Přemyslids. Trades were organized into corporations around 1318 and, around 1330, the first hygiene regulation was published and the first roads paved.

PRAGUE, METROPOLIS OF THE EMPIRE. Charles of Luxemburg, son of the last Přemyslid, Eliška, and heir to the throne, settled in Prague in 1333. He had the palace rebuilt within the Castle grounds, and in 1344 obtained from the Pope the right to make the bishopric of Prague an archbishopric. The Gothic cathedral's foundation stone was laid the same year. Even before he was crowned in 1346, Charles IV (whose seal is shown below) announced the establishment of the Universities of Prague and New Town, together with a wide-ranging plan for the town; work began on the two projects in the following year. In 1357, Petr Parléř, who was responsible for so many Gothic buildings in Prague, started work on a new stone bridge (modern Charles Bridge) with two towers, and by 1395, twenty-five new religious houses had been founded in Prague and the surrounding area. The population grew rapidly: with 40,000 inhabitants at the end of Charles IV's reign, it was the largest city in central Europe. Old Town was the bastion of the rich bourgeoisie while New Town attracted artisans and was the scene of the politicization of the corporations. Prague was spared the epidemic that followed the plague of 1348, fell victim to a similar disaster in 1380. In 1389, a huge pogrom against the Jewish inhabitants, who were accused of poisoning the water in the wells, took place.

Vladislav II Jagiello.

1300
Wenceslas II (1278–1305) is elected King of Poland. His monetary reforms included the striking of silver "groš" in Prague.

1306
The last of the Přemyslids, Wenceslas III (1305–6), was murdered at Olomouc at the instigation of his Polish enemies.

1325
The composer Guillaume de Machaut moved to the Court on the invitation of John of Luxembourg.

1348
The Carolinum University is founded in Prague.

1356
Charles IV's Golden Bull proclaimed the Czech State's absolute independence from the Empire, and made the King of Bohemia the first lay Elector of the Empire.

Crown of Bohemia.

The Hussite Crisis of the 15th Century

1402
John Huss begins preaching at Bethlehem Chapel.

Hussite troops

WENCESLAS IV COMES TO POWER. Under Wenceslas (or Václav) IV, Prague lost the supremacy it had enjoyed as Charles IV's Imperial residence. Trade slackened, the town grew poor, and social and religious disputes flared up.

Moreover, preachers such as Waldhauser of St Havel, Milíč of Kroměříž, John Huss, Jakoubek of Stríbro and Nicholas of Dresden denounced the Church's wealth and corruption, and called for a return to poverty and the values set out in the Gospels. Tensions began to mount in 1410. The execution in 1412 of three young men for encouraging people to demonstrate against the sale of indulgences was followed by the executions of both

JULY 6, 1415
John Huss dies at the stake in Constance.

1517
Luther starts to preach reform.

John Huss at the stake.

John Huss in Constance and Jeremy of Prague. At that point, the aldermen of Old and New Towns came out against the people; the latter were supported by the Taborites of South Bohemia. On July 30, 1419, the first defenestration at the Town Hall sparked off the revolution, and that same year Prague went to war with Wenceslas IV's successor, his brother King Sigismund. The people's victory, which led to the King's capitulation on June 7, 1421, enabled the town to become a decisive partner in the political life of the Kingdom.

A PARTING OF THE WAYS. The Hussite Wars lasted seventeen years, during which time New Town continued to be more extremist than Old Town; having become more moderate, the latter agreed to the terms proposed by the Four Articles of Prague which had been drawn up in 1419, and had served as the basis for the so-called "Compactata" (Compacts) between the Church, the Christian world, King Sigismund and the Czechs. In Prague, Church property was seized by the Town and no one was able to acquire bourgeois rights without taking Communion in both kinds; the people of Prague vowed that only Czechs should be entitled to this right.

From Utraquism to White Mountain

1526
Louis Jagiello (above), King of Bohemia and Hungary, is killed by the Turks at Mohács.

Utraquism takes its name from *sub utraque specie* (under both forms, i.e. bread and wine). The Utraquist George of Poděbrady, King of Bohemia from 1458 to 1471, endeavored to make Prague both more beautiful and economically successful, while at the same time respecting the freedom that had been won in the course of the Hussite Wars. In 1463, his councillor, Marini, produced a commercial plan based on the city's merchants more actively seeking business abroad, and in Venice in particular. It was not, however, until the reign of Vladislas Jagiello, also King of Hungary, that foreign merchants began to return to the Czech capital, and an agreement with Nuremberg once more accorded the city a central role in long-distance commerce. The 15th century was a prosperous period for Prague, but it ended with a number of uprisings in the name of the Reformation. In 1502, the

Rudolph II.

Behem

citizens reinforced the Utraquist union and the order of the towns against the power of the King. In 1526, the new King of Bohemia, Ferdinand of Habsburg, sought to bolster royal power by provoking a revolt of the nobility and the towns in 1547, and the repression of this uprising led to a withdrawal of the privileges that Prague had won during the wars. Later, Emperor Rudolph II (1576–1611) settled in Prague and, for twenty-eight years, the town was again one of the most politically important in Europe. However, the Habsburgs' Catholic absolutism began to weigh on the Czechs, and on May 23, 1618, two Catholic royal lieutenants from Prague were defenestrated at Hradčany. The episode marked the beginning of the Thirty Years' War and foreshadowed the Battle of White Mountain ● 34 in which the Estates of Bohemia were defeated by Catholic forces.

1556
The Jesuits arrive in Bohemia.

1583–1611
The Court of Rudolph II attracts learned men and artists to Prague, including astronomers Tycho Brahe and Johann Kepler, painter Giuseppe Arcimboldo and composer Filippo di Monti.

1686
Buda is wrested from the Turks by the armies of Emperor Leopold I, King of Bohemia and Hungary.

1729
Saint John Nepomuk is canonized.

UNDER THE HABSBURGS

The defeat of the Hussites at White Mountain meant that Protestants were forced to emigrate from Bohemia unless they converted to Catholicism. The victory of the Counter-Reformation was now complete, and the Peace of Westphalia (1648) ensured that Bohemia and Moravia remained under the Habsburgs' Imperial domination. The Kingdom of Bohemia continued to be Catholic until 1781. The Wars of the Austrian Succession (1740–8) against Frederick II of Prussia culminated in the election of Charles of Bavaria by the Diet of Bohemia. Until 1790, the reigns of Maria Theresa of Austria (the wife of Francis of Lorraine, who became Emperor in 1745) and Joseph II (1780–90) marked a period of enlightened absolutism, and the institutions of the Kingdom were fundamentally reformed. From 1749 onward, Bohemia and Moravia were administered in Vienna together with the Habsburgs' "hereditary countries", the future Cisleithenia. Joseph II introduced compulsory education throughout the Habsburg monarchy in 1775, and all schools had to use the vernacular, while in colleges and high schools Latin then German were spoken. He also abolished serfdom in 1780, and established a rule of religious tolerance in 1781 which was also applied to Jews ▲ 185 in 1782.

1784
The four towns of Prague are reunited in a single city.

OCTOBER 29, 1787
Mozart's "Don Giovanni" is premièred at the Nostitz Theater (formerly the Estates Theater).

Joseph II of Habsburg.

The Popular Guard and students standing side by side, 1848.

Czech National Awakening

1804
Francis I becomes Emperor of Austria.

December 2, 1805
Napoleon I defeats the armies of the Tsar and the Emperor of Austria at the Battle of

Austerlitz (Slavkov, near Brno).

1867
Birth of the Austro-Hungarian Empire.

December 8, 1870
Czech Deputies condemn the annexation of Alsace-Lorraine.

Tomáš G. Masaryk arrives in Prague, 1918.

1914
The Archduke Francis Ferdinand is assassinated at Sarajevo. World War One begins.

1938
Under the terms of the Munich Agreement, Czechoslovakia loses a third of its territory to Germany, Hungary and Poland.

The "Awakeners". The beginning of the 19th century was marked by the Czech "national awakening", a movement which received considerable impetus from a group of historians and linguists known as the "Awakeners". As early as 1791, Josef Dobrovský published a manifesto supporting the National Czech Movement, and a history of the Czech language and literature. The Awakeners founded the National Museum ▲ *175* in Prague in 1818; then, Josef Jungmann brought out the first manual of Czech literature (*Slovesnost*) and a history of literature (1825), and František Palacký (left) published a history of Bohemia (*Geschichte von Böhmen*, 1836), which was translated into Czech in 1848. It was during this period that Bohemia, Moravia and Silesia were industrialized.

1848. A pan-Slav congress was held in Prague following the Revolution in France. After forbidding all revolutionary movements, the Diet of the Austrian Empire abolished all feudal rights, putting an end to serfdom. However, following the return of a régime that had reneged on individual freedoms, František Palacký and František Ladislav Rieger sought to gain the support of Napoleon III and the Russians.

Leading up to World War One. The attempt to link Czechs to the Austro-Hungarian compromise of 1867 foundered, and Czech Deputies joined the opposition. Next, the Czech language acquired the same status as German, and a Czech-language university was re-founded in 1881. As Austrian subjects, the Czechs entered the war in 1914 on the side of their masters, albeit unwillingly, but by 1915 the idea of a Czech and Slovak federation was beginning to gain support in the United States, thanks to the efforts of Masaryk and Beneš.

A Republic. After the 1918 Armistice, Czechoslovakia became an independent republic, with Tomáš Garrigue Masaryk (1850–1937) as its first president. The country's constitution was influenced by the French model, and an alliance, with an undertaking to provide military assistance, was signed with France in 1925. Edvard Beneš succeeded Masaryk in 1935, and signed a treaty with the USSR.

World War Two. Under the Munich Agreement of 1938, Czechoslovakia was abandoned by the Allies and lost a third of its territory. The Czech Resistance began to form, and in London Beneš took over the Liberal Democratic Movement. Meanwhile, the leaders of the Czech Communist Party, including Gottwald ● *39*, fled to Moscow. Following the National Slovak Revolution, there was an uprising in Prague

Edvard Beneš and
Winston Churchill.

on May 5, 1945, and
four days later Soviet
troops allowed into
Prague by the American Army found a city that had already
liberated itself. On its return from exile, Beneš'
government persuaded the Allies to expel up to
two million Germans.

1945
*60,000 regular soldiers
and 40,000 members
of the Resistance
fought under the
Czechoslovak flag.*

FROM STALINIZATION TO NORMALIZATION.

The Communist Klement Gottwald formed a
coalition government in 1946 and, in February
1948, the ruling Communists established a Stalinist
régime of nationalization and political trials.
From 1953 to 1968 Antonín Novotný took
over from Gottwald. The historic
"Prague Spring" of 1968 ● *40* ended
with Czechoslovak resistance being
crushed by the USSR; then, the Slovak
Gustav Husák, First Secretary of the
Communist Party, took control of the
country and aligned himself with
Moscow. In 1970 and 1971, 500,000
Czechoslovak Communists were
expelled from the Party, and society
was "normalized". Charter 77, drawn up by Jan Patočka in
1977, was signed by 242 intellectuals, including Václav Havel.
In 1986, Jakeš replaced Husák, who stayed on as President;
the official slogan was "Perestroika" (*přesavba*).

Pro-Soviet
demonstration in
Prague in 1950.

ENGELS

AUGUST 1968
*Troops from Warsaw
Pact countries,
excluding Ceaucescu's*

PRAGUE, CAPITAL OF THE CZECH REPUBLIC

THE VELVET REVOLUTION. The huge demonstrations of
November 1989 (below, left) ▲ *173* were sustained by the
creation of the Civic Forum: the Velvet Revolution was under
way. On December 29, Václav Havel ● *41* was elected
President, and from 1990 things began to move quickly with
the departure of the Soviet army of occupation, the initiation
of parliamentary and local elections, an end to the friendship
treaty with the Soviet Union, and the removal of the
requirement for visas for most European countries.

TWO REPUBLICS. On June 8, 1992, the party of Václav Klaus
and that of Vladimír Mečiar in Slovakia won parliamentary
elections, and the process of separating the two countries
started. January 1, 1993 marked the end of the Czech and
Slovak Federal Republic and of Czechoslovakia, and the birth
of two independent States, the Czech and Slovak Republics.
Václav Havel (below, right) was elected President of the
Czech Republic. He was re-elected in January 1998.

*Romania, invade
Prague.*

JANUARY 16, 1969
*Jan Palach makes a
political statement by
publicly commiting
suicide.*

OCTOBER 1969
*Massive emigration.
Frontiers with the West
closed.*

1991
Dissolution of the USSR.

1991–2
*Success of the "small
privatization" program.*

Crown of the Kings of Bohemia.

The first Czech monarchs were members of the Přemyslid dynasty and were called dukes (Kníže). The title of Duke disappeared under Přemysl Otakar I, and the title of King, which two Přemyslid kings had already had conferred on them personally, became hereditary. If a king had no direct heir, his successor was elected by the Diet. The Jagiellos initiated the practise of having their eldest sons elected and crowned during their own lifetimes. After the Battle of White Mountain, Ferdinand II proclaimed the Kingship of Bohemia to be hereditary in the House of the Habsburgs. In 1804, Francis I became the first Emperor of Austria, a title which his successors retained even after the fall of the Holy Roman Empire (1806).

PŘEMYSLID DYNASTY
The story goes that the founder was a farm-laborer called Přemysl; he became the husband of Princess Libussa, daughter of the patriarch Čech who, legend tells us, led the Czechs to the gates of Prague. The Přemyslid line consists of BOŘIVOJ (9th century),

Barbarossa, PŘEMYSL OTAKAR I (1192–3 and 1197–1230), the first hereditary king after 1198, PŘEMYSL OTAKAR II (1253–78) (right), WENCESLAS I (1230–53), WENCESLAS II (1278–1305), and WENCESLAS III (1305–6), the last member of the Přemyslid Dynasty.

WENCESLAS (or VÁCLAV) (died 929 or 935), VRATISLAV II (1061–92) who was crowned king in 1085 by the Holy Roman Emperor Henry IV, VLADISLAV I (1140–72) who was crowned by the Holy Roman Emperor Frederick

GEORGE OF PODĚBRADY (1458–71), Regent from 1452 to 1458.

JAGIELLO DYNASTY
VLADISLAV JAGIELLO (1471–1516), King of Hungary from 1490. LOUIS JAGIELLO (1516–26) was also King of Hungary, but was killed by the Turks at the Battle of Mohács in 1526.

LUXEMBURG DYNASTY (14TH–15TH CENTURIES)
JOHN OF LUXEMBURG (1310–46) fought on the side of the French during the Hundred Years' War and died at the Battle of Crécy. CHARLES I, known as CHARLES IV (1346–78) (above): during his reign, the Czech State included Bohemia, Moravia, Silesia, the County of Glatz (now Klodsko, Poland), the fief of Cheb, Upper and Lower Lusatia, Brandenburg from 1373 to 1415, and the fief of Upper Palatinate from 1353 to 1373. WENCESLAS, or VÁCLAV IV (1378–1419); and SIGISMUND (1419–20 and 1436–7), who was King of Hungary from 1385.

HABSBURG DYNASTY

16TH–20TH CENTURIES
All the Habsburgs
were crowned Kings
of Bohemia in Prague,
with the exception of
Joseph II (who was
known in the Estates
as the "King wearing a
hat") and the last two
Habsburgs, Francis
Ferdinand I and
Charles I. Francis I
gave himself the title
of Emperor of Austria
on the grounds that,
although Emperor of
the Holy Roman
Empire, he was only
an Archduke of
Austria and King of
Bohemia and
Hungary.
FERDINAND I
(1526–64) (Opposite)
MAXIMILIAN II
(1564–76)
RUDOLPH II
(1576–1611)
MATTHIAS
(1611–19)
FERDINAND II
(1619–37)
FERDINAND III
(1637–57)
LEOPOLD I
(1657–1705)
JOSEPH I
(1705–11)
CHARLES VI
(1711–40)

RUDOLPH II OF HABSBURG
Rudolph was also King of Hungary until 1608.

HABSBURG-LORRAINE DYNASTY
When Maria Theresa married Francis of
Lorraine in 1736, the House of Habsburg
became the House of Habsburg-Lorraine.

MARIA THERESA (1740–80) (above)
JOSEPH II (1780–90)
LEOPOLD II (1790–92)
FRANCIS I (1792–1835)
FERDINAND V (1835–48)
FRANZ JOSEF I (1848–1916)
CHARLES I (1916–18)

● John Huss and the Hussite Movement

At the end of the 14th century, Prague University was the center of a reform movement favoring a return to fundamental Christianity, and poverty and humility for the clergy and the Church. This movement, influenced by the Oxford theologian, John Wycliffe (1320–84), was driven by a conflict between church and royalty. The leader of the reformers, John Huss, reinforced the movement through his powers of oratory and later as a martyr. In the 19th and early 20th centuries, the role of Hussite Reforms in the development of a national consciousness and Czech policy was as important as that of the Battle of White Mountain.

WENCESLAS IV (reigned 1361–1419, far right) King Wenceslas of Bohemia was one of John Huss' supporters between 1409 and 1412.
SIGISMUND OF LUXEMBURG (1368–1437, right) This king of Hungary, brother of Wenceslas IV, attended the Council of Constance.

JOHN HUSS AND REFORM. John Huss (1371–1415, left) studied at Prague University and became Rector in 1409. By 1400, he was a preacher and was two years later appointed Curate of the Bethlehem Chapel ▲ 286, where he remained until 1413. Excommunicated at the Council of Constance in 1411, Huss appeared there once more in 1414. Hussite Reform stated that the Bible was the supreme theological and legal authority, superseding human laws. The Church was to be divested of material goods and temporal powers, and the State should assume responsibility for them. Huss found an ally in Wenceslas IV, who wanted to re-establish his authority to the detriment of the Church; however, growing concerned at the prospect of seeing Bohemia in the grip of heresy, he withdrew his support in 1412.

"Pravda zvítězí"
(Truth shall overcome)

John Huss, at the stake

THE HUSSITE WARS
After Wenceslas IV died, both the Church and King Sigismund, Pretender to the Bohemian throne, were subjected to intense military pressure. The Hussite Wars raged around the country between 1419 and 1435, with the nobility taking arms and the University attesting Huss' integrity. In 1418, the Synod of Czech Priests approved both the articles of Hussite doctrine and its symbol, the chalice used in Holy Communion.

HUSS AT THE STAKE. John Huss attended the Council of Constance in October 1414 to defend his good faith. He was arrested, thrown into prison and convicted of heresy; on July 6, 1415, Huss was burned at the stake despite a royal safe-conduct and letters of protest from the nobility. As a result of his death, and that of his friend Jeremy of Prague, a year later, the situation intensified. Below: The arrest of John Huss, wearing the cap of a heretic.

● THE BATTLE OF WHITE MOUNTAIN

Ferdinand II of
Habsburg

At the end of the 16th century, the political initiative in the kingdom of Bohemia was held by Catholics, who were in a minority, and the most determined section of non-Catholics did not consolidate their position until 1609, when they persuaded Rudolph II of Habsburg to sign a Letter of Majesty which heralded a new era of religious tolerance. These ideological conflicts culminated in the Defenestration of Prague of 1618, and in the Battle of White Mountain of 1620 which brought defeat for the rebelious Estates of Bohemia.

A "COUNTER-KING"

Ferdinand II succeeded Matthias in 1617 but was officially deposed in August 1619; next came the Calvinist elector palatine Frederick V (below), known as the "Winter King".

THE DEFENESTRATION OF PRAGUE

After 1617, inter-religious antagonism sharpened as a result of the pro-Catholic policies introduced by the Emperor Matthias, successor to Rudolph II. On May 23, 1618, in an attempt to gain the support of those still undecided, radical elements threw two of the King's councillors, Jaroslav Bořita of Martinic and William Count Slavata, from the windows of the chancellery. This event sparked off the Thirty Years' War (1618–48).

MILITARY PRELUDE

The election of Frederick V gave the conflict with a dimension, and the formation of new political groupings duly gave rise to a military crisis.

DEFEAT AT THE BATTLE OF WHITE MOUNTAIN

Frederick V left the castle after the defeat on November 8, 1620, and the capital surrendered on November 11. On November 13

the Estates of Bohemia recognized Ferdinand II as king, and Bohemia was integrated into the Habsburg Empire, converting back to Catholicism and losing its political privileges. In the Czech camp, the defeat was followed by executions, including those of twenty-seven

insurgent leaders in 1621 (above), confiscation of goods, and forced conversion to Catholicism. The Marian Column (right) in Old Town Square symbolized the triumph of Catholicism.

A KEY HISTORICAL EVENT

The Battle of White Mountain was a major turning point in Czech history. Way beyond the immediate repercussions that helped to create the myth, the battle had long-term consequences. For those promoting the Czech revival, it was a disaster, and it became central to subsequent definitions of national identity during the 19th century. The creation of Czechoslovakia in 1918 was viewed by most Czechs as just reparation.

THE BATTLE OF WHITE MOUNTAIN

This decisive battle was fought on the outskirts of Prague around a knoll known as White Mountain (Bílá Hora) ▲ *321*; it lasted no more than two hours.

The Czechoslovak Republic emerged from the ruins of the Austro-Hungarian Empire, and was born without a single drop of blood being spilled. The new State – it included Czechs, Slovaks, Germans, Hungarians, Rutheno-Ukrainians and Poles – was democratic and secular, and the political spectrum took in everything from the Communist Party to the nationalist right. It was also over-industrialized in the west and under-developed in the east and, although in many ways well balanced, it was a country of great geographical contrasts. Czechoslovakia was a model democracy and was profoundly shaken by the economic crisis of 1929 and, on being abandoned by the western powers, it easily succumbed to pressure from Hitler.

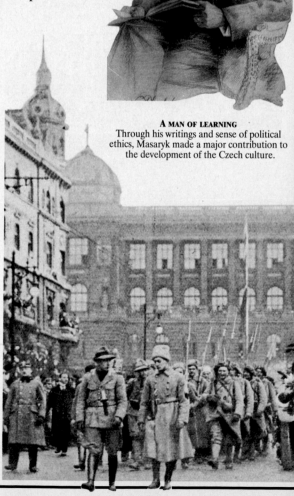

THOMÁŠ GARRIGUE MASARYK
(1850–1937)
This president-philosopher exercised a genuine "respectful dictatorship" because he was able to impress the people with his human and intellectual qualities. As a prominent figure of the expatriate Resistance during the War, he had fought for the emergence of the Czechoslovak State; he then became its President in 1918 and remained in this post until he retired in 1935.

A MAN OF LEARNING
Through his writings and sense of political ethics, Masaryk made a major contribution to the development of the Czech culture.

MASARYK ARRIVES IN WENCESLAS SQUARE IN DECEMBER 1918
Thomáš Garrigue Masaryk returned triumphantly to Prague after four years of exile. He is seen surrounded by Czech and Slovak troops who had fought in Russia on the side of the Allies.

"The Czech spirit was immediately sensitive to its European mission and . . . took all possible steps to show that it was worthy."

Jan Patočka

EDVARD BENEŠ

(1884–1948)
Edvard Beneš remains a key figure in Czechoslovakian history.

THE IMPORTANCE OF MINORITIES

Although the State accorded minorities the international rules of protection, it was sometimes difficult for these groups to accept inferior positions. This was particularly true of the Hungarians and Germans. From 1925 onward, democratic Germans adopted Czechoslovakia and from 1927 to 1938 joined the government, although this did not prevent minorities from being used by Hitler as a lever to overturn the State. The German population of the Sudetenland (above) began to adopt radical politics around 1933, and fell heavily under the influence of National Socialism. The independence of which some Slovaks had dreamed back in 1918 would not become reality until October 1938, with Josef Tiso as head of the government.

MASARYK'S SUCCESSOR

After playing a decisive role in securing recognition for his country, Beneš was Minister of Foreign Affairs until 1935, and then President of the Republic. Apostle of collective security, he was appalled by the Munich Agreement of September 1938, but he continued the struggle in exile and returned as leader of his country in April 1945.

Following the Munich Agreement of September 30, 1938, Czechoslovakia was forced to give way to German claims, and the Wehrmacht invaded the Sudetenland. The State was broken up and divided and, on March 14–15, 1939, Hitler invaded, turned Czechoslovakia into a protectorate and lent his support to Slovakian independence. The Slovaks' initial delight soon turned into rejection of their Fascist government, which became increasingly subservient to its protectors. The extermination of the Jews affected both parts of the country but on the whole their experiences were very different. The people therefore remembered things in dissimilar ways, and this meant that they retained different attitudes after the Liberation.

Arrival of Nazi troops in Prague in 1939. The Czech Resistance was harshly put down, and Czech Jews exterminated.

Territories claimed by Berlin before October 1

Regions subject to plebiscites

GERMANY

Prague

SLOVAKIA

GERMANY

A TIME OF ADVERSITY
In September and October 1938, the Czech lands lost their peripheral territories, inhabited by Germans since the 13th century, and Hungary annexed the prosperous areas in the south of Slovakia which had a Hungarian majority. On March 15, 1939, the Wehrmacht invaded the Second Republic and turned it into the Protectorate of Bohemia-Moravia and an independent Slovak State, a satellite of Nazi Germany. Many politicians, under the leadership of Beneš ● 37, fled to London; there, they sought assurance from the Allies that Czechoslovakia would be independent again.

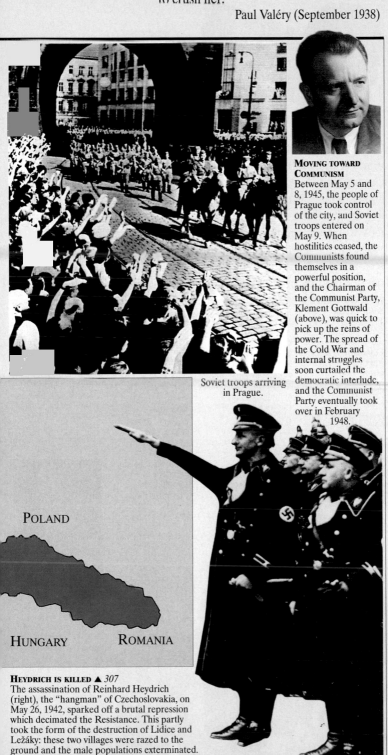

"Circumstances have made Czechoslovakia into a keystone . . .
Everything will collapse if she is unable to resist the attempts
to crush her."

Paul Valéry (September 1938)

MOVING TOWARD COMMUNISM

Between May 5 and 8, 1945, the people of Prague took control of the city, and Soviet troops entered on May 9. When hostilities ceased, the Communists found themselves in a powerful position, and the Chairman of the Communist Party, Klement Gottwald (above), was quick to pick up the reins of power. The spread of the Cold War and internal struggles soon curtailed the democratic interlude, and the Communist Party eventually took over in February 1948.

Soviet troops arriving in Prague.

POLAND

HUNGARY   ROMANIA

HEYDRICH IS KILLED ▲ 307

The assassination of Reinhard Heydrich (right), the "hangman" of Czechoslovakia, on May 26, 1942, sparked off a brutal repression which decimated the Resistance. This partly took the form of the destruction of Lidice and Ležáky: these two villages were razed to the ground and the male populations exterminated.

39

● CZECHOSLOVAKIA UNDER THE SOVIET UNION 1948–89

The Communists came to power in February 1948 when the government of the country was in serious crisis. Stalinization was quickly enforced and political repression intensified, affecting even the Communist Party itself. Following Gottwald's death and the waves of anti-authoritarianism that marked the 1960's, the Prague Spring brought real hopes of change, but these were smashed by the Soviet invasion of 1968. That signaled the beginning of normalization, but the Party did not fall until the time of the 1989 demonstrations. Although the new Republic sought European re-integration, it was not able to resist either the national tensions that had been smoldering for so many years, or the dynamic for separation which had been encouraged by politicians – but not noticed by the citizens.

1952: THE GREAT SHOW TRIALS

The trial of Slánský, Secretary General of the Czech Communist Party, was the culmination of a process of repression organized by the Party's upper echelons. Of the fourteen accused, only three escaped execution. This trial was marked by the struggle against "Titoism" in Yugoslavia and by a form of anti-Zionism that came close to anti-Semitism. The rehabilitation of the victims of these trials remained a major political issue until 1968.

1968–9: RESISTANCE

De-Stalinization reached Czechoslovakia late, illustrating the strength of the anti-authoritarian movement of the 1960's. Repression of the opposition did not impede the struggle. As *perestroika* took hold, and the people felt less frightened, the power of the Communists fell away, allowing dissidents to take control.

1968: THE PRAGUE SPRING

In January 1968, the Slovak Alexander Dubček (below) took over from Antonín Novotný as head of the Communist Party. From the spring onward, Dubček opted for reform and the country moved slowly toward liberalization.

NORMALIZATION

Czechoslovakia was invaded by Warsaw Pact troops on August 21, 1968. The country was subjected to a strict régime of normalization and, with the former GDR, became one of the most conservative members of the Soviet bloc. The divorce between power and opinion was now deep-seated.

> "I will take the risk of saying that, despite attractive appearances to the contrary. . . our society is plunging into deeper and deeper crisis."

> Václav Havel to Gustav Husák (1975)

1989 THE "VELVET REVOLUTION"

The gap between the official line and personal convictions had never been so great since 1969. Dissidence was born of this unrest, bolstered by a longing for ethical standards. A few hundred people were grouping

round Charter 77 ● 29, an organization that stood for the defence of human rights; they represented the feelings and aspirations that were now being increasingly shared by the population at large.

1969–89: FROM DISSIDENT TO PRESIDENT

The bourgeois origins of Václav Havel (born 1936) prevented him from having a university education although, as a playwright, he played an important role on behalf of the Writers' Union during the Prague Spring when he was banned from the theater, he became involved in setting up Charter 77, and his activities there earned him several terms of imprisonment. He led the demonstrations of November 17, 1989, and the crowd instinctively called on the man who had always spoken up to take over as President.

Pravda zvítězí: Truth shall overcome. The student struggles of 1989 echoed the last words that John Huss ● 32 uttered at the stake.

**THE KRALICKÁ BIBLE
1579–93**
During the 16th
century, the Unity of
Czech Brethren went
to considerable
lengths to restore the
characteristics of the
Czech language and
to establish them in
written form. As part
of this work, they
published grammars
and made important
contributions to a
consolidation of the
rules of spelling.
However, their finest
work was a
remarkable
translation of the
Bible; this was to
remain a touchstone
of the Czech
language's purity and
style.

INTRODUCTION

Czech is a Western Slavic language like Polish, Slovak and
Serb. It is the official language of the Czech Republic. The
Czech alphabet has thirty-four letters, which are pronounced
as follows:

a (ah)	f (eff)	l (ell)	r (err)	v (vay)
b (bay)	g (gay)	m (emm)	ř (rzh)	w (dvoyitay
c (tsay)	h (hah)	n (enn)	s (ess)	vay)
č (chay)	ch (chah)	ň (enye)	š (esh)	x (iks)
d (day)	i (ee)	o (oh)	t (tay)	y (ypsilon)
ď (diay)	j (yay)	p (pay)	ť (tiay)	z (zett)
e (ay)	k (kah)	q (kvay)	u (oo)	ž (zhet)

Czech makes distinctions between long and short vowels, the
main stress of a word being fixed and usually occurring on the
first syllable of each word. There are no articles in Czech. As
in Latin and German, nouns and adjectives are declined;
there are seven cases.

HISTORY OF THE CZECH LANGUAGE

Until the 14th century, Czech was essentially no more than a
spoken language, although during the 10th and 11th centuries
it sometimes combined with written languages, such as Latin
and Old Slav, to form occasional words (*Bohemica*) and
glosses. Following the political, economic and cultural
expansion that took place toward the end of the 13th century
(in the final years of the Přemyslid dynasty) and during the
14th century (particularly under the reign of Charles IV),
Czech rapidly became the kingdom's language of literature,
administration and law. From the 13th century onward, Czech
underwent major vocalic, consonantal and morphological
changes, and these extended into the 16th, and even the 18th,
centuries. Ultimately, they formed the basis of modern Czech.
Syntax developed under the influence of Latin. Czech
literature grew in stature in the course of the 14th century.
Many literary works of the period are notable for their
concentration on form and their search for elaborate syntax in
the style of medieval Latin prose; the theological works of
Tomáš de Štítný are fine examples of this. Other works drew
their inspiration from the spoken language and the flavor of
popular expressions. Under the influence of religious
reformers and the Hussite movement ● *32*, during a period
extending from the end of the 14th century to the 15th
century, the influence of the spoken language over literary

**JOHN HUSS,
CAMPAIGNER FOR A
NEW LANGUAGE**
"I have written here
as I normally speak,"
John Huss states in
one of his books.
Elsewhere he
recommends, "I ask
that anyone who
writes should not
write in any way
differently from me."

ď ch ň ř š ť ž

language became even more marked. As a result many preachers and theologians, such as John Huss and Petr Chelčický, used the spoken tongue as part of a deliberate policy to popularize the Church's teachings. In an attempt to unite the Czech language, John Huss gave pride of place to the dialect spoken both in Prague, a university city and economic and cultural center, and in the surrounding area. The standard features of Czech are based on this dialect.

JOHN HUSS AND SPELLING REFORM.
Until the time of John Huss, Czech sounds that did not exist in Latin were transcribed by means of two letters. For example, č was written cz (pronounced "ts") and the long a vowel was written aa; this made writing as complicated as it did reading. Huss suggested that spelling could be simplified by the use of diacritics placed over the relevant letter. He also introduced an acute accent to indicate a long vowel, and a dot to indicate a palatalized consonant. Huss's spelling reforms were revised by the Czech Brethren in the 16th century, and later on in the 19th century it was once again simplified by religious reformers.

THE SPREAD OF THE CZECH LANGUAGE. Interest in the Czech language grew toward the end of the 15th century, and even more so during the 16th century. Czech Humanists devoted many of their works to a defence of their mother tongue, which continued to develop throughout this period; for the most part, Latin served as a model for syntax. Lexicological works played a key role, and contained virtually every word in existence together with its Latin, Greek or German equivalent. The activities of the Unity of Czech Brethren also showed the reviving interest in the national language. Of no less importance were the didactic and pedagogical works of Jan Amos Komenský ▲ 262 (Comenius), the last bishop of the Unity of Czech Brethren.

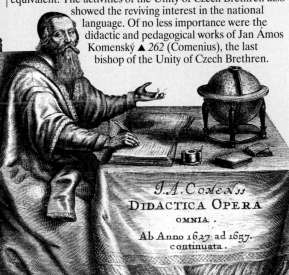

J.A. COMENII
DIDACTICA OPERA
OMNIA.
Ab Anno 1627 ad 1657.
continuata.

THE VYŠEHRAD CODEX
The manuscript of this Codex, which dates from 1085, is kept in the library of Clementinum University ▲ 150. The illustration above is of Saint Wenceslas. The Vyšehrad Codex, the Veleslav Bible, an extract from the Gutenberg Bible and John Huss' manuscripts are the oldest items held in the library. At the time of the Treaty of Versailles in 1919, the Codex was valued at 50 million gold francs.

J. Á. KOMENSKÝ (1592–1670)
Komenský's dictionary, the *Thesaurus linguae bohemicae*, was intended to provide an overall survey of language study during the 16th century. Unfortunately it was almost entirely destroyed in a fire at Lešno, where Komenský was living.

THE PRE-EMINENCE OF GERMAN. The development of literary Czech slowed down in the 17th century, and even more so during the 18th century. Defeat at the Battle of White Mountain (1620) ● 34 forced the non-Catholic intellectual élite to emigrate. Czech was gradually supplanted by German, particularly as the language used in government and in secondary and university teaching; however, it survived orally in religious chants, songs, poetry and popular stories.

REVIVAL. The Czech language began to be revived during the so-called period of "national awakening" which lasted from the late 18th century through the first half of the 19th century. This advance was both demanded and conditioned by various social developments, including the abolition of serfdom in 1781. It also led to an increase in the number of publications in Czech and to developments in literature and the theater. At the end of the 18th century, scholars, linguists, journalists and writers like F. M. Pelcl, J. Nejedlý, Josef Dobrovský, Josef Jungmann and A. J. Puchmajer allotted themselves the task of restoring self-respect to Czech; they aimed to do this by recalling its glorious past. They also produced works of considerable importance including grammars and dictionaries. It was not until the late 19th century that the language was decisively codified through the works of Jan Gebauer, Professor at the Czech University of Prague. These developments survive to the present day. After the Republic was founded in 1918 ● 36, Czech flourished without impediment and continued its process of modernization. Literary works from the inter-war period show both the language's richness and the enthusiasm that it stimulated in writers such as Karel Čapek, Vítězslav Nezval and V. Vančura. It was around this time that the word robot first appeared; this was a neologism created by Čapek for his play *RUR* (*Rossum's Universal Robots*) ● 55 and deriving from the Slavonic stem *rab* (to work, drudge). In 1926 the Prague Circle was founded; it numbered among its members many linguists, including V. Mathesius, B. Havránek, M. Weingart and Roman Jakobson.

AN INTERMINGLING OF LANGUAGES
In the early part of the 20th century, about 415,000 inhabitants of Prague were Czech, 100,000 were Germans, and 25,000 were Jews, of whom some spoke Czech and the rest German. The German minority enjoyed supremacy, but the various languages continued to influence one another: Czech abounded in German words, while German was full of Bohemian expressions. This was the origin of a new language which was far removed from pure German, although it shared the latter's constructions and pronunciation. Writers such as Rilke and Werfel fulminated against this underdeveloped language; by contrast, Kafka found something authentic in its poverty of expression, and this contributed to the purity of his written style.

The poster (right) was designed by Viktor Oliva in 1898 for the Prague review *Zlatá Praha*.

Arts and traditions

Latin Gregorian chant began to evolve in the 9th century. The existence of a canticle in Slavonian, *Hospodine pomiluj ný*, attributed to Saint Adalbert and dating from the same period, establishes that there co-existed in Prague two liturgies that were celebrated in two different languages and which derived from two quite distinct schools of music. Over the centuries, the advances made by Czech music were closely linked to the political, religious and cultural histories of Bohemia and Moravia; this also applied to the history of the whole of western and eastern Europe, of which Prague remained one of the major centers.

The training of cantors ensured the survival of Czech singing. Above: A music lesson.

ANTONÍN DVOŘÁK (1841–1904) Thanks to a cantor from Zlonice, this child of a peasant family, destined to be a butcher, came to Prague and enrolled at the Organ School. He later played viola with the Orchestra of the Provisional Theater under Bedřich Smetana. While Smetana was the musical standard-bearer, Dvořák was more successful at expressing the links that bound the original characteristics of a form of music that was both national and universal. He shone as a symphonist and composer of chamber pieces, and also in the field of oratorios. Only opera, despite his determination to succeed in this field, failed to bring him renown.

> ## "Czech life is in the music."
>
> Bedřich Smetana

The Hussite Movement ● *32* generated a style of canticles in the vernacular which was to have an undisputed impact nationwide. Above: John Huss at the stake; 15th-century gradual.

MUSIC AND HISTORY
Secular music of the Middle Ages reached its apogee during the reigns of Přemysl Otakar II ● *30* and of Charles IV, a man who had been brought up at the French Court. Later, despite defeat at the Battle of White Mountain, music prospered with the assistance of the Unions of Czech and Moravian Brethren, and thanks to the brilliance of the King's Court. During the time of the Thirty Years' War, Czechs made a major impact on the Baroque era. The period of the Enlightenment and the "national awakening" saw the rejection of Italian ideas and oppressive German influences.

BEDŘICH SMETANA
(1824–84). Smetana, who became famous through his *Má vlast*, was the most combative musician in the Czech National Movement. He fought for a National Theater in Prague ▲ *294*, his objective being to provide the theater with a Czech repertoire that was worthy of the patriotic ideas of the period.

CZECH SCHOOL
Many composers who followed Smetana contributed to the Czech school's reputation. They included Zdeněk Fibich (1850–1900), Karel Bendl (1830–97) and J. B. Foerster (1859–1951); the most celebrated,

however, was Antonín Dvořák. Later came Josef Suk (1874–1935) and Vítězslav Novák (1870–1949), but none of them challenged the uniqueness and power of Leoš Janáček (1854–1928, left). He was followed by Bohuslav Martinů (1890–1959, above). After Independence in 1918, new talents including Alois Hába (1893–1973) and Jaroslav Ježek (1882–1969) gave Prague an avant-garde reputation. Since World War Two, and in the face of fierce political pressures, a number of composers have made a deep impression through their daring and copious output.

Prague's international image as a musical capital has more to do with respect for certain places, monuments and institutions than with the reputation of its great composers. An example of this is the "Prague Spring" Festival which was founded in 1946 and attracts the world's great performing artists. This event is associated with the city's supposed image as the "conservatoire of Europe". The Museum of Musical Instruments which opened, in the Palace of the Order of Malta in 1954, contains three thousand instruments. It is currently closed, and will soon be moved to new premises.

VIOLIN
Made by Gasparo da Salo, Brescia (c. 1584). This violin, richly decorated, is carved from a single block of maple wood.

GREAT INTERPRETERS
The reputations of many great soloists, and the long line of Czech violinists, provide a rich counterpoint to the fame of Prague's musical institutions. The vitality of the School of String Quartets was demonstrated by the celebrated Czech Quartet founded by Josef Suk at the end of the 19th century. The tradition has been sustained to this day through the emergence of immensely talented groups.

IMPORTANT ORCHESTRAS
The Czech Philharmonic Orchestra ▲ *166* was founded in 1894 and gave its first concert in 1896 under Antonín Dvořák. It shares the Rudolfinum ▲ *194* and the Town Hall with the Prague Symphony Orchestra.

> "Master Poverty taught Dalibor to play the violin."
>
> Czech proverb

MUSICAL EDUCATION
The Academy of Music, the city's senior music school, grew out of the prestigious Prague Conservatoire (1811). When the Association for Musical Development in Bohemia took the initiative to establish the Academy, it was the first musical event linked to the period of "national awakening" ● 28.

"SEDIFONY" HORNS
J. Sediva, Odessa (1901–13). These instruments dating from the early 20th century were made by a Czech manufacturer who lived in Russia. They had two tubes and produced a shriller sound than modern horns.

GIRAFFE PIANO
The name of this early 18th-century instrument derives from the fact that it is shaped like the neck of a giraffe. It is one of the curiosities on display in the Museum of Musical Instruments.

AN 18TH-CENTURY HURDY-GURDY
A scene of the Annunciation is carved in relief on the lid. It is probably Bohemian.

49

● THE POLKA

The polka is often described as a dance of Polish origin, but in fact it is Czech; it was strongly influenced by the *écossaise* and the Polish *krakowiak*. The name was probably inspired by the presence of Poles in Prague following the 1831 uprising and the enormous feelings of sympathy that they engendered; some people believe, however, that the word derives from the Czech *pole* (field) or *pulka* (half). There were a number of regional variations of the polka that appeared after 1840, including the polka waltz and polka mazurka.

SMETANA'S "THE KISS" AT THE PROVISIONAL THEATER, PRAGUE (1876)
The patriotic composer Bedřich Smetana (1824–84) wrote many well-known polkas; he used this popular form in his large-scale symphonic works as well as in several of his operas, including *The Kiss*.

"BARREL BEER POLKA"
Cover of the score of the most famous polka in the world. It was composed in the 1920's by Jaromir Vejdova, and is known internationally by its American title, *Barrel Beer Polka*.

PIANO SCORE FOR THE "POLKA ESMERALDA"

After 1830, the polka replaced the waltz in the hearts of Czech people, particularly those who frequented the city's more popular meeting places. The first scores of this dance appeared in Prague in the form of loose sheets. F. M. Hilmar's *Esmeralda* was inspired by a character in Victor Hugo's novel *Notre-Dame de Paris*.

SCORE OF "THE BARTERED BRIDE"

Smetana started composing and playing polkas at the age of fifteen. He was an excellent dancer and, at a time when the polka was already sweeping the country, he used to entertain the bourgeois drawing-rooms of Prague and Plzen with demonstrations of the dance. *The Bartered Bride*, the first great Czech opera, made use of stylized polka tunes; the finale to the last act is a celebration of this popular dance.

The basic step, which is alternated and repeated in an unceasing swirl, had been used in several Czech dances since the beginning of the 19th century.

51

There is no question that music continues to play a major role in Prague life, but society balls are a thing of the past. Lively festivals and balls were once an integral part of the city's life: in the 19th century, the German and Austrian bourgeoisies would mingle at big society balls, while the city's parks played host to numerous, more popular festivals. However, festivals and balls did not simply provide sources of entertainment; for many years, they had a political objective, bringing together Czechs who yearned to affirm their nationalism. As early as 1848, Czechs were devising their own *besedas*; many years later, in the 1970's, soirées were being organized by Prague dissidents at the National House in Vinohrady and at other gatherings sponsored by Charter 77.

SOCIETY BALL IN PRAGUE (1830)
During the 18th century, the Austrian nobility and the German bourgeoisie held *Societäts-Bälle* and *Privat-Bälle* in their opulent residences. The most popular dances were the polonaise, the gavotte, the *ländler* and, later on, the waltz. At the beginning of the 19th century, they owned as many as sixteen dancing salons.

FUNFAIR IN HVEZDA PARK
In the early 19th century, the parks around Prague were thronged with Czechs enthusiastically indulging in the simple, catchy rhythms of popular dances like the *rejdovák*, *trasák*, *dupák* and *britva*. There had hardly been a Czech nobility of any description for two hundred years.

"POMNĚNKA", (MEMORIES), DANCE CARD
The first Czech *beseda* took place in April 1848. It was organized by the city's artists and intellectuals, who used the proceeds to build the National Theater.

FAN FROM THE PRAGUE STUDENTS' BALL, 1849
From 1840 onward, all sectors of Prague society, including cultural associations and professional bodies, had their own balls. Student *merendas* and masked *redutas* were the most popular.

PATRIOTIC BALLS
From 1830 onward, the Czech intelligentsia, led by the playwright Josef Kajetán Tyl ▲ *280*, organized private balls in aid of patriots, mainly in the Malá Strana district. The first "Czech ball" took place around 1840 in the Jesuit College ▲ *288* in the city center and in the Žofín Palace ▲ *302* on Bavířka Island, nowadays known as Slav Island.

BALLROOM AT THE TOWN HALL
The tradition of Prague society balls may not have survived the test of time, but dancing lessons remain very popular. Today, the Town Hall (*Obecní dům ▲ 164*) is one of the many places where large numbers of young people come to learn all about the polka, waltz, tango and samba – and even the paso doble.

53

The theater has always played an extremely important role in Prague, and this goes some way toward explaining how Czechs were able to protect their language and maintain their national identity while under Austrian rule. The theater was traditionally a place where people came together during important events, and dramatists always played decisive roles at these times. Both Karel Čapek and Václav Havel have been central figures in their country's destiny.

ABC THEATER
This was the home of the "Liberated Theater", Prague's most popular company during the years 1927–38 and 1946–8. The show had two singing clowns who put on a musical, usually anti-Fascist, revue. The duo was disbanded largely as a result of events in Munich in 1938 and the Prague Coup of 1948, but Voskovec and Werich nonetheless became legends in their own lifetime. Václav Havel first wrote for the theater in 1958.

NÁRODNÍ DIVADLO

Collections that formed part of the *Národ sobě* (Nation for the Nation) appeal paid for the construction in 1883 of what Czechs called "the Golden Chapel on the Vltava". The National Theater's curtain, painted by Vojtěch Hynais ▲ *295* and designed like a Gobelin tapestry, recounts this episode in allegorical style.

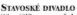

"DIVADLO NA ZÁBRADLÍ" ▲ *156*

For the most part, the Theater "on the Balustrade" (the costume above is from a 1972 production of *The Marriage of Figaro*) concentrated on the theater of the absurd when Václav Havel worked there as a playwright in the 1960's.

STAVOVSKÉ DIVADLO

The "Theater of the Estates", built by Count Nostic, was one of the most important theaters in central Europe at the end of the 18th century; the foundation stone was laid by Emperor Joseph II. Mozart wrote *Don Giovanni* for it in 1787, and Milos Forman filmed *Amadeus* here in 1984 with sets by Josef Svoboda. The theater was restored to its original appearance in building works in 1992.

"The theater must not simply be the mechanical sum of text, actors, directors, audience and usherettes. It has got to be something more than that – the spiritual home of its time."

Václav Havel

Left: A set by V. Novák for a 1921 production of *RUR* at the National Theater.

The Czech puppet theater tradition was born in the 17th century and rapidly became the favorite diversion of the country's middle classes. In the 19th century, Prague was the third most important puppetry center, after Bohemia in the south and the region of Mount Krkonoše (Mountain of Giants). Since the 1960's, a whole generation of professional puppet theater producers has emerged from the Faculty of Theater at Prague's Academy of Arts. They include Zdeněk Bauer, Pavel Kalfus, Petr Matasek and Jaroslava Žatková, who are particularly noted for bringing new ideas to the use of scenery.

THE REPERTOIRE

Puppets were hugely popular in Bohemia thanks to shows mounted by itinerant troupes from Britain, Germany, the Netherlands and Italy. Many early puppetry plays were influenced by Shakespeare, Molière and other famous playwrights. The fairy stories that are so typical of the present-day repertoire, including Božena Memcová's celebrated "The Grandmother", were neglected for many years.

The traveling puppet-master normally owned about a dozen puppets: six male, three female, Kašpárek (Punch), the Devil and Death. At one time in Bohemia, families of puppeteers passed their art on from father to son. One of the most popular and most skilled puppeteers of the second half of the 19th century was Jan Nepomucký Laštovka.

Poster for the Puppet Theater in Prague.

Group of musicians at the Špejbl and Hurvínek Theater.

OLD PUPPETS

Puppets have varied in size over the centuries. There have been times when heads and extremities were lengthened; sometimes, the bodies became no more than accessories. In the 17th century, puppets were approximately 20–32 inches tall, and the bodies were hollowed out to make them lighter. The 19th century saw numerous technical advances which facilitated more precise designs and a higher degree of realism.

THE ŠPEJBL AND HURVÍNEK THEATER

This theater, which was opened in 1945, is devoted to the adventures of two characters created by Josef Skupa. Špejbl and Hurvínek, father and son, use a technique and style of humor that are both grotesque and satirical, and portray immediately identifiable characters who are seeking remedies to the ills of the world. The production includes visual images, scenes from pantomime and musical numbers which accompany the dialogue.

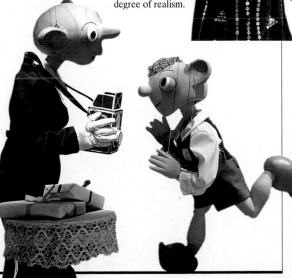

S·K·

It was a Levantine who introduced the idea of café life to both Prague and Paris. In Prague, this was just after the Siege of Vienna and the victory over the Turks at Kalhenberg in 1683. Then, in the early 18th century, one Theodat (or Deodatus) opened a café "At the sign of the Three Ostriches" near Charles Bridge, and shortly afterward another establishment called "Of the Golden Snake" in Karlova Street. By the 19th century, cafés in Prague were the equal of the "temples of the intelligentsia" patronized by Vienna's high society. For civil servants and obscure artists alike, a visit to a café was an essential element of daily life.

THE CAFÉ ARCO
This café was the rallying point for intellectuals with a German-language culture. They included Franz Kafka, Max Brod, Franz Werfel and Egon Erwin Kisch, cosmopolitan writers hostile to pan-Germanism. Members of the Devětsil Group took over the Café Arco in later years.

KAFKA'S CAFÉS
Franz Kafka used to sit in the Louvre Café, alongside the likes of Hugo Bergmann, Emil Ulitz and Ernst Pollak; he also enjoyed going to the less salubrious U Brejšků, a haunt of the "Young People's Circle", a group of Czech writers who sought to defend their culture and promulgate socialist ideas. On other evenings, he preferred the Savoy Café where Yitshak Löwy's Yiddish theater company sometimes gave performances. There was also the Stefan Café where Else Kornis attended a reading of the first version of *The Metamorphosis* given by Ernst Pollak.

PRAVÁ ZÁT

DEVĚTSIL

THE DEVĚTSIL GROUP
Poets and painters in the circle of Karel Čapek, Jaroslav Seifert, Vítězslav Nezval and Teige founded this innovatory movement in the *Café Union* ▲ *291* on November 5, 1920. In their search for a form of "new beauty", they chose cafés as their favorite observation points.

THE CAFÉ SLAVIA
Poets in the Devětsil Group often met at the Café Slavia ▲ *298*. According to Seifert, "Our table was crowded with the foreign poets and painters whom we talked about in our discussions and arguments. Apollinaire was often there, of course, with his head bandaged as in Picasso's painting. And Jakobson lured many others to our gatherings. That was how Mayakovsky would sometimes be seated amongst us, chatting away . . ."

Below, a caricature of the writer Rainer Maria Rilke.

OVA KÁVA.

THE NATIONAL CAFÉ
Rainer Maria Rilke was taken aback by the informality of these hospitable places, where people spent much of the night in an intimate club-like atmosphere, consoling each other for everything, or nearly everything. He preferred to patronize the National Café and "silently listen to older and more serious men who he could see were the local élite". A few years later, Jaroslav Seifert welcomed a newcomer, Roman Jakobson, as if he were "a celebrated guest".

The first brewery in Prague was probably established in 1082, but it was the town of Plzeň in Bohemia which became the undisputed capital of hop fermentation toward the end of the 13th century. The breweries of Plzeň were enormously successful, and in the 19th century they began exporting to the rest of Europe, and Paris and Vienna in particular. At that time, there were no fewer than 1,057 breweries in Bohemia-Moravia. Modern Prague boasts hundreds of taverns; they are the second homes for the city's inhabitants, who go there to make generous sacrifices to their household gods.

"VINO CORRUPTUS" Tacitus' scornful remark about German beer does not go down well with the Czech people, who have an inordinate passion for this beverage. The Italian Jesuit, Giovanni Botero, has described how enraged he was by the Bohemians who "never stopped drinking" – no doubt because of that "pestilential heresy", the Hussite reforms ● *32*.

Just as much beer was being drunk at the beginning of the 20th century. Jaroslav Hašek, the author of *The Good Soldier Schweik*, urged his compatriots to drink at least thirty-five glasses of beer a day.

TOP-QUALITY BEERS

Prague still produces a large number of beers, most of them made by craftsmen brewers. The best include "Flekovský ležák" made at the U Fleků tavern, "Staropramen" which dates from 1869, "Pražán" which has been produced at Holešovice since 1895, and "Special Braník", first brewed in 1898.

U FLEKŮ ▲ 306

The U Fleků is still typical of the old-style Prague tavern with its wood-paneling, long tables and huge courtyard. One of the oldest beers in Prague, "Flekovský ležák", has been brewed there since 1499; this dark beer made with roasted malt is 13° Balling, and is only produced in small quantities (3,650 barrels a year).

"In certain well-known bars in the Old Town (*U zlatého Tygra*), amidst the smoke and babble of voices, people stand elbow to elbow next to high, narrow shelves as if in the storage vaults of some arch spanning a sea of nothingness."

Petr Král

U KALICHA

This is the tavern where Jaroslav Hašek● *126* begins the tale of the Good Soldier Schweik's tribulations. On the day that the Archduke Ferdinand is assassinated in Sarajevo, Schweik goes to the U Kalicha for a chat with Palivec, the proprietor and an old friend of his. Sadly, this leads to them being arrested by a spy working for the political police. On his release, Schweik hurries straight round to his favorite bar: "I'm back!" he cries cheerfully, "Mine's a half!"

LOIN OF PORK WITH CABBAGE AND KNEDLÍKY

Loin of pork with cabbage and dumplings (*Vepřová s knedlíkem a se zelím*) is one of Czech cuisine's most typical dishes. Of course, pork, cabbage and dumplings are to be found in many central European cuisines – in Bohemia, Austria and Germany, for instance – but the cooking always varies slightly from one place to the next.

However, it is delicious wherever it is cooked and if, as is customary, it is preceded by soup, it is a complete meal in itself.

KNEDLÍKY. Ingredients:
3 cups of finely sieved flour, ¼ pint of milk, 2 egg yolks, ½ teaspoonful of baker's yeast, half a baguette cut into ½ inch dice, and a little salt.

1. Pour the milk into a shallow dish. Add the salt, the egg yolks and the flour mixed in with the yeast. Mold the mixture to cover the side of the dish with a wooden spoon for 3 mins.

SAUERKRAUT. Ingredients: 1½ lbs of sauerkraut, 1 tablespoonful of flour, 1 onion, ½ teaspoon of lard or margarine, 1 teaspoonful of vinegar, and 1 or 2 teaspoonfuls of sugar.

4. Sauté the onion in the lard until golden brown. Add the flour and mix, and then pour in one glass of water. Let the roux thicken, and allow to simmer until it sticks to the dish.

LOIN OF PORK

Ingredients for four people: 1½ lbs of fatty pork, 2 ozs of lard or margarine, 1 teaspoonful of caraway seeds, cooking salt, pepper.

6. Place the meat in a shallow dish with the lard. Add the salt and sprinkle caraway seeds. Cook at medium oven heat. After 15 mins, add some water regularly to prevent the joint from getting dry. The meat must be well cooked and golden brown on the outside.

2. Add the cubes of bread. Mix in well and leave. Put the water on to boil, and meanwhile cut the paste in half under running water to prevent it from sticking to your hands.

3. Roll each half into large sausage shapes approximately 6 inches long and 2½ inches wide. Leave the dumplings to cook in boiling water for 25–30 mins. Then cut them into equal, thick slices.

On each plate, place a helping of meat, 3 or 4 slices of dumpling and some cabbage. Add gravy. The best drink to go with this dish is a good light beer such as Pilsner.

5. Remove from the heat and leave for 5 mins for the crust to separate. Mix well. Lastly, add the salt, the sugar and the vinegar. Reheat before serving.

● SPECIALTIES

PUPPETS
The craze for puppet theaters that gripped Prague since the 17th century lives on. Wooden and string puppets are on sale in street stalls and in specialist shops.

COMPACT DISCS
Recordings of music by the great Czech composers performed by the world's top musicians are available on CD. These recordings are of excellent quality, and are on sale throughout Prague at competitive prices.

Toys made by craftsmen with untreated wood can be bought from street vendors and in specialist shops.

BOHEMIAN CRYSTAL
Crystal made Bohemia famous, and many shops in Prague have superb collections of glassware on sale.

NEWSPAPERS
In addition to Czech newspapers, there is a weekly English-language newspaper called *The Prag Post*. It is an English version of the weeklies *Přehled*, *Pro* and *Programm*, and provides a run-down of the city's cultural events.

BEER AND BECHEROVKA
These two national drinks are on sale in all food shops. Bohemian beer was first exported to other European countries in the 19th century, but brewing dates from the Middle Ages. "Pilsner" beer is one of the best known. Becherovka liqueur (38°) is best drunk cool as an aperitif or a digestive.

Architecture

● THE CONSTRUCTION OF PRAGUE

Libussa, legendary founder of Prague.

During the 9th and 10th centuries, the Slav peoples abandoned the hills overlooking the Vltava and built settlements down in the valley, now defended by two fortresses. The 13th-century ramparts around Staré Město were the beginning of a real medieval city. Space was limited, however, and this led to the construction of Nové Město in 1348 and an extension of the ramparts. Later, after coming under attack during the 17th century new ramparts reinforced by thirty-nine bastions were built around Prague. Industrialization in the 19th century also gave rise to a modern infrastructure with the first railroad station, numerous bridges and the first trams.

RELIEF MAP
Prague, like Rome, is encircled by seven hills and has often been compared with the Eternal City. The first Slav settlements in the 7th and 8th centuries were located in the fortified highlands. During the 8th century, the Slavs moved down toward the Vltava and, when Prague and Vyšehrad Castles were constructed in the 9th and 10th centuries respectively, they resolved to stay. The Malá Strana area was chosen because it afforded protection from flooding, and was also a healthier environment than the marshy district where Staré Město was eventually built.

PRAGUE CASTLE
The Přemyslids had this fortress residence built in about 880–90.

VYŠEHRAD
Legend has it that Libussa ▲ *324* lived in this 10th-century fortress.

EXTENSION OF THE FORTIFICATIONS

The Baroque fortifications built during the second half of the 17th century encompassed a larger area than the Gothic walls, although they observed the course of the original enclosure except to the west and north of the Castle where they incorporated part of Hradčany. Vyšehrad, for its part, was now transformed into an exclusively military citadel, and was provided with a new gate, known as the Leopold Gate, built by the architect Carlo Lurago between 1676 and 1678.

Prague and Vyšehrad Castles

Residential development (10th–12th century)

Residential development (1230–57)

Residential development (14th century)

Residential development (17th century)

19th- and 20th-century bridges

Railway

Staré Město fortifications: 1231 and 1250

Malá Strana wall

Nové Město's Gothic walls

Hunger Wall

Baroque fortifications (1648–54).
The inner suburbs first extended beyond the city walls; then, between 1871 and 1888, they were razed to the ground to make way for the city's urban development.

1. Hradčany
2. Malá Strana
3. Staré Město
4. Judith Bridge
5. Charles Bridge
6. Nové Město
7. Vyšehrad

PRAGUE'S BRIDGES

Charles Bridge (1357) was the only bridge connecting the two banks of the Vltava until the 19th century. Between 1868 and 1879, a series of new bridges were built across the river, facilitating journeys from one side of the city to the other. Right: Mánes Bridge (1911–14).

Romanesque art first appeared in Bohemia in the 11th century during the reign of the Přemyslid Dynasty; three stone rotundas and one basilica, St George's, remain. Later, as the Gothic style, which was popular in Prague during the reign of Charles IV (1346–78), developed, architecture became lighter. An example of this is St Vitus' Cathedral where the Swabian architect Petr Parléř married French influences and Bohemian Gothic. Buildings constructed thereafter were characterized by a search for greater luminosity.

Paving stones at St Laurence's Basilica in Vyšehrad.

ROMAN ROTUNDA
The 11th-century rotunda of the Holy Cross in Karoliny světlé Street perpetuated the Byzantine tradition of centrally planned buildings. It was a novelty for Prague in that it was circular, approximately 16 feet in diameter, and also had a choir. On the exterior, the stone cupola was covered with tiles and surmounted by a lantern ▲ 289.

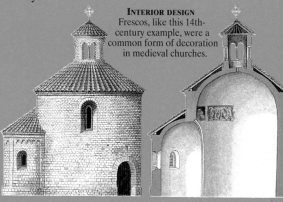

INTERIOR DESIGN
Frescos, like this 14th-century example, were a common form of decoration in medieval churches.

ROMANESQUE BASILICA
St George's Basilica ▲ 220 in Prague Castle was rebuilt after a fire in 1142. It is made of beautiful white stone and accords with the principles of a basilica groundplan: a nave bordered by two narrow aisles and a central apse with vaulting in the form of a semi-cupola.

ROMANESQUE STRUCTURE
(section)
The vault is supported by huge semicircular arches and massive square pillars. In line with traditional basilica design, the choir is raised above the level of the nave.

MODELED ON THE RHENISH SCHOOL
The influence of the Rhenish School is evident from the two square clock towers which frame the two lateral bays at the entrance to the choir.

Carved coats of arms of the
architects Matthew of Arras
and Petr Parléř, who were in
charge of work on St Vitus'
Cathedral.

MONUMENTAL GOTHIC WINDOW

The frame of this 16th-century window in
the south transept of St Vitus' Cathedral
▲ *214* is the work of Matthew of Arras. The
fine stairwell beside it is by Petr Parléř. The
stone armature with polylobed motifs dates
from the 20th century.

BOHEMIAN VAULTING

Petr Parléř introduced Europe to reticulated
vaulting; it is characterized by an
entanglement of ribbing.

PRIMACY OF CHURCH LIGHTING

The oriel window in
the Carolinum ▲ *278*
in Železná Street
dates from 1383. It is
an example of fully

blown Gothic design,
characterized by the
elegance of the walls
and the importance
of the bays; this was
made possible by the
vaulting with
intersecting ribs.

FROM FRENCH GOTHIC TO BOHEMIAN GOTHIC

Matthew of Arras introduced the canons of the French Gothic
to Bohemia and in 1344 built the choir of St Vitus'
Cathedral with an ambulatory and radiating chapels. The
two rows of flying buttresses neutralize the pressure
of the vaults on intersecting ribs, and return it to
ornate buttresses and blind arcades.
The Bohemian Gothic style is well
illustrated by Petr Parléř's
triforium
with
reticulated
vaults.

After the defeat of the Bohemian reformers in 1620, Catholicism became the State religion and the Baroque movement took on political and religious significance. In the hands of Caratti and Mathey, the so-called "Jesuit" Baroque sought balance within classical sobriety; then with the Dientzenhofers, the countries bordering the Danube breathed a new dynamism into spaces and volumes, and a tension and sensuality into lines. Under Maria Theresa, the Baroque began to evolve toward an affected delicacy known as the "Rococo".

WREATHED COLUMNS in U Svatého Jiří Square. The Baroque enthused over wreathed columns, like those (right) framing the door to a chapel adjoining St George's Basilica. The spiral design of the columns emphasizes their architectural function, and skilfully brings them to life.

INTERRUPTING THE FLOW
The door (1740) to Břevnov Abbey ▲ *320* is a good example of Baroque art at the height of its maturity. This work by Kilián I. Dientzenhofer (1689–1751) is notable for the fact that the architectural flow is broken without altering the balance: a curvilinear pediment overlaps with a broken pediment with scrolls, columns set at an angle, a broken cornice, and a contrast between the curves of the consoles and straight lines. Standing in isolation like a triumphal arch, it was the final touch to the reconstruction of the Abbey.

JESUIT STYLE. Between 1638 and 1640, Carlo Lurago carried out alterations to the Church of St Savior ▲ *153* in Křížovnické Street, taking as his model Church of Il Gesù in Rome. Its austere, triumphant façade is decorated with a porch and gallery (1653–9) by Francesco Caratti; the statues glorifying mystical life observe the façade's vertical organization.

DRAMATIC STYLES
The tormented treatment of the folds on this statue of Saint John Nepomuk are a good illustration of the Baroque movement's taste for theatricality.

OVERLAPPING SPACE
In the Church of
St-John-Nepomuk-
on-the-Rock
(1729–39) (left)
interactive space
generates unusual
tensions (see
groundplan below)
▲ *313*. It was built by
Kilián I.
Dientzenhofer.

CENTRALIZED PLAN
The Baroque greatly
preferred centralized
plans to cruciform
plans. Examples
include the Churches
of St Joseph (top)
and St Francis
Seraphim (above).

**A THEATRICAL
FAÇADE**
It is claimed
by some that
the crooked
corner towers
curve the façade
in such a way as to
encourage the faithful
to come into the
church. This
presentation is
accentuated by a four-
flight staircase which
partly compensates
for the difference in
level in relation to
the street.

ONION DOMES
Onion-shaped clock
towers like that of St
Giles' (above) are
typical of the
Baroque.

THE ROCOCO
narrow façade of the Loreto Church is
ravagantly carved with biblical scenes,
luding the theme of the Annunciation.
church was built by the Dientzenhofers
in 1721.

● St Nicholas' Church, Malá Strana

St Nicholas' Church in Malá Strana Square is one of the most dazzling examples of Baroque style in Prague. The surface, the elegance and balance of the exterior, and the opulence of the trompe l'oeil Rococo decoration, all reflect the supreme technical skills of the Czech artists who worked on it. The façade and nave were built between 1703 and 1711 by Kryštof Dientzenhofer; his son, Kilián Ignác, added the choir in 1713 and the cupola in 1752. Anselmo Lurago added the clocktower in 1755. Artists involved in the decoration included the sculptors Jan Kohl, Ignác Platzer and members of the Prachner family.

IMITATION MARBLE
The general decoration and the pulpit (1765) are in polished stucco in imitation of marble.

TROMPE L'OEIL
Baroque art, a spearhead of the Counter-Reformation, sought to rouse souls by favoring luxuriant decoration enriched by illusions. The osmosis between architecture and décor is here sublimated by the use of trompe l'oeil, a device widely used in the decoration of St Nicholas' Church. In fact, the marble is false, and the pictorial perspective alters the cornice by making it undulate, and even creates an illusion of space in the vaults covered with figurative frescos.

A STATELY ART
A fascination with form and color characterizes Baroque style.

ROCAILLE
The conch on which the Rococo pulpit stands is a common motif in rocaille style.

DIDACTIC ART
Through its taste for ostentatious opulence, the Baroque reminded humanity of its mortal condition and the "Vanity" of worldly goods. This death's head is on the carved corbels of St Nicholas' Church.

CLASSICAL HERITAGE
The cupola, which reaches a height of 230 feet, is built according to a circular centralized plan inherited from the classical Renaissance.

CURVES AND COUNTER-CURVES
Baroque style frequently used curved lines to express movement both in architecture and in ornamentation. This 130-foot-long façade comprises a continuous display of curves and counter-curves. Inside the church, there are curved lines painted in trompe l'oeil.

EMPHATIC BODY MOVEMENT
This statue in the choir, of a saint fighting heresy, twists and turns in a manner characteristic of the Baroque.

"JESUIT ARCHITECTURE" AND ROCOCO DÉCOR
The façade is organized in three parts, and the unity of the axial and centralized plans testify to the Jesuits' austere, classical tastes. The plastic elements of the décor, by contrast, anticipate Rococo style.

A PROFUSION OF LITTLE ANGELS
The organ is adorned by as many groups of little angels as there are families of instruments in an orchestra.

73

The lower part of Staré Město was banked up during the 13th century to protect it from flooding when the Vltava overflowed. In this way, what had been a ground floor in Romanesque times became a cellar in the Gothic period; what is more, since 1230, the design of dwellings had changed substantially with houses becoming taller, narrower and deeper. After the fire of 1316, they were rebuilt on a larger scale and in stone. Many buildings retained their Gothic infrastructure over the centuries, as in later periods architects simply remodeled the façade in Renaissance or Baroque style.

THE GOTHIC FAÇADE
The house "At the sign of the Stone Bell" (U kamenného zvonu) ▲ 143 in Starometské Square is a somewhat controversial re-construction of a patrician Gothic residence. It has three stories, and the alternating niches and windows are surmounted with a décor consisting of gables. The Gothic façade, which is covered with a Baroque facing, was discovered in 1965.

MEDIEVAL DWELLINGS
Arched passages and gabled walls are characteristic of the façades of medieval houses. Ground plans show that the first floors had barrel or groined vaults; they were often used as workshops.

GABLES SURVIVE
The Nové Město Town Hall dates from the Renaissance, but the medieval tradition of gables was artificially preserved.

THE TRADITION OF ORNAMENTAL TILING
Streets have been paved since the Middle Ages. In the 19th century, pavements were covered with white, blue and pink marble, and some have survived despite heavy wear.

Barrel vault   Ribbed vault

ROOFS
During the Gothic period, flat and curved Roman tiles were fixed to the lattice with lugs.

MEDIEVAL TO BAROQUE
A series of façades attached to medieval buildings: here, the façade was remodeled in the Renaissance by the addition of a decorative gable with scrolls and sgraffito. In the Baroque era, the façade was altered to suit tastes of the time by adding stucco moldings which covered the Renaissance sgraffito.

ROMANESQUE TO GOTHIC
In the Gothic period the outward appearance of houses changed though their infrastructure, consisting of an arcaded ground floor and two upper stories, was not altered.

Arched pediment in the Venetian style.

With the accession of the Catholic Habsburg Dynasty to the throne of Bohemia in 1526, the Kingdom acquired a powerful political personality in the person of Ferdinand I. He soon established his influence by giving commissions to Italian artists, and one result was the Royal Summer Palace which introduced the estheticism of the Italian Renaissance to Prague. In the reign of Rudolph II (1576–1611), Prague became the capital of the Empire and attracted the greatest minds in Europe. Bohemian art then established its own style with brick and elaborated gables and sgraffito decoration.

A UNIQUE CURVED LINE
The façade of Martinic Palace sweeps round in a continuous curve.

RENAISSANCE DOOR
Two carved wolves are just one unique feature of this townhouse in Kožná Street (1580). The elegant doorway is framed by an arch resting on pilasters, but the clumsily made foliage is more reminiscent of northern than of Italian workmanship.

RENAISSANCE FAÇADE OF FORMER MARTINIC PALACE, HRADČANSKÉ SQUARE
During the Renaissance period, three Gothic houses were converted into a palace (1618–24). The gables continue the medieval tradition while the décor, particularly the sgraffito ▲ 232, is in the Renaissance style.

ROYAL BELVEDERE "IN THE ITALIAN MANNER"
Paolo della Stella built this summer pavilion (1538–64) at the request of King Ferdinand I for his wife, Anne. This rectangular two-story building encircled by a gallery of Ionic capitals recalls the Foundling Hospital in Florence. The alternating niches and windows on the first floor are the work of Bonifác Wohlmut, who completed the building between 1554 and 1564. Its copper roof in the shape of an inverted ship's hull seems to have been inspired by the Palladian Basilica in Vicenza. The garden, which is laid out in the Italian manner, has geometrically shaped flowerbeds that contain exotic plants.

THE CZECH RENAISSANCE

Schwarzenberg Palace (1545–63) in Hradčanské Square, a fine example of the Czech Renaissance, imitated not only the massive structure of Florentine palaces but also the false bosses decorated with diamond-point sgraffito. Northern influence is concentrated on the gables: three levels of pilasters are superimposed on them, their entablature set with urns.

GABLES IN THE VENETIAN STYLE

Gables in Týn Courtyard ▲ *160* and Husova Street are topped by semicircular gables in the Venetian style.

HOUSE "AT THE SIGN OF THE GOLDEN LION" (U ZLATÉHO IVA)

The façade (1608) of this house ▲ *248* in Malá Strana Square is an example of the purity of the late Czech Renaissance. It consists of an arch, on two stories pierced by windows, and lastly a gable adorned with scrolls surmounted by a broken pediment.

TROMPE L'OEIL DÉCOR
This mullioned window in the old Martinic Palace has sgraffito decoration in the form of trompe l'ocil garlands and foliage.

● Sgraffito

The technique of sgraffito decoration was imported from Italy, and it spread rapidly throughout Prague and Bohemia round the middle of the 16th century. Palaces and residences belonging to the bourgeoisie were swathed in sgraffito decoration, particularly their exteriors. Sgraffito was especially well adapted to trompe l'oeil imitations of stone designs such as diamond-point bosses, but was also used to depict figurative scenes based on mythological, biblical or historical themes. Neo-Renaissance style in the 19th century revived the use of sgraffito to illustrate the Czech National Awakening with the representation of historical scenes and allegorical figures.

1

3 **4**

5 **6**

7

2

against a black background.
7. Bad weather and atmospheric humidity can lead to deterioration.
8. The design peels and then falls off.

HISTORIC PORTRAIT
Right, unidentified portrait of a monarch, applied in 1610 to the cornice of the House "Of the Minute" (Dum U minuty), 3 Old Town Square.

8

APPLICATION AND DECOMPOSITION

1. First, either black mortar (ground charcoal) or blackish-brown mortar (pigments of ferric minerals) is applied.
2. A second, white, lime-based coating (the *intonaco*) is then smoothed on with a trowel.
3. and **4.** The design is transferred onto the coating by means

of perforations.
5. and **6.** The white coating is scratched with small mattocks and scrapers to obtain a design in two colors, in this case, white

BIBLICAL THEME
The House "Of the Minute" ▲ *146* is covered in early 17th-century sgraffito decoration. A frieze (below), so finely etched it might be a copper engraving, relates the story of Joseph being taken out of a pit to be sold to the Ishmaelites. The sgraffito on this house was discovered at the beginning of the 20th century and has been frequently restored.

A MYTHOLOGICAL THEME
This 16th-century representation of Hercules at 4 Old Town Square was preserved after the house was rebuilt by Pavel Janák in 1938.

THE CZECH NEO-RENAISSANCE
The Renaissance bossage on the Schwarzenberg Palace (above, right) was restored by Josef Schulz at the height of the Czech National Awakening in the 19th century ● 28.

FRIEZES IN THE ANTIQUE STYLE
These sgraffito friezes on the cornice of Schwarzenberg Palace ▲ 230 could be mistaken for reliefs. The motifs used derive from designs popular in antiquity.

FLORAL AND ANIMAL DECORATION ▲ 232
This decoration on the main façade of Martinic Palace dates from the late 15th century.

ALLEGORICAL THEMES
The neo-Renaissance Hlávka houses (Hlávkovy domy) ▲ 291 date from 1889. The façades are adorned with allegorical sgraffito figures, including Vanity (below).

INFLUENCE OF PAINTING
In the Martinic Palace ▲ 232, a technique of linear perspective on a convex surface ● 76 is used to represent the episode of Joseph and Potiphar's wife.

79

Urns provide the finishing touch to gardens of Prague.

The ravages caused by the Thirty Years' War provided the new aristocracy with an opportunity to fill Malá Strana with huge palaces and gardens. During the 17th century, these palaces, many of them built by Italian architects, were characterized by simple, geometrical spaces marked by rich decoration. As early as the beginning of the 18th century Prague had become one of the leading Baroque capitals in Europe. Dientzenhofers, Santini-Aichl, and other great masters who had trained in Vienna including Alliprandi and Fischer von Erlach, conceived of space in terms of curves and countercurves that stimulated the play of light and shade. The Baroque also gave prominence to colossal orders of columns of the type favored in Prague by the architect Kaňka. The decorative exuberance of the Rococo appeared after 1740.

BAROQUE PEDIMENT
A stucco molding of curves and countercurves on the pediment of 2 Celetná Street ▲ *158*.

ČERNÍN PALACE
This palace (1669–79) in Loretánské Square ▲ *234* was built by Francesco Caratti on an earlier plan by Bernini (1598–1680).

FROM THE GOTHIC TO THE BAROQUE
The House "At the sign of the Two Suns" (U dvou slunců) (1673) at 47 Nerudova Street has a Baroque façade with two attics topped by pediments; they replaced the gables that had adorned the earlier Gothic façade ▲ *254, 256*.

AMBIVALENCE OF BAROQUE SCULPTURE

It is difficult to draw the line between sculpture and architecture on this Baroque door (1714) to Clam-Gallas Palace ▲ 149. The sculptor, Matthias Bernhard Braun, constructed two pairs of atlantes that act as columns and which contort beneath the weight of the upper balcony. This kind of presentation, and the expressiveness of the figures, owe much to the influence of Bernini. The remainder of the façade overlooking Husova Street is classical.

MONUMENTAL ARCHITECTURE

The impressive façade of Černín Palace is notable for an order of thirty huge columns that rest on a high crepidoma adorned with diamond-point bosses, a direct reference to the work of Palladio (1508–80).

TRANSITION BETWEEN CLASSICISM AND THE BAROQUE

Černín Palace's high, embossed crepidoma and huge orders derive from the classical Renaissance, while its porches with their concave and convex lines foreshadow the Baroque.

LIGHT AND SHADOW

The façade of Alliprandi's Lobkowicz Palace (1703–13) that overlooks the street is flat. By contrast, on the garden side, the Baroque has imbued the façade with great movement and, together with the central oval pavilion flanked by the two concave wings, it provides opportunities for plays of light and shadow. The curb roof and the urns which crown the building are typically Baroque devices.

PASSAGEWAYS AND GALLERIES

Houses have incorporated passageways since the Middle Ages, but there were huge changes in Prague between the late 19th century and World War Two when galleries and many new passageways were built. This more modern style of town planning was appended to older methods in such a surprising manner that, for Surrealists poets, Prague represented the urban archetype of wandering and melancholy. A specifically Czech hallmark of the galleries came from their architectural boldness and the avant-garde ideas propounded by the theater and the cinema.

STARÉ MĚSTO
This map reveals the dense network of passageways and galleries criss-crossing Staré Město.

SECRET PASSAGEWAY
The typically Prague passageway, *pruchod* in Czech, is supposed to "shorten" one's journey by enabling the walker to pass through a number of buildings instead of having to walk round them. According to a medieval tradition,

the passageway took its name from the owner of the house the walker was passing through, or from the coat of arms that sometimes surmounted the entrance. The entrance to a passageway was only marked by an anonymous door which was no different from an ordinary house door; in this way, these doors were ambiguous in that they both announced and concealed the presence of these pedestrian ways.

GALLERIES, AN IDEAL OF MODERN DESIGN
The Prague gallery was first known as *bazar* and then as *pasáž*. It constitutes an ideal of modern design in that it forms part of large urban dwellings referred to locally as "palaces", a modern concept with commerical, social and cultural uses. Important characteristics are pomp, functionalism and versatility. The gallery's luxurious interior contrasts sharply with the sobriety of the entrance (below Novak Gallery).

J.NOVAK

82

KORUNA GALLERY, WING AND CUPOLA
The gallery was built between 1911 and 1914 to plans by Antonín Pfeiffer (1879–1938) to a commission by the Koruna company, the first Czech limited company specializing in life insurance ▲ 174. It stands on the corner of Wenceslas Square and Na Příkopě Street. This perfect illustration of Secession ● 86 style is joined to an enormous town palace, one of the earliest buildings in Prague to be built of reinforced concrete. There were once offices, businesses and apartments upstairs, but a café downstairs was replaced between 1931 and 1978 by a self-service restaurant by the architect and stage designer, Ladislav Machoň (1888–1973). The basement contained a swimming pool and a movie theater. The gallery's overall décor includes tall stained-glass windows and bronze reliefs on the walls.

GLASS CUPOLA
The original cupola, which was restored in 1980, comprised 3,800 pieces of glass cut diamond-style, and was held in position by ribs of reinforced concrete. The prismatic range of the glass generated enough light to illuminate the underground swimming-pool through the translucent concrete floor.

Ionic capital at the Villa Kinský.

The renovation of Prague Castle in 1740–80 announced the arrival of neoclassicism and the decline of Baroque estheticism. At the time, Georg Fischer (1768–1828) was advocating a more austere approach to architecture, but neoclassical sobriety was soon to be supplanted by neo-Gothic Romanesque styles, themselves inspired by Romanticism. Around 1848, a spirit of Historicism quickly prompted a variety of new styles and the rise of nationalism in the 1860's promoted a Czech neo-Renaissance style which rehabilitated the ideas of decoration and local traditions. In the end, Historicism usually meant an eclectic range of different styles applied to a single building.

ITALIAN NEO-RENAISSANCE

The Italian Renaissance directly influenced the architects Josef Zítek and Josef Schulz in the construction of the Rudolfinum (1872). This building houses a concert hall and exhibition facilities.

CZECH NEO-RENAISSANCE

Novotného lávka

Some of the inspiration for the façade of the Smetana Museum (1883) ▲ *156* in Novotného Passage is to be found in Bohemia's Renaissance architecture. The elaborate gable is typically North European, and the relief decoration is also adorned with sgraffito in the Italian manner.

HISTORICISM IS BORN

The birth of Historicism was here marked by the resurgence of a decorative technique, sgraffito ● *78*, and by the representation of a historic subject, the story of the battle against the Swedish Army on Charles Bridge in 1648.

NEO-BAROQUE
This building in Old Town Square designed by Karel Osvald Polívka in 1900 is decorated in the Baroque style. There is a protruding porch, medallions, a rocaille frieze, scrolls, and some urns and genuine Baroque statues on the roof.

CHRONOLOGY OF NEO-STYLES
Late 18th-century neoclassicism was fired by the need for archeological authenticity. However, around 1850, Romanticism emphasized a more Romanesque vision, and was challenged by fin de siècle Historicism, which in turn led to neo-Renaissance.

NEO-GOTHIC STYLE
This building at 8 Masaryk Quay illustrates how a wall containing decorative, rather than architectural, neo-Gothic elements, like the lancet windows, can evoke an image of real Gothic style.

NEOCLASSICAL STYLE
Georg Fischer's Customs House (1808–11) in Republiky Square is decorated with Antique motifs including Doric columns framing the entrance, metopes and triglyphs on the entablature, and a classical pediment. The tympanum, carved by Lederer, takes the form of a two-headed eagle, the symbol of the Holy Roman Empire.

FALSE KEYSTONE
This Art Nouveau device does not fulfil its role as a keystone.

Art Nouveau in Prague was influenced by Symbolism and looked to Paris for inspiration, but it also derived in part from German Jugendstil (1894–1914), the Viennese Secession (1897–1907) and the School of Otto Wagner where many Czech architects were trained. In Prague, these artistic trends were initially to be found in the applied arts; later, they found expression in architecture where they were combined, concordantly or conflictingly, on façades of buildings, many of them Historicist in design.

URN WITH GARLANDS OF PLANT MOTIFS.
Na příkopě 7

GILDED STUCCO
In its pursuit of Symbolism, Art Nouveau returned to the ornamental themes of the classical and Baroque periods, imposing on them curvilinear forms of plant motifs.

THE PEACOCK
Pelikán Building (1904–6), Na příkopě 7

UNDULATIONS AND BROKEN LINES
Extravagantly undulating spaces give way to the sobriety of geometrical lines and simply defined spaces. The combination of curves and broken lines prefigure Art Deco.

THE SECESSION
Tower of the Koruna Gallery (1912–14) Wenceslas Square Outlines remained classical (square towers, octagonal drums and circular coronas), and the only concessions to Secession styles were symbolic subjects ▲ *171* and plastic applications (plays of materials and of colors and light).

PLANT MOTIFS
Like the peacock, the Ginkgo biloba was a recurrent motif in Art Nouveau decoration.

DECORATIVE MOLDING
Decoration in the form of molding also of classical inspiration, at Na příkopě 7.

MOSAICS
Ceramic or glass mosaics adorn a number of façades completely or in part; here they recall a pier glass. Above: Mosaic by Jan Preisler (1872–1918) ● *104*, ▲ *311*.

SECESSION DECORATION (1899–1901). The only real innovation at 10 Hybernská Street is the décor, as the building itself is very classical in its organization (crepidoma with bosses, a central torso and pediment) and harmoniously merges with much older buildings ▲ *168*.

IRONWORK AND STAINED GLASS
A superb example of Secessionist design seen in a doorway to the Town Hall in Prague. Wrought iron and stained glass were gral to the style.

"Architectural creation has two functions: first the creation of space, and then the decoration of that space. The creative conception of space is truth itself, and decoration is the expression of that truth." This is how Jan Kotěra, the founder of modern Czech architecture, described the role of ornamental composition in space. The inventiveness of artists working in different decorative spheres – painters, graphic artists, sculptors, decorators, artisans – is expressed in both the solicitude they bring to the play of form and color and their choice and treatment of materials. This "global art", which was to culminate in Cubism, developed with astonishing stylistic diversity.

PAINTING (1910) Alfons Mucha (1860–1939) A painting decorating the Mayor's Room in the Town Hall (Obecní dům) ▲ 164.

WALLPAPER (1900) Vojtěch Preissieg (1873–1944) An example of the search for novel symmetries by which to produce stylized motifs, and of the dynamic relationship between pattern and background (Museum of Decorative Arts ▲ 195).

CERAMIC TILES

PAINTED STUCCO
Glass and gilting used to enhance stucco scrolls on the Town Hall ▲ 164.

STAINED GLASS
Stained glass in the main entrance to the Praha Insurance Company building (1905–7) by Osvald Polívka (1859–1931) ▲ 176, ▲ 293.

CUBIST
ARCHITECTURE
1910–20

Prague was the only city   in which an
architectural style inspired by Cubism developed.
Evolving in the wake of Secession in decline and
invigorated by Prague's late Gothic and Baroque
heritage, Cubist architecture influenced the design
of both furniture and everyday objects. Although
shortlived, it foreshadowed Art Deco, and
carried the seeds of modern,
post-war architecture.

BENCH AND STREET LAMP
(1912–13) 310 Jung-
mann Squarc by
Matěj Blecha.
▲ *310.*

CUBIST BUILDING
(1913) 30 Neklanova
Street by Josef Chochol
(1880–1956) ▲ *326.*

VAULTS

Though medieval vaulting spread throughout Europe, in Prague it became an art form in the hands of such innovative architects as Petr Parléř (1333–99) and Benedikt Ried (c. 1454–1534). Central to Czech tradition, vaults remain in the forefront of 20th-century design, whether made of reinforced concrete, or decorated with glass or multifaceted.

A TRADITION OF VAULTS IN PRAGUE
Vaulted arcades are a prominent feature of Prague. Above: Malé náměstí ▲ 148.

FAN VAULTS. Church of the Ascension, Bechyně (1490–1513).

Gilt and polychrome boss with a carving of a heraldic lion. Vladislas II Jagiello's room in Prague Castle.

LIERNE VAULT
The Riders' Staircase in Prague Castle (left) ▲ 205 leads to Vladislav Hall (right). It is the work of Benedikt Ried.

Banisters round the stairwell in the Evropa Hotel, 25–7 Wenceslas Square ● 86, ▲ 174.

Balcony of a residential building at Na příkopě 7, Secession style ● 86.

Balcony of the Jewish Town Hall, Maislova Street, Rococo style ▲ 193.

Décor beneath the eaves of the Belvedere ▲ 224.

Balcony of the Church of Our-Lady-of-Perpetual-Succor-of-the-Gaetani, Nerudova Street, Baroque style ▲ 255.

Railing in the garden of Strahov Monastery ▲ 237.

Railing of the Royal Mausoleum at St Vitus' Cathedral ● 68, ▲ 216.

Panel of a lift shaft in Malé náměstí ▲ 148, (detail, above).

Prague
as seen by painters

> "I love to go for walks in Prague at night time:
> it is like gathering in each gasp of its soul."
>
> Jiří Karásek

Jakub Schikaneder (1855–1924) first studied in Munich (1886–7) and then at Prague Academy. At first he was attracted to the post-Impressionists, but later he moved toward Symbolism. In letters, he explained how he wanted to turn the landscape into an expression of states of mind: "Man watches and forgets everything . . . He only sees kinds of phantom colors leaning further and further out as they get nearer. At that moment, the tree has neither branches nor leaves; it has only spots of fire describing ornaments which we had never even suspected."

No one has been more successful than Schikaneder at enhancing the myth of Prague's obscure, ghostly beauty, a beauty that has survived until today. He recalls the Belgian Symbolist painter, William Degouve de Nuncques (1867–1935). He produces a powerful effect with his rarefied, unreal atmospheres, his detached, meticulous style, and the profound sense of mystery in which he wraps compositions such as *Carriages in the Night* (1911)

95

● Antonín Slavíček

Schikaneder gave expression to Old Prague, but it was left to Antonín Slavíček (1870–1910) to reinvent it; this he did within the radiant perspective of pure colors based on post-Impressionism and a very personal technique. He spent much of his time roaming the streets of Prague, and strove to reproduce its paradoxical beauty – luminous yet changing, and enamored with shadow. *Square in the Old Town, St Mary's Square* (1906) (**2**, detail **4**), and *Tower of St Vitus' Cathedral at Hradčany* are evocations of the more charming corners. Slavíček hoped to eulogize Prague in a cycle of paintings with one panorama for each season that was sadly never completed. Encouraged by the success of his "blue Prague", he painted *View of Prague from Letná* in 1908 (**1**, detail **3**), and then started work on a third panorama using the mixed, nostalgic tones of autumn rain.

1	
	3
2	4

«ADDENTARE IL PAESAGGIO AVIDAMENTE
E DIGERIRLO, ACCOGLIERLO IN OGNI GOCCIA
DEL SUO SANGUE.»

ANTONÍN SLAVÍČEK

> «MI PIACEVA MOLTO PRAGA [...] ERA RIDIVENTATA
> UN CENTRO COSMOPOLITA, NEL QUALE L'EUROPA
> SI RITROVAVA PER L'ULTIMA VOLTA.»
>
> OSKAR KOKOSCHKA

	1	
2		3

Stanco dell'instabilità politica e sociale che regnava a Vienna all'inizio degli anni Trenta, Oskar Kokoschka (1886-1980) decide di stabilirsi a Praga, dove resta per quattro anni, fino a quando le vicissitudini della storia non lo cacciano. Vi realizza il ritratto del presidente Tomáš G. Masaryk. Nelle sue memorie ricorda così questo soggiorno: "Paragonata alle metropoli moderne con i loro grattacieli uniformi e le loro baracche in cemento, Praga era rimasta, o era ridiventata, la creazione di una società colta." Si è impegnato a fare il "ritratto" di questa piccola città, sempre nell'ottica dei panorami e mettendo l'accento sul suo carattere misterioso, tormentato e di natura quasi magica. "In quattro anni", scrive, "ho dipinto [...] sedici quadri, quasi tutti di Praga, da luoghi sempre diversi, dai quali potevo avere una vista sulla Moldava; questo fiume mi aveva stregato, come il Tamigi..." Nel 1934 realizzerà *Veduta di ponte Carlo e Hradčany* (1) e *Ponte Carlo a Praga* (3). In esilio a Londra si dedica nel 1938 alla composizione dell'ultima veduta di Praga. *Nostalgia* (2).

«L'IMPORTANZA DEL COLORE STA NEL FATTO CHE HA VERAMENTE
UNA PROPRIETÀ ARMONICA E UNA NATURALE MISTICA SIMBOLICA
PROPRIA DELLA VITA MODERNA.»

BOHUMIL KUBIŠTA

Dopo avere trascorso diversi mesi a Parigi nel 1910, durante i quali realizza alcune opere con una tecnica nuova, dovuta alla profonda influenza del cubismo francese e particolarmente a quella di André Derain, Bohumil Kubišta (1884-1918) rientra a Praga alquanto trasformato. Pur non rinnegando la propria inclinazione per la pittura espressionista e fauvista, applica con determinazione i principi costruttivi appresi alla scuola

francese. Il suo percorso estetico si traduce in tele che annunciano la nascita di un cubismo tipicamente ceco. Una di queste può essere considerata indiscutibilmente il suo manifesto: *Motivo della vecchia Praga*, 1911 (a lato). I monumenti seguono una geometria complessa, mentre le nuvole sono risolte sommariamente con linee sinuose ed energiche. L'insieme del quadro è trattato in una tonalità grigio-blu cui fanno da contrappunto solo il bianco e il nero. È questa l'unica opera che Kubišta dedicherà a Praga, città disdegnata anche dai suoi amici pittori, ma che invece gli architetti cubisti si impegneranno a trasformare.

● JIŘÍ KOLÁŘ

Partendo da fotografie Jiří Kolář ● 125 ha realizzato una serie di distorsioni dei monumenti praghesi (sotto, *La porta delle Polveri*). Accompagnate da citazioni di Franz Kafka, queste singolari deformazioni danno della città una visione distorta e inquietante, simile a quella divulgata dall'autore del *Castello*.

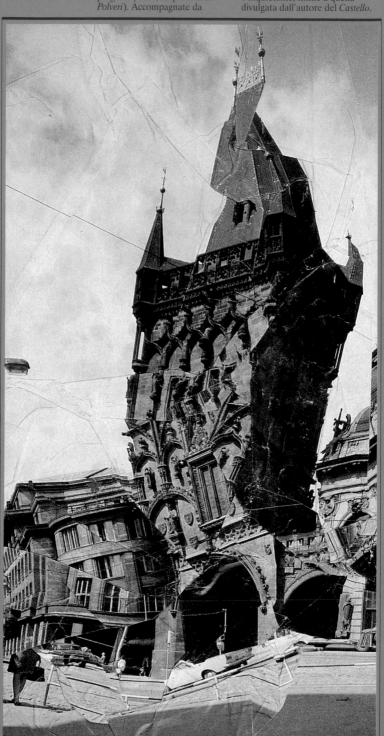

102

PRAGA,
L'ARTE ALL'INIZIO
DEL NOVECENTO

Frantíšek Bílek (1872-1941), *L'aratura è l'espiazione delle nostre pene* (1892).

Se si deve indicare una data che segni la nascita dell'arte moderna in Boemia, bisogna fare riferimento al 1894, anno della pubblicazione del primo numero della *Moderní revue*. Creata per iniziativa del critico Arnošt Procházka e dello scrittore Jiří Karásek ze Lvovic, questa incarna l'arte decadente e simbolista. I vari movimenti che le succedono si apriranno sempre più verso la cultura europea: l'intensificazione degli scambi culturali porterà così a nuove concezioni artistiche che, ispirate alla Secessione viennese prima, al cubismo e al surrealismo di Parigi poi, tradurranno la volontà di dare all'arte ceca una sua specificità culturale.

«LA MOSTRA MUNCH È CADUTA
COME UNA BOMBA IN MEZZO AI NOSTRI SOGNI
E AI NOSTRI DESIDERI.»

VÁCLAV ŠPÁLA

L a retrospettiva di Edward Munch a Praga nel 1905 provoca un vivo interesse per l'espressionismo, così che nel 1908 artisti cechi e tedeschi fondano il gruppo OSMA, composto da Emil Filla (1882-1953), che nel *Lettore di Dostoevskij*, 1907, a fronte, esaspera il pathos e l'estremismo dei propri sentimenti attraverso la congiunzione di colori violenti; da Antonín Procházka (1882-1945) e da Bohumil Kubišta (1884-1918), che rispettivamente con *Il circo*, 1907 (sopra) e *Il triplice ritratto* sono impegnati a loro volta nella ricerca di un adattamento figurativo specifico delle tematiche espressioniste. Tutti vogliono rompere con il simbolismo e con il postimpressionismo e adottare una rappresentazione drammatica del mondo da esprimere con e nel libero gioco dei rapporti di forza plastici al di fuori di ogni riferimento col reale. Jan Preisler (1872-1918), che si è liberato abbastanza rapidamente dal neoimpressionismo, comincia dal 1902, con *Il quadro di un ciclo più grande* (sotto), un'opera innovatrice. Il suo stile spoglio, che sottende una concezione sintetica e una semplificazione significante della forma, si era già affermato nel 1894 con *Il lago nero*. L'Osma corrisponde all'avvento dell'arte moderna a Praga.

BOHUMIL KUBIŠTA (1884-1918)
Natura morta con teschio, 1912.

BOHUMIL KUBIŠTA
San Sebastiano, 1912.

EMIL FILLA (1882-1953)
Piatto con grappolo d'uva, 1915.

«L'OPERA D'ARTE È L'ESPRESSIONE
IMMEDIATA DELL'ESSERE INTIMO DELL'ARTISTA.»

EMIL FILLA

BOHUMIL KUBIŠTA
Il fachiro, 1914.

Il cubismo ceco non è in alcun modo soggetto al suo modello francese; la sua tecnica infatti consiste in una sintesi molto originale di diversi principi estetici e persino in una singolare reinterpretazione del barocco, come dimostra il dinamismo del *San Sebastiano* di Kubišta. Gli artisti cechi raccolgono l'insegnamento formale della concezione cubista solamente durante il periodo bellico o poco prima: *Natura morta con bottiglia*, 1913-1914 (sotto) di Antonín Procházka (1882-1945); *Piatto con grappolo d'uva*

JOSEF ČAPEK (1887-1945)
Il suonatore di fisarmonica, 1913.

di Filla, oppure *Testa di donna* (gesso del 1913) di Otto Gutfreund (1889-1927) esprimono il bisogno di passare attraverso una rigorosa costruzione dello spazio. Nessuno di questi artisti, però, accetterà i limiti di una formula rigida: le loro ricerche si orientano infatti in direzioni divergenti, come evidenzia *Il canto di primavera* di Špála, costruito sulla geometrizzazione delle figure e sul registro cromatico che gioca esclusivamente sui toni del blu, del bianco e del rosso.

VÁCLAV ŠPÁLA *Il canto di primavera*, 1915.

Verso la fine della guerra il contesto artistico cambia radicalmente: Čapek e Špála si uniscono al gruppo degli Ostinati, che ora porta la fiaccola dell'arte moderna. Il Devětsil ● 59, fondato nel 1920, continua questa corrente grazie ai suoi artisti proiettati sia verso il dadaismo tedesco sia verso i futuristi italiani. Profondamente antiborghesi, campioni di un'arte proletaria, suggerita dagli eroi della fantasia popolare e dall'arte folclorica, esaltano la freschezza dell'ispirazione e lo stile naïf. Il Devětsil si spegne per dar vita nel 1924 al poetismo, che raggruppa Štyrský, Toyen e Teige, suo teorico e catalizzatore. Gli stessi pubblicheranno nel 1927 il manifesto dell'artificialismo, in opposizione al surrealismo di André Breton, da loro considerato uno "splendore infrarosso sul limitare della coscienza", mentre l'artificialismo "vive nel mondo ultravioletto della piena coscienza". Soltanto nel 1934 nascerà, sotto l'egida di Breton, il gruppo surrealista praghese che riunirà la maggior parte dei membri del poetismo. A Parigi Josef Šíma (1891-1971) intrattiene strette relazioni con *Il Grande gioco*, gruppo dissidente di Breton, e si impegna in una ricerca che coniuga l'onirismo surrealista con una concezione metafisica del mondo. Nel 1927 dipingerà *Europa* (in alto) e *Alle quattro del pomeriggio* (in basso).

Praga
VISTA DAGLI SCRITTORI

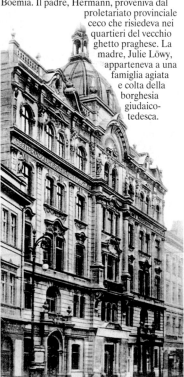

Franz Kafka a 5 anni.

"Kafka era Praga e Praga era Kafka. Niente era mai stato così completamente e tipicamente Praga, e mai più niente potrà esserlo, come quando Kafka era vivo", affermava Johannes Urzidil. "E noi, i suoi amici, gli *happy few*, noi sapevamo che questa Praga era contenuta dappertutto nell'opera di Kafka, in particelle minuscole... è proprio merito di Kafka se questa Praga che sparì con lui non fu seppellita assieme a lui." Tutta l'esistenza dello scrittore si svolgerà nello stretto intreccio delle vie della Città Vecchia praghese. Una vita tutto sommato "provinciale", a dispetto dei suoi sogni infantili che lo portavano verso paesi lontani, nei quali però non andrà mai.

UN'ATMOSFERA FAMILIARE "OPACA, VENEFICA, CORROSIVA"

Franz Kafka nacque a Praga il 3 luglio 1883 in una famiglia ebrea rappresentativa della mescolanza sociale e linguistica della vecchia Boemia. Il padre, Hermann, proveniva dal proletariato provinciale ceco che risiedeva nei quartieri del vecchio ghetto praghese. La madre, Julie Löwy, apparteneva a una famiglia agiata e colta della borghesia giudaico-tedesca.

IL NEGOZIO PATERNO

La gestione del negozio di chincaglierie (il cui marchio, la cornacchia, *kavka* in ceco, è omofono del cognome della famiglia) permise rapidamente ai Kafka di conoscere il benessere. I genitori affidarono allora il figlio al personale di servizio, tra cui una cuoca che ogni giorno ripeteva imprecazioni e lo riprendeva. Questo motivo di angoscia e di tormenti divenne uno dei temi ossessivi delle opere di Kafka.

HERMANN KAFKA
PRAG I.,
ALTSTADTERRING No. 16
Palais Kinsky.

GALANTERIEWAREN EN GROS.

Sachverständiger des k. k. Landes- als Strafgerichtes.

Postsparkassen-Konto No. 2.131.
TELEFON No. 141.

LE COMPAGNIE DI ASSICURAZIONI

Un breve apprendistato da un avvocato e un anno di pratica legale si confusero con i diversi progetti impossibili di fuga lontano da Praga. Kafka si rassegnò a un impiego alle Assicurazioni Generali prima e all'Istituto di assicurazioni (a lato) poi, che manterrà fino al 1922.

Über jeden Tag soll zumindest eine Zeile
gegen mich gerichtet werden wie man die
Fernrohre jetzt gegen den Kometen richtet. Und
wenn ich dann einmal vor jenem Satze erscheinen
würde ... von jenem Satze so wie ich
z. B. Weihnachten gewesen bin und wo
... daß ich mich nur noch grade
... und wo ich, wircklich auf
der ... meiner Leiter schien, die
aber ... auf den Boden stand und an
... was für ein Boden, was wir
... fiel jene Leiter nicht,
... an den Boden,
... an die Wand.

CREATIVITÀ
Fu durante notti di
veglia e di solitudine
che nacque questa
prosa acida e
grottesca, capace
di sedurre André
Breton, Albert
Camus e Jean-Paul
Sartre.

LA TOMBA DI KAFKA
Il monumento
funerario della
famiglia Kafka si
trova nel cimitero
ebraico di Olšany,
non lontano dalla
tomba di Max Brod.

PRIMI SCRITTI
Quelli che lo
conobbero all'epoca
del liceo imperiale di
lingua tedesca di palazzo
Kinský ricordano un
adolescente molto stimato e
amato dai compagni, ma nello
stesso tempo strano e distante.
Fu in questo periodo che
cominciò a scrivere le sue prime
opere. In seguito, giudicandole
troppo vane e ampollose, le
distrusse in preda al bruciante
desiderio di un salvataggio
spirituale. Egli credeva infatti che
solo nella scrittura e con la scrittura
si potesse accendere "un fuoco col
quale scaldare lo spazio glaciale del
nostro mondo", un mondo che a
volte gli pareva un "cumulo di
oggetti", muto e inerte.

Dr FRANZ KAFKA
1883–1924

HERMANN KAFKA
1854–1931

JULIE KAFKA
1856–1934

MILENA

Molto presto in Kafka la scrittura assunse la dimensione di un'esistenza a parte; scriveva nei *Diari*: "... non sono altro che letteratura e non posso né voglio essere altro ." Persino i diversi tentativi da lui fatti per instaurare dei rapporti sentimentali durevoli, di cui è testimonianza la corrispondenza con Felice Bauer e Julie Wohryzek, si conclusero con una tragica rinuncia Solamente, forse, il tardivo incontro con Milena Jesenská ● *116* avrebbe potuto modificarne l'atteggiamento: le bellissime lettere che le scrisse rimangono l'unica dolorosa traccia di questa relazione.

MAX BROD, L'AMICO DI SEMPRE

L'iscrizione alla facoltà di giurisprudenza dell'università tedesca di Praga, impostagli dal padre, doveva assegnargli grandi responsabilità in seno alla burocrazia austriaca. Per lui fu invece una tortura. L'amicizia con Oskar Pollak gli fu di conforto, così come in seguito quella fedele e nobile di Max Brod, che poi dedicò la propria vita alla missione di portare a conoscenza del mondo intero l'opera dell'amico. Il 28 giugno 1906 Kafka ottenne la laurea in legge.

UNA VITA FECONDA DI SCRITTI

Kafka non cessò mai di scrivere. Il 4 settembre 1917 gli venne diagnosticata la tubercolosi: cominciarono allora le sue peregrinazioni da un sanatorio all'altro, confortato da Ottla, la sorella prediletta. Si spense a Kierling, presso Vienna, il 3 giugno 1924. Anche in questi anni dolorosi egli non rinunciò alla passione della scrittura. Nel 1922 scrisse *Il castello*, *Primo dolore*, *Il digiunatore*, *Indagini di un cane*. Nel 1923 visse un breve periodo d'indipendenza e di serenità con Dora Diamant, a Berlino, dove redasse i suoi ultimi testi in prosa, *Una donnina*, *La tana* (1923), *Josefine, la cantante* (1924).

«SONO ALLE ASSICURAZIONI GENERALI, CON LA SPERANZA TUTTAVIA D'ANDARMI A SEDERE, PROPRIO IO, NELLE SEDIE DI PAESI MOLTO LONTANI, DI VEDERE DA UNA FINESTRA D'UFFICIO CAMPI DI CANNA DA ZUCCHERO O CIMITERI MUSULMANI.»

UN UOMO DEL SUO TEMPO

La sensibilità per i problemi sociali e politici si rafforzò nel corso della sua vita. Frequentava le riunioni pubbliche, durante le quali i più importanti uomini politici cechi prendevano la parola, e seguiva questi dibattiti nella rivista *Čas*, diretta da Tomáš G. Masaryk. Partecipava alle manifestazioni dell'associazione dei lavoratori Vilém Körber e a quelle del gruppo social-rivoluzionario Klub mladých. Nel giugno 1912 assistette anche alle conferenze del socialdemocratico Soukup sul sistema americano, che ebbero poi profonda influenza nello sviluppo delle scene sulle elezioni contenute nel suo ultimo romanzo, *America*.

"LA METAMORFOSI"

L'opera fu pubblicata nel 1915. Un disegno di Hans Fromus (1948) ne illustra una scena.

KAFKA SCOMPARSO

Gli avvenimenti che seguirono la morte di Kafka relegarono la sua opera nell'oscurità. La prima edizione integrale, cominciata nel 1935, fu ostacolata e infine vietata. L'appartamento berlinese di Dora Diamant fu messo sotto sequestro e numerosi manoscritti vennero distrutti. A Praga gli occupanti nazisti saccheggiarono archivi, documenti e lettere. Le tre sorelle di Kafka, come numerosi amici e parenti che erano stati testimoni della sua vita, morirono nei campi di concentramento. Fu solo negli anni Cinquanta che la sua opera finalmente riemerse.

A lato, una scena del film *Kafka*, girato nel 1992 a Praga da Steven Soderbergh.

LA CITTÀ TRIONFANTE

GRANDEZZA E SOLITUDINE

Chateubriand (1768-1848) si recò due volte a Praga nel 1833 per rendere omaggio a Carlo X in esilio. Questi infatti risiedette al castello di Praga dal 1832 al 1836.

❝ Mi inerpicai su strade silenziose, scure, senza lampioni, sino ai piedi dell'alta collina che corona l'immenso castello dei re di Boemia. L'edificio disegnava la propria massa nera sul cielo; nessuna luce usciva dalle sue finestre; vi era qualcosa della solitudine, del luogo e della grandezza del Vaticano, o del tempio di Gerusalemme visto dalla valle di Josafat.

Non si sentiva altro che il rimbombo dei miei passi e di quelli della mia guida; a intervalli, tanto la salita era ripida, ero obbligato ad arrestarmi sulle piattaforme del lastricato distribuite lungo il cammino.

Mano a mano che salivo, scoprivo la città al di sotto. Le concatenazioni della storia, la sorte degli uomini, la distruzione degli imperi, i disegni della Provvidenza, si presentavano alla mia memoria, identificandosi con i ricordi del mio destino personale ❞

FRANÇOIS-RENÉ DE CHATEAUBRIAND,
MÉMOIRES D'OUTRE-TOMBE (LIBRO XXXVIII, CAP. I).

FINO AL CUORE

R.M. Rilke (1875-1926) nacque a Praga, dove passò l'infanzia e la fine dell'adolescenza. Le sue opere giovanili sono segnate dal carattere di questa città, dalla sua atmosfera singolare e ammaliante, vicina a quella dei romanzi di Kafka, di Ungar, di Meyrink. In un articolo apparso il 10 giugno 1899 sul settimanale berlinese Die Zukunft, *parlando di* Due storie praghesi *Rilke dice: "Il proposito di questo libro era di avvicinare in qualche modo la propria fanciullezza. Poiché ogni arte tende a questo giardino remoto per arricchire i suoi profumi e oscurità e per dare la parola al suo fruscio. Il pretesto era rappresentato da due piccole storie praghesi. Lo scenario è Praga, questa città piena di vicoli bui e di cortili misteriosi."*

❝ Nelle prime serate di primavera l'aria che si posa lieve su tutti i colori, rendendoli luminosi e più simili gli uni agli altri, è fresca e umida. Le case chiare sul lungofiume hanno assunto quasi tutte la pallida tonalità del cielo e solo le finestre di tanto in tanto mandano guizzi di luce ardente per poi spegnersi placate nel crepuscolo, non appena il sole non le molesta più. Allora solo la torre di San Vito continua a stagliarsi ritta nel suo antichissimo eterno grigiore. "È veramente un emblema", disse Bohusch allo studente taciturno. "Resiste a ogni crepuscolo ed è sempre identica. Intendo nel colore. Non è vero?"

Rezek non aveva sentito niente. Guardava dalla parte della Città Piccola in direzione della torre sul ponte dove in quel momento si accendevano le luci.

Bohusch continuò: "Conosco la mia mammina Praga fin dentro al cuore, fin dentro al cuore", ripeté, come se qualcuno avesse messo in dubbio la sua affermazione, "infatti proprio questo è il suo cuore, la Città Piccola con il Hradschin [il castello]. Nel cuore c'è sempre la parte più segreta, e senta, ci sono tanti segreti in queste vecchie case." **"**

RAINER MARIA RILKE, *DUE STORIE PRAGHESI*,
EDIZIONI E/O, ROMA 1985.

A IMMAGINE DELL'UOMO

Josef Škvorecký è nato a Náchod in Boemia nel 1924. Dopo l'invasione sovietica del 1968 emigra in Canada dove dirige una casa editrice in lingua ceca. È autore di numerosi romanzi e novelle, nonché di saggi e di sceneggiature cinematografiche. Ha tradotto i principali scrittori americani contemporanei.

" Crepuscolo. Color miele e sangue. Senza alcun rapporto con la situazione storica della nazione e della città, parlava, a me diciottenne, al riparo in un angolo riparato d'Europa dove la morte era più clemente, più modesta. Stavo in piedi davanti alla facciata di un albergo costruito alla fine del secolo, in un'epoca di sforzi ostinati per creare qualcosa di totalmente nuovo, al quale però non si era saputo dare forma, e gli si era perciò conferita l'impronta di una grande inettitudine che, in fondo, aveva una sua bellezza, non essendo imitazione di Dio ma immagine dell'uomo; me ne sto dunque in piedi davanti a quella facciata con un mosaico verdognolo tutt'attorno alle grandi vetrate del caffè incise a motivi floreali, e intanto la sera, pozzanghera color miele, vi gocciola sopra. […]; e la luce del sole color miele (che, sospeso sopra la torre panciuta del castello vecchio, divampava nelle ampie finestre della torre quadrata del castello nuovo del milionario Domanín, la cui figlia amavo, per il solo fatto che viveva in quella torre da dove ogni notte la luce delle lampade di alabastro filtrava in direzione dei quattro punti cardinali passando attraverso quattro acquari, e lei era pallida, malata, in un mondo di pesci viola, anche lei solo un'illusione, solo un sogno, solo il sogno patologico di una patologica infanzia) si era riflessa sul corpo enorme e incredibile di un sax basso, grande quanto un pentolone da bucato.

Non immaginavo che cose simili esistessero realmente. Le ultime testimonianze risalivano all'epoca in cui vivevano i poetisti e i dadaisti, forse negli anni remoti della Prima Repubblica qualcuno aveva fabbricato un simile pezzo da museo, espediente pubblicitario troppo costoso e in seguito riposto in qualche magazzino dimenticato. Poi non se n'erano più fabbricati; era solo un sogno, un calcolo teorico forgiato chissà quando nei variegati anni Venti; noi avevamo solo sax alti e sax tenori. **99**

JOSEF ŠKVORECKÝ, *IL SAX BASSO*, ADELPHI, MILANO 1993.

LA CITTÀ VOLUTTUOSA

ELOGIO DEL KITSCH

Il nome di Milena Jesenská, nata a Praga nel 1896 e morta nel campo di concentramento di Ravensbrück nel 1944, è entrato nella storia della letteratura grazie alle lettere che Kafka le indirizzò (Lettere a Milena, *Mondadori, Milano 1980). Questa donna per venti anni perseguì la carriera di giornalista: redasse numerose cronache per giornali praghesi (*Tribuna, Národní Listy*), poi* reportages *politici per il settimanale liberal-democratico* Přítomnost *e, in seguito all'invasione del suo paese da parte delle truppe hitleriane, per un giornale clandestino,* V boj. *Fu la prima traduttrice di Kafka in ceco. Sia per la sua storia sia per la sua opera, Milena Jesenská è una grandissima testimone della propria epoca e del proprio paese, particolarmente di Praga, alla quale era attaccata "con tutte le fibre del suo cuore", come scrive Margarete Buber-Neumann nel libro che le ha dedicato (*Milena, l'amica di Kafka, *Adelphi, Milano 1986). Questo brano è tratto da un suo articolo,* Vivere.

66Ho deciso di fare l'elogio del Kitsch, anche se è ben lontana da me l'idea che questo sia degno di rispetto e positivo. Tanto meno ho in mente la pretesa di definirlo bello; e mi vedreste in gran difficoltà se dovessi enumerarne le virtù. Tuttavia, dopo aver bighellonato due ore nella mattutina città inondata dal sole, sono stata presa dalla voglia di fare qualcosa di un po' folle. Il Kitsch? Del superfluo, un non so che di vano, una sorta di bolla alla superficie del tempo; ma una bolla magnifica, multicolore. Non c'è del buono o del cattivo Kitsch. Esiste, punto e basta. [...]

Prendete una banale giostra, variopinta di colori chiassosi, nei dintorni della città – nel fossato dietro il ponte Palacký. Non attira affatto gli sguardi. Non perché essa sia spoglia di una qualche meravigliosa bellezza, ma perché i passanti si intimidiscono di fronte al Kitsch. Alle loro anime che essi portano a spasso in giacca e in colletto bianco da un ufficio all'altro, questa giostra con le sue frange e le sue campanelle, questa giostra volteggiante tappezzata di velluto rosso e di galloni dorati non evoca affatto un castello incantato e una principessa bella come il sole – anche se è proprio ciò che questo ragazzo, succhiandosi il pollice, contempla piantato davanti alla giostra. Eppure questa giostra è un pezzo della vostra giovinezza che è svanita. [...] E, il giorno di Tutti i Santi, le coccarde bianche nel cimitero di Olšany e le cornici di perle azzurre che attorniano le rose di latta celebrano con magnificenza questo lutto. **99**

MILENA JESENSKÁ, *ŽÍT*, 1922.

DALLA PARTE DEI SOBBORGHI

Bohumil Hrabal ▲ 163 è nato a Brno nel 1914 e morto nel 1997. Laureato in legge non ha mai esercitato la professione di avvocato, ma ha svolto parecchi lavori negli ambienti più diversi, sempre scrivendo i propri romanzi pubblicati solo a partire dal 1963. Tra gli scrittori cechi contemporanei viene considerato uno dei più importanti. A.M. Ripellino lo situa "alla convergenza della linea metafisica Kafka/Meyrink e di quella, grottesca ed eloquente, di Hašek e la sua opera riunisce quindi due aspetti fondamentali dell'essenza praghese."

66 E quando il tram imboccò il ponte di Libeň, mi alzai, mi appoggiai al finestrino e sgranai gli occhi, che cosa non vedo al di là del fiume? La Bulovka, quell'ospedale e le case gigantesche sparpagliate sui pendii, questo mi ricordava le immagini delle riviste sul Tibet, castelli stupendi ci sono là sulla Bulovka, tessere sparpagliate di un domino... E poi il tram svoltò nel viale principale di Libeň, arrossii leggermente, nemmeno un negozio mi sfuggì, passavo con lo sguardo da una vetrina a quella che mi veniva incontro e così, anche se volevo scendere al teatro, sul marciapiede di quella fermata dove subito dietro l'angolo c'è la via na Hrázi, così avevo l'impressione che come stavo percorrendo quel viale principale, mi sembrava di attraversare Břeclav quella volta che avevo sedici anni, tanto bello mi appariva quel viale principale di Libeň. [...] E così scesi, mi inteneriva la piccola pasticceria u Bulovky, una pasticceria in una casetta bassa, c'era una fermata

del tram e già me ne andavo di nuovo giù, non potevo saziarmi di quel viale principale di Libeň, ma più di ogni cosa mi commuoveva la Červená Báň, alcune casette e alcune officine smantellate e una fabbrichetta, e tutto affondava nel verde dei cespugli e degli alberi e sullo sfondo si ergeva ritto sulla collina un cascinale in rovina. [...] Mentre scendevo giù a Libeň, ancora questa Libeň mi pareva come Hodonín dove avevo abitato fino ai sedici anni, veramente questa Libeň era una cittadina di campagna ma molto diversa da Žižkov, dove abito. Qui, quando prendo il tram, vedo piccoli parchi e alberelli e il fiumiciattolo Rokytka, mentre a Žižkov tutto è solo e soltanto di pietra e anche quei nomi delle vie di Žižkov mi terrorizzano, come le messe dell'Avvento e il riformatorio e la caserma e la galera... [...] Mi stupii di quanto fosse bella la periferia di Libeň e anche di quanto fossero ben vestite qui le giovani donne. **99**

BOHUMIL HRABAL, *LE NOZZE IN CASA-
ROMANZETTO FEMMINILE*,
EINAUDI, TORINO 1992.

LA CITTÀ TRADITA

Il patto di Monaco ● 38, concluso nel settembre del 1938 fra Germania, Gran Bretagna e Francia, mise brutalmente fine alle illusioni diplomatiche di Beneš, allora presidente della Repubblica, e alle speranze del popolo ceco, che si trovò inerme di fronte all'espansionismo della Germania nazista. Gli scrittori cechi hanno espresso la collera e la disperazione provocate nel loro paese da questo tradimento.

SAPORE DI LACRIME

Vítězslav Nezval (1900-1958) è autore di un'opera vasta e diversificata (romanzi, racconti, saggi, opere teatrali, articoli, traduzioni...), ma è famoso soprattutto come poeta. Negli anni Venti aderì al partito comunista, fu membro del Devětsil con Karel Teige, Jaroslav Seifert, Vladislav Vančura... e fondatore del gruppo surrealista cecoslovacco. Monaco è il laconico titolo di questa poesia del 1938.

❝È un giorno in cui anche il canto di un uccello vi fa male al cuore
dove sono passati i carri schizza il fango viscido
come il sangue di un bue sprizza nel mattatoio
In questo giorno anche il mendicante trova un sapore di lacrime nella sua cicca

Invano le folle si adunano per ascoltare la voce che vuole consolarle
Si assembrano si separano e di nuovo abbassano la testa
rifuggendo la voce che li proclama o cechi cechi o cechi

invano le folle si ribellano levando in alto il pugno abbronzato
invano le folle si riuniscono e si assembrano sulle piazze
È la fine finita la speranza ed è la fine della felicità

Mentre la sera cupa pesa sull'orizzonte grave
le voci nascoste nella nebbia si levano all'unisono
Voci che gridano Traditi traditi che gridano al tradimento❞

VÍTĚZSLAV NEZVAL, *MNICHOV*, 1938.

SAPORE DI VERGOGNA

Jaroslav Seifert (1901-1986) nel periodo fra le due guerre aderì al Devětsil e al poetismo. Militò nel partito comunista, che lasciò nel 1929. Nel 1956, al congresso dell'Unione degli scrittori, difese pubblicamente i poeti imprigionati. Fu poi uno dei firmatari di Charta 77. Nel 1984 ricevette il premio Nobel per la letteratura. Roman Jakobson ▲ 305, che giunse a Praga nel 1920 e frequentò i poeti del Devětsil, scrisse a proposito di lui: "Non è solamente il più grande poeta lirico dei mille anni della letteratura ceca [...] è il più grande maestro della poesia mondiale." Seifert è tra gli autori cechi più tradotti in Italia. Questi versi sono tratti dalla poesia Il castello di Praga, *che rievoca la tragedia di Monaco a trent'anni di distanza.*

> «Città che ha sofferto, città purificata!
> So quale oscuro anello cerchia il tuo orizzonte
> e come fosti sola nell'amara veglia tra il pane
> dell'angoscia e l'acqua del tradimento.»
> Suzanne Renaud

> La Francia un tempo ci era cara,
> e la Francia ci ha traditi.
> Alla finestra che dava sui giardini
> Hitler è apparso per dare, con una smorfia,
> a Praga l'ordine di inginocchiarsi. [...]
>
> Per l'angoscia correvo qui e là sul ponte.
> Ai pilastri aderivano, leggere,
> le lingue umide delle onde.
> Il castello era striato di vapori grigi
> e macchiato del sangue delle rose raccolte.
> Il cielo lo teneva in braccio.
> Persino le feritoie delle torri, drizzate in arco di cerchio,
> volevano difenderlo dall'assalto
> delle stelle invisibili.
> Ma nessuno dava l'ordine. **99**
>
> Jaroslav Seifert, *Pražský hrad*, 1968.

SAPORE DI COLLERA

Vladimír Holan è nato e morto a Praga (1905-1980). Nel 1926 cominciò a pubblicare componimenti poetici influenzati dal surrealismo. Dal 1933 al 1940 è redattore della rivista Život*, poi della rivista* Program D 40. *A partire dal 1940 si dedica esclusivamente alla scrittura e alle traduzioni. Tra il 1948 e il 1963 ogni pubblicazione gli fu vietata. Nel 1948 si stabilì a Kampa, isoletta della Moldava nel centro di Praga, dove visse in completo ritiro, nella solitudine e nel silenzio. "Poeta elegiaco ma epico, intimo ma sconcertante, lirico ma triviale, barocco ma risolutamente moderno", Holan è considerato, con Seifert di cui fu amico, uno dei più grandi poeti cechi. Questa poesia porta il titolo eloquente* Risposta alla Francia.

> Nessuno si cura, laggiù da tutti voi,
> che questo paese nel quale io vivo ancora tranquillamente
> possa essere oggi o domani per il vostro orgoglio
> pelle di cane buona per la cornamusa
> Francia, l'infamia di qualcuno dei tuoi
> è profonda come il disonore che ci tocca.

Perché sei bandiera che si aggrappa all'onta,
sei voce senza voce.

Sei l'avvenire che non sarà,
la misura postuma dei codardi.
Il solo fatto che oggi soffi il vento
dà forma ai tuoi brandelli. **"**
VLADIMÍR HOLAN, *ODPOVĚĎ' FRANCII*, 1938.

L'ARTE DELLA DERISIONE

UN EROE BURLESCO

Jaroslav Hašek (1883-1923), vagabondo, anarchico e giornalista, scrisse numerosi articoli e racconti umoristici e satirici. Ma soprattutto ha creato il personaggio, divenuto leggendario, del "Buon soldato Švejk, eroe derisorio, insieme naïf e scaltro, che accorda lo spirito di Don Chisciotte col pancione di Sancho Panza." Questo vasto romanzo eroi-comico "così irreligioso, così lutulento e sfacciato, macchina che sgonfia i miti, romanzo che si fa gabbo di tutto, tuttavia non rinunzia a una sua storta metafisica, a un suo ridicolo soprannaturale" (A. M. Ripellino). La sua arte del sarcasmo evoca i quadri di O. Dix, di G. Grosz, di M. Beckmann, di L. Meidner, mostrando gli orrori della guerra come un'assurda e crudele buffonata, e la sua opera illustra alla perfezione questi versi di Vladimír Holan: "L'ironia non muore per amor di tragedia."

" E fu così che un bel giorno si vide per le strade di Praga un esempio di commovente eroismo. Una vecchia donna spingeva dinanzi a sé un carrozzino, su cui stava seduto un uomo col berretto militare e il "franceschiello" luccicante, che agitava un paio di grucce. E sul suo pastrano splendeva un iridescente ciuffetto di piume da recluta.
E quell'uomo, agitando incessantemente le grucce, gridava per le strade di Praga: "A Belgrado, a Belgrado!"
Gli veniva dietro una gran turba di gente, ingrossava senza posa il piccolo capannello che s'era raccolto dinanzi alla casa, per vedere Švejk che andava alla guerra.
Švejk poté constatare che le guardie di polizia di servizio ai crocicchi gli facevano il saluto militare.
Sulla piazza di san Venceslao la folla che circondava il carrozzino di Švejk era salita a parecchie centinaia di persone. **"**
JAROSLAV HAŠEK, *IL BUON SOLDATO ŠVEJK*, FELTRINELLI, MILANO 1971.

NEL PAESE DEL SIMULACRO

Václav Jamek è nato nel 1949 e ha studiato a Digione e a Parigi, poi alla facoltà di lettere di Praga. Poeta e traduttore, lavora alla casa editrice Odeon a Praga e collabora a numerosi giornali e periodici letterari. Questo brano è tratto da un suo saggio pubblicato in Francia.

"L'umanesimo socialista: respirare è fidarsi del regime; in altre parole, significa non fidarsi di niente e di nessuno. A maggior ragione, bisogna essere folli per fidarsi della propria immagine nello specchio, rasandosi, al mattino.
Pertanto non cesso di rimanere colpito dalla buffa giustezza di questa farsa di studenti della quale, ben prima che a me si imponesse, con la forza di una necessità interiore, la figura di Narciso-Minotauro, fusi insieme e personificanti nella loro identità tutta una faccia della mia più torbida realtà, io sono stato uno degli istigatori e dei partecipanti: il 7 maggio 1970, un piccolo gruppo di studenti,

DUBČEK AND HAVEL

Timothy Garton Ash's book "We The People" celebrates the revolutions of 1989, as witnessed in Warsaw, Budapest, Berlin and Prague.

"In the early afternoon comes Dubček. He looks as it he has stepped straight out of a black-and-white photograph from 1968. The face is older, more lined, of course, but he has the same grey coat and paisley scarf, the same tentative, touching smile, the same functionary's hat. Protected by Havel's bodyguards – lead on, John Bok – we emerge from the belly of the Lantern, Dubček and Havel side by side, and scuttle through covered shopping arcades and tortuous back passages to reach the balcony of the Socialist Party publishing house and the offices of *Svobodné Slovo:* the balcony of the free word. Along the arcades people simply gape. They can't believe it. Dubček! It is as if the ghost of Winston Churchill were to be seen striding down the Burlington Arcade.But when he steps out on to the balcony in the frosty evening air, illuminated by television spotlights, the crowds give such a roar as I have never heard. 'DUBČEK! DUBČEK!' echoes off the tall houses up and down the long, narrow square. Many people mourn his ambiguous role after the Soviet invasion, and his failure to use the magic of his name to support the democratic opposition. He has changed little with the times. His speech still contains those wooden newspeak phrases, the *langue de bois*. (At one point he refers to 'confrontationist extremist tendencies'.) He still believes in socialism – that is, reformed communism – with a human face. The true leader of this movement, in Prague at least, is Havel not Dubček. But for the moment none of this matters. For the moment all that matters is that the legendary hero is really standing here, addressing a huge crowd on Wenceslas Square, while the emergency session of the Central Committee has, we are told, been removed to a distant suburb. 'Dubček to the castle!' roars the crowd – that is Dubček for president. The old man must believe he will wake up in a moment and find he is dreaming. For the man who supplanted him and now sits in the castle, Gustav Husák, it is the nightmare come true.After Dubček comes Havel. 'Dubček-Havel,' they chant, the name of '68 and the name of '89.**"**

TIMOTHY GARTON ASH,
WE THE PEOPLE, PUB. GRANTA BOOKS
IN ASSOC. WITH PENGUIN BOOKS, CAMBRIDGE 1990

GC

ARCHITECTURE

Dr Charles Burney (1726–1814), a musical historian, visited the city shortly after the battle of Prague in 1757 gave Frederick the Great his first success against the Austrians in the Seven Years' War.

❝This city is extremely beautiful, when seen at a distance. It is situated on two or three hills, and has the river Mulda running through the middle of it. It is divided into three different quarters, or districts, which are distinguished by the names of Ult Stadt, Neue Stadt, and Kleine Stadt, or Old Town, New Town, and Little Town; the Kleine Stadt is the most modern, and the best built of the three. The houses are all of white stone, or stucco, in imitation of it, and all uniform in size and colour. The hill of St. Laurence, the highest about the town, commands a prospect, not only of the whole city, but of all the adjacent country: the declivity of this hill is covered with wood, consisting chiefly of fruit-trees, and vineyards. A great part of the town is new, as scarce a single building escaped the Prussian batteries, and bombardment during the blockade, in the last war. A few churches and palaces only, that were strongly built, and of less combustible materials than the rest, were proof against their fury; and in the walls of these, are still sticking innumerable cannon balls, and bombs, particularly, in the superb palace of count Czernin, and in the Capuchin's church. This palace, which is of the Ionic order, and built of whitestone, has thirty windows in front, the chapel, at the Capuchins, is an exact copy, in stone, of that at Loretto, in Marble.

The inhabitants are still at work throughout the city, in repairing the Prussian devastations, particularly at the cathedral and imperial palace, which were both almost entirely demolished; these are situated on a high hill, facing that of St. Laurence.❞

DR BURNEY'S MUSICAL TOURS IN EUROPE, VOL. II,
PUB. OXFORD UNIVERSITY PRESS,
LONDON 1959

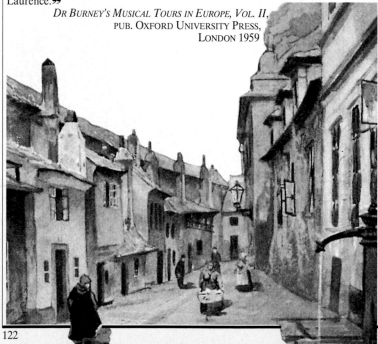

FOREIGN INFLUENCE

The writings of V. S. Pritchett (b. 1900), the British novelist and short-story writer, are full of shrewd observations of human nature and culture.

❝Prague, or more particularly old Prague, which is very large, is one of the noblest cities in Europe. Its hundred Gothic spires prick the sky, its medieval towers, its baroque belfries and cupolas bring their graces to the city panorama. One has an impression of another Paris of the Latin quarter. The broad river curves through the tree-lined embankments. One can see from the war between Gothic and Baroque that this city is marked at every corner by historical struggle. It is a difficulty for the Czech to admire the Baroque because it is the architecture of a foreign conqueror, though some of the art historians are beginning to weaken and point out that it was also the work of Czech artisans. One could see why L—— claimed that the Czechs had the highest level of political education in Europe; they have learned in the bitter school of oppression.❞

V. S. PRITCHETT, *FOREIGN FACES,* PUB. CHATTO & WINDUS, LONDON 1964

ARCHWAYS AND VAULTS

Patrick Leigh Fermor (b. 1915) describes the staircase leading to the citadel and King Vladislav's Hall of Homage.

❝The city teems with wonders; but what belongs where? Certainly that stupendous staircase called the Riders' Steps, and all that lay beyond them, were part of the great castle-palace. The marvellous strangeness of the late gothic vaults enclosing this flight must have germinated in an atmosphere like the English mood which coaxed fan-tracery into bloom . . . These vaults are almost impossible to describe. The ribs burst straight out of the walls in V-shaped clusters of springers. Grooved like celery stalks and blade-shaped in cross section with the edge pointing down, they expanded and twisted as they rose. They separated, converged again and crossed each other and as they sped away, enclosed slender spans of wall like the petals of tulips: and when two ribs intersected, they might both have been obliquely notched and then half-joggled together with studied carelessness. They writhed on their own axes and simultaneously followed the curve

of the vault; and often, after these contorted intersections, the ribs that followed a concave thrust were chopped off short while the convex plunged headlong and were swallowed up in the masonry. The loose mesh tightened as it neared the rounded summit and the frantic reticulation jammed in momentary deadlock. Four truncated ribs, dovetailing in rough parallelograms, formed keystones and then broke loose again with a wildness which at first glance resembled organic violence clean out of control. But a second glance, embracing the wider design, captured a strange and marvellous coherence, as though petrifaction had arrested this whirling dynamism at a chance moment of balance and harmony.

Everything here was strange. The archway at the top of these shallow steps, avoiding the threatened anticlimax of a flattened ogee, deviated in two round-topped lobes on either side with a right-angled central cleft slashed deep between the cusps. There had been days, I was told, when horsemen on the way to the indoor lists rode in full armour up these steps: lobster-clad riders slipping and clattering as they stooped their ostrich-plumes under the freak doorway, gingerly carrying their lances at the trail to keep the bright paint that spiralled them unchipped. But in King Vladislav's vast Hall of Homage the ribs of the vaulting had further to travel, higher to soar. Springing close to the floor from reversed and bisected cones, they sailed aloft curving and spreading across the wide arch of the ceiling: parting, crossing, re-joining, and – once again – enclosing those slim subdivided tulips as they climbed. Then they cast their intertwining arcs in wider and yet wider loops with the looseness and the overlap of lassoos kept perpetually on the move, accelerating, as they ascended, to the speed of coiling stockwhips . . . Travelling the length of that arched vista of ceiling, the loops of the stone ribs expanded and crossed and changed partners, simultaneously altering direction and handing on the succession of arcs until the parabolas, reaching the far limit of this strange curvilinear relay-race, began to swing back. Nearing home and completing the journey in reverse, they rejoined their lost companions at their starting point and sank tapering and interlocked. The sinuous mobility entranced the eye, but it was not only this. Lit by the wintry chiaroscuro of the tall windows, the white tulip-shaped expanses that these stone ribs enclosed so carelessly seemed to be animated by an even more rapid and streamlined verve. Each of these incidental and sinuous facets reflected a different degree of white, and their motion, as they ascended the reversed half-cones of the vault and curled over into the ceiling, suggested the spreading and upward-showering rush of a school of dolphins leaping out of the water. **99**

PATRICK LEIGH FERMOR, *A TIME OF GIFTS – ON FOOT TO CONSTANTINOPLE, FROM THE HOOK OF HOLLAND TO THE MIDDLE DANUBE*, PUB. JOHN MURRAY, DATE?

NATURAL ATTRACTIONS

THE RIVER MOLDAU

Arthur Symons (1865–1945) was a British poet and critic and a leading spirit of the Decadent movement.

66The Moldau, which cuts Prague in two, is broad and swift, golden under sunlight, as it hurries under its five bridges, between the green banks and the quay. Long rafts of floating timber, on which men run to and fro with tall poles, pass slowly, hurrying as they shoot the weir. Boats cross from side to side, and one sees the slow, crossing gesture of men with long-handled scoops, dredging in a barge. A man stands on a heap of stones, in the very middle of the weir, fishing. Half-naked figures, or figures in bathing-gowns, move to and fro on the big brown floating baths, or swing out on a trapeze over the water. A sound of music comes from one of the green islands, where people are sitting at café tables under the trees. People drowse on the benches by the side of the river.

Warm, full of repose, heavy with happy sleep, at midday, at night the riverside becomes mysterious, a romance. The water silvers; with its islands, from which lights glimmer, it might be a lake, but for the thunder of the weir, which comes to you as you walk under the trees, or go out on a kind of platform beside a dusty mill, from which you see the water rushing violently towards the great wooden stakes by the bridge. Lights move on the opposite shore, at the foot of what seems a vast mountain, dimly outlined. The bridge, at first invisible, a detached line of lights, comes out gradually, as your eyes accustom themselves to the night-mist, in the palest of grey, like the ghost of a bridge. Beyond and above, the Hradčin emerges in the same ghostly outline, a long grey line against the sky, out of which the cathedral spire points upward. It is a view which seems to have been composed, almost too full of the romantic elements to be quite natural; and it has something of whatever is strange, placid, and savage in the character of the Bohemians.**99**

ARTHUR SYMONS, *CITIES*, PUB. J. M. DENT & CO., LONDON 1903

PRAGUE IN THE SNOW

Karel Čapek (1890–1938), the Czech novelist and dramatist, decided to write this article about snow because he could no longer build snow men or snow castles.

66When the snow comes down, Prague at once becomes a little old-world town; overnight we go back fifty or a hundred years and it is suddenly all countrified and old-fashioned, all quaintly baroque, straddling, naïve, and antique; for no reason at all one thinks of old women with seven petticoats, apples baked in their jackets, the smell of burning wood, old interiors, and flowered curtains. The folk in the street are happy, stamping their footprints in the snow, crunching it and waving their hands as they did a hundred years ago. And it is so still! the stillness of a little country town. Even the Vltava does not move; the tram tinkles like a sledge, and one would not be a bit surprised if motor cars began sounding little bells as sleighs used to once upon a time. Old world! Suddenly it is a world of old things and old dimensions. The charm of the quaint little town. The weather which brings old times back.

That is why, as you will understand, the only real snow is what we get on Malá Strana. That is why it lasts there longer than in other places; and when it is all blown away from other parts of the town (because there it is nothing special, just idle and good-for-nothing) on Malá Strana, thank God, it still lies in banks and drifts just wherever it can. For here it has a special right, here and up yonder round the Castle. . . .

Then when the moon shines on it all, what happens cannot even be expressed: Prague crouches down and makes herself quite little; she holds her breath; the snow rings like glass under-foot, the roofs press themselves down to the ground, everything huddles together icily, and it is so light, so strangely light, that you are startled at the darkness within you.99

KAREL ČAPEK, *INTIMATE THINGS*,
TRANS. BY DORA ROUND, PUB. GEORGE ALLEN & UNWIN LTD., LONDON 1935

LIVING IN PRAGUE

FOOD

Hester Piozzi (1741–1821) found that in Prague "everything seems at least five centuries behind-hand", but she was impressed by the food.

66The eating here is incomparable; I never saw such poultry even at London or Bath, and there is a plenty of game that amazes one; no inn so wretched but you have a pheasant for your supper, and often partridge soup. The fish is carried about the streets in so elegant a style it tempts one; a very large round bathing-tub, as we should call it, set barrow-wise on two not very low wheels, is easily pushed along by one man, though full of the most pellucid water, in which the carp, tench, and eels, are all leaping alive, to a size and perfection I am ashamed to relate; but the tench of four and five pounds weight have a richness and flavour one had no notion of till we arrived at Vienna, and they are the same here.99

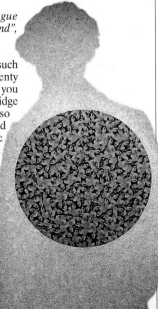

HESTER PIOZZI, *OBSERVATIONS AND
REFLECTIONS MADE IN THE COURSE OF A
JOURNEY THROUGH FRANCE, ITALY AND
GERMANY*, EDITED BY HERBERT BARROWS,
PUB. UNIVERSITY OF MICHIGAN PRESS,
ANN ARBOR, 1967

CRIME

Czech novelist Jaroslav Hašek (1883–1923) describes the streetwise Cetlička, an outlaw who loves Prague.

"Cetlička was banished from Prague . . . All went well in the daytime. He sauntered about Prague, no one recognised him, that is not until the terribly disastrous evenings.

Once when he was in *The Stars* he had wanted to run off with an overcoat; on another occasion he had wanted to slip away from the *California* without paying the bill. Then there were the fist fights in *The Wreath*. It all added up to a month of gaol for each incident because he had disobeyed the law.

Nevertheless, he loved his native Prague, because he as able to take full advantage of this city which had so much to offer.

No other city had as many skirts hanging outside the shop windows, nor did ne know any other town that had locks which were so easily pried open. Nowhere was it easier to steal than in Prague.

Whenever something happens on the streets, no matter how silly, a crowd of people will gather, all of them deaf and blind, jostling and elbowing their way to see for themselves that it was really a sparrow's egg that fell from the eaves of the roof right onto the hat of a respectable gentleman who was now indignantly showing his black bowler with a yellow stain on the crown to the inquisitive throng that had gathered about him.

Those were such opportune occasions for emptying pockets of overcoats, for hardly anyone ever carries wallets in breast-pockets as it saves them the trouble of unbuttoning jackets; to say nothing about the pleasure people get in being robbed.

Cetlička would plunge into the midst of a mob, they might be a horde of admirers watching a couple of monkeys race each other; wooden, mechanical monkeys in toyshops, in front of which adults would be pushing one another, although the display was meant for children who could not get near enough to see anything because of the hobbledehoy grown-ups.

He was among those who struggled to get seats in tramcars.

And wherever he went, he would reach down deep into people's pockets and depart unobserved.**"**

JAROSLAV HAŠEK, *THE TOURIST GUIDE*, PUB. ARTIA, 1961

AN ANTIQUE ARMOIRE

Czech novelist Ivan Klima (b. 1931) writes of a travel courier observing his own city.

"The repairs to the façades on the Old Town Square were almost finished, and the square gleamed with newness and colour like a grand Sacher cake; I liked it, and I got enormous pleasure out of just being able to wander about there. Before I found this job I came downtown twice a month at most, and then I was in a hurry to get back home and back to work. But now this job brought me here every day, and I could study the slow progress of repairs to the Týn Church, and peer into the exhibition room of the Town Hall. I could even have gone in, but felt reluctant to do so, for as long as I was moving through the streets with my pushcart in the general direction of my destination, I was working and no one could complain. But I had no business at an art show.

I stopped in front of the Town Hall tower. The first tourists of the morning were beginning to gather on the pavement below the astronomical clock. Tourists from the West were still asleep or perhaps having breakfast, whereas those standing beside me, already burdened with parcels and waiting for the Twelve Apostles to appear when the clock struck the hour, were a group from the empire of our eastern neighbours. I likened to their soft speech, a language that had seduced some of our reckless and gullible ancestors into dreaming dreams of a brotherhood of the strong and the weak. But the conversation didn't seem to be about anything that made sense. The clock struck, the apostles paraded one by one past the tiny portals, but as always, they remained silent, telling us nothing and then vanishing into their darkness again.

I walked along Ironmonger's Street to Mustek where, in an antique store, I saw a Renaissance armoire costing 180,000 crowns. Doing the work I was doing now, this was the accumulated salary of ten years. I began to plan the story of a courier who decided not to eat, drink, live anywhere or even read so he could save all his money to buy this antique armoire. Several endings suggested themselves. The courier, who all that time had slept in a cellar and lived on the leftovers he picked off plates in the stand-up buffets, could die of exhaustion. Or he survives but meanwhile – and this was the most plausible outcome – the armoire is sold to someone else. Or, and this was my favourite: he finally drags himself to the shop, where he finds the armoire still waiting for him, but in the meantime the price has doubled. **"**

IVAN KLIMA, *MY GOLDEN TRADES*,
PUB. GRANTA BOOKS IN ASSOC WITH PENGUIN BOOKS, 1992

KAFKA'S DIARIES

Franz Kafka (1883–1924) wrote the following diary entries on November 18, 1911, and March 14, 1915, respectively

"Yesterday in the factory. Rode back on the trolley, sat in a corner with legs stretched out, saw people outside, lights in stores, walls of viaducts through which we passed, backs and faces over and over again, a highway leading from the business street of the suburb with nothing human in it save people going home, the glaring electric lights of the railway station burned into the darkness, the low, tapering chimneys of the gasworks, a poster announcing the guest appearance of a singer, de Treville, that gropes its way along the walls as far as an alley near the cemeteries, from where it then returned to me out of the cool of

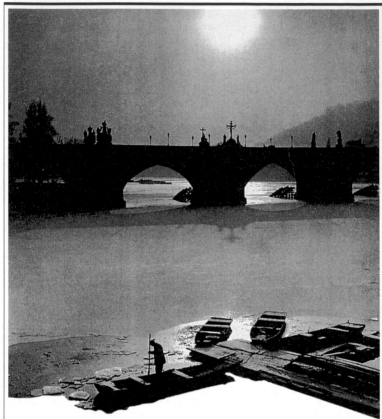

the fields into the liveable warmth of the city. We accept(ed) foreign cities as a fact, the inhabitants live there without penetrating our way of life, just as we cannot penetrate theirs, a comparison must be made, it can't be helped, but one is well aware that it has no moral or even psychological value, in the end one can often even omit the comparison because the difference in the condition of life is so great that it makes it unnecessary.

The suburbs of our native city, however, are also foreign to us, but in this case comparisons have value, a half-hour's walk can prove it to us over and over again, here live people partly within our city, partly on the miserable dark edge of the city that is furrowed like a great ditch, although they all have an area of interest in common with us that is greater than any other group of people outside the city. For this reason I always enter and leave the suburb with a weak mixed feeling of anxiety, of abandonment, of sympathy, of curiosity, of conceit, of joy in travelling, of fortitude, and return with pleasure, seriousness, and calm, especially from Zizkov.❞

❝A morning. In bed until half past eleven. Jumble of thoughts which slowly take shape and hardens in an incredible fashion. Read in the afternoon (Gogol) in the evening a walk, part of the time the defensible but untrustworthy ideas of the morning in my head. Was in Chotek Park. Most beautiful spot in Prague. Birds sang, the Castle was its arcade, the old trees hung with last year's foliage, the dim light.❞

THE DIARIES OF FRANZ KAFKA, 1910–13,
ED. MAX BROD, TRANS. JOSEPH KRESH, PUB.
SECKER & WARBURG,
LONDON 1948

Itineraries in Prague

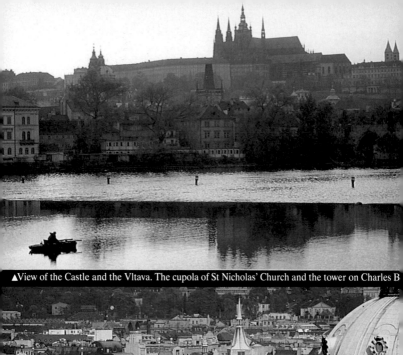

▲View of the Castle and the Vltava. The cupola of St Nicholas' Church and the tower on Charles B

▼ Prague by night, with St Nicholas' Church, Malá Strana in the foreground

▲ Church of Our Lady of Týn,   ▼ Statues on Charles Bridge

▼ "There are said to be as many churches here as there are days of the year." (Ingvalt Undset)

▲ Černínská Street, Hradčany

▼ Baroque façades in Old Town Square

▼ The old Jewish cemetery in Josefov

▲ The Nový Svet district

▼ A Secession façade in the Old Town

▼ Kampa Island seen from Charles Bridge

▲ Archways near Loretánská Street

▲ Restaurant in the Town Hall   ▼ A road on Kampa Island

From Old Town Square to Charles Bridge

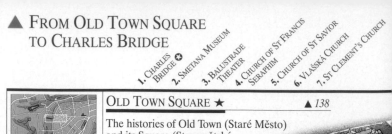

1. CHARLES BRIDGE ❂ 2. SMETANA MUSEUM 3. BALUSTRADE THEATER 4. CHURCH OF ST FRANCIS SERAPHIM 5. CHURCH OF ST SAVIOR 6. VLAŠSKÁ CHURCH 7. ST CLEMENT'S CHURCH

OLD TOWN SQUARE ★ ▲ 138

🕐 **One day**
◆ **B** A4-B4-C4

The histories of Old Town (Staré Město) and its Square (Staroměstské náměstí) are closely inter-related. Much of our knowledge of the city in its earliest days is based

OLD TOWN SQUARE, THE HEART OF PRAGUE ❂
Old Town Square, an open space in the midst of narrow streets, is dominated by the soaring spires of the Church of Our Lady of Týn, Goltz-Kinský Palace and the statue of Jan Huss. It is worth climbing the clocktower of the Old Town Hall for the 360° view over Prague that it offers. From ground level, the performance of the Apostles in the astronomical clock is an entertaining spectacle. For a drink afterwards, avoid the cosmopolitan café terraces in the square in favor of the quieter ones to be found in Týn Courtyard.

on a document written by an emissary of the Caliph of Cordoba, the diplomat and merchant Ibrahim Ibn Jacob. His stay from 965 to 966 inspired him to write of his journey, during which he came to realize that the city was an important center of commercial exchange. The opening of the city to the west and the development of commerce encouraged Soběslav I (1125–40) to play a more active role in the commercial Týn Courtyard (Ungelt) ▲ 160 behind the Church of Our Lady. This was the start of Prague's role as an important commercial center.

NEWCOMERS. New communities from Piedmont, Burgundy, Germany and Flanders settled in Prague during the 12th century, and their arrival increased the amount of business transactions, already stimulated by the needs of the Royal Court. At this time, the Germans occupied an area that was to become Old Town Square; there, they founded a church dedicated to St Nicholas ▲ 145, the patron saint of merchants, and they also built a hospital, houses and shops. The square began to look a little as it does today: the houses on the north, east and south sides, including Kinský Palace, are aligned on axes already determined in the 12th and 13th centuries.

AIMING FOR MUNICIPAL STATUS. In 1230, Old Town acquired the status of a town, but it was not entitled to have a Town

An old engraving (above) showing the execution of rebel leaders in 1621.

Scenes of the liberation of Prague (below) in Old Town Square, May 1945.

Hall, the decisive symbol in the Middle Ages of city freedom. It was not for another hundred years, in 1338, that John of Luxemburg granted the right to erect a Town Hall in Old Town Square. With political and judiciary power now hand in hand, the bourgeoisie sought to install a prison inside the Town Hall and stocks in the square. As the town's political center, the square established itself as the economic and social epicenter, and it was inhabited by the wealthiest families. Apart from commercial activities, the square also hosted festive occasions, including tourneys.

HISTORIC EVENTS. Down through the centuries, Old Town Square has been the scene of momentous and bloody events: after his victory at White Mountain on November 8, 1620 ● *34*, Ferdinand II sent twenty-seven noble and bourgeois rebels to the scaffold (today marked by a rectangle of black stones). Twelve of the heads were hung on the tower on Charles Bridge and were not buried until 1631. On May 8–9, 1945, the partisans fought a ferocious battle here to liberate the city from the Nazis, and then on February 21, 1948, Klement Gottwald proclaimed the victory of Soviet Communism ● *39* from the balcony of Kinský Palace ▲ *143*. By 1968 the square had come to be known as "Hyde Park" and was soon the favorite venue for student meetings. Today, more people meet and walk here than in Wenceslas Square or any other square in Prague.

KINSKÝ PALACE. In a previous age, the Palace housed the German-language Imperial High School attended by German-speaking intelligentsia, notably Max Brod and Franz Kafka ▲ *110*. Today it houses the National Gallery collection ▲ *227*.

137

KRIZ HOUSE. The building features an interesting window, or loggia, dating from 1520 and bears the inscription *Pragua caput regni*.

Historic Old Town Square (Staromětské náměstí) is the very heart of the city. It also contains some of the finest examples of Prague's artistic riches; indeed, no other part of the city can boast such an extraordinary collection of architectural styles and periods. The square offers an amazing juxtaposition of different schools, mixing Gothic porches with Renaissance sgraffito, and Baroque pediments with classical monumental windows and Art Nouveau décor.

2

TOWN HALL CLOCKTOWER

This clock, built in 1410 by Mikuláš of Kadaň and renovated in the 16th century, has two faces. Above is the astronomical face whose operation is controlled by scientific theories of the 15th century, so that the Earth is in the middle and the planets circle round it. The face below, containing a calendar of months and signs of the zodiac, was painted by Josef Mánes in the 19th century; the original hangs in Prague City Museum. The calendar moves forward one day at midnight and completes a revolution once a year. When the hour strikes a mechanism above both of the faces is activated. First, Christ and the Apostles emerge one by one; then, when they have disappeared, the skeleton of Death inverts the hourglass. Finally, the cock flaps its wings and crows.

"Death pulled the cord, and rang by nodding its head. Other small statues stirred while the cock flapped its wings, and the twelve Apostles glanced impassively down at the street through the open window."

Guillaume Apollinaire

1

2

N

THE FORMER TOWN HALL (1)
All the buildings from the clocktower to the House "Of the Minute" (2), with its sgraffito decorations ● 78, were once occupied by Staré Město's former Town Hall ▲ 146.

1

THE HOUSE "OF THE MINUTE" (2)
This house is one of the finest examples of architecture with sgraffito decoration ● 78. Like other houses in the square, it was built in the Gothic period but its façade was remodelled in the 17th century in the Renaissance style. The mythological and biblical scenes on the façade display a mixture of Italian and German influences.

DETAIL OF THE SGRAFFITO DECORATION ON THE HOUSE "OF THE MINUTE"

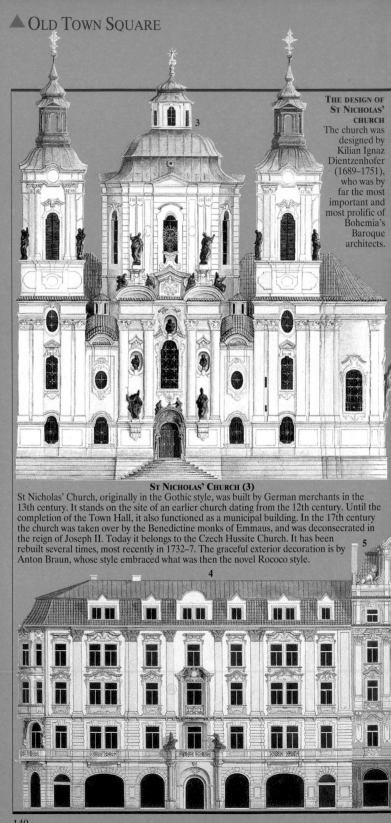

THE DESIGN OF ST NICHOLAS' CHURCH
The church was designed by Kilian Ignaz Dientzenhofer (1689–1751), who was by far the most important and most prolific of Bohemia's Baroque architects.

ST NICHOLAS' CHURCH (3)

St Nicholas' Church, originally in the Gothic style, was built by German merchants in the 13th century. It stands on the site of an earlier church dating from the 12th century. Until the completion of the Town Hall, it also functioned as a municipal building. In the 17th century the church was taken over by the Benedictine monks of Emmaus, and was deconsecrated in the reign of Joseph II. Today it belongs to the Czech Hussite Church. It has been rebuilt several times, most recently in 1732–7. The graceful exterior decoration is by Anton Braun, whose style embraced what was then the novel Rococo style.

Until the end of World War Two the elegant façade St Nicholas' was obscured by the Krenn House.

3. St Nicholas' Church (1732–7)
4. House at 934 Old Town Square
5 and **6.** Ministry of Internal Trade, 932 Old Town Square, built by the architect O. Polívka in 1900.
7. Former Pauline convent, 930, Old Town Square, built by the architect Giovanni Domenico Canevale in 1684.

N

THE INTERIOR OF ST NICHOLAS' CHURCH:
MAGNIFICENT SCULPTURES

St Nicholas' may well have the most beautiful church interior in Prague. It is impressively sculpted with architectural elements including tribunes, balconies, uneven cornices, arches, and curvilinear broken pediments set with scrolls. Such extraordinary complexity of design is quite unique. The high point of the decoration is Pater Asam's cupola fresco depicting the Life of Saint Nicholas and scenes from the Old Testament, notably *Joseph and Potiphar's Wife*. Asam's fresco in the small cupola in the choir recounts the Legend of Saint Benedict.

THE NORTH SIDE OF THE SQUARE

This part was substantially altered at the end of the 19th century when the Jewish quarter was pulled down. The neo-Baroque building on the left (**4**) has a fine door framed by columns surmounted by statues. The two central buildings in the neo-Baroque style (**5, 6**), occupying the site of three houses, are used by the Ministry of Internal Trade. They were built between 1898 and 1900 and their façades are not uniform. The former Pauline convent on the right (**7**) has Gothic foundations, the present Baroque construction dating from the late 17th century; it is linked to the Church of St Savior by a passageway.

8. Goltz-Kinský Palace
9. House "Of the Stone Bell"
10. Týn School
11. House "Of the White Unicorn"
12. Church of Our Lady of Týn

HOUSE "OF THE STONE BELL" (9)
This Gothic house (below) ● *74* was built in the 14th century. It was remodelled and for a long time was fronted by a Baroque façade. The present appearance of the house is the result of extensive restoration, and the façade has been returned to its original form.

N ◄—

To the left of Goltz-Kinský Palace (**8**) stands a Renaissance house.

GOLTZ-KINSKÝ PALACE (8)
The Rococo palace was built in 1755–65 by Anselmo Lurago for Count Goltz. It stands on the site of several Romanesque houses, some of whose cellars survive. The palace projects from the alignment of buildings on this side of the square, so that its monumentality is enhanced. It has a double-fronted façade and the arrangement of pediments, pilasters and doorways flanked by columns simultaneously emphasize the building's vertical axis and preserve the uniformity of the narrow façades that line the square.

TÝN CHURCH AND SCHOOL (12 AND 10)
Týn Church is the most important religious building in Prague after St Vitus' Cathedral. During the 10th century a church was built in the Týn courtyard ▲ *160*; it belonged to the foreign merchants' hospice. A new church in the early Gothic style was built in 1270 but was rebuilt from 1380. The roof was not completed until 1457 and the north gable only added in the reign of George of Poděbrady (1458–71). In front of the church stand Týn School (**10**), dating from the 14th and 16th centuries, and the House "Of the White Unicorn" (**11**), which was built in the 18th century.

THE SOUTHWEST SIDE OF THE SQUARE

On this side of the square almost all the vaulted Romanesque cellars and Gothic doorways, vestiges of successive phases of rebuilding around the square ● *74*, survive. The façades, several times remodelled according to the style of the period, date mostly from the late 17th century. Although the Baroque style predominates, many Gothic and Renaissance details can be identified, as in Stepan House, with a Gothic doorway and Renaissance gables (**19**), and the former Servite convent (**20**), which has an early 17th-century Renaissance doorway.

THE SOUTHEAST SIDE OF THE SQUARE

Štorch House (**13**) was built in the neo-Renaissance style in the late 19th century on the site of a Gothic house. The architect Bedřich Ohmann decorated the façade with a representation of Saint Wenceslas on horseback. The

House "Of the Stone Sheep" (**14**) has an entrance dating back to 1520. The House "Of the Stone Table" (**15**) was built in the 14th century, although the façade was later remodelled in the Baroque style. The next building, which houses a

tavern, has well-preserved Romanesque foundations, although the façade was rebuilt in the neoclassical manner. The House "Of the Golden Unicorn" (**16**), which stands on the corner of Železná Street, has a 12th-century

Romanesque basement. It was converted into a tower house in the 14th century and was rebuilt in the Late Gothic style in the 15th century. Finally, Late Baroque alterations were added to the façade in the 18th century.

13. Štorch House
14. House "Of the Stone Sheep"
15. House "Of the Stone Table"
16. House "Of the Golden Unicorn"
17. House "Of the White Angel"
18. House "Of the Blue Star"
19. Stepan House
20. Former Servite Convent
21. House "Of the Golden Angel"

N

MONUMENT TO JOHN HUSS
This statue by Ladislav Šaloun (1870–1946) ▲ *165, 176* was unveiled in 1915 to commemorate the quincentenary of the death of John Huss ● *32*, by then a major symbol of Czech national identity. The proximity of the Marian Column ● *35*, which recalls the defeat of the Habsburgs (it was pulled down in 1918), encouraged Šaloun to use more horizontal space so as to strike a contrast with the Column's height. The power of the statue, which owes much to Rodin, shows the great preacher standing surrounded by the fighters of God, the Exiles and a mother and child expressing a wish for national renewal.

OLD TOWN'S FORMER TOWN HALL

AN ANCIENT BUILDING. The heterogeneous complex of buildings that now make up the Former Town Hall accumulated only gradually. In 1338, the municipality purchased WOLFLIN HOUSE on the corner, adding a belfry in 1364 and an oriel chapel by Petr Parléř in 1381. The Gothic door, which is the main entrance, dates from the era of Vladislav II Jagiello, as does the window in the vestibule, while the surround of carved figures and floral decoration are fine examples of the genius of the stonemason Matěj Rejsek ▲ *167*. Over the years, various houses have been added, including KŘIŽ HOUSE with its lovely Renaissance window (1520) and Baroque railing (1731) decorated with the inscription *Praga caput regni*. The coats of arms are those of municipal councillors of the second half of the 15th century, except for the one in the middle which is that of the town itself. COCK HOUSE, connected to MIKEŠ HOUSE by a series of broken arches, was integrated into the Town Hall in 1835. The HOUSE "OF THE MINUTE", with its early 17th-century sgraffito, was the last to be added, in 1896, and the Kafka family lived there. Later, the main development was to the north wing, when offices were added. These were destroyed during World War Two ▲ *137*. The early 15th century astronomical clock (left) dominates the façade. Parts of the building open to the public include the vestibule, decorated with a mosaic representing Princess Libussa, the Old

> "John Huss' long shadow stood out fleetingly
> against the front of his bronze stake."
>
> Sylvie Germain

Council Chamber (1470) and the meeting room, which was restored in 1879. The buildings left standing at the end of the war were not big enough to accommodate the various administrative services, which were transferred to another building ▲ 149. The Town Hall has been listed as a historic building and is now used for official receptions and exhibitions; the marriage parlor has not been removed.

CHURCH OF OUR LADY OF TÝN
▲ 145

After St Vitus' Cathedral, Týn Church (Týnský chrám) is the most important place of worship in Prague. There is evidence of there having been a church on this site since 1135, when it formed part of a hospice constructed by foreign merchants in Týn Courtyard ▲ 160. A new Early Gothic church was built here in 1220, but it was replaced in the 1380's; the roof was not completed until 1457 and the north pediment not added until the reign of George of Poděbrady (1458–71).

A MUSICAL VENUE
Týn Church had the finest organ in Prague in the 17th century; it was made by H. Mandl of Cologne. Josef Ferdinand Norbert (1716–82) was the church's most notable musical

A REFORMERS' CHURCH. The Church of Our Lady of Týn had links with the Hussite Movement, and early Reformers including Konrad Waldhauser, Jan Milíč of Kroměříž ● 26 and Matthew of Janov frequently preached here. Its successor continued the tradition and became the Utraquists' main church. Jan Rokycana, the only Hussite archbishop, was a priest here, and here the Utraquist King George of Poděbrady attended the first mass of his reign.

figure. His reputation as a contrapuntist was such that Joseph II asked him to be organist to the Royal Chapel in Vienna, but confirmation of his appointment arrived the day after he died. The funeral of Bedřich Smetana took place here on May 15, 1884.

BAROQUE RENOVATION. As Catholicism regained the ascendancy after 1626, the chalice which had adorned the pediment was removed and most of the early decoration destroyed. Baroque style was on the march. The finest elements of the new décor included the altars, many of them adorned with paintings by Karel Škréta (1610–74) ▲ 167, 220, the greatest Baroque painter in Bohemia; the high altar with an Assumption and a Holy Trinity; and the altars of Saint Barbara, Saint Joseph and Saint Adalbert. In the main nave, level with the third pillar on the right, is a fine altar of St John the Baptist (c. 1520). In contrast with the custom of the time, the reliefs were not painted, color being subtly suggested by the use of different materials. The artist has identified himself only with the monogram "IP". A fine canopy by Matěj Rejsek (1493) near the fourth pillar on the left decorates the tomb of the Hussite Bishop Augustine of Mirandola, and the tombstone of the astronomer Tycho Brahe is to be found on the fifth pillar

A MAJESTIC MADONNA
This wooden Madonna dating from 1420 is one of the many statues in the church.

ROTT HOUSE
The house was commissioned by the Rott steel company, and the façade is covered with representations of the various tools made in its factories; other motifs include allegories of skilled

artisans and agriculture. The decoration was executed after cartoons by Mikoláš Aleš.

Pharmacies have concentrated in Malé náměstí since the 14th century. The pharmacy on the corner of Karlova Square and Karlova Street is the best known in the city.

on the right. The oldest baptismal fonts in Prague (1414) are at the bottom of the south nave; the covers were not made until the 19th century. A curiosity of the church is a window in the south wall over the right-hand aisle and level with the third chapel. Our Lady of Týn is next door to a house in Celetná Street that was inhabited by a bigoted woman who insisted on the window being built. The Kafka family also lived here for a time.

AROUND MALÉ NÁMĚSTI (LITTLE SQUARE)

The HOUSE "OF THE TWO GOLDEN BEARS" (U dvou zlatých medvědů), a short walk from Old Town Square in Kožná Street, has one of the most beautiful Renaissance doors in Prague ● 76.
ROTT HOUSE ★. The center of the square is marked by a well dating from 1560, and decorated with a Renaissance railing surmounted in the 17th century by a gilt Lion of Bohemia. The House "At the sign of the Three White Roses" (or Rott House) at no. 3 has some remarkable Romanesque remains. In the 15th century, it belonged to a printer named Jan Pytlích who, with financial assistance from members of the Utraquist bourgeoisie in Old Town, published the first Bible in Czech in 1488. The house was then rebuilt in the Renaissance style and decorated with sgraffito ● 89 but, when it was restored in 1890, it was decorated in the neo-Renaissance manner ● 84. Today it houses a shop selling jewelry and cut glass. Visitors can look inside, admiring the interior, which dates from 1922–3, and the glass dome that covers the old interior courtyard.

KARLOVA ULICE. Karlova Street starts off at Jilská Street and ends at Cross and Red Star Square (Křížovnické náměstí), forming a direct link between Charles Bridge and Old Town Square via Small Square (Malé náměstí). It consists of three sections which protrude slightly one in front of the other. The street used to be part of the "Royal Route" or "Coronation Route" followed by the Kings of Bohemia when they were to be crowned at St Vitus' Cathedral. They went from Powder Tower to the Castle via Celetná Street, Old Town Square, Karlova Street, Charles Bridge, Mostecká Street, Malá Strana Square and, lastly, Nerudova Street. Many of the Gothic houses, including nos. 175/3, 156, 147, 452 and 451 which were renovated in the Baroque style, have preserved their Romanesque basements. Karlova ulice runs alongside the Clementinum, providing one of the many means of access to this building, and borders directly on the Italian Chapel and St Clement's Church. During the 16th and 17th centuries, it was known as Jesuit Street (Jezovitská ulice). One of the most beautiful Renaissance houses is at no. 175/3: the House "OF THE GOLDEN WELL" (U zlaté studně) was renovated in the 17th century and further decorated in 1714, as the last plague to ravage Bohemia and Austria was finally dying out. The decoration consisted of stucco figures representing the two intercessors, Saint Roch and Saint Sebastian, the Virgin, and the country's two patron saints, Saint Wenceslas and Saint John Nepomuk. The first café in Prague ● 58 was opened in 1714 at no. 181/18, the House "Of the Golden Snake" (U zlatého hada), whose interior has only recently been renovated. From 1607 to 1612, Kepler lived at no. 188/4, a Renaissance building known as the House "Of the Crown of France", it was here that he wrote *The New Astronomy*, setting out the laws that bear his name.

CLAM-GALLAS PALACE. Clam-Gallas Palace is at 20 Husova Street on the corner of Marianské náměstí and Karlova Street. It is one of the most important buildings that the Viennese architect Johann Bernhard Fischer von Erlach produced for Prague; he designed it around 1700 for the Emperor's Ambassador Count Jan Václav Gallas, and it was built between 1713 and 1729 by Giovanni Domenico Canevale and Tomáš Haffenecker. The irregular groundplan is that of a building with several wings encircling two courtyards. The interior staircase is one of the most beautiful in the city, and Santin Bossi executed the stucco decoration in the hall. Since 1945, this palace has housed the city archives.

OLD TOWN'S NEW TOWN HALL. After passing the splendid Clam-Gallas Palace, enter Marianské Square with the Clementinum on the left, the Municipal Library (František Roith, 1924–8)

SCULPTURE AT CLAM-GALLAS PALACE
The atlantes flanking the entrance (1714) (below) and the sculpture decorating the pediment are the work of M. B. Braun ▲ 220, 224, 244, 276. Three copies of the sixteen originals, Jupiter, Mercury and Venus, are there; the others are on display in the Lapidarium in the National Gallery ▲ 227. The interior staircase is one of the most beautiful in Prague.

opposite and
on the right, Old
Town's new Town Hall built
by Karel Osvald Polívka ▲ *176*
between 1905 and 1912. It comprises a

Layout of the
Clementinum. Below:
Karlova Street with
the towers of the
Italian Chapel and
the entrance to
St Clement's.

subtle blend of neo-Baroque and Secessionist elements ● *84,
86*. The decoration on the façade was the work of three of the
greatest sculptors of the age: Stanislav Sucharda did the
reliefs around the entrance and the two allegories on the
right-hand cornice ('Bookkeeping' and 'Management
Control'); Ladislas Šaloun sculpted the splendid Rabbi Löw
▲ *186* on the right and the Iron Knight, a character from
ancient Prague legends, on the left; and Josef Mařatka ▲ *165*
carved the groups on the balcony and the left-hand cornice.

THE CLEMENTINUM ★

The Jesuit Clementinum is an enormous complex built over
the course of more than a century, between the end of the
16th century and 1726. It stands on the site not only of a
former Dominican Monastery given to the Jesuits when they
arrived in Prague in 1556, but also of three churches and over
thirty houses. It has three entrances: two are main entrances,
one of them giving onto Křížovnické náměstí and the other
Marianské náměstí, and there is also a less important
entrance in the very long wall that lines Karlova Street. The
Jesuits entrusted the task of building their first college in
Prague to Francesco Caratti. Today, it is the site of the
National Library. The Clementinum Library has more than
4½ million works, of which 6,000 are manuscripts and 3,000
are incunabulae.

A room in the
Clementinum
Library.

REINFORCEMENTS. The Jesuits arrived in Prague
in 1556, on the invitation of Ferdinand I of
Habsburg, who wished to re-establish Bohemian
Catholicism and minimize the influence of the
University. The same year, they founded a
school for the gentry to which Ferdinand sent
his pages and his son, Prince Ernest of Bavaria-
Munich. A Jesuit education suddenly became
fashionable among the Czech aristocracy, but it
was also a strategy for achieving a Catholic re-
conquest. The Jesuits were soon granted the
right to award doctorates, and this enabled
them to compete with Charles University, which
was Utraquist and therefore non-Catholic.
**AN ARCHITECTURAL TREASURE SECOND ONLY TO
THE CASTLE.** The building consisted of four
central wings organized around four interior

courtyards with an observation tower where they intersected. In the first courtyard, there is a statue of a *Student* by Josef Max, erected in memory of the Prague students who, with the Jesuit Ferus, defended Old Town against the Swedes in 1648. **LIBRARIES.** At the far end of this first courtyard is the former Jesuit College, now the National Library. In 1773, following the abolition of the Society of Jesus, the buildings were handed over to the Observatory and the Academy of Fine Arts and then, from 1800 onward, to Charles University. In 1924, the buildings began to be converted to house the National Library; these premises are also occupied by the University Library and Slav Library. Many of the rooms have preserved their Baroque magnificence: on the second floor, the vault of the former College Library, known as the "Baroque Hall", is decorated with frescos representing the arts and sciences, and in the center there is a remarkable trompe l'oeil by Johann Hiebl (1727); the Mozart Room in the wing that overlooks Platnéřská Street boasts elaborate Rococo ornamentation; the summer refectory is now a lecture room, and is adorned with paintings by Krištof Tausch dated 1710; the second courtyard has a Baroque fountain, and the Observatory tower, built in 1721, was renovated by Anselmo Lurago in 1778 and is surmounted by a statue of Atlas. The astronomer Joseph Stepling founded the Observatory in 1751, and the monument erected in his honor by Ignác Platzer stands in the third courtyard.

Ripellino describes the Clementinum as "[an] ill-tempered fortress, a protruding, provocative, haughty bastion, a mirror of supremacy and hard-line indoctrination."

CHAPEL OF MIRRORS
The Chapel of the Annunciation, also known as the Chapel of Mirrors owing to its stucco decoration incorporating mirrors, is in the third courtyard. It was built by František Maximilián Kaňka, who was also responsible for the Library. The Chapel is now used for concerts.

CROSS AND RED STAR SQUARE

The square (Křížovnické náměstí) takes its name from the convent of the Order that settled here. The building was raised to its current level only in the 16th century, and it did not acquire its present appearance until the 17th century. Although of only modest proportions, it is remarkable for its architectural unity. In the center of the square stands a statue of Charles IV erected by the University to commemorate the 500th anniversary of its foundation.

CHURCHES IN THE CLEMENTINUM

The Clementinum has three churches: St Clement's (Kostel sv. Kliment) and the Italian Chapel (Vlašská kaple), both accessible from Karlova Street through a Baroque portico executed by František M. Kaňka in 1715, and St Savior's (Kostel sv. Salvátora) which opens onto Cross and Red Star Square and Charles Bridge.

ST CLEMENT'S ★. St Clement's belonged to the Dominicans before it was handed over to the Jesuits when they first came to Prague, and the Clementinum took its name from this church. As it met neither the artistic criteria of the period nor the needs of the Jesuits, it was rebuilt between 1711 and 1715, probably by Kaňka to plans by Kilián Ignác Dientzenhofer. The sense of monumentality derives from the bays crowned by cupolas, and resembling huge canopies. The decoration includes pillars adorned with paintings of the saints by Ignác Raab ▲ *241*, and niches containing statues of the Four Evangelists and Fathers of the Church by Matthias Bernhard Braun (1684–1738). The statuary comes in the main from the workshop of Braun and his six companions which, in 1725, was the greatest in the city. Braun was also responsible for the sculptures of Saint Louis of Gonzaga, St Stanislas Kostka on the ALTAR OF THE CIRCUMCISION, the Prodigal Son and the group depicting the Plague. The high altar was painted in trompe l'oeil by Josef Kramolin, and the ceiling fresco recounting the life of Saint Clement is by Johann Hiebl. The building now belongs to the Greek Orthodox Church.

THE ITALIAN CHAPEL. This atypical building is sometimes known as the Italian Chapel of the Assumption of the Virgin Mary. It was built between 1590 and 1597 for the first Italians to settle in Prague, and has an oval groundplan, a rarity in Bohemia. The designer was probably Ottavio Mascherino, a builder in the employ of the Pope.

St Savior's. This, the oldest of the three churches, has three Renaissance naves and dates from the years 1578–1601. It was restyled in the Baroque manner between 1638 and 1659 by the addition of a huge octagonal cupola by Carlo Lurago and Francesco Caratti, and acquired its present appearance in 1714 when František M. Kaňka added two towers. The church has fifty-five windows, the façade is decorated with fifteen statues by Jan Jiří Bendl and his workshop, and the beautiful and elaborate decoration in the interior includes stuccowork by Domenico Galli and Bendl. Bendl was also responsible for the wooden statues of the twelve Apostles that adorn the confessionals, and which are among the finest works of the period. The ceiling has a fresco by Kovář entitled *The Four Corners of the World* (1748), and the painting on the high altar is *The Transfiguration of Christ* by Hering.

CHURCH OF ST FRANCIS SERAPHIM

This belongs to the Monastery of the Brothers of the Cross, a Czech hospital Order founded in the 12th century by Agnes of Bohemia. Brunn's façade of the monastery overlooking the river (1850), to the left of the church, is classical; it gives onto Platnéřská Street, which is in the Art Nouveau style and was decorated by Josef Šakař ▲ *194* between 1910 and 1912. The church is the work of J.-B. Mathey (c. 1630–c. 1695) ▲ *141, 231, 272, 318* and is now used for concerts.

A MAGNIFICENT CUPOLA
The Brothers of the Cross were overawed by the overwhelming proximity of the Clementinum and, when they commissioned Mathey to build the Church of St Francis Seraphim, they asked him to rectify the imbalance. Accordingly, he designed a building on an oval, compact ground plan with a conspicuous cupola. This restrained structure is supported by giant pilasters which easily embrace the five horizontal registers, and even the concave corners cause the cupola to protrude even further through a compression of space. The interior, with its pilasters made of purple Slivenec marble, is superbly balanced. The cupola fresco of *The Last Judgement* by Reiner is quite remarkable for the twisting bodies which give a vivid impression of floating in space. The other paintings are by Michael Lukáš Willmann (including the one over the high altar) and Jan Kryštof Liška ▲ *241*.

Statue of Saint Francis Seraphim on Charles Bridge.

▲ From Old Town Square to Charles Bridge

Charles Bridge ★

Charles Bridge has been a major thoroughfare ever since it was first built in the 14th century; until the 19th century, it was the only bridge across the Vltava, and is today a scene of constant animation. At night, the gaps between the

CHARLES BRIDGE AND ITS STATUES ✪
Supported by sturdy pilasters and protected by wooden ice-breakers, Charles Bridge gives an impression utter immobility. It is decorated with statues of richly garbed figures commemorating the triumph of the Counter-Reformation and it majestically links the banks of the Vltava. The statues are uncannily lifelike; according to legend, they engage in learned theological debates at midnight. The citizens of Prague will tell you that anyone who touches the statue of Saint John Nepomuk will have their wish fulfilled.

street lamps create shadowy areas that encourage all manner of mysteries, mirages and surprises. When there is a mist, the whole place becomes magic or terrifying, according to one's temperament.

JUDITH BRIDGE. Prague's oldest bridge was made of wood and lay parallel to modern Charles Bridge. It is mentioned as far back as 1118. After it was destroyed by a flood in 1157, Vladislav I had a stone bridge built, which he named after his wife, Judith of Thuringia. It was completed some thirteen years later. At the time, it was the oldest stone bridge in central Europe after the bridge at Regensburg. It was destroyed again by floods in 1357.

CONSTRUCTION OF CHARLES BRIDGE. When Petr Parléř accepted Charles IV's commission to build Charles Bridge in 1357, he was only twenty-seven years old; work was not completed until 1402. It was known as the "Stone Bridge", and only took Charles' name in 1870. Charles Bridge was built with blocks of sandstone; it is 1,700 feet long and 30 feet wide, and rests on sixteen pillars. It was longer, wider and – above all – higher than Judith Bridge, and has survived numerous floods. Since being renovated in 1974, it has been restricted to pedestrians.

THE ROW OF SCULPTURES. The row of statues in front of the Jesuit College of Kutná Hora is reminiscent of the Ponte degli

The tower on the edge of the Old Town, guarding Charles Bridge.

> "Charles Bridge is disastrous to God's chosen ones."
>
> Roger Grenier

Angeli in Rome. The statues were brought together over a period of time. In the 17th century, the collection was limited to the Crucifix, Saint John Nepomuk, a Pietà and a Saint Wenceslas, the remaining statues dating from the first half of the 18th century, the high point of the Counter-Reformation; the most recent works were executed in the 19th century.

Many of the sculptures displayed today are copies of copies made in the 20th century.

CALVARY. The first Calvary adorned the bridge from its earliest days, but it disappeared at the time of the Hussite troubles. The present cross on the third pier is the fifth to be made, having been cast in Dresden in 1627–8. An inscription in Hebrew recalls a case of desecration in 1695 in which a Jew is alleged to have registered his contempt for the Calvary while he passed by; he was then ordered to pay for the gold-plated Hebrew inscription which reads "Holy, Holy, Holy God". The punishment is written below in German, Czech and Latin.

ST JOHN NEPOMUK. This bronze statue was the first statue to be placed on the bridge on the central pier on the north side. It was made in 1683 by Jan Brokoff, thirty-eight years before the saint was beatified ▲ *233*, but it lacks force and is of little stylistic worth. The bronzes on the pedestal recall scenes that are said to have happened during his life: the Queen's confession, and the moment when his body was thrown into the river. The second of these contains an allusion to the Massacre of the Innocents, with a soldier ill-treating a mother and her child.

THE TOWER ON CHARLES BRIDGE. For military reasons, Charles IV charged Petr Parléř with building a strong

laughing-stock for years to come.

View of Charles Bridge crossing the Vltava and Kampa Island, and rejoining Staré Město at Malá Strana.

tower 130 feet high that closed the bridge off on the Staré Město side. By the early 15th century, it was already considered to be one of the most beautiful gates in

Europe, and Viollet-le-Duc referred to this Gothic masterpiece on a visit to Prague. The tower had carved decorations added by the workshop of Petr Parléř at the beginning of the 15th century. The west face was badly damaged by Swedish cannon in 1648, but the east face is still adorned with strikingly realistic figures of Charles IV (on the left) and Wenceslas IV brought from St Vitus' Cathedral. **THE TOWERS ON MALÁ STRANA BRIDGE.** It was probably intended that there should be a similar tower on the left bank, but Wenceslas IV's indecisiveness, and the start of the Hussite Wars ● *32*, delayed the project. The complex consists of a Gothic gate (1410) and two towers, the smaller of which is the oldest as it formed part of the fortifications of Judith Bridge. The bigger of the two towers was built in the reign of George of Poděbrady in 1464, and imitates Parléř's masterpiece without the decoration.

SMETANA MUSEUM

NATIONAL OPERAS
After achieving some success with his opera *The Brandenburgers in Bohemia*, *The Bartered Bride* brought Smetana huge popularity. He then wrote *Dalibor* in 1868, a tragic opera recalling the struggles for national independence. But his style, considered to be too Wagnerian, attracted criticism and, by way of reply, he composed *Libuše* (1872), a glorification of the Czech nation. Smetana's writing was steeped in the folklore of Bohemia, and he devoted his genius to the six symphonic poems that made up *Má vlast*. His interest in chamber music is less well known but his compositions in this field no less remarkable.

Since 1936 the Bedřich Smetana Museum has been housed in a neo-Renaissance building of 1885 (below, left) on Novotný Lane (Novotného lávka), close to the end of the bridge. The exterior decoration ● *78* depicts battles against the Swedes that took place on Charles Bridge in 1648. The objects in the museum's collection are mostly the great musician's belongings. Bedřich Smetana (1824–84) ● *47, 50*, ▲ *195, 296* is a national figure and Bohemia's most representative composer. The whole country holds him in exceptionally high esteem, and every Prague Spring Festival opens with a performance of his *Má vlast* (*My Country*). Not only was he a composer of genius, he was also very active in the National Awakening after 1848 ▲ *296* and, in 1849, with the help of Liszt and Clara Schumann, founded a private music school where the use of Czech was compulsory. This was one of his methods of indicating his opposition to the official teaching of German. He also fought in an armed group called the "Concord", and there met Karel Sabina who was to be the librettist of his first two operas.

BALUSTRADE THEATER

The Theater "on the Balustrade" (Divadlo na Zábradlí) ● *55*, one of the most famous in Prague, is tucked away in discreet Anenské Square. Since it opened in 1958, the Theater has put on lively, unusual works, and Václav Havel worked there as a technician before becoming a prolific and talented playwright. The other great name in the theater's history is the mime artist Ladislav Fialka, a pupil of Marcel Marceau.

Around
Wenceslas Square

1. Staroměstské Square   2. Church of Our Lady of Tý...   3. Týn Courtyard   4. St James' Church   5. Black Virgin House   Celetná Street   7. Hotel Paříž

◱ Half a day

◆ **B** C4-C5-D4-D5-D6-E5-E6

Celetná Street is pedestrianized and is one of the most popular streets in Prague. Mary Wortley Montague, who was staying there around 1715, complained of the lack of privacy, the overcrowding and the uncomfortable surroundings of the aristocratic houses.

CELETNÁ STREET

Celetná Street, one of the most important roads in the Old Town, leads out of Old Town Square toward Powder Tower. Like Karlova Street, it once formed part of a route taken by the Kings of Bohemia on their way to their coronations at St Vitus' Cathedral, and has been a major commercial thoroughfare since Roman times. The Gothic and Renaissance buildings that line Celetná Street are hidden behind façades dating from the Baroque period; some of them have preserved elements from earlier periods and offer lovers of architecture curious examples of stylistic superimposition. At basement level, many of the houses have retained vestiges of Roman times: the most interesting are the cellars at nos. 558–I/12, 53–I/12 and 603–I/12. Other houses incorporate passageways ● *82* linking them with Štupartská Street on one side and Kamziková Street and Ovocný Street on the other. At one end of Celetná Street is Sixt House ● *80*, named after Jan Sixt of Ottersdof, a celebrated Old Town Chancellor who bought it in 1567. His son, Jan Theodor, a leader of the 1618 revolt ● *34*, was one of the twenty-seven condemned to death in 1621. He was granted a pardon on the scaffold, but did not undergo religious conversion, and emigrated to Dresden in 1626. His house was then scized, and subsequently bought by the third person to be thrown out of the Hradčany window on May 23, 1618: the Aulic secretary, Filip Fabricius, thereafter known as "Long Drop". Since 1991, the premises have been occupied by a pleasant café named after

"Prague seemed ... not only one of the most beautiful places in the world, but one of the strangest. Fear, piety, zeal, strife and pride, tempered in the end by the milder impulses of munificence and learning and *douceur de vivre*, had flung up an unusual array of grand and unenigmatic monuments. The city, however, was scattered with darker, more reticent, less easily decipherable clues. There were moments when every detail seemed the tip of a phalanx of inexplicable phantoms."
Patrick Leigh Fermor,
A Time for Gifts

Egon Erwin Kisch, and by the "Sixt" restaurant in the basement. The building was restored in 1725; it contains a barrel-vaulted Romanesque room and Gothic elements in the courtyard.

HOUSE OF THE THREE KINGS. Opposite Sixt House is the House of the Three Kings (U tří králů), a building that has retained a number of Gothic elements including vaults, gables and framework. It was once inhabited by the Kafka family ● *110*, and it is likely that Franz occupied the room that overlooks the interior of Týn Church. Hrzán Palace (1702) at no. 12 is one of the most beautiful buildings in the whole street, and is the work of Giovanni Battista Alliprandi who was also responsible for Lobkowicz Palace ▲ *243* in Malá Strana (Lesser Town).

ARISTOCRATIC HOMES. In the 19th century, the former Caretto Millesimo Palace at no. 597/13 was a casino patronized by the Prague nobility. Although it was built in 1750 for Count Cavriani, whose coat of arms still adorns the main entrance, this house still boasts Gothic brick gables which are visible from the inner courtyard, and a Romanesque doorway. Buquoy House at no. 562/20 combines a Baroque façade, and a Mannerist doorway whose wreathed columns recall Ammannati's Florentine work. At no. 595/17 stands Menhart House which was rebuilt at the beginning of the 18th century; its outstandingly beautiful inner courtyard contains a wooden statue of Hercules and a Baroque statue of a saint. The building's superb vaulted chambers now house a fine

Celetná Street derives its name from *calta* (from the German *Zelten*), a 14th-century plaited bun or flat cake made by the street's many bakers.

159

BERNHARD BOLZANO (1781–1848)
This philosopher, a disciple of Leibnitz, died at no. 25 Celetná Street. Bolzano supported the idea of a Czech nation in which Czechs and Germans lived side by side, and was accordingly dismissed from his professorship at the Carolinum ▲ 278 in 1819.

In the early 20th century, Celetná Street was lined with a large number of very fashionable shops.

Black Virgin House houses the Czech Museum of Cubism ● 106.

restaurant, the "U Pavouka" (At the sign of the Spider).
MORE MODERN COMPETITION.
A later addition to Celetná Street was Friedrich Ohmann's *U české orlice* (1897) at no. 567/30. This neo-Renaissance house has gables in the "Venetian" style and, on the other side overlooking Ovocný trh, a splendid oriel window. The polychrome sgraffito ● 78 is the work of Alois Drýak, who also designed the Evropa Hotel ▲ 174. This house is an excellent example of the "eclectic" or "historicist" style. More avant-garde is the newly renovated BLACK VIRGIN HOUSE on the corner of Celetná Street and Ovocný trh. Built by Josef Gočár in 1911–12, the façade is in the Cubist style. Since 1994, this extraordinary building has housed the Museum of Cubism along with collections of decorative art paintings and architectural projects. The polyhedral profiles of the dormer windows, the cut-off sections of glass and the form of the pillars at the main entrance are wholly Cubist in style. The house at no. 589/29, U Templu (In the temple), is what remains of restoration work carried out in 1801 when a small Baroque church and a hospice adjoining the façade were removed. Opposite is the front of the former Pachta Palace (1759), which includes a balcony with telamones and terms by Ignác Platzer. This building housed the mint from the 15th to late 18th centuries.

TÝN COURTYARD (UNGELT)

The entrance is in Malá Štupartská almost opposite St James' Church. From the 11th century, the courtyard was a shelter for foreign merchants to unload their carts and pay their taxes. It was also used as a warehouse, market and city toll until the 18th century. The original plan has been preserved. Most buildings around the Tyn courtyard have now been restored: the most remarkable is Granovský House, built in 1560 on the model of an Italian Renaissance palazzo with an open loggia on the second floor. Chiaroscuro frescos on biblical and mythological themes are soon to be revealed.

ST JAMES' CHURCH

Access to St James' Church is along the passageway ● 82 belonging to the houses at no. 29 or no. 17, both of which overlook Štupartska Street. The Franciscan Friars Minor lived in the first St James' Convent on the invitation of Wenceslas I in 1232. The original church was not built for another hundred years, between 1335 and 1374.

> "One might praise it even more for its individuality than for its beauty. It is a most personal town."
>
> Hilaire Belloc

THE FAÇADE. The façade was rebuilt after a fire in 1689, and is somewhat restrained in style: the main body of the church is set off by double columns with highly ornate capitals, and by the cornice and the superimposed pediments of the second level and the attic. This contrasts with extraordinary stucco compositions executed by Ottavio Mosto in 1695: on the left is Saint Francis, founder of the Friars Minor, in the center Saint James, and on the right St Antony of Padua. The walls have been hollowed out in places to heighten the effect of depth and chiaroscuro. Mosto introduced to Prague the artistry of Bernini, the brilliant sculptor who had been such an influential figure in the Roman Baroque. Mosto's period of creativity was short-lived, but his influence was considerable mainly thanks to his great expressiveness and the vivacity of his works. Overall, the church exudes magnificence without excess, and the pulpit (1738) is a fine example of this; it is well worth comparing with the pulpit in St Nicholas' Church in Malá Strana. The nave and choir are punctuated by tall, browny-red pilasters topped by opulent, gold capitals, and the eye is drawn to the "guard of honor" that these pilasters form. No less impressive is the effect of perspective which takes the eye from the cornice, at the bottom of the windows, to the upper part of structure framing the altar. Jan Šimon Pánek's

THE ENTRANCE TO ST JAMES' CHURCH
An extraordinary feature of Mosto's Group of St Francis is how quickly the initial impression of disorder, even of

overcrowding, disperses on close examination. Each group is executed with simplicity, and benefits from the effects of symmetry; only the little angels flying over the saints create any confusion. Unquestionably, the swarms of plump children are the fruit of a powerful imagination: two of the putti are embracing passionately, another is flying downward head first, while yet another is searching for something beneath a coat of arms.

ST JAMES' CHURCH
St James' Church has superb acoustics, and the organ recitals are not to be missed. The church is frequently used for recordings, and is also noted for its magnificent masses at Christmas time.

Bar-Vinárna. Otevřeno od 8ʰ več.
Franc. kuchyně ⚜ Grill ⚜ Koncert

HOTEL PAŘÍŽ

The Hotel Paříž was built in 1907 by Jan Vejrych (1856–1926), who also designed several buildings in Pařížka Avenue ▲ *190*.

"I SERVED THE KING OF ENGLAND"

The narrator has just obtained a job at the hotel, and describes his arrival: "The Hotel Paříž was wonderful to behold – so beautiful, in fact, that I almost fell over. The mirrors on the walls, the copper banisters, the door handles, the impeccably polished chandeliers. . ! You would think you were in a golden palace, what with all these red carpets and glass doors!"

Baroque restoration of 1689–1702 did not totally conceal aspects of the building's original Gothic structure such as the height of the nave and the length of the choir.

THE HIGH ALTAR. The ceiling was painted by František Maxmilián Voget in 1736; the life of the Virgin covers the nave, while the glory of the Holy Trinity is over the choir. The light yet warm colors suit the overall harmony admirably well. The painting over the high altar, and a Martyrdom of Saint James (1739) by Václav Vavřinec Reiner ▲ *285*, all but disappear next to the opulent frame by the Tyrolian Matthias Schönherr. The high altar is a truly monumental composition which sweeps upward toward the vault, where angels lift up a hanging to reveal the monstrance for all to contemplate.

TOMB OF COUNT VRATISLAV MITROWICZ. This tomb (1714–16) is situated in the left aisle, level with the choir; it is the work of the Viennese architect Fischer von Erlach. The sculpted figures are by Ferdinand Maxmilián Brokoff (1688–1731), the most beautiful piece undoubtedly being the figure of Chronos, identified by an hourglass. Brokoff trained in the workshop of his father Jan, and during this time worked on groups adorning Charles Bridge. He completed his studies in Vienna in the workshop of the Strudel brothers, where he appears to have been introduced to Italian art. Ferdinand Brokoff inherited the style of Bendl and, with Braun, represented the apogee of Bohemian Baroque sculpture.

ST JAMES' CONVENT. This convent stood adjacent to the church and was once one of the major musical centers in Bohemia. Unfortunately, few scores survived the fires of 1689 and 1754 to tell us of the convent's impressive musical activity. However, some musicians of the period are known: they include Bernard Artophaeus (died 1721), Česlav Vaňura (died 1736) and Bohuslav Černohorský (1684–1742). Works by these composers are available on a compact disc on sale throughout Prague entitled "Music at Prague's St James' Church".

HOTEL PAŘÍŽ

This is one of the most famous hotels in Prague. Stylistically, it is a mixture of Secession (the awning over the entrance), neo-Gothic (particularly the corner gable) and highly elaborate architectural style in general. The interior has been renovated and is worth a visit: the restaurant is decorated with Art Nouveau mosaics and the café boasts splendid paneling and furniture of the utmost refinement.

BOHUMIL HRABAL AT THE PAŘÍŽ. The writer Bohumil Hrabal, who was born in 1914 in Brno and who has recently died, was one of the most popular Czech writers. He immortalized the "Paříž Hotel" in his novel *I Served the King of England*

hotel Paříž
LVOVSKÁ ULICE

(1981). After an eventful life as a student, Hrabal, the son of a brewery manager, managed to obtain a doctorate in law in 1946, before embarking on a series of jobs including railway worker, commercial traveler, steel worker, packer of old papers, and property master in a theater. He had keen powers of observation, and his experiences provided the inspiration for his works, although they were not published for many years due to censorship. In 1963 he came into the public eye with *A Pearl in the Background*. It was a success: critics and readers alike saw him as the true successor to Jaroslav Hašek; the brewery anecdote, a minor genre of story closely associated with Prague folklore, forms an important element in the work of both writers. Hrabal also had exceptional skill with words, combining literary language, neologisms, the spoken language and slang. His best-known works include *Closely Watched Trains*, *Dancing Lesson for Adults and Advanced Pupils* (1969), *Sacrificed Head of Hair* (1987), *Tender Barbarian* (1988), *Wedding in the House* (1990) and his masterpiece *Too Lonely a Solitude*.

The restaurant and bar of the Hotel Paříž, which are nowadays situated on the corner of Obemího domu and Královdorská streets, were enormously popular in the early part of the 20th century.

KOTVA SHOPPING CENTER

Jakubská Street leads away from St James' Church toward Královdorská Street and the Kotva shopping center. It was constructed and internally designed between 1972 and 1974 with the help of Swedish capital by Vera and Vladimir Machonin, and is one of the biggest of its type in eastern Europe. When the foundations were being laid, relics were found. They throw interesting light on the locality's history. This includes a palace in the Middle Ages, a church of the Order of St Benedict dating from the Roman era, and a 13th-century monastery of Teutonic Knights.

ST JOSEPH'S CHURCH

St Joseph's Church, which stands in náměstí Republiky (Republic Square) opposite the Kotva shopping center, dates from 1636–53 and is one of Prague's earliest Baroque churches. It was built as the chapel for a Capuchin convent, and its sober decoration recalls that Order's love of simplicity. The statue of Saint Francis (1708), overlooking the square, is by František Preiss ▲ *293* and originally stood on Charles Bridge. It was brought here in 1855, and the angels that once flanked it are now in the courtyard. The statue of Saint Jude Thaddeus (1741) is traditionally surrounded with tokens of thanksgiving, and inside the church, by the side altars, there are two paintings of Saint Anthony and Saint Felix by Karel Škréta.

ST JOSEPH'S CHURCH
The main entrance is surmounted by the Questenberg coat of arms (above). The former Capuchin monastery next to the church was pulled down in 1795 and, at that time, only the hospital was restored. This, too, was eventually demolished and replaced by the military barracks where Josef Kajetán Tyl ▲ *280* composed the Czech national anthem *Where is my home?* (*Kde domov jůj?*) in 1834.

A table at the Hotel Paříž (left).

163

EXTERNAL VIEW OF OBECNÍ DŮM
The mosaic on the central pediment, *Homage to Prague*, was the work of Karel Špillar who had acquired Puvis de Chavannes' taste for subdued, stilted scenes during his stay in Paris. Ladislav Šaloun's Baroque-inspired allegories above the metal awning represent the nation's Despondency and Uprising.

INTERIORS
Despite objections from his colleagues, Alfons Mucha was given the task of providing painted decorations for the Mayor's Room (below) ● 88.

TOWN HALL

AN UNUSUAL DECISION. In many ways, the construction of the Obecní dům between 1905 and 1911 was one of the high points in the history of Prague's architecture and decorative arts. It was also a hugely demanding task. The municipal authorities wanted a prestigious building which could accommodate not only the everyday public services, but also various cultural events. In particular, it had to comply with the complex limitations of an irregular lozenge-shaped area of land which had been the site of a former royal palace pulled down in 1903–4. The palace had been badly damaged by fire in the 17th century and had been rebuilt, but now housed only a military academy. The members of the jury selecting the final plan argued long and hard, and in the end agreed to award the prize to two architects: Antonín Balšánek, who was made responsible for the exterior, and Karel Osvald Polívka ▲ *176*, who was commissioned to do the interior. Such a decision risked an element of disparity in the design, and the construction of a building that lacked unity of style. However, it is now difficult to identify which parts were done out by which architect, although a comparison with Antonín Balšánek's other work suggests that he was responsible for the overall design, and that Osvald Polívka concentrated on conceptualizing the dominant forms and executing the interior design. In building the façade, Balšánek, who had the benefit of historicist training, used traditional decorative styles and adapted them to modern tastes. The overall result is somewhat neo-Baroque. By contrast, the interior is completely Art Nouveau: it consists of the ceremonial rooms including the Mayor's Room with its allegory of Prague just above the line of chairs painted by Alfons Mucha (facing page, bottom), the exhibition halls, a concert hall (the Smetana Hall), a café (opposite, top right) and a restaurant with a mixture of decorations.

AN ARTISTIC MELTING-POT. As with the National Theater ▲ 294, decorating the Town Hall succeeded in mobilizing all the artistic talent that Prague could muster. This included the painters Mikoláš Aleš, Alfons Mucha, Karel Špillar, Jan Preisler and Maxmilián Švabinský, and the sculptors J. Mařatka, Bohumil Kafka, František Úprka and Ladislav Šaloun. However, unlike the National Theater, where esthetic and political plans had gone hand in hand, the construction of *Obecní dům* relied on a wide range of decorative styles. Careful examination reveals signs of the exuberant inventiveness that characterized Prague in the early years of the 20th century and that is best appreciated by a close attention to the detail. There are two trends here that exist side by side: elegant Art Nouveau plant décors ● 86, and geometrical designs inspired by the Secession and the Wiener Werkstätte (Viennese Arts and Crafts Workshops). The lift cars, for instance, comfortably combine naturalistic floral motifs and strict geometrical designs, but are nonetheless able to incorporate the subtlest of transitions and echoes. The result is one of the many astounding interplays of form that Prague abounds in. In the restaurant, the characteristically Secessionist clock combines well with the botanical stucco on the archway where a plump young woman appears to be using her generous endowments to challenge the flat, frontal bodies of the other painted allegories. As luck would have it, as soon as the Town Hall was finished it seemed out-of-date to the new generation of artists, and it was opened in 1912 in an age which was already being swept along by new currents such as Cubism ● 89 and Viennese rationalism. Perhaps the décor was too severe. The geometry of the elegant iron awning over the entrance, which has been further embellished by the renovation work on the whole building, and many of Osvald Polívka's decorative motifs do not, however, clash with the new, modern works.

A THWARTED GENIUS. Of all the artists involved in the decoration of the Town Hall, the most controversial by far was Alfons Mucha ▲ 232 who, fortified by his successes in Paris, wanted to do all the interior decoration himself. His colleagues saw things differently and rebuked him for placing his talents so rarely at the service of his own city.

Decorative details from the Mayor's Room (Primátorské salon). Above, from left to right: a stucco scroll, part of the railing of the reception room and a blue stained-glass window.

TOWN HALL
Detail (above) of the ceiling of the Mayor's Room painted by Alfons Mucha between 1910 and 1911, after he returned from the United States.

PRAGUE SYMPHONY ORCHESTRA

Václav Smetáček (1906–86) was a frequent conductor of the Czech Philharmonic but from 1942 to 1972 he devoted much of his career to conducting the second of Prague's three orchestras, the

Prague Symphony Orchestra, the third one being the Czech Radio Orchestra. Smetáček also taught at the Conservatory and the Academy of Music.

THE SMETANA HALL. The second floor of the Town Hall houses one of Prague's largest concert halls, the 1,500-seater Smetana Hall. On either side of the stage are two sculpted groups by Ladislav Šaloun, one of them symbolizing Smetana's *Má vlast* (*My Country*) and the other representing Dvořák's *Slavonic Dances*. Statues of Czech composers adorn the escutcheons decorating the boxes, and the paintings on the walls and ceilings are the work of Karel Špillar. In the small, second-floor ceremonial rooms at the front of the building, music takes pride of place in Maxmilián Švabinský's frescos, a testament to the crucial role that music played in the nation's rebirth. The vestibule contains busts of the conductors Václav Talich (1883–1961) and Václav Smetáček, both of them key figures in the history of Czech music.

THE CZECH PHILHARMONIC ORCHESTRA. The Czech Philharmonic Orchestra (CPO) and the National Theater are the most important institutions in the musical life of Prague ● *46, 48*. The CPO regularly performs in the Smetáček Hall although its official home is now the Rudolfinum ▲ *194*. Founded in 1894, it was originally made up of musicians from the National Theater, but became independent in 1901. As a private organization, times were sometimes difficult and the orchestra performed many concerts and undertook a large number of tours to survive. Later on, under the first Republic, the government came to appreciate its importance as an ambassador of Czech culture, and the Czech Philharmonic was nationalized by Edvard Beneš' government in 1945. Under Václav Talich, who was conductor from 1917 to 1954, the CPO became one of the world's great orchestras; Talich proudly promoted the music of Otakar Ostrčil, Josef Suk, Vítěslav Novák, Bedřich Smetana and Antonín Dvořák, and also of Bohuslav Martinů, the first performance of whose opera *Juliette* he conducted in 1938. Talich was also involved in the formation of the Slovak Philharmonic Orchestra in 1952.

POWDER TOWER

This tower (PRAŠNÁ BRÁNA) was built in honor of Vladislas Jagiello II on the site of one of the gates that had formed part of the old fortifications. Work was commenced in 1475, but this was abandoned when the king transferred his residence to the castle in 1484. It was not finished until the 19th century. The decorations by Matěj Rejsek (c. 1450–1506) have been well preserved, thanks to the integrity of Josef Mocker (1835–99) who was also responsible for St Vitus' Cathedral ▲ 214 and rebuilt the Church of St Peter and St Paul at Vyšehrad ▲ 325. Mocker completed the upper story, raised the roof and decorated the net vault, and enthusiasts will enjoy guessing which parts were done by Rejsek and Mocker respectively. The depictions of the Kings of Bohemia on the east and west walls are the work of sculptors invited by Mocker: Čapek, Seeling and Šimek ▲ 290.

NOVÉ MĚSTO

AMBITIOUS TOWN PLANNING. Nové Město (New Town) stretches beyond Republic Square. The Old Town was no longer large enough to contain the growing number of inhabitants and, on his ascent to the throne, Charles IV ● 66 combined the various districts that stood outside the Old Town into a "new" town which was founded in 1347 and designed in accordance with his ideas of breadth and space. It was the biggest piece of town planning in the Middle Ages, and included streets 60 to 70 feet wide and a main thoroughfare 200 feet wide and 5 miles long. Furthermore, the building plan was notable as much for its insistence on the rules and time constraints of construction as for the geometrical structures of the streets.

ENORMOUS MARKETS. The plan for the New Town included three vast areas which adjoined the former districts and were designed as markets: they were the cattle market (later to become Charles Square ▲ 308), the horse market (later renamed Wenceslas Square ▲ 172) and the hay market (Senovážné náměstí).

CAPITAL OF BOHEMIA AND THE EMPIRE. It was Charles IV's ambition to make Prague into a second Rome, and he went some way to achieving this aim by founding the University ▲ 278 by a decree of April 7, 1348. By 1355, he had become Holy Germanic Emperor and was at the height of his powers, and Prague had become the imperial capital. In 1378, the last year of Charles' reign, Prague had a population of forty thousand and was one of the biggest cities in Europe.

FORMER U HYBERNŮ CHURCH
The "Hibernians" were Irish Franciscan monks who came from "Hibernia"(the classical name for Ireland) in 1629; Their church was built between 1652 and 1659, almost certainly by Giovanni B. Orsi; it was rebuilt in the Empire style between 1808 and 1811 by the Viennese architect Georg Fischer (1768–1828) and used as a customs office. The convent has retained its Baroque appearance.

"We wish and command that a town shall be built called New Town, and that its inhabitants shall be the owners of the entire area between the Old Town and the walls with which we shall encircle the New Town. We also command that they shall be free to build houses and outhouses . . ."
Decree announcing the foundation of Nové Město (New Town), April 3, 1348.

POWDER TOWER
Up until the 17th century gunpowder was stored in this tower.

Former Central Hotel

The early days of Art Nouveau. Art Nouveau, with its floral motifs that proliferated in the Central Hotel, was characterized by its French-style naturalism; there are many examples of this in Prague, particularly in buildings of overwhelmingly large proportions. However, Prague's version of Art Nouveau took as long as ten years to develop, and did so on the basis of ideas which had been developed by Ohmann but which were only to find truly Baroque vigor beyond simple neo-Baroque styles. Not far away, on the corner of Havlíčkova Street, is the neoclassical Masaryk Station; it was Prague's first railway station, and was built in 1845.

Façade of the Central Hotel
A short walk along Hybernská Street, past what was once the U Hybernü Church, leads to the former Central Hotel. The hotel was built between 1899 and 1902 (that is the Corso Café) to plans by Friedrich Ohmann; the whole building has been recently restored, with the exception of the second floor.

Former Café Arco

Max, Franz & Co . . .
For many years at the beginning of the 20th century, the Café Arco ● *58* at no. 16 Hybernská Street was the meeting place for the great names of German-language Czech literature. Max Brod (1884–1968) made the acquaintance of Kafka ● *110* here while still a student; he used to go to the Café Arco in his university days, and it was also there that he met the younger Franz Werfel (1890–1945), and became one of his supporters. Werfel, too, was a student at the Carolinum and a habitué of the Arco, and in this way he became friends with Jan Urzidil, Ernst Pollak, Kornsfeld and Haas. In 1911, thanks to Brod, he published his first, and highly successful, novel, *Friend of the World*.

Sweets-Sporck Palace
This building at nos. 3–5 Hybersnká is in fact two Baroque buildings combined. It has a façade built by Antonín Haffenecker c. 1780, and the doors and the roof statuary are by Ignác Platzer. In 1912, it hosted the 6th Conference of the Russian Social Democratic Party where the Bolsheviks, led by Lenin, founded an independent party. For many years, the Sweets-Sporck Palace housed a Lenin Museum.

Former Legio Bank

This curious building, which was built in 1922–5, stands in Na Poříči Street, and is approached along Havlíčkova Street. It is the work of Josef Gočár (1880–1945), who was a student of Kotěra and became the first President of the Group of "Plasticians". It is an astonishing mixture of the spirit of Cubism and of local tradition, and the enormous doorway with pilasters recalls entrances to many Renaissance and Baroque buildings. The decorated frieze and the telamones depict the world of work and industry, fields of endeavor that the bank did much to foster.

FORMER MORTGAGE BANK

Dlážděná Street leads into Senovážné Square, the former hay market. The former Mortgage Bank at no. 13 is a building in the neo-Renaissance style. Kafka was employed here.

A DYNAMIC BANKING CENTER. From 1860 onward, Prague was gripped by a fever for investment, with mechanical industries and banking establishments in the forefront, and the Czech middle classes were particularly active in the economic development of Bohemia. Initially, all the major financial operations were in the hands of the Viennese banks that had branches in Prague, but this period also saw the establishment of the first Czech banks; these included the Discount Bank (1863) and the Mortgage Bank (1864). In one corner of the square, in Jeruzalemská Street, stands the JUBILEE SYNAGOGUE which was built in 1906 in a half-Art Nouveau, half-Moorish style. At right angles to the synagogue is ST HENRY'S CHURCH; it is one of the biggest churches in the New Town and was restored during the Baroque period.

FRIEDRICH OHMANN (1858–1927)
The architect trained in Vienna and became a professor of the second "special class" at the Academy of Fine Arts. Otto Wagner, who was working in the first "class", was therefore a colleague of his. Ohmann taught for ten years at Prague's School of Arts and Crafts before returning to Vienna in 1899. There, he became a leading architect although, as the years went by, his style tended toward bombast. This led him to embrace historicism, and his work of this period includes the neo-Gothic Štorch House (1896–7) in Old Town Square and the Czech neo-Renaissance *U české orlice* house (1897) in Celetná Street ▲ *160*. However, it also includes examples of Art Nouveau which he introduced to Prague, particularly the Corso Café (1897–8), which has now been pulled down. In the view of K.B. Madl, a leading critic of the Secession, Ohmann was the "John the Baptist" of Modernism in Prague.

PRAGUE CITY MUSEUM

Prague City Museum lies about five minutes away, on the edge of the New Town and on the other side of the ramparts now replaced by the city's internal freeway. It is unjustly ignored by visitors – a visit here is an excellent introduction to the Czech capital. The Museum is opposite the Jan Šverma Gardens (Sady Jana Švermy, Prague 8), and occupies a neo-Renaissance building (1895–8) designed by Antonín Wiehl and Antonín Balšánek. The rooms on the ground floor contain Gothic and Roman statues, frescos and illuminated manuscripts, along with models and objets d'art; these are displayed chronologically and trace the city's history. The museum's most important piece, however, is on the top floor: a huge model of

**COMMERCE AND CRAFT
INDUSTRY BANK**
This neo-Renaissance buillding stands at
no. 20 Na příkopě Street. It was built in
1894 by Polívka ▲ 176.

EARLY 20TH-CENTURY HOUSES
Dorfler House, (above), at no. 7 Na příkopě Street,has retained elements of the Secession despite its "modernized" floors. Also known as the "Pelikan Building", it was designed by Blecha and Justice. Koruna House, which stands opposite between nos. 4 and 6, probably has the narrowest façade in Prague. Like Koruna Palace ▲ 174, Koruna House was built by Antonín Pfeiffer and is notable for its marked Art Nouveau decoration.

Prague made by Antonín Langweil between 1826 and 1834. A proper examination requires at least half an hour and the use of binoculars is recommended; the model shows the city limits and its architectural styles during the 19th century, and it is quite possible to visualize what the Jewish quarter, Na příkopě Street, Wenceslas Square and Masaryk Quay looked like during that period. The room also contains an old map of Prague which makes study of the model even more intriguing.

NA PŘÍKOPĚ

This pedestrianized shopping street has some wonderful buildings, and a superb panorama of styles stretching from 1860 to today. It actually goes back further than that as it was initially built in 1760 after the ditch which surrounded the Old Town's ramparts was covered over. This is the origin of the name of the street, which means "over the ditch".
NATIONAL BANK. The imposing building that houses the Bank of the Czech State (1936–8) at nos. 24–8 is the work of František Roith (1876–1942), who also designed the Municipal Museum (in Marianské náměsti.). After studying under Otto Wagner in Vienna, Roith settled in Prague where his taste for monumental and restrained styles revealed the influence of his Austrian teacher's principles.
SLAV HOUSE. Czech Communists held meetings of the Central Committee in the Přichovsky Palace between 1945 and 1948. The neoclassical façade designed by Filip Heger (c.1734–1804) conceals an earlier Baroque façade dating from the late 17th century, but in 1873 the building was turned into a casino which became popular with Germans. As a reaction to this, the building was renamed "Slav House" (Slovanský dům) after the war. Prague's first Art Nouveau building was constructed opposite; it was designed by Friedrich Ohmann, and the Corso Café occupied the first floor.

FORMER INVESTMENT BANK. The Živnostenská (Commerce and Craft Industry Bank), which opened in 1868 at no. 20, was the leading financial institution of the Czech bourgeoisie, and many of its administrators played key political roles. The present building was constructed in 1894–6 for the National Bank: the monumental staircase and the enormous hall on the second floor are well worth a visit.

SYLVA-TAROUCCA PALACE. This extremely beautiful example of Rococo architecture at no. 10 Na příkopě is the work of the architect K. I. Dientzenhofer and was built between 1743 and 1751. It was intended for Prince Ottavio Piccolomini whose family had settled in Bohemia after the Battle of White Mountain ● *34*. All the carved decoration is from the workshop of Ignác Platzer, while the frescos on the ceiling over the staircase were executed by V. B. Ambrozzi. The Savarin Palace Casino can be found on the second floor.

STATE BANK. At nos. 3–5 Na příkopě, there is another building belonging to the Czech National Bank; this is clad in beautiful polished granite. It represents an early 20th-century example of a form of re-discovered and refined classicism inspired by Viennese styles, and the powerful influence of Otto Wagner in particular. Another instance of this is the extraordinary Adria Palace ▲ *291* by Joseph Zasche, a German architect who lived in Prague. Franz Metzner's massive and severe sculptures in marble marry very well with the architecture. Opposite Adria Palace, at no. 4, is the FABRIC HOUSE, the oldest of Prague's big department stores, built in 1870. From the roof terrace of the Universal building on the corner of Na můstku there is a lovely view out over the neighboring districts.

ALFONS MUCHA (1860–1939) Mucha started out as a theater designer.

He then entered the service of Count Karl Khuen-Belasi, whose Emmahof Castle he decorated, before being sent to Paris to complete his training. After his patron committed suicide, Mucha earned his living through contributions to various illustrated magazines, including La Vie Parisienne. His career took off in 1894 thanks to a fortunate meeting with the celebrated actress Sarah Bernhardt for whom he created some famous posters. The one above was designed for Lorenzaccio (1899).

VÁCLAVSKÉ NÁMĚSTÍ MANY YEARS AGO
This photograph dated 1876 shows the square after the Horses' Gate was pulled down and before the National Museum was built. The square had been a popular and busy area since the beginning of the 19th century, and gradually the royal vines planted behind the gate were removed to make way for the new buildings which make up the Vinohrady district. On either side, large magnificent buildings replaced the small, low houses at the top of the square, and elaborate street lamps were erected

MUCHA MUSEUM

Housed in Kaunicky Palace at no. 7 Panská Street, behind Wenceslas Square, the Mucha Museum opened in February 1998. Dedicated exclusively to the unique works of Alfons Mucha (1860–1936), the famous Art Nouveau Czech painter ▲ *171*, it was created in cooperation with the Mucha Foundation ▲ *232*. More than eighty items, including decorative panels, posters, charcoal drawings, pastels, lithographs and personal objects, are on display. The prestigious Parisian period (1887–1907) is particularly well represented, and Mucha's workshop, with its original furniture and the artist's own photographs, has been reconstructed as part of the exhibition.

WENCESLAS SQUARE

ORIGINS OF VÁCLAVSKÉ NÁMĚSTÍ. This former horse market is the longest of the three huge squares that Charles IV ● *25* planned for his New Town. It forms a cross with the others (Senovážné and Karlovo náměstí) which are in turn linked by roads at right angles: Jindřišská Street and Vodičkova Street. The square was originally closed off at one end by the Horses' Gate, which formed part of the city's fortifications; in 1885–90, the gate was replaced by the monumental National Museum.

down the middle from 1868 onward. The city fortifications and the gates began to be removed in 1875.

THE STATUE OF WENCESLAS. The original statue of the patron saint of Bohemia was executed by Jan Jiří Bendl in 1680, and it was situated in the middle of the square before being taken to Vyšehrad in 1879. The modern statue of the saint on horseback is the work of Josef Václav Mylsbek and was erected in 1912; this Wenceslas is surrounded by five patron saints of Bohemia: saints Ludmila, Procope, Adalbert, Vojtěch and Agnes. The words of a piece of 13th-century choral music are written on the plinth: "May we and our descendants not perish." Czechs have always sung this piece in difficult times and at important moments in their history.

DOWN THROUGH HISTORY. Wenceslas Square has played an important role in the history of the people of Prague. It was during the Revolution of 1848 ● *28* that the square received its current name, symbolizing the identity and durability of the Czech nation. In 1918, the square was the scene of huge demonstrations in favor of national independence, and then, in August 1968, it was where the inhabitants of Prague tried to

172

PRAGUE SPRING ● *40*
On August 21, 1968, the five countries of the Warsaw Pact invaded Czechoslovakia, and in Prague, Soviet tanks took up positions in Václavské náměstí. Opponents of the invasion made the square into a symbol of national resistance, some of them opting for confrontation and others remaining seated at the foot of the statue of Saint Wenceslas.

THURSDAY NOVEMBER 23, 1989
Not even the bitter cold prevented hundreds of thousands of inhabitants of Prague from coming to hear Václav Havel speak. The following day, excitement reached new heights when Dubček appeared on the balcony, and the great mass of people surged forward to hear the great Slovakian reformer continue a speech that had been interrupted back in August 1968. On this day twenty-one years later, many people were in tears and Wenceslas Square proved far too small to accommodate all those who yearned for freedom.

stop Russian tanks advancing into their city. In January 1969, a student, Jan Palach, set fire to himself at the foot of the statue of Saint Wenceslas ▲ *198*. To prevent groups of people gathering there, the authorities reacted by building the new innercity motorway (*magistrala*) which runs between the National Museum and the statue; the statue was also surrounded by chains to stop people approaching. All demonstrations during the 1980's either began or finished in Wenceslas Square. It was also here that May Day marches took place during the forty-one years of Communist rule.
FOCAL POINT OF THE VELVET REVOLUTION ● *40*. The savage suppression of the first demonstration of November 19, 1989 – it commemorated a demonstration that had taken place on November 19, 1919 – followed by the setting up of the Civic Forum, led to several consecutive days of demonstrations. It attracted up to a million people on November 23 and 24,

Right:
the National Museum

Museum království Českého

LUCERNA
Lucerna Palace is the work of a well-known architect and former resident, Václav Havel, grandfather of the President. The drawing room is used for concerts, and famous musicians including Chaliapin, Bronislaw Huberman, Pablo Casals and Toscanini have all played here. Prague's younger generations also come to learn the waltz and the tango in the vast rooms with their parquet floors.

PETERKA HOUSE
Peterka House at 12 Václavské náměstí was the first building that the architect Jan Kotěra (1871–1923) designed in Prague; it signaled the start of the geometrizing phase of the Prague Secession. Kotěra studied in Vienna under Otto Wagner, and his arrival in the capital of Bohemia was warmly welcomed by the supporters of Modernism.

when workers and young people addressed the well organized and peaceful crowd from the balcony of the Melantrich publishing house; they were flanked by the dissident priest Václav Malý, the politicians Havel and Dubček, other representatives of the Civic Forum, and even the Archbishop of Prague.

KORUNA PALACE

Koruna Palace ● *84, 86*, a former commercial and administrative building on the corner of Na příkopě Street, was designed by Antonín Pfeiffer. It is a good example of the buildings of "Babylonian" inspiration that were constructed at the end of the 19th century in the wake of the new, widespread interest in eastern civilizations. Archeological digs in Mesopotamia started in 1899, and discoveries made there encouraged a fashion for so-called "Babylonian" monumental motifs. Sucharda's sculptures are most impressive.

EVROPA HOTEL

This hotel, which is unquestionably the most famous in Prague, was built by Bendrich Bendelmayer and Alois Drýak ▲ *288* between 1903 and 1906. It embodies the best of Prague's Art Nouveau ● *86, 92*, particularly the plant motifs and geometrical design. The entire gamut of Art Nouveau devices are to be found here, both on the exterior and inside: they include carved balconies, mosaics, ornamentation characteristic of Kotěra, and gilt.

WIEHL HOUSE

In 1896, the architect Antonín Wiehl built himself a large four-

174

story house on the corner of Wenceslas Square and Vodičkova Street. It is one of Prague's finest examples of neo-Renaissance style. The façade is decorated with sgraffito ● 78 and frescos depicting national stories and legends; they were painted by L. Novák and F. Urban after cartoons by Mikoláš Aleš and Josef Fanta.

EVROPA HOTEL
The café has an oval gallery. The restaurants are curiously outdated but extremely refined.

NATIONAL MUSEUM ★

The only way to reach the National Museum is by crossing the motorway that runs through the city or by walking through the underpass. Like the National Theater, the National Museum embodies the nation's rebirth ▲ 194. It was founded in 1818 following encouragement from Czech patriots spurred on by Count Kašpar Šternberk and the philosopher Josef Dobrovský ● 28, ▲ 267; since then, many leading figures in Prague life including the historian František Palácky, the philologist Josef Jungmann and the naturalist Jan Evangelista Purkinję ▲ 308 have contributed to its continued success. The modern building, which dates from 1885, was constructed at the top end of Wenceslas Square to designs by the architect Josef Schulz. The fountain at the foot of the slope incorporates a number of sculptures by Antonín Wagner, including an allegory of Bohemia towering above personifications of the Rivers Elbe and Vltava. The interior has a main staircase consisting of four flights leading up to the pantheon, a vast room crowned by a dome decorated with statues of leading figures in Czech artistic and intellectual life. The museum comprises three departments including an immense library that contains precious medieval manuscripts. Some of the displays on the second floor deal with the region in prehistoric times, as well as modern history and popular traditions; there are also sections on mineralogy and petrology, and a particularly interesting collection of precious and semi-precious stones. The third floor consists of sections devoted to zoology and paleontology. There is a delightful café at the far end of the entrance hall, and concerts of classical music are regularly given on the main staircase.

NATIONAL MUSEUM ★
The imposing façade of the national museum, set with statues, conceals great riches within. The lobby, grand staircase and galleries are graced with works glorifying the evolution of the arts and sciences. As well as an extensive library, the museum contains collections devoted to mineralogy, anthropology and natural history. The busts in the dome of the pantheon depict famous Czech artists, scholars and writers. After so absorbing so much information, the little café at the back of the lobby provides visitors with very some welcome refreshment.

Much of the artistic endeavour of Karel Osvald Polívka (1859–1931) took place in Prague. He was a student at the Polytechnic School and then an assistant to Josef Zítek, the architect of the National Theater and the Rudolfinum, before collaborating with Antonín Wiehl, who designed the Prague City Museum. After forsaking historicism, Polívka established himself as a leading representative of Art Nouveau architecture, and threw all his energies into this form. His best works include the interiors of the Town Hall, the U Nováku building, the former Praha Insurance building and the Topíč publishing house.

"Praha"

The building occupied by the former "Praha" insurance company is at 7 Národní třída and dates from 1905–7; it stands next to one of Polívka's later works, the Topíč publishing house (1910). The ornamentation on the Praha Insurance building, particularly Ladislav Šaloun's allegorical and figurative designs, recalls Viennese Secession styles. It was through this free and inventive use in both subject matter and form of façade stucco that Art Nouveau in Prague retained links with the Baroque.

Čelda Klouček

This sculptor and interior designer was one of Polívka's more important collaborators; he also taught at the School of Applied Arts in Prague between 1888 and 1916. Klouček was one of the first interior designers in Prague to use naturalistic formulas for his ceramics. A measure of his importance can be gained from the warm welcome accorded to his students at the International Exhibition in Paris in 1900.

Working with Polívka

Polívka demanded that collaborators employed on decorative work took the greatest of care. He was able to gather around him the most talented artists in Prague but, as a result, this occasionally went too far in the direction of another form of abundance typical of the florid style associated with Symbolism.

STATUES AT THE MINISTRY OF INTERNAL COMMERCE

This building, dating from 1900, is at 7 Old Town Square, and is one of Polívka's best examples of neo-Baroque design. Particularly noteworthy are the monumental doorway, the characteristic undulation of the façade, and the mock-Baroque stucco ornamentation. Even the statues framing the mosaic, the sole concession to Art Nouveau, recall the roof statuary of Baroque palaces.

The Praha building avoids this because of the care that Polívka took to mark out the ornamental motifs. He seems to have harbored a positively jealous concern that the almost Wagnerian signature of the façade should not be compromised.

COMMERCE AND CRAFT INDUSTRY BANK
(20 Na příkopě)

Here, Czech neo-Renaissance style combines with an upper level decorated with mosaics by Mikoláš Aleš, Čelda Klouček and Stanislav Soucharda; they depict allegories of technology, commerce, industry and agriculture. The main hall is decorated with frescos by Maxmilián Švabinský.

CENTRAL STATION
Built between 1901 and 1909 to plans by Josef Fanta (1856–1954), the Central Station is a fine example of unity of design. The towers and the central arcade give the whole building an unusual strength. The carved decoration is by Šaloun.

GUSTAV MAHLER (1860–1911)
For a time, this great musician was second-in-command at Prague's German Theatre.

STATE OPERA

THE FRUITS OF RIVALRY. When the national movement culminated in the building of the National Theater ▲ 294 with the help of donations from all over the country, the powerful German bourgeoisie did not want their choice to be limited to the Estates Theater ▲ 281, which was a hundred years old and smaller than the Theater of the Czechs. This conflict led to the building of a new theater, the "German Theater", on the site of the New Town Theater on the ramparts, and between Wilson Station and the National Museum. This theater, which opened in 1888, is still the biggest in Prague and is an exact, though smaller, replica of the Vienna Opera.

DISTINGUISHED MUSICAL DIRECTORS. The first director was the celebrated Angelo Neumann. The first conductor was Karel Muck, and he was followed by Gustav Mahler, Leo Blech, Georges Szell, Bruno Walter, Erich Kleiber and Richard Strauss. The opera house traditionally opted for a German repertoire, but it changed direction under Alexander

Zemlinsky (1911–27), who was not only a fine conductor but also a composer of operas including *The Dwarf* and *The Florentine Tragedy*. He also promoted Richard Strauss' operas and Mahler's symphonies. His time in Prague was noted for appearances by some of the greatest exponents of German opera including Alfred Piccaver, Leo Slezak, Richard Tauber, Lotte Lehmann and Max Laurenz, and a number of Czech singers including K. Burian. The theater was partly destroyed in 1945 and when it reopened it was named the "Smetana Theater", and became the country's second most important theater. It was restored between 1968 and 1973 but, with the rebuilding of the National Theater, it has again achieved independence. Its new name, the State Opera (Státní Opera Praha), acknowledges that it is the only theatre in Prague to perform opera exclusively. The State Opera has an international repertoire, while the National Theater concentrates on the Czech repertoire.

From the Na Františku Quarter to Josefov

⏲ **Half a day**

◆ **B** A2-A3-A4-B2-B3-B4-C2-C3-C4

6 VĚŽEŇSKÁ STREET
The entrance to this building in Věžeňská Street is one of the most remarkable in the whole district.

ARCHITECTURAL TOUR

GOLDEN TRIANGLE. This is the part of the Old Town which, from 1892 onward, was most affected by the rebuilding program usually referred to as the "clean up". Here, as elsewhere in Prague, architecture enthusiasts can walk along street after street and marvel at the extraordinary beauty of so many of the houses. Two of the city's main attractions are Masaryk Quay ▲ *300* and Paris Avenue ▲ *186*. Some of these fine constructions, which include entire roads in the Secession and Art Nouveau ● *86* styles, such as Vinohrady Street, are not very well known because they are some distance from the city center; but there are others, very close to Old Town Square, that are still hardly known at all. Dlouhá, Kozí and Haštalská streets form a triangle made up of 19th- and early 20th-century buildings with wonderfully imaginative façades.

KOZÍ ULICE. The designer of the neo-Baroque building on the corner of Kozí Street and V. Kolkovně Street appears to have been obsessed with a desire to include every component of the Baroque repertoire. The result is a house topped by an onion-shaped dome, a pediment pierced with a bull's-eye window, masks and

SECESSION STYLE
In the early years of the 20th century, Art Nouveau was the art form that encapsulated modernity and supplanted the neo-Renaissance and neo-Baroque styles that had dominated the previous decades. As Petr Wittlich has remarked, "During the characteristic period of the neo-Renaissance, the architect played a representative role; by contrast, and in a complex manner, the Secession took control of the very functioning of the city itself." Polívka ▲ 176 made the greatest contributions to the Secession movement in his role as Prague's official architect; he was involved in the design of banks and other official buildings, as well as districts, such as Vojtěšská, Karlova and Haštalská streets, that were being "cleaned up" but whose architecture looked back to the neo-Baroque.

garlands.
Is this
neo-Baroque? Perhaps it is
more neo-Rococo as, apart from the
doorway, this façade lacks the monumental proportions of so many others. The next two buildings are quite different. No. 7 is an imposing structure which recalls the period of sgraffito, and is also decorated with busts of medieval architects. No. 9, which was built in about 1907, is a minor Art Nouveau masterpiece; the fine, curvilinear pediment is elaborately ornamented and pierced by a bull's-eye window, and the whole structure is a free creation containing innumerable allusions to Baroque architecture. Ornamentation on the lower floors combines two aspects of Secession style: the rich floral décor of the pediment and the window frames contrasting with geometric elements. Significantly, the roughcast stops short at the windows, and the "brutalist" appearance thereby achieved recalls certain Modernist theories of Kotěra, Novotný and Bílek dating from the second decade of the century. On the other side of the street, the façade of no. 4 Haštalská Street is in the Secession style, and is the work of Polívka (c. 1907).
VĚZEŇSKÁ ULICE. This street is as richly decorated as Kozí Street. Of particular interest is the Secession façade by A. Stárek at no. 6 decorated with a statue of Saint Wenceslas.

181

ANEŽSKÁ
STARÉ MĚSTO - PRAHA 1

CHURCH OF ST HASTAL
A Gothic church with two naves was added to this 14th-century building in 1375. The sacristy walls are adorned with frescos.

ST AGNES' CONVENT
Below are the archways of the cloister, and to the right is one of the convent's two churches; the Church of St Francis which was in ruins until 1981 and is now a

The patron saint's presence may partly account for the Gothic form of the narrow windows and the consoles suggesting covered ways. The doorway is the most beautiful in the whole street.

V. KOLKOVNĚ. The contours of the building at no. 6, which dates from 1905, are almost pure in this setting. The house next door has more in common with neo-Baroque styles.

ST AGNES' CONVENT

A TROUBLED HISTORY. St Agnes' Convent (ANEŽSKÝ KLÁŠTER) comprises two churches: a convent belonging to the Poor Clares and a Franciscan monastery. It was founded in 1233, and was one of the first religious buildings in Prague constructed in the Gothic style; the architecture, like that of St Giles' Church ▲ 285, is clearly inspired by Cistercian Burgundian art. Building work on the whole convent lasted from 1233 to 1280, and the Franciscan monastery founded by Agnes of Bohemia was completed in 1240. In time, the Convent was to become an extremely important place of worship and, in the 14th century, consisted of as many as seven churches. However, the occupants were forced to leave at the time of the Hussite troubles ● 32, and the complex then remained empty until it was handed over to the Dominicans. They had been living in the Convent of St Clement, which stood on the site of the Clementinum and had been given to the Jesuits in 1556. The Poor Clares returned in 1627. The Convent was then dissolved and, in 1782, during the reign of Joseph II, was

turned into workshops and a refuge for the poor. A Union for the Restoration of St Agnes was established in 1892 and it paid for plans to rebuild both churches; the work was begun by A. Cechner. After a long interruption, work was resumed in 1940 under Oldřich Stefan until archeological digs in 1941, and later in 1953–5, revealed the original remains. This allowed a more thorough program of restoration work to begin in 1960.

MUSEUM OF ANCIENT BOHEMIAN AND CENTRAL EUROPEAN ART Laid out in the Convent at the end of 2000, the museum presents a magnificent collection of paintings and sculptures that were formerly on display in St George's Convent, as well as pieces that were newly restored for the opening of the museum.

MUSIC AT AGNES'. Today, the Convent houses a splendid and well-appointed

popular concert hall. The Convent is attached to the National Gallery and houses collections of art of the medieval era (1200–1550).

arts complex. During the time that the buildings that had been handed over to the National Gallery were undergoing restoration, the chapel was turned into a concert hall, work having been done to improve its acoustics. This charming room is a great favorite with chamber music lovers. It is notable for a sculpture entitled *Music*, by Josef Václav Myslbek, which originally stood in the foyer of the National Theater ▲ 294.

THE GREAT MASTERS OF BOHEMIAN GOTHIC ART

The Convent's collection includes works by three important painters: the Masters of the Vyšší Brod and Třeboň altarpieces, and Theodoric. The *Madonna of Roudnice* (left) is attributed to the Master of the Třeboň Altarpiece, an anonymous painter who was active in Prague in the 1380s and who's exquisite work marks the apogee of Gothic painting in Bohemia. He is named for an altarpiece painted for the Augustine Convent at Třeboň and which is now on display at St Agnes'. *Saint Vitus* (below, left) was painted by Theodoric, from whom Charles IV commissioned a series of portraits for the chapel at his castle at Karlštejn, not far from Prague.

AGNES OF BOHEMIA

Agnes of Bohemia, daughter of Přemysl Otakar I and sister of Wenceslas I, brought the Poor Clares and the Franciscans to Prague and founded the Crusaders of the Red Cross. Her letters are kept in the Church of St Clare of Assisi. According to legend, her canonization, which took place one week before the Velvet Revolution in 1989, would shower Bohemia with blessings.

183

HOSPITAL OF ST SIMON
In 1761, this famous hospital was the first medical lecture theater in Bohemia to be equipped with a display of anatomical specimens. By 1780, it was acknowledged to be one of the finest in Europe.

SPANISH SYNAGOGUE
This synagogue was originally built to cater for the descendants of Spanish Jews. The interior is in a neo-Moorish style directly influenced by the Alhambra in Granada.

CHURCH OF ST SIMON AND ST JUDE

A short walk from St Agnes' Convent along U milosrdných Street and past the hospital leads to the Monastery of the Brothers of St John of God (U milosrdných). The 18th-century façade is by Jan Josef Hrdlička, but the church itself goes back to 1615–20. It was built by the Union of Czech Brethren on the site of a chapel belonging to the Gothic hospital, but alterations in the Baroque style dating from 1751 have obscured its original Renaissance features. Both Haydn and Mozart played the organ here.

SPANISH SYNAGOGUE

Further down Dusní Street, on the corner with Bílkova Street, stands a building with three extraordinary atlantes in the Babylonian style by František and Václav Kavalír (1910–11). Dusní Street itself is the center of one of the oldest Jewish colonies in Prague. The Spanish Synagogue (ŠPANĚLSKÁ SYNAGÓGA) was built in 1867–8 to plans by Vojtěch Ignác Ullmann (1822–97) ▲ 289 on the site of the Old School, Prague's oldest synagogue, which had been pulled down in 1867. It was in the Old School in 1837 that the Reformed Service had been introduced to Prague, and Jewish liturgical music first performed: the composer František Škroup ▲ 281 was organist there for ten years and made important contributions to the development of this music. The land occupied by the synagogue is separate from the ghetto and defines the boundary of the Sephardic community. An exhibition on the history of Jewish emancipation between the 18th and 20th centuries is currently planned. Almost opposite is the Church of the Holy Spirit (Kostel sv. Ducha) constructed in the Gothic style (1346) and later restored in the Baroque manner (1689). It contains Jan Jiří Heinsch's *Saint Joseph*.

CHURCH OF ST SAVIOR

At the bottom of Dusní Street is the Church of St Savior. It was originally built in 1611–14 in the Renaissance style as a temple for German Lutherans. According to a 17th-century chronicle, eleven of the conspirators executed in 1621 ● 35 were buried here after their heads had been exhibited on one of the towers at the end of Charles Bridge ▲ 154.

FORMER GHETTO

Kostečná Street leads directly into Paris Avenue, the boundary of the former ghetto.
SITUATION. Geographically, the ghetto was bound by Elišky Krásnohorské Street to the east, 17 Listopadu Street to the north and northwest (parallel to

> "Prague rivals Vienna for its palaces,
> Dresden for its gardens and
> Cracow for its ghetto."

Paul Morand

the river), and Kaprova Street in the south. It was one of the oldest in central Europe and of great importance to other communities in Bohemia. A Jewish community is referred to in the year 965 by the merchant Ibrahim ibn Jacob, but at that time it stood at the foot of the Castle. Another colony settled there around 1091 on the road to Vyšehrad. A third colony appeared no later than the 12th century close to Old Town Square on the Josefov site.

AN ENLIGHTENED SOVEREIGN. Despite the early pogroms and the anti-Jewish interdictions issued by the Lateran Council of 1215, Jewish people did receive some protection from certain sovereigns. One of these was Přemysl Otakar II who, in an edict in 1254, accorded them privileges, banned anti-Semitic violence and slanderous suggestions, forbade forced baptisms, and guaranteed freedom of worship, administration and justice. In spite of this royal protection, several sovereigns abused their power, confiscated goods and made scant efforts to put down pogroms; the 1939 Easter pogrom in Prague left 3,000 dead. It was not until the reign of Joseph II that the Jews were able to enjoy rights and participate fully in Bohemia's cultural and economic life, particularly agriculture and industry.

DESTRUCTION OF THE GHETTO. In the early years of the 19th century, the more prosperous Jews slowly began to settle in the immediate vicinity of the former ghetto, but complete equality throughout the Empire was not granted until 1867. In the meantime, the ghetto became Prague's fifth district in 1861; it was called Josefov after Joseph II, and was restricted to the poor

ŠTENC HOUSE
The printworks and former graphic art establishment at 931/8–10 Salvátorská Street is the work of

the architect Otakar Novotný. The building is made of brick and is one of the earliest examples of the Rationalist style. The first floor is punctuated by enameled pillars, and the windows are arranged asymmetrically. The right-hand façade in the neo-Baroque style is by Polívka ▲ 176.

Prague's sense of magic and the fantastic finds one more echo in the memories of its ghetto. The Jews are said to have come here after the destruction of the Temple in Jerusalem but, whether or not that is the full story, they have always been an essential component of the cultural mix that Prague boasts. Until it was pulled down, the Fifth District was a labyrinthine skein of narrow, sombre lanes crammed with tumbledown houses. That was how Gustav Meyrink described it in his novel *The Golem* which linked the Jewish legend for ever to the Prague of Emperor Rudolph II.

"The hidden nooks and crannies, the secret passageways, the blind windows, the grubby courtyards, the noisy taverns, the sinister inns live on inside us . . . The insalubrious Jewish Old Town is a lot more real than the hygienic new town that surrounds us."

Franz Kafka
(Letter to G. Janouch)

ŠIROKÁ STREET

The most famous of Prague's Jews lived at no. 90 of what used to be Josefovská Street, a road that followed the course of modern Široká Street almost exactly. He was Jehuda Liwa ben Bezabel ben Chaïm, known as Rabbi Löw, born at the beginning of the 16th century and at one time a Rabbi in Mikulov in Moravia. Legend links him closely with Rudolph II. Some see Rabbi Löw as a Jewish Faustus, a conspirator who brought to life a creature made of mud (i.e. the Golem); He was still the first Jew in Prague to have an audience with the King, when Rudolph received him at the Castle on February 16, 1592 and promised to give protection to the Jewish community.

THE GOLEM

This giant, made by
Rabbi Löw ▲ *190* out
of a mixture of earth
and clay is still
legendary in Prague.
The Golem, who was
intended to protect
the Jewish community
and became the
Rabbi's devoted
servant, came to life
through a *chem*, a
parchment marked
with a holy sign which
his master placed in
his mouth. One
evening, however, on
the eve of the
Sabbath, the Rabbi
forgot to remove the
talisman and the giant
angrily went round
the ghetto terrifying
everybody. Löw
eventually retrieved
the *chem* and
managed to mollify
the monster, who
turned back into a
mound of mud.
Opposite. a still from
Paul Weneger's film,
The Golem (1920).

OLD TOWN SYNAGOGUE

Legend has provided many accounts of the
origin of Prague's oldest synagogue. Some
people believe it was built with the stones of
the Temple that Jews brought over from
Jerusalem; others say that the stones were
transported by protecting angels. Another
version claims that an old man showed the
elders of the community a mound under
which the synagogue had already been built.

Members of the burial society attend the dying man during his last moments.

The undertakers carry the body, while the man in the black gown collects gifts.

The cortège arrives at the new cemetery where the minister gives a funeral eulogy.

THE HOLY COMPANY OF PRAGUE
A cycle of fifteen paintings illustrates the
activities of this religious charitable
organization. They are by an anonymous artist
and were probably executed in about 1780.

The new Jewish cemetery with its broad, well-kept avenues was situated outside the city.

Some Jewish men gather in front of the funeral monument of Maharal, the Rabbi Löw.

The leader of the burial society was elected by his peers at the annual dinner.

18

PAŘÍŽSKÁ TŘÍDA
The many fascinating buildings in Paris Avenue include a neo-Baroque structure by Jan Koula (1902) at no. 1; a group of houses by Jan Verych, the architect of the Hotel Paříž, at nos. 7, 9, 10 and 13; and, at no. 17, a strange corner building (below) by Weyr and Klenska, two designers with a strong interest in the unexpected.

Interior of the Klaus Synagogue, which now houses one of the collections of the National Jewish Museum.

of all denominations. However, the maze of tiny lanes and courtyards and backyards was insalubrious, and they began to be pulled down in 1892, although many years passed before the level of the land could be raised, water piping installed and new streets built. By the beginning of the 20th century, all that remained were six synagogues, the cemetery and the Jewish Town Hall. The demolition of the ghetto was not the only change to Prague's layout: the quarter round St Adalbert's Church ● *303* and the Na Františku and Podskálí districts were rebuilt, and the area near the quays was renovated.

PARIS AVENUE

MODERN TIMES. Paris Avenue (Pařížská třída) is one of the most famous streets in Prague. It starts in Old Town Square level with St Nicholas' Church ▲ *145*, runs down to the Vltava and offers a view over to Letra ▲ *316*. The neo-Baroque and Secession buildings are unusually elegant, and the Avenue is a favorite place for walks. A corner building at 14 Bílkova Street by Otakar Novotný (1917–18) is one of the finest examples of Cubist architecture ● *89* in Prague. Paris Avenue was built at the end of the 19th century, and its construction was considered to be a matter of exceptional prestige.

OLD-NEW SYNAGOGUE

This Gothic synagogue (STARONOVÁ SYNAGÓGA), which was constructed in 1270–5, is the oldest building in the ghetto and is the center of the district. This synagogue was originally called the New School but when other places of worship were built, it became the Old-New. Unlike the ghetto's other religious buildings, the Old-New Synagogue was never closely surrounded by houses, and in that way avoided any fires that broke out. It was not until the late 19th century that any rebuilding work was done, and this was carried out in the "purist" style by Josef Mocker. Further restoration took place after 1920 and in 1966–7. The interior decoration is restrained. The synagogue has always been an active place of worship, even under Communist rule.

"RABBI LŐW". As this has always been the Jewish community's most important synagogue, its Rabbis have always been selected from amongst the most brilliant candidates. The most famous of these was the erudite Jehuda

Liwa ben Bezabel ben Chaïm (1512–1609), who was known as the Rabbi Löw and created the legendary Golem ▲ 187.

KLAUS SYNAGOGUE

This synagogue (KLAUSOVÁ SYNAGÓGA), which is in U starého hřbitova Street (At the Old Cemetery) and very near the old cemetery, was built in the late 17th century. Today, the former Burial Guild Ceremonial Hall (obřádní síň Pohřebního bratrstva) houses an exhibition of Jewish festivals and traditions. At one time, Prague boasted the oldest Jewish printing center north of the Alps, and its workshops were famous throughout Europe. The first Hebrew print works opened at the beginning of the 16th century; it belonged to Gershom Kohen and ran for almost three hundred years. The collection contains manuscripts done by copyists in the 18th and early 19th centuries. There are many old books in Hebrew on sale in the bookshops along Celetná Street ▲ 158.

The tympanum over the doorway of the Old-New Synagogue, with fig-leaf carving (below).

FORMER BURIAL GUILD CEREMONIAL HALL. This neo-Romanesque building dates from 1906, and contains a number of works of art in addition to documents, particularly children's drawings, from Terezín. Before the war, Terezín was a fortified garrison town with 6,000 inhabitants; it lay some 38 miles to the north of Prague. In 1941, the Nazis expelled the inhabitants and replaced them with Jews from Czechoslovakia, Germany and Austria with the aim, so they said, of building a "thermal spa" ghetto. They also allowed musicians to put on symphony concerts, operas and chamber music recitals, thereby seeking to persuade international opinion of the benefits that they were providing the detainees. Goebbels himself went so far as to organize a visit from the Red Cross, and the place was swept, repainted and smartened up for the occasion, inmates in poor health being sent off to the concentration camps. The Reich's propaganda department even produced a film entitled *The Führer gives the Jews a Town*. In fact, Terezín was a transit camp from which prisoners were sent to the death camps. Food shortages and dysentery killed up to 150 people a day, and altogether about 140,000 people, including 15,000 children, passed through. In 1945, there were only 17,000 survivors. Buses bound for Litoměřice depart from the Na Florenc bus station and pass through Terezín.

FORMER JEWISH CEMETERY

LAYERS OF GRAVES. This cemetery (STARÝ ŽIDOVSKÝ HŘBITOV) dates from the 15th century. Earlier cemeteries on

THE JEWISH CEMETERY ✪
The old Jewish cemetery, set in the heart of the former Ghetto and encircled by a great wall, contains some 12,000 tombstones. In use from 1439 to 1787, it is one of the oldest in Europe, and is a testament of the Jewish community's great influence on the history of Prague. It is reached via the Pinkas synagogue, then by following the path that meanders between the tombstones, which seem to be planted in the ground like so many crooked teeth. According to legend Rabbi Löw's golem wanders about the cemetery at night. On Starého Hřbotova Street, just outside the cemetery, street stalls offer an interesting range of local handicrafts.

the same site disappeared after the Middle Ages.
This is true of a cemetery which lay where Spálená
and Jungmannova Streets now stand in Nové Město,
and where the bodies of people of all faiths were laid
to rest. The cemetery took up a very small amount of
land, and soon there was no more room for any new graves.
Where a religion permitted bodies to be exhumed, they were
placed one on top of the other, sometimes ten deep.

ELABORATE DECORATIONS. From the early 17th century
onward, important people were entitled to graves with four
walls, and these were covered in texts that glorified the lives
of the deceased. Examples of this practise are the tombs of
Mordechaï Maisel (1528–1601) and Rabbi Löw. Over the
centuries, these inscriptions became more elaborate and
varied: a few words were deemed sufficient in the Middle
Ages, but by the 15th century the texts detailed the dead
person's profession and celebrity. Later, the Baroque period
saw the introduction of lengthy texts which included poems,
rhetoric and quotations from the Bible.

ŠIROKÁ STREET

Maislova Street runs downhill from the cemetery, and the first
turning on the right, Široká Street, is notable for a wide range
of the most interesting buildings. They include a neo-Gothic
building at no. 11 (1906) by Matěj Blecha which is visible

MAISELOVA ULICE
This street in the
Jewish quarter is
named after
Mordechai Maisel, a
former mayor of the
old city. It contains
two buildings that the
Rabbi commissioned:
the Town Hall and
the Maisel
Synagogue. The pink
outline of the Jewish
Town Hall is at no.
18; the present
building by Josef
Schlesinger dates
from 1763–5, and
replaced the former
Town Hall built in
1580 by Pankrác
Roder and destroyed
by fire in 1754. The
tower contains a clock
adorned with Hebrew
figures, on which the
hands turn from right
to left. The new Town
Hall is now the home
of a number of
official institutions in
the Jewish
community, and
houses the Sefer
publishing house and
an important library.

גמלי חסדים

from the climb up Paris Avenue, neo-Baroque designs at nos. 12 and 14, and a house in the Secession style at no. 7 by František Weyr (1867–1939). In sharp contrast is no. 5, a fine building by a student of Otto Wagner ▲ *170*, the Rationalist designer Antonín Engel (1879–1958).

HIGH SYNAGOGUE

This synagogue (VYSOKÁ SYNAGÓGA), which lies at the back of the Town Hall in Cervená Street, was built in the 16th century by Pankrác Roder. Restoration work to the building was carried out a few years ago. The fine collections of Jewish textiles, including thousands of curtains, fabrics, mantles, bindings for the Torah, and other draperies from all the Jewish communities of Bohemia and Moravia, covering a period extending from the 16th century to the present day, are no longer held here. Some items are temporarily on display at the Maisel synagogue and others are in the Klaus synagogue. The most interesting pieces are curtains that are hung inside the Arks in front of the Torah scrolls.

JEWISH TOWN HALL

(ŽIDOVSKÁ RADNICE). The Jewish community in Prague had administrative and legal independence for many years, but there is no documentary evidence of there being a Town Hall on this site until 1541. In 1648, after Jewish people had played an active part in the defence of the city against Swedish troops, Ferdinand III showed his gratitude by granting them the right to build a clock tower over their Town Hall. This was a very considerable privilege as only Christian buildings were allowed to add towers.

MAISEL SYNAGOGUE

Nearby, at 10 Maislova Street, is the Maisel Synagogue (MAISELOVA SYNAGÓGA), which was completely remodeled in neo-Gothic style between 1893 and 1905 by Alfred Grotte. In 1591, Rudolph II had granted the Jewish leader, Mordechaï Maisel, permission to build a synagogue. According to David Gans, it was a magnificent building with twenty pillars; unfortunately it was destroyed, together with 316 ghetto houses, the synagogues and the public buildings, in a fire in the Old Town started by French emissaries in 1689. The synagogue now houses a permanent exhibition on the history of Bohemian and Moravian Jews (from Czechoslovakia) from the 14th to the 18th centuries. **RABBI MAISEL.** Mordechai Maisel was considered to be one of the richest men of his time. He died in 1601. He is almost as famous as Rabbi Löw, and is the subject of numerous legends; he is also one of the main characters in Leo Perutz's *By Night under the Stone Bridge*, a novel set in Prague in the time of Rudolph II. This great financier negotiated terms with

PINKAS SYNAGOGUE (Široká ulice)
This synagogue was originally built in 1535 in the Late Gothic style. Despite alteration in 1625, the vault's Flamboyant Gothic design has

survived. Since 1959, the synagogue has been a memorial to Bohemian and Moravian Jews murdered in Nazi concentration camps, and the walls are covered with almost 80,000 names together with dates of birth and the dates on which they died. After restoration work on the building, the names were carefully re-copied on the walls (above).

ŠIROKÁ ULICE
The house at no. 9 has a Secession façade decorated with allegorical statues of two plump women carved by Karel Vítězslav Mašek in 1908.

The exterior is decorated with statues of composers (Palestrina, Orlando di Lasso, Vittoria, Handel, Cherubini, Auber, Bach, Gluck, Mozart, Haydn, Beethoven, Schubert, Mendelssohn and Schumann), sculptors, painters and architects (Bramante, Della Robbia, Masaccio, Brunelleschi, Donatello, Ghirlandaio, Apelles, Phidias and Ictinus).

Emperor whereby he would improve the living conditions of Jewish people in Prague; in return, half of his fortune would revert to the King on his death. The day after he was buried, bailiffs came to take away his goods, but the amount of money that they found was considered to be insufficient. This led to a civil action against Prague's Jewish community, who were asked to pay up what Maisel owed. The content of this action, which lasted for over 180 years before it was officially closed during the reign of Joseph II, is held in the Vienna Archives.

RUDOLFINUM

Jan Palach Square is dominated by three important buildings. They are Josef Sakar's FACULTY OF PHILOSOPHY (1929), which is at the end of Široká Street and also overlooks Kaprova Street; the SCHOOL OF DECORATIVE ARTS (1884), to the left, in the neo-Renaissance style by F. Schmoranz the Younger and J. Machytka; and the

Rudolfinum to the right, also known as the House of Artists (Dům umělců). The latter is a neo-Renaissance building conceived as a "Temple to Beauty" by its architects Josef Zítek ▲ 294 and Josef Schulz, who were also responsible for the National Theater ▲ 294. It was built between 1875 and 1884 to a commission by the Czech Savings Bank to celebrate their fiftieth anniversary. It was then renamed the Rudolfinum after Crown Prince Rudolph, the tragic hero of the Mayerling episode of January 1889.

DVOŘÁK HALL. This large concert hall, noted for its fine colonnades and magnificent decoration, is situated on the south side of the Rudolfinum. It has an organ by the Rieger Brothers of Krňov which replaced the original instrument made by the Frankfurt-an-der-Oder firm of Sauer. Behind the Dvořák Hall is a

smaller concert hall used for chamber recitals. The
north end of the building used to be reserved for the
plastic arts and exhibitions and, until restoration
work in 1990–2, also housed the Conservatory and
the Academy of Music. The exterior is notable for
sgraffito executed after cartoons by the painter
Petr Maixner. The Rudolfinum is also the home of
the Czech Philharmonic Orchestra ▲ 166. During
the time of the Third Republic, the concert hall
and the rest of the buildings housed the National
Assembly, and the Academy of Music had to find
quarters in Na Slovanech (Emmaus Monastery
▲ 312). Since the recent work, the Academy has
been accommodated in Liechtenstein Palace
▲ 250, and the Conservatory has been in Palffy
Palace ▲ 262, in Valdštejnské Square.

PRAGUE SPRING. The House of Artists has become the home
of the Prague Spring International Music Festival ● 48,
founded in 1946 to celebrate the fiftieth anniversary of the
Czech Philharmonic. The Festival traditionally opens on May
12, the anniversary of the death of Bedřich Smetana, with a
performance of *Má vlast* (*My Country*), and closes on June 3
with Beethoven's *Ninth Symphony*. It is a choice that
underlines both the durability of Bohemia and its place in a
fraternal world. The Festival's scope and reputation go way
beyond the boundaries of the Czech Republic.

ARTISTS NO LONG WITH US. No visit to the Rudolfinum is
complete without a moment's thought for the musicians who
were deported to Terezín Camp ▲ 191. The most celebrated
were the composers Viktor Ulmann (born 1898, died at
Terezín), Gideon Klein (1919–45), Pavel Haas (1899–1944),
and Hans Krase (1899–1944) who composed the famous
children's opera *Brundibar*. The singer Karel Berman and the
conductor Karel Ančerl (1908–73) both survived.

MUSEUM OF DECORATIVE ARTS

Prague's Museum of Decorative Arts (Uměleckoprůmyslové
muzeum – UPM), built by Josef Schulz between 1897 and

HOUSE OF ARTISTS
This poster by Jan
Konůpek was for the
Krásná Praha
exhibition at the
Rudolfinum in 1906.

"Fortunately, it was
enough simply to wait
at the top of the
Rudolfinum's grand
staircase, one's back
relishing the gentle
murmur coming from
the brightly lit rooms,
and one's face turned
to the other side of
the square toward the
trams . . ."

Petr Král

▲ MUSEUM OF DECORATIVE ARTS

JOSEF CHOCHOL
Drawing-room
armchair (1910–11)

Prague's Museum of Decorative Arts houses fine collections of glassware, furniture, posters and jewelry, besides large numbers of precious and other assorted objects. Glass objects from the Middle Ages to the 19th century are currently displayed in rows in glass cases as enticing as Ali Baba's caves. Other collections, including splendid Art Deco and contemporary glassware, can only be seen in temporary exhibitions.

PENDANT (1909)
This pendant by Marie Křivánková was influenced by the geometrical and spiraliform styles which, in that period, also characterized the paintings of Klimt. This style claims to imitate Byzantine and Egyptian forms.

JOSEF GOČÁR
Secretaire made in 1913. Gočár was one of Prague's leading representatives of the Cubist movement.

"AT THE WINDOW"
(1932)
This Art Deco glass object is the work of Josef Drahonovský. It is 10½ inches high and consists of three panels of engraved glass. Drahonovský (1877–1938) opened his own workshop in 1904 and started teaching at Prague's School of Decorative Arts in the same year. He was one of the few 20th-century artists to devote his career to the revival of glass engraving. Some of his work is in the Cabinet des Médailles of the Bibliothèque Nationale, Paris. At the Paris Exhibition of 1925, he won the "Grand Prix" for glassware.

> "After functionalism comes thought and abstract expression."
>
> Pavel Janák

JAROSLAV HOŘEJC
This vase, which is made of ceramic covered with one black and white coat of enamel, dates from 1911. Hořejc was a member of the Artěl Cooperative which brought together many young designers. He also made many glass objects.

Poster for the 1910 Czech Gardening and Horticulture Exhibition in Prague.

DRINKING VESSEL IN FILIGREE GLASS (early 17th century)
This beautiful object was highly prized on aristocratic tables for its superb Venetian design. Bohemian glass had been produced since the Middle Ages, but crystal did not appear until about 1670.

VASE BY PAVEL JANÁK (1911) The graphic decoration of this simple, elegant object is an early example of Art Deco.

GLASS OF THE BOR SCHOOL (after 1915)
The uncolored glass is decorated with two narrow bands of different colors of enamel.

MUSEUM OF DECORATIVE ARTS
On entering this museum, visitors are immediately struck by

the monumental stairway, the ceiling (above), and the windows designed by the architect Josef Schulz.

Before his death, Jan Palach wrote, "My action has achieved its aim, but I do not want anyone to imitate me . . . The living must keep up the fight." When he was buried, students led by the Rector, Dean and Professors of the Faculty of Philosophy marched through Prague holding up photos of their friend who had died for freedom.

1901, houses fine collections of glassware, furniture, posters and jewelry, besides large numbers of precious objects. Glass objects from the Middle Ages to the 19th century are displayed in rows in glass cases as enticing as Ali Baba's caves. Other collections, including splendid Art Deco and contemporary glassware, can only be seen in temporary exhibitions.
COLLECTIONS IN THE MUSEUM OF DECORATIVE ARTS. The museum's very extensive collection consists of more than 250,000 pieces of glassware, pottery and porcelain, graphic art and photographs, furniture and other wooden artefacts, metalware, jewelry and textiles. The permanent displays trace the history of the decorative arts in Europe from antiquity to the 20th century. The techniques of glassmaking go back a long way in Bohemia's history, the earliest examples of local art forms dating from the 14th century. Bohemian glassmaking began to achieve widespread fame in the reign of Rudolph II, who invited to his court Kaspar Lehman, the most celebrated gem engraver of his day. The museum also mounts temporary exhibitions focusing on a single material, technique or period.

JAN PALACH SQUARE

Until 1989, this square (Jana Palacha náměsti) was dedicated to the soldiers of the Red Army; it was then renamed after Jan Palach, a martyr of the Prague Spring ● *40*.
A TRAGIC END. On the afternoon of January 16, 1969, a twenty-one-year-old student tried to commit suicide in the manner of Vietnamese bonzes, at the foot of the statue in Wenceslas Square. A tram conductor managed to put out the flames, but the young man was in a critical state by the time he reached hospital. He was suffering from 85 percent burns, and died on January 19. Jan Palach was one of fifteen students who had decided to protest against the invasion of Soviet troops by setting fire to themselves; Palach's name had been drawn by lot. His death sparked off tumultuous reactions throughout Europe, and the Czech people gave him a national funeral.

The Castle

The building known as Prague Castle is a series of vast structures whose history of over a thousand years invests them with a character of marked complexity. It incorporates a palace containing hundreds of apartments, a cathedral, churches, a convent, museums and gardens. Prague Castle has been the seat of supreme temporal and spiritual power since the earliest days of the Czech State, as well as being an important cultural center. Today, as the Republic's seat of power, it is an impressive symbol of the Czech nation.

BEYOND STAG MOAT:
ROYAL GARDENS
Pacassi Gate leads to parts of the Castle outside the fortifications, including the Royal Gardens and the riding school ▲ 224. They were laid out in the reign of Ferdinand I. The Castle's south façade is lined with terraced gardens ▲ 214.

ST VITUS' CATHEDRAL

KOHL FOUNTAIN

SPANISH HALL

STATUE OF SAINT GEORGE

OLD PROVOST'S HOUSE

HOLY CROSS CHAPEL

FIRST COURTYARD

SECOND COURTYARD

ACCESS TO POWDER BRIDGE

GARDEN ON THE BASTION

MATTHIAS GATE

GARDEN OF PARADISE

One of the "giants" at the entrance ▲ 2.

The Castle seen from the Belvedere

THERESIAN BUILDINGS

During the reign of Maria Theresa (1740–80), the architect Niccolo Pacassi erected the buildings in the First Courtyard and transformed those around the second and on the south side of the third into a three-story building in the Viennese Rococo style, giving them a stylistic uniformity.

Above, left to right: the buildings seen from the Garden "Over the Ramparts", the Garden of Paradise and the Garden on the Bastion.

BLACK TOWER

DALIBORKA TOWER

NEW PROVOST'S HOUSE
ST GEORGE'S SQUARE
ST GEORGE'S BASILICA
ST GEORGE'S CONVENT (MUSEUM)

HOUSE OF CZECHOSLOVAK CHILDREN
GOLDEN LANE
WHITE TOWER

LOBKOWICZ PALACE

ST GEORGE'S STREET (JIŘSKÁ ULICE)

FORMER INSTITUTE FOR NOBLE LADIES

ALL SAINTS' CHAPEL

OLD ROYAL PALACE

LOUIS WING
STAIRWAY LEADING TO THE GARDEN "OVER THE RAMPARTS"
THIRD COURTYARD
GARDEN "OVER THE RAMPARTS"

🥾 **One day**

◆ A C2-D1-D2-E1

THE CASTLE, SYMBOL OF NATIONAL POWER ✪

Allow at least one day to visit this monumental complex, consisting of a palace, religious buildings, museums and gardens, that dominates the city of Prague. Let the splendors of the past come alive in the former Royal Palace, St Vitus' Cathedral, the basilica and the museum in St George's Convent. Leaving Golden Lane and its tiny houses, walk through the terraced gardens laid out below Lobkowicz Palace toward Wallenstein Square, taking the opportunity to admire the red rooftops of Malá Strana.

MATTHIAS GATE

The imposing Matthias Gate, which stands at the end of the First Courtyard, was built in 1614 by G. Maria Filippi to a design by V. Scamozzi of Vicenza. It is situated opposite palaces built by Rudolph II and was at that time an isolated entrance forming a triumphal arch between the bridges which until the 18th century straddled the ditches. It is the only Mannerist work that preceded the Baroque period. It also marked the Castle perimeter, and helped transform the western section of building into a residence that was worthy of a king.

THE ROSE WINDOW
The rose window covers an area of 1066 square feet, and depicts the creation of the world. It was constructed in 1927–8, based on cartoons by František Kysela, and in collaboration with the glass artist, Josef Vlasak, who used 26,740 pieces of glass. Beneath the window are reliefs by Stanislav Sucharda representing the builders of the cathedral.

A BELATED COMPLETION
The vaulting over the nave, the final bays, the west front with its ornate rose window, the triple entrance with its three great bronze doors and the twin towers, 270 feet high, were completed in 1929. This put the finishing touches to the cathedral while also respecting the building's original Gothic conception.

PLAN AND ELEVATION OF THE CHOIR
The chevet of the cathedral bears the mark of the first architect, Matthew of Arras, whom Charles IV called Matthew of Avignon in 1344. By the time he died in 1352, Matthew had only managed to build as far as the triforium; he also completed the polygonal choir with five radiating chapels, the north and south side chapels and the ambulatory.

PHASES OF CONSTRUCTION

926. Wenceslas founds the original church, a simple rotunda surrounded by apses.
1061–96. The Romanesque basilica is constructed, in the form of a nave flanked by aisles.
1344–52. Charles IV orders the building of the first Gothic cathedral. The architect is Matthias of Arras, and from 1356 to 1397 Petr Parléř.
1861–1929. The western part of the cathedral is finally completed by Josef Kranner, Josef Moker and Kamil Hilbert.

DISASTERS STRIKE

The Hussite rebellion of 1420 hampered the progress of the building program. Work resumed in 1509, when the foundations of the Black Tower were laid. Construction of other parts of the cathedral also went ahead, although none reached completion. The cathedral was damaged by several fires, including a major one in 1541.

CATHEDRAL TOWER

The main tower, which reaches a height of 325 feet, was covered by a Renaissance dome in 1560–2, but this was replaced in 1770 by an onion-shaped Baroque roof by Pacassi. It is illuminated through a window decorated with an extremely beautiful Renaissance railing ● 68. The tower contains two rows of bells.

▲ Prague Castle: the Old Royal Palace and Provost's Houses

PHASES OF CONSTRUCTION
12th century. Original Romanesque royal palace.
1370–87. The Chapel of All Saints is built by Petr Parléř in the Gothic style.
1493–1509. Benedikt Ried builds the great rooms of the Old Palace in the Late Gothic style.

THE PROVOST'S HOUSES
The Old Provost's House (right) is Romanesque and has a façade dating from the 1660's. The New House (above) is neo-Gothic and was built between 1878 and 1881 on the site of several old houses.

ALL SAINTS' CHAPEL (5)
The chapel's complex vaulting was removed during rebuilding that took place in the 14th century.

THE OLD ROYAL PALACE
The foundations of this palace, which served as a residence for the Kings and Princes of Bohemia until the 16th century, date from the 12th century. Gothic structures were built over Soběslav's old Romanesque palace, but Vladislav II Jagiello's reconstruction in 1430 included the first Renaissance elements, as well as a new story dominated by a Hall called after the King himself.

THE VLADISLAV HALL (1)

The vault above the Banqueting Hall has no central supporting structure, and comprises five areas resembling flat cupolas; the surface consists of a network of intermeshed ribbing which creates an extraordinary sense of space.

THE RIDERS' STAIRCASE (2)
AND THE VLADISLAV ROOM (3)

The Riders' Staircase ● *90* features a highly complex pattern of interlaced ribbing (right). The Vladislav Room above it is decorated with deeply sculptured motifs.

LOUIS WING (4)

This transverse block in the Renaissance style was built in 1502. It housed the Chancellery of Bohemia, famous for being the site of the Defenestration of Prague. It was this event that sparked off the Thirty Years' War.

GOLDEN LANE

A line of houses of Lilliputian dimensions are backed up against the wall between White Tower and Daliborka Tower. Some of them have stories less than three feet high and used to be inhabited less well off. At the end of the 19th century the appearance of the lane changed, living conditions improved, and artists arrived. Franz Kafka lodged at no. 22 in 1917, and Jaroslav Seifert, winner of the Nobel Prize for Literature, lived here in 1929.

ST GEORGE'S BASILICA

By the end of the 19th century, the appearance of this Romanesque basilica had been completely distorted by a series of renovations, and a decision was taken that it should revert to its original style. The only features retained were the Baroque façade decorated with statues of Vratislav and Abbess Mlada (the statue of the latter had its original red, ocher and white polychromy restored).

ST GEORGE'S CONVENT

Founded in 973, the Benedictine convent was the earliest religious establishment in Bohemia. It was rebuilt or remodelled several times, and now has a double cloister. Closed in 1782, the complex was converted into barracks. Restoration began in 1962, and today it houses the Museum of Czech Art.

PHASES OF CONSTRUCTION

912. A wooden church is built.
1142. The Romanesque church is built.
End of the 14th century. A Gothic chapel, built by Petr Parléř, is added.
1657–1680. The Baroque façade is added.

THE BASILICA

The Baroque façade obscures one of the oldest Romanesque buildings in Bohemia ▲ 220. Twin towers frame the basilica. The three-tiered nave, flanked by aisles, leads up to a choir built to a square plan and crowned with a dome. The barrel-vaulted apse is raised over a crypt.

THE BASILICA'S SIDE ENTRANCE

The side entrance, dating from the early Renaissance, has a relief depicting St George and the Dragon.

THE LEGEND OF GOLDEN LANE

According to an 18th-century legend, Rudolph II ordered the construction of alchemists' laboratories and workshops for artisans working in gold and making elixirs of life. These were to be near the Castle in a mysterious lane with tiny houses, known as Golden Lane. In Rudolph II's time, this lane was inhabited by archers and the less well off ▲ 223, but legend has it that it was known for activities relating to the occult sciences.

It was indisputably the site of esoteric practices and became the city's "soul", giving Prague that "devilish" aura which it has never shaken off. Many 19th-century writers sought to perpetuate the legend. One of them, Gustav Meyrink, states in *Golem* ▲ 187: "I was in the Street of the Goldsmiths where, in the Middle Ages, those who were skilled in alchemy burnt the philosopher's stone and poisoned the moonbeams."

A statue of the Přemyslid Princess Eliška in the Triforium of St Vitus'.

Prague in the late 15th century.

A THOUSAND YEARS OF HISTORY

DISPUTED ORIGINS. Recent research by archeologists and historians somewhat contradicts the view expressed by Kosmas (in the oldest Czech chronicle dating back to the 11th century) that the first residence of the Dukes of Bohemia was at Vyšehrad. In fact, the Castle was probably founded earlier, between 880 and 890; at all events, we know for sure that it was built by the Přemyslid Prince Bořivoj. The Castle's oldest church, the small stone chapel to the Virgin Mary founded by Bořivoj and Saint Ludmila, has disappeared.

ROMANESQUE FOUNDATION. The second church built within the Castle walls was dedicated to Saint George (905) ▲ 220, but this was supplanted by the Rotunda of St Vitus erected in the middle of the Castle by Duke Wenceslas in 925. Around 973, St Vitus' became the cathedral of Prague's new bishopric. The Castle was where dukes were elected and monarchs crowned, but it was also a cultural center of great importance because of the Chapter Choir and St George's Convent.

EARLY FORTIFICATIONS. It was not until after 1041, during the reign of Břetislav I (1034–55), that a stone rampart was built, and a new ducal palace, also made of stone, was constructed in the Roman style. Between 1060 and 1074, Spytihněv turned St Wenceslas' Chapel into a magnificent Ottonian-Roman basilica 250 feet long. Vratislav I, the first King of Bohemia, was crowned here in 1085, and the rebuilding of the Castle

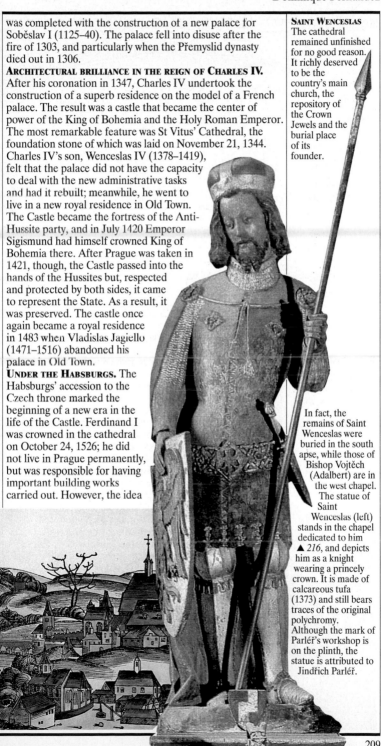

> "Above us, wherever we happen to be in the town, the Castle is omnipresent and omnipotent. Not just a building built on a hill, but a miniature city overhanging this city."
>
> Dominique Fernandez

was completed with the construction of a new palace for Soběslav I (1125–40). The palace fell into disuse after the fire of 1303, and particularly when the Přemyslid dynasty died out in 1306.

ARCHITECTURAL BRILLIANCE IN THE REIGN OF CHARLES IV.

After his coronation in 1347, Charles IV undertook the construction of a superb residence on the model of a French palace. The result was a castle that became the center of power of the King of Bohemia and the Holy Roman Emperor. The most remarkable feature was St Vitus' Cathedral, the foundation stone of which was laid on November 21, 1344. Charles IV's son, Wenceslas IV (1378–1419), felt that the palace did not have the capacity to deal with the new administrative tasks and had it rebuilt; meanwhile, he went to live in a new royal residence in Old Town. The Castle became the fortress of the Anti-Hussite party, and in July 1420 Emperor Sigismund had himself crowned King of Bohemia there. After Prague was taken in 1421, though, the Castle passed into the hands of the Hussites but, respected and protected by both sides, it came to represent the State. As a result, it was preserved. The castle once again became a royal residence in 1483 when Vladislas Jagiello (1471–1516) abandoned his palace in Old Town.

UNDER THE HABSBURGS.

The Habsburgs' accession to the Czech throne marked the beginning of a new era in the life of the Castle. Ferdinand I was crowned in the cathedral on October 24, 1526; he did not live in Prague permanently, but was responsible for having important building works carried out. However, the idea

SAINT WENCESLAS
The cathedral remained unfinished for no good reason. It richly deserved to be the country's main church, the repository of the Crown Jewels and the burial place of its founder.

In fact, the remains of Saint Wenceslas were buried in the south apse, while those of Bishop Vojtěch (Adalbert) are in the west chapel. The statue of Saint Wenceslas (left) stands in the chapel dedicated to him ▲ 216, and depicts him as a knight wearing a princely crown. It is made of calcareous tufa (1373) and still bears traces of the original polychromy. Although the mark of Parléř's workshop is on the plinth, the statue is attributed to Jindřich Parléř.

BAROQUE SPLENDOR
At the height of the Baroque period in the reign of Charles VI, both the Castle and the cathedral were the scenes of magnificent ceremonies. The coronation shown here in 1836 recalls the pomp that dated back to the 16th and 17th centuries.

of turning Prague into the sovereign's main and permanent residence was abandoned following the fire in Malá Strana of June 2, 1541. After his victory over the revolt of the Estates of Bohemia in 1547, Ferdinand appointed his youngest son Viceroy, and the time he spent in Prague witnessed some major cultural advances. The Castle was rebuilt and modernized, and once again became a residence that was actually lived in; the architect, Bonifác Wohlmut, placed the building containing the Bohemian archives next to the palace.

ARCHITECTURAL ACHIEVEMENTS DURING THE REIGN OF RUDOLPH II. Prague properly became the capital when, in 1583, Rudolph II chose to make his permanent residence there. The Castle was soon the home of immense Imperial collections as well as the King's stables of Spanish horses, and the last decade of Rudolph's reign saw the high point of the castle's renovation under the architect, Giovanni Maria Filippi. A new entrance, known as the Matthias Gate and completed during the reign of Rudolph's successor, marks the Castle's present-day boundary. However, Emperor Matthias (1611–19) went back to live in Vienna, and thereafter none of the Habsburgs ever returned to live in Prague permanently.

THE "WINTER KING". In 1618, the Castle was the scene of an event which sparked off the Thirty Years' War ● 34. For a year, the Castle had become the seat of the "alternative" Calvinist King Frederick, who was made Elector Palatine by the rebellious Diet in 1619. From 1634 to 1637, the future Ferdinand III (1637–57) lived at Prague Castle as Viceroy, and had alterations carried out both in the so-called

[Map legend text in German at bottom of illustration, partially legible]

Empress's Rooms overlooking the third courtyard and in the
north-south wing between the second and third courtyards.
The "New Way", which later became Nerudova Street and
linked Prague and the castle, was built after 1640.

BEGINNINGS OF A DECLINE. The Castle was renovated after
the Peace of Westphalia in 1648 ● *27*, and following the
departure of the Swedes, who had mercilessly pillaged
it. The accession of Leopold I marked the
beginning of the Imperial residence's decline.
Maria Theresa (1740–80) was responsible
for a major administrative reorganization
and by attempting to turn the castle into
a modern, up-to-date residence. The
modernization work changed the
building's appearance substantially ▲ *201*,
but after 1775 the Castle was unable to find
an appropriate role for itself; it simply lay on
the side of the hill like a kind of fossilized enclave
amidst a rapidly expanding city.

20TH-CENTURY REVIVAL. After the creation of the
Czechoslovak Republic in 1918, Prague Castle acquired a new
lease of life as the Head of State's residence. Renovation
work during 1920–34 was entrusted to the Slovenian architect,
Josip Plečnik ▲ *213, 327*. The Castle escaped damage during
World War Two, and was accessible even during the time it
served as the residence of Communist presidents. Building
works, which continued between 1950 and 1980, mainly
involved the transfer of some of the National Gallery's
collections to St George's Convent and the establishment of a
historical museum in Lobkowicz Palace ▲ *223*. Václav Havel
was solemnly proclaimed president here during the "Velvet
Revolution". Building and renovation work has been
resumed, and the most recent has taken place in the grounds.

**PLAN OF THE CASTLE
AND GROUNDS IN THE
18TH CENTURY**
The royal gardens
were laid out in the
reign of Ferdinand I
(1526–64).

**COMPLETION OF
ST VITUS'**
The construction of
St Vitus' Cathedral
was resumed after
1860 by an
association of Czech
patriots led by Josef
Kranner. The
cathedral was
completed under the
Czechoslovak
Republic in 1929 to
celebrate the saint's
thousandth
anniversary.

"ZÁMECKÉ SCHODY"
Two stairways lead up to the castle. The stairway on Thunovská Street climbs the hill, reaching the royal residence near Hradčanské Square and the garden over the ramparts.

The Changing of the Guard takes place every day at noon. This slightly uninspiring ceremony is improved by the bright new uniforms designed by Pištěk, the costume designer who won an Oscar for *Amadeus*, which was filmed in Prague by Miloš Forman.

THE GIANTS
The entrance to the castle is decorated by pairs of statues representing Čeněk Vosmik's early 20th century "Fighting Giants". They are copies of statues made by Ignác Platzer the Elder in 1768.

THE FIRST COURTYARD

The first courtyard adjoins Hradčanské Square, and is separated from it by monumental railings bearing the monogram of the Empress Maria Theresa and eight carved groups; the most imposing of these are on the entrance columns. This courtyard is the newest part of the castle, having been built over the moats during the 18th century and used as the main courtyard; the buildings lining it are in the Viennese Rococo style. Fresh from renovating Rožmberk Palace and houses in Jiřská Street, the architect Niccolo Pacassi effectively joined the buildings to the west of the palace into a uniform grouping as far as the first courtyard. In this way, Prague Castle lost the picturesque charm that the Renaissance and medieval buildings had provided and at a stroke, the Castle's development over a thousand years came to an end. A side entrance to the Castle on the left of the main courtyard leads to the "NA BAŠTĚ GARDEN" (Garden over the Bastion), which takes its name from the bastion that formed part of Vladislas Jagiello's fortifications.

THE SECOND COURTYARD

Access to this courtyard is through the Matthias Gate ▲ *207*. It was built in the second half of the 16th century, but its current appearance dates from the end of the 18th century. The southern end contains buildings that belonged to the new Imperial palace in Matthias' time, while the northern end consists of the remains of a Renaissance wing from the reign of Rudolph II; it includes the Renaissance stables which now house the Picture Gallery, the Spanish Hall and Rudolph's Gallery. The two ends are linked by a central structure put up during the reign of Ferdinand III around 1645.

THE PRAGUE CASTLE PICTURE GALLERY. This is on the first floor in the north and west wings, in what were once the royal stables. The collection derives from previous royal collections, although it now comprises only a very small part of them. After Rudolph II's superb collection was pillaged by the Swedes in

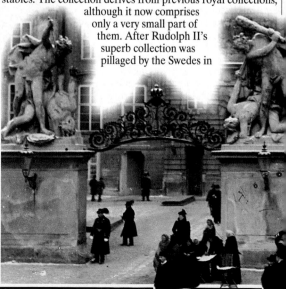

> "The leaves of gold which Charles IV used to cover the roof
> of his castle have long ago been taken away and melted down.
> But the fame they brought the city lives on."
>
> Jaroslav Seifert

1648, it was replenished by Ferdinand III before being
dispersed by the Habsburg Charles VI; the most valuable
paintings were transferred to Vienna and Dresden, and the
rest were sold by auction in 1782. Inventories of the period
described the remaining paintings as merely anonymous
items, and it was not until the 1960's that art historians were
able to establish the exact identities of the artists responsible
for many dozens of them.

THE SPANISH HALL AND THE RUDOLPH GALLERY. These
reception rooms are situated on the second floor of the north
wing. The Rudolph Gallery, formerly known as the German
Room and ultimately the home of the royal collections, dates
from 1586. Lit by a thousand candles placed in gold
chandeliers, it is as long as the Spanish Hall but not so wide.

THE THIRD COURTYARD

This courtyard is completely overlooked by St Vitus'
Cathedral and the Royal Palace. Various 10th- and 11th-
century remains, including ramparts, roads and houses, were
preserved beneath a concrete framework constructed by the
architect Josip Plečnik between 1925 and 1928. The granite
monolith, the work   of the same artists, was
erected in memory of   those who died in
World War One.

THE NEW PALACE. This   huge building
brings together a   number of
constructions that   were gradually

SPANISH HALL
This magnificent
banqueting room is
160 feet long, 80 feet
wide and 40 feet high.
It was built in the
Renaissance style by
G. Filippi between
1601 and 1606, and is
decorated with
stucco, mirrors, and
with bronze
chandeliers bearing
three thousand
candles. The most
recent alterations to
the décor date from
1865; they were
carried out in
preparation for the
coronation of Franz-
Josef as King of
Bohemia, which did
not ultimately take
place.

HOLY CROSS CHAPEL
This chapel, situated
in the south wing and
protruding into the
courtyard, was built
between 1756 and
1763 by Anselmo
Lurago. It is richly
decorated with
paintings and neo-
Baroque sculptures
and is the site of the
castle's information
center. It once
housed the major
part of the St Vitus'
Cathedral Treasury
(a unique collection
of liturgical objects
and ecclesiastical and
secular jewelry; this
was assembled by
Charles IV, who was
passionately keen on
holy relics). The
collection of jewelry
has now moved to the
Cathedral Treasury.

The belltower, dating from the Renaissance, is sometimes open to visitors, offering a breathtaking view over Malá Strana.

THE DOORS
Today, the main entrance consists of three porches on the west side which incorporate bronze doors (below, top). The Golden Door, which was the cathedral's main entrance for five hundred years, includes a beautiful, decorative railing made by J. Horejc in 1954.

turned into a single residential palace. It now houses the office of the President of the Republic and some reception rooms. A staircase in the southeast wing leads to the garden "Over the Ramparts" (Na valech), and from the terrace in the Garden of Paradise (Rajská zahrada) there is a fine view over the city.

ST VITUS' CATHEDRAL (CHRÁM SVATÉHO VITÁ) ★

After succeeding in making Prague the seat of an archbishop, Charles IV undertook the construction of a new cathedral ● 68 on the site of the rotunda put up by Wenceslas and the early Romanesque basilica. Work was commenced by the French architect Matthias of Arras in 1344, and was continued by Petr Parléř, the greatest Gothic builder in central Europe, and his sons; however, the building was not completed for another five hundred years. First, work was held up by the Hussite Wars, and it was not resumed afterward through lack of money; although consecrated in 1385, St Vitus' Cathedral was not actually finished until 1929. In the course of this work, the earlier Gothic part was restored and the non-Gothic furnishings removed, while the newer neo-Gothic part was decorated as it is today. The church is 400 feet long, 200 feet wide and 110 feet high; the vault is supported by twenty-eight pillars.

THE WEST FAÇADE. This was the last façade to be finished, and it was only in 1929 that the West Door

> "There, contrasting with the Baroque of Malá Strana below, and with splashes of green here and there, is the Gothic Cathedral of St Vitus."

Angelo Ripellino

became the main entrance. The new neo-Gothic façade is adorned with fourteen statues of saints and Charles IV, and busts of the later architects. The three bronze doors were executed in 1927 by Otakar Španiel, and are decorated with carvings: the story of the cathedral over the central entrance, the life of Saint Adalbert (Vojtěch) over the right-hand door, and the life of Saint Wenceslas over the left-hand door.

THE SOUTH FAÇADE AND THE GOLDEN DOOR. In 1406, the completed part of the cathedral was simply shut off by a wall at the level of the Golden Door. For five hundred years, then, the south façade was the main façade, and the Golden Door gave access to the cathedral. The door takes its name from the red and gold background of the mosaics depicting the Last Judgement. Charles IV and his last wife, Elizabeth of Pomerania, may be seen kneeling in the tympana of the central arch, their hands joined in solemn supplication. Parléř's main tower is 300 feet high, and is topped by a cupola by Pacassi dating from 1770.

THE VAULT. The cathedral has three naves, a transept, an ambulatory and radiating chapels. The ribbed vault is Petr Parléř's masterpiece. On returning to the site where he was to remain for almost fifty years, Parléř reworked the plan originally produced by Matthias of Arras, but when he came to the vault, he opted for innovation. He was no longer content with a simple ogive with crossed ribs. Instead, he prolonged the arch which was punctuated with windows, and the ribbing then formed new ogives which became entangled; they project over the shortest ribs as far as the

STATUE OF SAINT GEORGE
This is a copy; the original is kept in St George's Convent.

It was made by Jiří and Martin of Cluj in 1373. When it was damaged by the fire of 1541, parts of it were recast in the Renaissance style by the celebrated metal caster, Tomáš Jaroš of Brno.

St George's Square in 1830, showing the apse of St Vitus', the old Royal Palace on the left, and the beginning of Vikářská Street on the right.

215

ROYAL MAUSOLEUM
(1566–89)
This is the work of the
Flemish artist
Alexandre Colin de
Malines. The
recumbent statues
represent Ferdinand I,
his wife Anna Jagiello,
and his son
Maximillian II, all of
whom were buried
here. Ferdinand I,
who ruled Bohemia
from 1526 to 1564, is
considered to be the
founder of the
Habsburg dynasty
in Bohemia and
Hungary.

Below: the tomb of
Saint John Nepomuk.

keystone which is in turn transformed into the middle of a
magnificent star. It would be difficult to list all the priceless
objects to be found in the cathedral; we shall confine
ourselves to the most important. A visit begins with the
various chapels, including the Chapel of St Wenceslas (below)
shortly before reaching the choir.

THE HIGH ALTAR. This neo-Gothic altar by Josef Kranner
dates from 1868–73. The Renaissance pulpit dates from the
17th century, and the sides contain wooden reliefs made by
Jan Jiří Bendl between 1625 and 1650. The relief on the left
shows the flight of the "Winter King" ● 34, while that on the
right depicts a fascinating view of Prague dating from 1620.

TOMB OF SAINT JOHN NEPOMUK. Two tons of silver were
required to complete this tomb (1733–6) to plans by the
architect Josef Emanel Fischer von Erlach, the sculptor
Antonio Corradini and the Viennese goldsmith Johann
Joseph Würth. The paving of this section of the ambulatory
covers the tombs of fourteen bishops of Prague.

ROYAL VAULT. From the HOLY CROSS CHAPEL (last chapel in
the right-hand aisle), a staircase leads down to the vault
where there are remains of the original Rotunda of St Vitus.
The royal vault contains the tombs of Charles IV, his four
wives and his children, King Wenceslas IV, Vladislav,
Wenceslas' son who was born after his father died, George of
Poděbrady and Rudolph II, and Maria Amelia, the daughter
of Maria Theresa. Their remains were placed in new
sarcophagi during the 1930's.

ROYAL ORATORY. Vladislav Jagiello's oratory, which was
designed by Benedikt Ried in 1493, is one of the finest
examples of Flamboyant Gothic in the whole cathedral. The
gallery rests on vaults adorned with stylized branches forming
ribs which incorporate the coats of arms of the countries
conquered by Vladislas. The oratory is linked to the Royal
Palace by a covered way.

ST WENCESLAS' CHAPEL. This is the most impressive
and most venerated of all the chapels. It is an
undisputed Gothic masterpiece of the period
1362–7 and is an example of the impressive esthetic
standards attained by Czech artists. The chapel was
constructed by Petr Parléř on the site of the 10th-
century Romanesque rotunda where the martyr
prince was interred. The decoration, which consists
entirely of murals from 1509 and comes
from the workshop of the so-called
Master of the Litoměřice Altar, is
appropriate to its function as a
reliquary. The upper parts of
the walls are devoted to the life
of Saint Wenceslas; the lower part
includes a cycle of the life of Christ,
and ornamental sections consisting of
more than 1,000 semi-precious Czech
stones (jasper, amethyst, chalcedony and
chrysoprase) set in gilded plaster. The
main altar, whose walls were renovated at
the beginning of the 20th century and
which are also covered with precious
stones, lies on the site of the saint's tomb.
On the door to the chapel there is a heavy

> "These ancient wrongs must have lost much of their bitterness in the baleful light of modern times when the only evidence to survive is an heirloom of luminous architectural beauty."
>
> Patrick Leigh Fermor

THE CHAPELS

Starting with the first on the right after entering the cathedral by the main entrance, there are three neo-Gothic chapels which precede the old part of the cathedral. The circuit of the chapels concludes with three more 20th-century chapels: these new chapels have mosaic and glass decoration by the most famous Czech Art Nouveau artists, including Alfons Mucha.

THE TRIFORIUM: A PORTRAIT GALLERY

The old interior of the triforium, a kind of passageway above the aisles which opens up over the nave, is decorated with twenty-one busts of male and female members of the Luxemburg dynasty, the first archbishops of Prague and the two architects of the Gothic part of the cathedral. This collection, which dates from the 14th century, is the finest example of Czech sculpture from the Gothic period. The new part of the triforium contains busts of people who have contributed to the construction of the cathedral.

Opposite: the walls of the Land Registry Hall decorated with the coats of arms of magistrates who held positions there.

"Terrified, you see yourself portrayed in the rubies of St Vitus'. You saw yourself mortally sad the day you saw yourself there. You look like a beggar frightened by the daylight."

Apollinaire, *Zone*

knocker which bears a symbol: legend has it that, when Wenceslas was murdered at Stará Boleslav on the orders of his brother Boreslav, he hung on to the door knocker and stayed upright even after he had died. The knocker was later found and placed in the chapel.

ROYAL TREASURY. A stairway in the St Wenceslas Chapel leads to the Royal Treasury. The door has seven locks, the keys to which are held by seven different institutions. The Treasury has housed the Czech Crown Jewels since 1791, but unfortunately the collection cannot be seen although facsimiles of the most important pieces are on view in the Historical Museum at Lobkowicz Palace ▲ *223*.

THE OLD ROYAL PALACE

STOVES
The castle was heated by large stoves (opposite) which were supplied with fuel from a corridor or a neighboring room. They were usually covered with green, glazed bricks.

The entrance to the Old Royal Palace (Starý Královský palác) ▲ *202* is underneath the balcony at the far end of the courtyard. The palace was a residence of princes and kings from the 12th century onward, but the Habsburgs deserted it in the mid-16th century for the newer parts of the castle. The Old Palace continued to be occupied by central State organizations until the late 18th century, but is now only rarely used.

VLADISLAV HALL. This room, the largest secular hall in Europe, was built by Benedikt Ried of Piesting between 1493 and 1503. It occupies almost the entire second floor of the palace and is 200 feet long, 50 feet wide and 40 feet high. The interior, and the vault's complex ribbing ▲ *203* in particular, are good illustrations of the vitality of Gothic architecture in the late Middle Ages; the exterior, the entrances, and the huge windows, announce the Renaissance.

VLADISLAV HALL
Banquets and jousts were once held in this ceremonial hall. It

ALL SAINTS' CHAPEL. At the far end of the Vladislav Hall, a rood screen overlooks the interior of All Saints' Chapel. It was originally built by Petr Parléř in 1370, but was destroyed by fire in 1541 and not restored until the end of the 16th century. At that point, it was joined to the Vladislav Hall. The painting of All Saints on the high altar is by Václav Reiner (c. 1732).

THE LOUIS WING. After completing the Vladislav Hall, Benedikt Ried started work on a Renaissance transverse block sometimes known as the "LOUIS PALACE", after Vladislav's son ▲ *201*.

DIET HALL. Although this room was constructed by Benedikt Ried toward the end of the 14th century, its current appearance dates from the mid-16th century by Bonifác Wohlmut. The 19th-century furnishings are faithful copies of the original 17th-century pieces, and they give an idea of how the sessions were organized: the royal throne, with the archbishop's seat to the right of the King's and just behind the prelates' bench; then, along the walls, places reserved for senior functionaries; and lastly, opposite the throne, the bench occupied by lords and knights. Near the right-hand window is a gallery for representatives of the royal cities.

was also used for important meetings of the Diet. Since 1935, the results of Presidential elections have been announced from here.

THE NEW LAND REGISTRY HALL. A stairway beside the knights' bench leads to this hall. The registers contained information relating to land ownership, and detailed all the property rights of the Superior Estates (or Orders) of the Diet as well as decisions handed down by the Court of Justice and the Diet itself. They were destroyed in the fire of 1541. A beautiful chest in one of the rooms dating from 1562 contains a few of the registers.

RIDERS' STAIRCASE ▲ *202*. This ramp opens into the Vladislav Hall through an accoladed gateway; its broad steps enabled knights to climb it on horseback.

GOTHIC PALACE OF CHARLES IV. The same ramp also gives access to the Gothic Palace situated under Vladislav Hall. The new tiles of the so-called CHARLES HALL are imitations of the original paving stones, while the walls are decorated with copies of busts from the cathedral triforium.

The spines of the country's registers were adorned with drawings – distinctive signs that could be recognized by the illiterate staff who looked after them.

Wonderful sketches tracing the various stages of construction tell the story of how the area has changed since work began.

St George's Square

Despite its restricted size, St George's Square (JIŘSKÉ NÁMĚSTÍ) was the Castle's central area throughout the Middle Ages. As can be seen from old engravings ▲ *214*, the square had numerous shops and wash houses until about 1870.

St George's Basilica   ● *68*

Beneath the Baroque façade (below) of St George's Basilica (Bazilica sv. Jiří) lies the façade of a real Romanesque church. Apart from the archeological remains of the tiny Church of the Virgin of Bořivoj and St Vitus' Chapel, this is the oldest monument from the Romanesque period in Bohemia. It was originally built of wood, and was founded in 912 by Prince Vratislav I. It was enlarged in 973 and, in 1142, following a major fire, was rebuilt in a late Romanesque style with two towers. In 924, the church had received the remains of Saint Ludmila, Saint Wenceslas' grandmother; it subsequently housed the remains of other 10th- and 11th-century members of the Přemyslid family, including the church's founder, Vratislav I, and the founder of the nearby convent, Boleslav II.

RESTORATION. The basilica was renovated during the Gothic period by the workshop of Petr Parléř, and later during the Renaissance and Baroque periods; it was then restored during the 19th century ▲ *206*. The interior has been frequently redone and dates from the second half of the 12th century; the exception is the Gothic Chapel of Saint Ludmila to the right of the choir, where there is a late 14th-century tomb hewn out of the limestone by the workshop of Petr Parléř.

THE CRYPT. Beneath the stairway leading to the choir is the crypt (1142) which is covered by a vault resting on pillars with cubic capitals. It contains the tombs of the convent's first abbesses, including that of Mlada; it was Mlada who obtained from Pope John XIII a letter making Prague the seat of an archbishop. To the right, on the altar table, is a statue of Saint Bridget (*Vanitas*), with her entrails full of snakes and lizards; this is a Baroque naturalist allegory of vanity. According to legend, an Italian stone-cutter called Spinetti carved it in penance for an act of violence he committed in the church. Between 1718 and 1722, the ST JOHN NEPOMUK CHAPEL was built by František Maxmilián Kaňka and the Dientzenhofers, beside and adjoining the basilica.

ST GEORGE'S CONVENT (KLÁSTER SV. JIŘÍ) ★. This, the earliest religious establishment in Bohemia, was founded according to the Benedictine Rule by Mlada, the sister of Prince Boleslav II, in

BUST OF A YOUNG GODDESS
Fragment of the attic decoration of Clam-Gallas Palace, executed by Matthias Bernhard Braun in 1716.

The simple, narrow, long nave is connected to the square, semicircular apsidal choir by a beautiful Baroque staircase. Unusually for Prague, the 10th- and 11th-century arches are made of splendid light-colored stone that has not been decorated.

MASTERS OF CZECH BAROQUE PAINTING IN ST GEORGE'S CONVENT
The collection of paintings on display in St George's Convent certainly deserves a visit. It includes works by such major artists as Karel Škréta, P. Brendl, M.B Braun, M. Brokof and Václav Vavřinec Reiner (1689–1743), one of the greatest Czech exponents of the Baroque style. Among his works on display in the Convent is *Still Life with Skull.*

VIKÁŘSKÁ ULICE
Vicars' Street is situated between the fortifications and the north side of the cathedral. In the middle is the Powder Tower, an artillery bastion built in the 15th century by Vladislas Jagiello. The Castle's information office is at no. 2, the house of the Old Dean: the ceiling of this house is decorated with portraits of the Deans of St Vitus'.

HISTORICAL MUSEUM
This 2nd–1st-century BC man's head made of stone was found at Msecke Zehrovice. It is considered to be one of the most accomplished pieces of Celtic art.

973. The convent's abbesses had long enjoyed the privilege of crowning the Queens of Bohemia, this function being reserved for virgins in the princely and royal Přemyslid families. The cross-shaped corridor was built in the 14th century, but the convent itself has been frequently rebuilt, following the same development as the church. St George's was an important cultural center and, in the years to come, many valuable manuscripts later kept in the Clementinum ▲ *150* were to be written here. The convent was closed down by Joseph II in 1782 and used as a barracks. Between 1962 and 1974, it was renovated by František Cubr and Josef Pilár and underwent alterations before becoming the MUSEUM OF CZECH ART. The exhibits, from the basement to the top floor, span the centuries from the Mannerist period, and the work of painters active during the reign of Rudolph II, to the Baroque era of the 17th and 18th centuries.

AN ESTABLISHMENT FOR NOBLE LADIES.
This building at the beginning of St George's Street (Jiřská ul.) was originally the Rožmberk family's palace (1545). In 1600, the owner exchanged it with Rudolph II for Schwarzenberg Palace in Hradčanské Square. The palace was then rebuilt by Tomáš Haffenecker between 1723 and 1731 and, on the orders of Maria Theresa, became an Institute of Noble Ladies for the benefit of female members of poor aristocratic families.

GOLDEN LANE (ZLATA ULIČKA)

Golden Lane is approached by going halfway down Jiřská Street and turning left into a passageway called U Daliborky. Rudolph II's name, and the fashion for occult sciences during his reign in the 18th century, inspired a legend surrounding this lane of alchemists ▲ *207*. In fact, Golden Lane derived its name rather more simply from some craftsman gold-beaters who took refuge there after the Malá Strana fire of 1541. After that, Rudolph had wooden houses built for his archers who somehow found space to live there with their families. The situation deteriorated during the succeeding centuries as some of them built a first floor less than four feet high, and houses sprang up on both sides although the lane was no more than four feet wide. In the 18th century, Maria Theresa ordered the inhabitants to replace their slums with houses made of brick, or at the very least cover them with roughcast. Between 1952 and 1955, the street was entirely renovated to plans by Pavel Janák; the choice of colors for the houses was entrusted to Jiří Trnka, a painter well known for his animated cartoons, and the street subsequently became popular with tourists.

WHITE TOWER AND DALIBORKA TOWER. These towers, which are situated to the east and west of Golden Lane respectively, were built as artillery bastions under Vladislas Jagiello in 1485. Both were used as prisons until the 18th century. The second tower takes its name from Dalibor of Kozojedy, who was imprisoned here in 1498 and whose story inspired a famous opera by Smetana.

The small houses in Golden Lane are now souvenir shops.

DALIBOR THE KNIGHT Dalibor of Kozojedy was imprisoned in the Castle for supporting an uprising by a neighboring knight's serfs. To ease the boredom, Dalibor used to play the violin; according to legend, his music cast a spell over the whole town, and the people pleaded that he be set free, but he was later beheaded.

JIŘSKÁ ULICE

After Golden Lane, St George's Street (Jiřská ul.) on the left leads to the Black Tower.

LOBKOWICZ PALACE. This palace (Lobkovický palác), at no. 1/3 on the right, was built after 1570 by Vratislav of Pernštejn. It came into the possession of the Lobkowicz family in 1651 and has remained there until the 20th century. The late Renaissance interior is well preserved, although the façade was redone in 1791 in order to merge with other parts of the castle. In 1973, the palace was turned into a department of the NATIONAL MUSEUM dealing with Czech history.

FORMER PALACE OF THE BURGRAVES. This building stands opposite, and contains the "House of Czechoslovak Children". In the 16th century, it was the home of the Chief Burgrave, chosen from among the great aristocratic families of Prague; he was the leading citizen in the country after the king, and his official representative in the latter's absence.

THE BLACK TOWER. Jiřská Street is closed off by a huge ogival door flanked by a high, square courtyard, the Black Tower. It formed part of the castle's system of fortifications during the first half of the 12th century; then, Wenceslas I had the tower walled up and he opened the present door in the 13th century. It had been given a golden roof during the reign of Charles IV, and it was known as the Golden Tower; it was damaged by the fire of 1541, which blackened it completely – hence its current name. Through the door is an observation terrace from which it is possible to take in all of Malá Strana.

Above: the Powder Tower and gateway to the former Palace of the Burgraves with nobles' coats of arms.

223

REAL TENNIS ★
This Renaissance
structure in the Royal
Garden was built by
Bonifác Wohlmut
between 1567 and
1569. It was used as a

real tennis court, then
as a royal stable, and
finally as a military
store. It was
destroyed during
World War Two, but
an identical copy was
then put up; this now
serves as an official
building. In front of
the house is a carved
group by Anton
Braun, the nephew of
Matthias Bernhard
Braun. The façade is
decorated with
allegorical sgraffito of
the sciences, virtues
and earthly elements.
Concerts are
sometimes given
here.

The Belvedere.

BEYOND POWDER BRIDGE

From the second courtyard, POWDER BRIDGE (PRASNÝ MOST)
leads to those parts of the castle outside the fortifications that
were added in the reign of Ferdinand I after 1526.

RIDING SCHOOL. The riding school (JÍZDÁRNA), to the right of

the bridge, is a fine example of
utilitarian architecture in the heyday of
the Baroque style. It was designed by
Jean-Baptiste Mathey in 1694. After
being partly rebuilt by Pavel Janák, it
was turned into an art gallery in 1948–9.
THE ROYAL GARDENS. These gardens
(Královská zahrada) were laid out for
Ferdinand I by G. Spatio and the court
gardener, Francesco, and are one of the
most beautiful examples of Renaissance
art. Exotic trees like fig and grapefruit were grown here, and
tulips were also introduced. Destroyed by the Swedes and the
Saxons, they were redesigned in the 18th century. After being
devastated yet again by the French army of occupation in
1743 and by Prussian bombardment in 1757, they were once
more laid out during the 19th century, and then abandoned,
before being restored by the architect Pavel Janák after 1918.
The pathways in the park are adorned with statues from the
workshop of Matthias Bernhard Braun.
THE ROYAL SUMMER PALACE (KRÁLOVSKÝ LETHORÁDEK). This
huge one-story building with a curved roof, also known as the
"Belvedere" (Belvedér), was commissioned by Ferdinand I
for his wife Anna, and built in 1535–64 to designs by Genoese
architect Paolo della Stella and completed by Bonifác
Wohlmut. It is considered to be an example of the purest
Renaissance architecture to be found outside Italy ▲ 80. The
first floor is bordered with a gallery of arcades with elegant
columns supporting seventy-four reliefs. Nearby is a statue of
Victory (above, right) by J. Stursa, dating from 1921. In the
small garden, there is a bronze, "singing" fountain: a few
moments spent beneath its basin suffice to justify its name.

From Hradčany
to Malá Strana

▲ FROM HRADČANY TO MALÁ STRANA

1. STRAHOV MONASTERY ✿
2. ČERNIN PALACE
3. CHURCH OF OUR LADY OF LORETO
4. LORETÁNSKÁ STREET
5. TOSCAN PALACE
6. MARTINIC PALACE

🕐 **Half a day**

◆ **A** A2-A3-B2-B3-C2-C3

Coat of arms of the Archbishopric of Prague.

The Hradčany district is relatively modern in that it did not become a "town" until 1320 during the reign of John of Luxemburg. It was built on the orders of Berka of Duba, Burgrave of Prague. Originally, the district only consisted of what is now Hradčanské Square (Hradčanské náměstí) and a group of houses scattered round present-day Kanovnická and Loretánská streets; only in 1598 did Hradčany benefit from the royal privileges that other royal towns enjoyed, and it remained under the monarchy's strict control for many years. In June 1541, a fire destroyed Malá Strana and spread as far as the Castle and Hradčany, and the land thereby made available enabled the Church and the aristocracy to build fine Renaissance, and later Baroque, houses and palaces. Hradčany is probably better known than any other part of Prague for its peaceful atmosphere, its gardens and its exceptionally well preserved 17th- and 18th-century architecture. For the writer, Jiří Karásek, a visit to Hradčany is like a walk into times gone by; the past "blows over you from green shadows in the huge gardens with their thick foliage. It envelops you from the shade of a doorway and the depths of a palace hallway."

ARCHBISHOP'S PALACE

Hradčanské Square is lined with several palaces; the Archbishop's Palace (ARCIBISKUPSKÝ PALÁC) is at the bottom near the Castle. The architectural history of this building is complex because it has been added to and redecorated on many occasions. It was designed by Bonifác Wohlmut and built by Udalrico Aostalli between 1562 and 1564. A century later, between 1675 and 1694, it was renovated by Jean-Baptiste Mathey, and the façade is the work of Jan Josef Wirch (1732–87) although the main entrance is attributed to Mathey. The palace is now the most beautiful in the whole square. The decoration on the piano nobile (the third level) is a superb example of balance. It is articulated not only by the

Archbishop's Palace.

slight projection of the lateral wings and the central body of the building, but also by the display of half-columns and pilasters; the balconies, bull's-eye windows and pediments are in the Rococo style.

STERNBERG PALACE (ŠTERNBERSKÝ PALÁC)

NATIONAL GALLERY. Access to Sternberg Palace is by a passageway that runs along the left-hand side of the Archbishop's Palace. From what remains today, we can see that it originally formed part of a more ambitious, yet never completed, project on which a number of celebrated architects collaborated. These included Domenico Martinelli of Lucca, the workshop of Krištof Dientzenhofer and, in the final phase, Giovanni Battista Alliprandi. The building is remarkable for the elliptical pavilion overlooking the garden. Today, Sternberg Palace houses the National Gallery's collections of European art. The majority of its collection comprises works from the Italian and northern European schools ▲ 228. The fine collection of 19th- and 20th-century French art, which was exhibited, up to 1995, in an annexe of the Palace, is now housed in the Museum of Modern Art at Veletržní Palace ▲ 317. The museum also houses the collection of the art critic and collector, Vincenc Krámář (1877–1960).

RESTORED TO THEIR RIGHTFUL OWNERS. At one point, the collection was threatened by the 1990 Law of Restitution. This law gave people whose goods had been seized by the Communists after February 1948 the right to repossess them. But it proved to be very difficult to implement these rights in the art world. Krámář's heirs claimed a right to sixteen Picassos, two Braques, two Derains and a dozen Czech Cubist painters, but the Curator of the National Museum relied on correspondence from Krámář to show that the great collector, an ardent Communist, had knowingly donated his paintings to the State.

THE NATIONAL GALLERY COLLECTIONS
Six museums in Prague have a permanent exhibition of part of the collection of the National Gallery. The Convent of St Agnes ▲ 182 houses the collections of medieval Bohemian and Central European art. St George's Convent ▲ 220 exhibits the works of Bohemian artists from the reign of Rudolf II to the end of the Baroque period. The Sternberg Palace exhibits European art from the 14th to the 18th centuries. The Veletržní Palace ▲ 317 houses art of the 19th and 20th centuries. Asiatic art is exhibited at the Zbraslav Convent ▲ 328. The Kinský Palace ▲ 137 houses the information center of the National Gallery, as well as temporary exhibitions.

227

At the end of the 18th century, Prague was quite unlike Vienna, Munich or Dresden in that it did not have an art gallery worthy of the name. Count František Josef Šternberk decided to rectify this sorry state of affairs by founding the Society of Patriotic Friends of the Arts in Bohemia in 1796, with the aim of creating a public art gallery. Gifts flowed in immediately both from the aristocracy and from the enlightened bourgeoisie and, during the 19th century art collections were further enhanced by bequests from Dr Josef Hoser, particularly paintings of the Dutch School. In 1937, the gallery was acquired by the Czechoslovak State, and since 1945 it has been part of Prague's National Gallery.

«Portrait of Éleonora of Toledo»
This portrait by the Florentine Agnolo Bronzino (1503–1572) depicts the daughter of the Viceroy of Naples.

"Feast of Rose Garlands"
This is the Sternberg Museum's greatest work. It was painted in 1506 by Albrecht Dürer and was hung in the Church of St Bartholomew. It was later purchased by Rudolph II and transported across the Alps. The work escaped the ransacking Swedes, but was sold in 1782, then bought back by the abbey of Strahov in 1793. In 1934 it was bought by the state.

«JASPER SCHADE VAN WESTRUM»
Frans Hals (c. 1582–1666)
A masterly work from the Dutch school.
The painter has captured the haughty
personality of this young Utrecht
nobleman with ingenious
subtlety. The highlights on the
costume also highlight the vanity
of the wearer, and give the painting
a nervous vitality.

«ST BRUNO»
Antony van Dyck (1599–1641)
one of the most influential painters of the
XVII century. A prolific portraitist, he
also executed a number of mythologicial
and religious works, such as this
St Bruno. Here we can see the
elegant touch of the great
master. The work is characterized
by a sentimental piety.

«CHRIST»
Doménikos
Theotokópoulos
(1541–1614), who
was born in Crete,
acquired the name
El Greco (the Greek)
after he settled in
Toledo in 1577.
It was in the Spain of
the late 16th century,
imbued with religious
mysticism, that his
genius reached its
height. This *Christ*,
painted around
1595, was one of
the most important
acquisitions made by
the National Gallery
while it was under
the direction of
Vincenc Kramář
in the years
1919–39.

The square has hardly
changed in two
hundred years. In the
center stands
Ferdinand Macmilián
Brokoff's Column of
the Plague erected in
1726 to
commemorate the
end of the 1679
epidemic. At the far
end of the square is
Toscan Palace, which
served as
headquarters for
Marshal Count de
Bellisle, commander
of the French army
that occupied Prague
in 1741–2.

FORMER SCHWARZENBERG PALACE

This building is opposite the Archbishop's Palace and
once formed part of Lobkowicz Palace. Today, it
houses the Swiss Embassy. The palace was built by
František Pavíček (1776–1861) between 1795 and
1810, and its design is in the Empire style which was
so popular at the beginning of the century.

SCHWARZENBERG-LOBKOWICZ PALACE

Schwarzenberg-Lobkowicz Palace (1545–63)
easily makes a big impression beside its
somewhat insipid neighbor. It was built by
Augustin Vlach to a commission by Prince
Johann Lobkowicz, and is a magnificent example
of Czech Renaissance style. Vlach invested the
palace's grandeur and refinement with great
originality, while the gables, the cornices with their
curious lunettes, and the sgraffito ● *78* established
Schwarzenberg-Lobkowicz as an architectural
touchstone when Czechs began to rediscover their
architectural heritage in the 19th century. There are
many neo-Renaissance buildings in Prague that
include elements that are characteristic of this
building. It now houses a military museum ▲ *231*.

CONVENT OF THE DISCALCED CARMELITES

"ST MICHAEL"
This carving by
Ottavio Mosto (1693)
adorns the façade of
Toscan Palace on the
corner of Loretánská
Street.

Next to Schwarzenberg-Lobkowicz Palace stand a number of
buildings that made up the former Barnabite Convent in the
17th century. It was closed down in 1786 and handed over to
the Discalced Carmelites in 1792. The Church of St Benedict,
once Hradčany's parish church and restored in the 16th, 17th
and 18th centuries, is in the middle. In his *Magic Prague*,

Angelo Ripellino quotes from *A Gothic Soul* (1900), a novel by Jiří Karásek, in which the hero is a hypochondriac terrified at the prospect of going mad. The Convent of the Discalced Carmelites, with its myriad legends, particularly attracted him: "At midnight, before taking his vows," each novice "had to remove the ring from the crushed hand of the mummified Saint Elekta ... During the ceremonies, the voices of the living dead could be heard singing psalms, as if from the depths of an abyss". Today, the palace is used to accommodate visiting dignitaries.

TOSCAN PALACE

The west side of Hradčanské Square consists of Thun-Hohenstein Palace, otherwise known as "Toscan" Palace (TOSKÁNSKÝ PALÁC) and originally owned by the Grand Dukes of Tuscany who bought it in 1718. The palace, built in 1689–91, is attributed to Mathey and is a skilful combination of Romanesque architecture and French classicism. The decoration of the impressive façade consists of two belvederes projecting from the balustraded attic story. The statues of the seven liberal arts are from the workshop of Jan Brokoff.

LORETÁNSKÁ STREET

There are some interesting buildings in this lesser known street. The first is the FORMER HRADČANY TOWN HALL (1601–4), built in the Czech Renaissance style, and notable for its sgraffito ● 78, some pieces of Imperial armor, and a representation of Justice. At no. 4 is Martinic Palace by Bartolommeo Scotti, who worked to plans by the architect, Carlo Fontana; it is one of Prague's rare examples of design influenced by Roman styles. At the end of Loretánská Street, there are steps leading to Nerudova Street ▲ 254.

Above left: the magnificent Schwarzenberg Palace seen from Nerudova Street, details of the façade decorated with sgraffito decoration in diamond point. Right: sgraffito of biblical motifs on Martinic Palace.

"The broad façade of the old Royal Palace ... is the most powerful. The family castle of the princes of Schwarzenberg and another building ... stand on the other side [of the square] as if regarding them with perpetual reverence."
R. M. Rilke,
Histories from Prague

In the 19th century, Hradčanské Square was lit by street lamps in the form of candelabra.

MILITARY MUSEUM
An interest in military matters is not essential to enjoy a visit to this museum. The ceilings are splendidly frescoed, and the magnificent collections of arms and uniforms are fascinating. Left, *The Battle of Solferino* (1859). The museum is currently closed for renovation.

MARTINIC PALACE

● 78

This fine Renaissance building (MARTINICKÝ PALÁC),
somewhat restrained in appearance despite its sgraffito
decoration employing biblical and mythological themes,
has an entrance dating from 1560; the gables date from
the 17th century. The part of the building overlooking
the courtyard is also decorated with sgraffito. The palace
was once the property of Jaroslav Bořita de Martinic,
one of the Councillors thrown from the Hradčany in
1618 ● *34*.

MUCHA'S HOUSE

Alfons Mucha's old house, one of the most beautiful
buildings in Prague, is situated at 6 Hradčanské Square,
and abounds in evidence of the painter's lyricism and
refinement ▲ *171*. Today it houses the Mucha
Foundation. Visits are only by request, via the
Mucha Museum ▲ *172*.

LEADING FIGURE IN PRAGUE ART NOUVEAU.
Mucha had unparalleled skill at adapting the
heady convolutions of modern design to the
language of drawing and posters, and he
managed to revive the genre with his
peerless command of color, his placement
of figures and his decorative arrangements.
His success was limited, however. A trip
to the United States in 1904 did not live up to his
expectations, and his return to Bohemia was only
moderately successful ▲ *165*, as a new, more radical
generation was already guiding Czech painting
in new directions. Nonetheless, his best
posters are true masterpieces, and many less
well-known works are interesting, particularly
the pastels he completed in the early 1900s.

MUCHA FOUNDATION. Jiří Mucha has faithfully
recaptured the atmosphere of his father's house. Nearly
all of the works that took Paris by storm – and made the
actress Sarah Bernhardt such a famed beauty – are now
mostly in the Mucha Museum ▲ *172*. However the
Foundation still houses a few gifts from friends, including

Poster from 1898

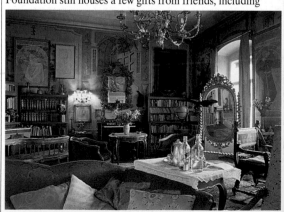

A TOUCH OF 1900
The lyrical, turn-of-
the-century world of
Alfons Mucha is
much in evidence in
the painter's house,
one of the most
beautiful in Prague.

a somewhat risqué sculpture of two women from Rodin, and a harmonium from Gauguin. Alfons Mucha died in 1939. His works were miraculously spared during the period of Communist rule, but his son, Jiří, a celebrated writer, spent many years in prison. He later divided his time between Paris and Prague tracking down his father's works. In 1991, ten years after Jiří's death, his son and his widow created the Mucha Foundation with the support of the Minister of Culture. The Foundation organizes exhibitions of the painter's works.

CHURCH OF ST JOHN OF NEPOMUK

Kanovnická Street leads to this church, which was built between 1720 and 1728 by Kilián Ignác Dientzenhofer to a commission by the Ursuline nuns. Inside, Václav Vavřinec Reiner's frescos (1728) depict the legend of St John of Nepomuk, a leading figure in central European culture and one of the patron saints of Bohemia.

JOHN OF POMUK. In 1393, the Vicar-General of the diocese of Prague, John of Pomuk, was arrested and tortured on the orders of King Wenceslas IV following a violent argument between the king and Archbishop John of Jenzenstein. He died under interrogation, and his body was thrown into the Vltava under cover of darkness. Legend has it that stars began to sparkle round the body on the surface of the water, and this is the origin of the crown of stars that statues of St John always wear. He was later buried at St Vitus' Cathedral.

CONFUSION. Around 1450, the Viennese chronicler Ebendorfer claimed that the reason for the Vicar-General's death had been his refusal to reveal to the king what his wife, the queen, had said in the confessional. This new version was somewhat embellished and became the basis of the legend of St John of Nepomuk. A confusion of dates that came to light in the 15th century had him dying in 1383, and Václav Hájek's *Kronika Česka (Czech Chronicle)* of 1541 ▲ *324*, which drew freely on contradictory sources, even recounted the death of two characters, St John of Nepomuk and John of Pomuk, despite the fact that the Vicar-General died in 1393. However, it was the former, the supposed martyr of the confessional, who was beatified in 1721 and canonized in 1729. Veneration of Saint John of Nepomuk was widespread in the 17th and 18th centuries. A number of versions of his legend were published in the 17th century: the most famous, by the Jesuit Bohuslav Balbín, appeared in the *Acta Sanctorum*, published by the Bollandists of Louvain in 1680.

A SYMBOL OF SILENCE. On April 15, 1719, when Saint John's tomb was opened up, something was found which was thought

ST JOHN NEPOMUK
"The tongue's . . . burning ruby rising out of . . . the house of verses burns with constancy/from the divine depths spared by the all-powerful dust."

J. Zahradníček

ČERNIN PALACE
The 500 feet-long façade includes an impressive line of thirty huge columns; they are in two rows and rest on a crepidoma decorated with diamond-head bosses.

to be his tongue, although it was subsequently established in 1980 that it was nothing more than a piece of dried out brain. Back in 1725, this scrap of moistened organic tissue had been examined by experts charged with the task of instituting the process of canonization, and the "tongue", the martyr's symbol of silence, became his emblem; this emblem is now found in all the churches in Prague dedicated to Saint John of Nepomuk. Nowadays, John of Pomuk is no longer thought to have been the queen's confessor, and it seems that it is his more legendary double who has been canonized.

ČERNIN PALACE ● 80

From the Church of St John of Nepomuk, Nový Svět Street and then Kapucínská Street on the left lead into Loreto Square (Loretánské náměstí). The formidable Černin Palace (ČERNÍNSKÝ PALÁC) (1669–79) is the main work of Francesco Caratti. The interior decoration (1717–23) was by F. M. Kaňka ▲ 274, also responsible for the Baroque garden; the main entrances were executed by Anselmo Lurago in 1747–9. Count Humprecht Černin of Chudenice, who had commissioned the palace, hoped his residence might vie with Prague Castle: in his favor, only a few modest buildings stood between it and his palace, the area having been laid waste during the Thirty Years' War.

IMMODERATE TASTES. The Count originally asked Bernini to design his residence, but he subsequently chose another architect, Francesco Caratti. His time as ambassador in Venice seems to have turned his head, and he wanted to have his palace built on an elevated spot so as to make an even more striking impression. The count's monumental architectural tastes almost cost him his fortune; particularly as his son, Hermann Jacob, was having yet another palace built in Vienna. In his Prague residence, the latter amassed such a magnificent collection of paintings that it was thought to be one of the finest in the Empire.

SUICIDE OR ACCIDENTAL FALL? In 1779, by which time the palace had fallen into a state of considerable decay, it was offered for sale but did not find a buyer. It was turned into a hospital during the Napoleonic Wars, and then a barracks in 1851. In 1919, it became the headquarters of the Ministry of Foreign Affairs, and it also housed the Nazi "protectorate" during World War Two. Tragedy again visited the palace on March 10, 1948, when the body of Jan Masaryk (1886–1948), son of the first President of the Republic and then Minister of Foreign Affairs in the Gottwald cabinet, was found nearby. It wsa never established whether he had committed suicide or had been pushed out of a window.

CHURCH OF OUR LADY OF LORETO ● 71

This church (LORETA) is both an important religious building and a highly regarded example of architectural design. It is constructed around a *Casa Santa* (Holy House), a replica of an Italian sanctuary at Loreto, near Ancona in Italy, which, according to legend, was a house of the Virgin Mary that had been transported there by angels in 1294.

CASA SANTA. The Prague replica is not the only one in Bohemia, where there are about fifty altogether. The Casa Santa was built to celebrate the Catholic victory at the Battle of White Mountain ● *34* by venerating the Virgin Mary and is the architectural and ideological center of the Church. Of the buildings left standing, it was the first to be constructed. It was built between 1626 and 1631 by Giovanni Battista Orsi with money

NOVÝ SVĚT ★
Nový Svět (New World) Street is one of the most delightful in Prague. The surrounding area was originally very poor (it was where Castle staff used to live) and was frequently ravaged by fires, but it was later rebuilt in the Renaissance style and often renovated. Today, it is home to many artists and writers.

LORETÁNSKÉ SQUARE ★ is bound by Černin Palace to the west, the Church of Our Lady of Loreto to the east, and the former Capuchin Monastery to the north.

The slope in front of the Loreto Church is decorated with statues of *putti*.

PRINCESS LOBKOWICZ
After a visit to the "Casa Santa" in Mikulov, Moravia, the Princess built a similar shrine in Prague. It later became the most famous in Bohemia.

provided by Princess Benigna Catherine of Lobkowicz. The façade is articulated by sixteen columns with Corinthian capitals, which also include niches containing statues of prophets and sibyls; the reliefs recount the life of the Virgin Mary. Inside, the silver altar and the limewood statue are dedicated to the Virgin. The rest of the church was completed shortly afterward, and the courtyard was surrounded by cloisters before 1664; an extra floor was built above them by Kilián Ignác Dientzenhofer in 1747–51.

THE FAÇADE. Krištof Dientzenhofer, Kilián's father, started the façade shortly before he died in 1722, and it was completed by his son, who added the terrace. This consists of two side pavilions and a central structure with a bell tower topped by an onion-shaped dome. The décor, which resembles that of a carved reredos, features the theme of the Annunciation; Mary is kneeling on the left-hand gable and there is an angel on the right-hand gable. They are accompanied by statues of the saints and evangelists on the balustrade and above the main entrance.

CHURCH OF THE NATIVITY. This is the largest chapel in the church, and one of the best examples of Baroque style in Prague. In 1734, Jan Jiří Aichbauer (1685–1737) enlarged the church which the Dientzenhofers had also worked on, Václav Vavřinec Reiner ▲ *162, 184, 285* painted his fresco, *The Presentation in the Temple*, over the choir, while Jan Adam

Schöpf (1702–72) painted more frescos in the nave. The paintings in the side altars are by Antonín Kern (1709–47), a leading exponent of the Rococo, whose works can also be seen in St George's Convent in the Castle ▲ *220*. The abundant statuary is beautifully situated and gives the church a slightly theatrical air.

CHAPEL OF OUR LADY OF SORROWS. This chapel is situated in the southeast corner of the cloister. A side chapel dating from 1730, which is dedicated to a Spaniard, Saint Wilgefortis, depicts a curious scene. According to legend, this virtuous princess asked God to save her from a marriage that her father had arranged with a pagan. God obliged by giving her a magnificent beard, but the father was so furious that he had the unfortunate woman crucified. This Spanish saint has never been significantly worshipped in Bohemia any more than other imported saints like Saint Felix and Saint Marcia whose remains are kept in the side chapels of the Church of the Nativity. Popular tradition replaces this picture of Saint Wilgefortis with one of the medieval Czech saint, Saint Starosta, who boasts an identical legend.

The Casa Santa the high altar of the Church of the Nativity, and a general view of the church.

FORMER CAPUCHIN CONVENT

Loreto Square also contains the former Capuchin Convent, the Order's first monastery in Bohemia. It was built between 1600 and 1602 on land donated by the powerful Lobkowicz family; the adjoining Church of the Virgin and Our Lady of the Angels is designed in the restrained style that the Capuchins particularly favored. The cycle of fourteen Gothic paintings that once adorned the church are now in the National Gallery. At Christmas, the convent is home to the biggest crib in Prague; it dates from the 18th century.

STRAHOV MONASTERY ★

The Premonstratensian Strahov Monastery (STRAHOVSKÝ KLÁŠTER) is not far from Loreto Square. This is no longer Hradčany, but the Malá Strana district to which the monastery properly belongs. It is more pleasant to walk through the maze of passageways than along noisy Pohořelec Street. The Premonstratensians occupied the convent from the 12th century until 1952, the year when religious orders were abolished by the Communists. The monastery was returned to the order after the Velvet Revolution.

THE PREMONSTRATENSIANS. The order was founded in the 12th century, at a time when a sense that the Church had strayed too far from the spirit of the Gospels encouraged a number of individuals to seek reforms. One of these was Saint Norbert; born in 1080, this aristocratic chaplain to the German Emperor was a key political figure, and he participated directly in the dispute over Investitures. He abandoned temporal struggles in 1115 and, like many

STRAHOV MONASTERY AND ITS BAROQUE TREASURES ✪
Strahov Monastery, which crowns Pétřín Hill, is one of the largest in Bohemia and seems to rival the nearby Castle. Its finest features are the Church of the Assumption, with its profusion of Baroque decoration, the picture gallery and the library (visits by arrangement). Not only does the library contain 130,000 volumes and illuminated manuscripts; it is also notable for its Theology and Philosophy Rooms, which impress by their size and their magnificent ceilings. Afterwards, it is worth going out onto the terrace behind the church, which overlooks orchards and commands a panoramic view of the plain of Prague.

Ever since its foundation in 1143, Strahov Monastery has been famous for its library. The collections have been frequently ruined, but on each occasion they have been built up again, and in the 17th and 18th centuries respectively, the Theology and Philosophy Rooms were added to house extra books. The library continues to receive gifts and bequests: in 1950, it contained 130,000 volumes, including 3,000 manuscripts and 2,000 incunabula, a remarkable number for an abbey library.

SAINT JOHN THE EVANGELIST
Fifteenth-century
wooden statue.

LECTIONARY FROM STRAHOV
The oldest manuscript in the
Monastery (left), is a fine example
of Ottonian art. This 9th-century
document contains illuminations
which probably come from the
scriptorium of Saint Martin
of Tours.

**THEOLOGY
ROOM (1671)**
This room contains 16,000
books, many of them bibles,
including the famous Kralice Bible
(1579–93), and writings of Fathers of the
Church and leaders of the Counter-Reformation. It
was enlarged in 1721 and redecorations by a local monk,
Siard Nosecký, consist of seventeen large scenes depicting the
thoughts of the then Abbot, J. Hirnhaim.

PHILOSOPHY ROOM (1783)

This room contains 50,000 volumes including philosophy, history and philology, and which include Diderot's *Encyclopédie*. Following Joseph II's decision to close down the monasteries, the Abbot, J. Mayer, managed to save his house from secularization and acquired the wonderful carved wood cabinets from the Monastery at Louka. Abbot Mayer's intention was to recreate the room at Louka by employing the same painter, the Austrian master Franz Anton Maulbertsch. The theme chosen expressed the optimism of the Age of Enlightenment: the upward journey of humanity under the guidance of Providence toward philosophical and religious knowledge.

members of the nobility, took Holy Orders and became a priest, and embarked on his career as a reformer. He founded his first abbey in 1120 at Prémontré, near Laon in northern France. More monasteries were opened, and in 1126 Norbert was elected Archbishop of Magdeburg; he subsequently became Chancellor of the Empire and died in 1134.

A NOTABLE HISTORY. The year 1140 saw the foundation by Prince Vladislav II of the Premonstratensian monastery at Strahov; this came about at the suggestion of Jindřich Zdik, Bishop of Olomouc. The monastery was ideally situated close to the commercial route that ran between Nuremberg and Krakov. It is also the oldest Premonstratensian monastery in Bohemia, and is known as "Mount Sion" because the layout of the town on the hill is reminiscent of Jerusalem. The first occupants of Strahov Monastery came from Steinfeld Convent, and the wooden buildings rapidly gave way to stone structures, beginning with the primitive church which was completed in 1150 and dedicated to the Assumption. The monks enjoyed a certain degree of comfort: water, for example, came from springs on Petřín Hill along an ingenious system of wooden canals. At the end of the 16th century, Rudolph II ordered the construction of a votive church, and work took place between 1603 and 1612 on this sanctuary dedicated to SAINT ROCHE. The church was built next to the main entrance, and is often attributed to Giovanni Maria Filippi ▲ 271; it manages to combine elements of both Gothic and Renaissance styles. Substantial additions were made during the 17th and 18th centuries; these included the

Strahov Monastery seen from Petřín Hill ▲ 269.

Abbot's Library, the present-day Theology Room (1671–9) by Giovanni Domenico Orsi, Jean-Baptiste Mathey's summer refectory (1679–90) decorated with a brilliant trompe l'oeil fresco (1728–31) by Siard Nosecký, and the new library's Philosophy Room (1782–92) by Ignaz Johann Palliardi. The Philosophy Room's ceiling fresco, the Austrian painter F. A. Maulbertsch's last great work ▲ 239, depicts the upward advance of humanity based on the Old and New Testaments, symbolized respectively by Moses and Aaron before the Ark of the Covenant and by Saint Paul before the unknown god in Athens. Special cupboards covered with wire mesh and placed above the doors contained prohibited publications, the *libri prohibiti*. Strahov Monastery had little to fear from the secularization of religious orders decreed by Joseph II; he was greatly impressed by the Order's way of life and, in the event, it was only closed briefly toward the end of his reign.

The Premonstratensians followed the Rule of Saint Augustine. Their main aims were to propagate solemn liturgy and a life of penance, and to devote their lives to the apostolate.

MAIN ENTRANCE. The majestic doorway, a Baroque masterpiece by Johann Anton Quitainer made in 1742 on plans by Anselmo Lurago, is surmounted by a statue of Saint Norbert.

CHURCH OF THE ASSUMPTION. What survives of this Romanesque building (right) dates from 1758. The Assumption of the Virgin at the main entrance (1744) is one of J. A. Quitainer's greatest works. Leading figures of 18th-century Baroque art took part in the decoration of the church.

ABBEY BUILDINGS. These are situated to the right of the courtyard, and take the form of four wings surrounding a closed yard known as the Paradise Courtyard. The buildings are predominantly Baroque in style, and were built over Roman foundations which had in turn replaced earlier wooden constructions. They were discovered in the course of archeological digs which are still in progress.

MUSEUM OF CZECH LITERATURE. The main door leads to the various second-floor rooms belonging to the library ▲ *238*. Another door situated behind the Abbey Church gave access to the Museum of Czech Literature, founded by the Communists, that presented a historical perspective of Czech literature. The library and its archives are now open to the public and temporary exhibitions are organized on a regular basis.

VLAŠSKÁ STREET

Vlašská Street (Italian Street) leads down the hill away from Strahov Monastery; about halfway down, there are some benches where the visitor may rest, admire the view and enjoy the countryside.

A HOSPITAL AT THE FOOT OF PETŘÍN HILL. This is an enormous building. At one time, there were vines and bourgeois homes here but, between 1851 and 1864, the Sisters of Charity of St Carlo Borromeo had a hospital built to plans by A. Gudera. The Empire style building was enlarged during the 19th century and modernized in 1970; today, it is a university hospital. The Church of St Carlo Borromeo (1855), which forms part of the hospital, is in the late Empire style. It is decorated with paintings by V. Kandler and sculptures by V. Lev, and now also houses a medical library.

VLAŠSKÝ ŠPITAL AND THE ITALIAN HOUSE. A large colony of Italians emigrated to Prague during the second half of the 16th century, and an Italian religious order was founded in 1573. At the beginning of the 17th century, it had a hospital built on the site of a number of old houses; the architect was Domenico de Bossi. Today, the buildings are used by the Italian Cultural Center.

LOBKOWICZ PALACE ● 80

Slightly further down and to the right is Lobkowicz Palace, now the home of the German Embassy and one of the most beautiful Baroque buildings in Prague. It was built between 1703 and 1713 by Giovanni Battista Alliprandi, and another floor was added in 1769 by Ignaz Johann Palliardi. Altogether, the building offers a curious contrast between the almost severe façade that overlooks the street and is very classical in style, and the other façade overlooking the gardens which was influenced by Bernini's project for the Louvre (1655). The garden was laid out at the same time as the palace on plans by J. J. Kapula; it covered land where vines had once grown. After 1793, it was converted into a natural English Garden, and this is how it has remained to the present day. The landscape gardener J. V. Skalnic, already noted for his work on the gardens at Marienbad, established the first alpinum in Bohemia. The gardens are not open to the public, but a few feet further up the street, visitors can turn left into an overgrown garden, and walk along behind the palace gardens. The railings are decorated with two beautiful sculptures depicting the abductions of Persephone and Oreithyia. The protruding, rounded central building houses frescoed halls. On leaving the palace, Šporkova Street leads into a charming little square with a large number of trees and some delightful houses.

Top, left to right: a general view of Lobkowicz Palace; painted entrance hall with stucco decoration; on the façade, the coat of arms of the Lobkowicz family, owners of the property since 1753. Above: statue in the Church of St Carlo Borromeo.

SCHÖNBORN-COLLOREDO PALACE

Further still along Vlašská Street is Schönborn-Colloredo Palace, now occupied by the United States Embassy. The palace was commissioned by General Count Rudolph Colloredo (1587–1657), whose family settled in Bohemia during the Thirty Years' War. He amassed a fortune after 1620 and inherited a vast Renaissance residence, entrusting its entire restoration to Carlo Lurago. This palace, with beautiful wooden doors and huge grounds, was renovated by Jan Blažis Santini-Aichl in 1715, but is not open to the public.

Lobkowicz Palace and grounds in 1740.

"ÚVOZ STREET" BY VINCENC BENEŠ
This splendid work shows a clearing toward the south, the Strahov orchard in the foreground, and then Petřín Hill. This oasis of complete calm in a quite unexpected rural setting is only a few minutes from Charles Bridge.

VRTBA PALACE

Vrtba Palace is at the end of Tržiště Street, but the entrance is in Karmelitská Street. It is on the site of two Renaissance houses joined together by Sezima of Vrtba around 1631, and was rebuilt in the late Renaissance style which it has retained to this day. The house originally belonged to Kryštof Harant of Polžice (1546–1621). He was one of Bohemia's most important composers and also one of the leaders of the rebellion against the Habsburgs. He was beheaded in 1621 in Old Town Square ▲ *136*. His house was seized, and later given to Sezima of Vrtba. The painter, Mikoláš Aleš, also lived here from 1886 to 1889. The old road that separated the two houses is still there, and is now the passageway that leads to the garden. The grounds, which are adorned by an Atlas, were laid out by F. M. Kaňka in 1720; they comprise some of the most beautiful Baroque gardens (Vrtbovská zahrada) in Prague ▲ *274*. The statues are the work of Matthias Bernhard Braun, and the paintings on the first floor are by Reiner.

Above: entrance to Vrtba Palace garden. Right: bust of the Moon decorating "Stone Column House" in Úvoz Street, where there is also a Sun.

ÚVOZ ULICE

Úvoz Street is an alternative, and very pleasant, road to Strahov Monastery. The southern side of the road is shut off by the wall running along the monastery garden, while the northern side is lined with attractive houses as well as house signs ▲ *264*. The end of Úvoz Street marks the beginning of the panoramic route that goes to Petřín Hill. Vines were once grown on these slopes; later, gardens such as Na Nebozízku, Seminářská zahrada and the Kinsky Gardens (Kinského zahrada) were laid out, but after 1945 they were joined up to the gardens of Petřín Hill.

Malá Strana 1:
at the foot of
the Castle

1. MALÁ STRANA SQUARE ✪
2. ST NICHOLAS' CHURCH ✪
3. SMIŘICKÝ-MONTAGŮ PALACE
4. STERNBERG PALACE
5. FORMER TOWN HALL
6. LIECHTENSTEIN PALACE
7. NERUDOVA STREET
8. THUN PALACE

MALÁ STRANA: OFF THE BEATEN TRACK ✪

Renowned for its churches and palaces, Malá Strana has a self-contained atmosphere, so that it seems to be quite separate from the Castle and even the river. The district's houses, lanes and taverns, their names imbued with legend, make it certainly the most charming and magical of Prague. A walk through carriage gateways and along narrow passages will reveal delightful gardens and many secret courtyards. A day's exploration of Malá Strana will invariably end with a tankard of Pilsen, savored in one of the district's many beer cellars.

HISTORY

THE EARLIEST INHABITANTS.
There is archeological evidence that there were people living in what is now Malá Strana in prehistoric times; it is also thought that, no later than the 8th century, there were a number of markets down the hill from the Castle, the oldest of which extended over the site of present-day Sněmovní Street. The first major medieval exercise in town planning was carried out by Vladislav I who, after 1157, began the construction of Judith Bridge ▲ 154 ; the effect of this was the creation of a new thoroughfare now known as Mostecká Street. Around this time, the Knights of St John of Jerusalem erected a hospital and the Church of Our Lady Under the Chain ▲ 272, and the Premonstratensians established their monastery on the hill at Strahov ▲ 237. Bishop Jindřich Břetislav, the King's nephew, also had his residence transferred to a palace built on the site of what is now Dražikého Square. There were already

🕐 **Half a day**

◆ **A** D2-D3-E2-E3

fourteen churches
in Malá Strana by the middle of
the 13th century. In 1257 King Přemysl
Otakar II founded the royal town of Malá Strana and
drove the existing inhabitants out into neighboring villages,
replacing them with German settlers, and merchants and
artisans attracted by tax and legal benefits; the new arrivals
remained subject to the laws of their town of origin,
Magdeburg. He also had the Archbishop's Palace and the
JOHONITES COMMANDERY fortified, and completed the
ramparts started by his father, Wenceslas I, in 1253: these now
extended from the Castle to the river, and were later altered
during the reign of Charles IV in the 14th century.

A TIME OF WAR AND RECONSTRUCTION. The Hussite Wars ● *32*
were the cause of widespread devastation: Malá Strana was
burnt down, the Archbishop's Palace was destroyed, a
Carthusian monastery near Ujezd Gate was razed to the
ground, and many other buildings were badly damaged.
Worse, the battles between Hussites and royal troops by the
Castle walls caused the destruction of one third of all of Malá
Strana. After being rebuilt at the end of the 15th century, the
Lesser Town (Malá Strana) was laid waste once again in 1541
by a fire that also reached the Castle and the site where the
Cathedral was being built. The Gothic buildings were
replaced by architecture in the Renaissance style, and
numerous Italians – masons, architects and stuccoists – came
to Malá Strana and settled in Vlašská Street and the
surrounding area. Former Hrzán Palace in Velkopřevorské
Square and the House "At the sign of the Golden Swan"
▲ *259* in Sněmovní Street both date from this era.

LEADING FAMILIES
After the Battle of
White Mountain
● *34*, aristocratic
Catholic families, and
others that had
converted to
Catholicism and
rallied to the
Habsburgs, bought up
plots of land from
Protestants cheaply
and built their palaces
on them. Malá Strana
owes much of its
reputation as the
Baroque jewel of
Prague to the
magnificence of these
and later buildings.

A PERIOD OF INERTIA. Following the Battle of White Mountain and throughout the 18th century, Malá Strana was the scene of much building work: the aristocracy enthusiastically had palaces and gardens built and the Church was only slightly less energetic. Malá Strana's building expansion came to a halt toward the end of the 18th century, something the visitor may well be grateful for. Prague's four main towns were brought together administratively by Joseph II in 1784, but Malá Strana continued to be inhabited by the lesser folk, most of them Czechs. For most of the year, the palaces of the aristocracy stood empty; most aristocrats lived near the Emperor in Vienna, even though the institutions and offices of the Government of Bohemia remained in Prague. During the second half of the 19th century, architectural activity on the other side of the river increased. The closing years of the century saw plans for a railroad and building works that included the ghetto, but only the Straka Academy at the foot of Letná Hill ▲ 316 was actually built.

"Although the Castle is turned toward Malá Strana lying at its feet, Malá Strana itself does not seem to be looking at the Castle; it is not even looking at the river. Its buildings adorned with belvederes, roof decorations, towers, garrets and chimney stacks are deep in slumber, turned in on themselves, and as dour as strongboxes; its narrow lanes resemble green spaces, poky recesses and mysterious passageways. . ."

Angelo Ripellino,
Magic Prague

MALÁ STRANA SQUARE

Malostranské náměstí lies on the route followed by the Royal Way between Mostecká Street and Nerudova Street, a road that climbs up toward the Castle; the square is laid out around St Nicholas' Church. From the 10th century, a Romanesque church dedicated to Saint Wenceslas has stood in the square, along with a few other buildings. In 1283, a Gothic parish church dedicated to Saint Nicholas bisected the square dividing it into an upper part and a lower part. In the 16th century this division was emphasized by the construction in the

HOUSE "AT THE SIGN OF THE GOLDEN LION" ● 77
This house (U zlatého lva), in a pure Renaissance style, once housed an oast house whose façade is at 14 Tržiště Street; under the arcades is At Maecenas (U mecenáše), an old bar named in connection with from Václav Trost, a noted defender of the arts.

century of a Jesuit college on the site of St Wenceslas' Church; then, in the 18th century, the monumental Baroque St Nicholas' Church was built on the site of an earlier church of the same name that had been handed over to the Jesuits in 1625. The houses and palaces lining the square form a wonderful blend of Renaissance and Baroque styles; most of them were built after the fire of 1541.

COLUMN OF THE PLAGUE. This monument was erected in 1715 by F. W. Herstorfer on a plan by architect Giovanni Battista Alliprandi. Standing in the middle of the Square, it commemorates the end of the plague epidemic that decimated the population of Prague between 1713 and 1714.

FORMER TOWN HALL

Malá Strana's former Town Hall (Malostranská beseda) stands at the end of the east side of the square, and partly gives onto Letenská Street; built in 1478, it was remodeled in 1617–22 on plans by Giovanni Campione de Bossi. The interior was then altered in 1660, and the third floor fitted out as a chapel. It was not until the 19th century that the characteristically Renaissance corner towers were removed. The building is now used for concerts, exhibitions and plays.

THE "CZECH CONFESSION". In 1575, the evangelical Estates of the Diet of Bohemia presented to Maximilian II a document that had been drawn up in this Town Hall by representatives of the various currents of Czech Reform: the Union of Czech Brethren, the Lutherans and the Utraquists. It had been modeled on the Confession of Augsburg which, on Charles V's initiative, allowed Protestants to produce their own statement of belief, and now claimed freedom of confession on behalf of non-Catholics in Bohemia. The Emperor, who was also King of Bohemia, undertook to observe the terms but refused to sign the document.

PALACES IN MALÁ STRANA SQUARE

SMIŘICKÝ-MONTÁGŮ PALACE. This palace, which stands at no. 18 on the corner of the square and Sněmovní

16th

GRÖMLING PALACE
This palace (no. 28) was built behind the church about 1772, and is usually known as the House "At the sign of the Stone Table" (*U kamenného stolu*) ▲ *143*; on the second floor there is a café called *Malostranská kavárna* where Kafka ● *110* and writer Urdizil used to go. Until 1918, it was known as the *Radetsky Café*.

THE SMIŘICKÝ PALACE PLOT
It was within the walls of Smiřický Palace that opponents of the Catholic League met on May 22, 1618 before going up the hill to the Castle to meet the Imperial Governors. The episode sparked off the famous Defenestration of Prague ● *34*.

Street, was built in 1606 and is one of the best preserved from Renaissance times; the façade was renovated in the Baroque manner in 1763 by František Josef Jäger ▲ *267, 272*. The owner, Albrecht Smiřický, was head of one of the richest families in Bohemia; he had studied at the Calvinist University of Heidelberg and was a fierce opponent of Ferdinand II. He died in 1618. After the Battle of White Mountain ● *34,* his house was seized and Wallenstein gave it to one of his relatives, Maximilian of Valdštejn.

STERNBERG PALACE. This palace, at no. 19, is situated to the right of Smiřický Palace. Architect Giovanni Battista Alliprandi built it in 1720 on the site of three Romanesque houses.

KAISERSTEIN PALACE. This palace, built by Alliprandi in 1700 on the grounds of two houses, is also known as the *U Petzoldů* house. The rear overlooks Josefská Street and dates from 1536; the attic is decorated with allegories of the seasons by Ottavio Mosto.

ACADEMY OF MUSIC
The Academy's reputation rests on its trumpet and horn classes. It has also produced violinists of the caliber of Ševčik, Kubelík, Ondříček, Kocián and Suk, and pianists including Jan Hermann, Rudolf Firkušný and

Josef Páleníček. Other artists, specializing in ancient music, include Vachulka and Veselka, and Venhoda who has formed the Prague Madrigalists' Ensemble.

View of Charles Bridge and Malá Strana.

LIECHTENSTEIN PALACE

This enormous palace at no. 13 takes up the entire west side of the upper part of Malá Strana Square. Until the beginning of the 17th century, the site was occupied by five separate houses that the Liechtenstein family gradually acquired after the Battle of White Mountain, and had turned into a palace after 1638. The fifth house, the largest of all, was purchased in 1598 by Václav Popel of Lobkowicz, a *hejtman* (captain) of the Old Town. Karl von Liechtenstein, who lived in the palace until his death in 1627, was known as the "Bloody Governor": as Governor of the Kingdom and, Steward Extraordinary, the King's representative, he ordered the execution of the leaders of Ferdinand II's representatives on July 21, 1621 ● *34*. On the orders of Ferdinand II, he also found himself, together with Wallenstein, at the head of the Confiscation Commission set up in the aftermath of White Mountain playing a major role in the redistribution and sale of the rebels' goods to the Emperor. He had previously received the hereditary title of Prince from the Emperor Matthias. The palace was renovated in 1791 by Matthias Hummel who was responsible for the neoclassical façade executed in the style of Niccolo Pacassi's work at Prague Castle ▲ *201*. Philosopher Josef Dobrovský, who was prominent early on in the National Awakening Movement ● *28,* lived in this palace. Subsequently it was closely linked to significant moments in the city's history: these include the military element of the coup d'état that took place when Czechoslovakia ● *36* was created in 1918.

ACADEMY OF MUSIC. The Academy of Music has been housed in Liechtenstein Palace since the House of Artists (Rudolfinum ▲ *194*) was rebuilt; it is difficult to dissociate it from the Conservatory, which was based in Palffy Palace in Valdštejnské Square ▲ 262. Until the 19th century, musical education was mainly provided by churches and convents, or simply by village schools under the direction of teacher-cantors ● 46. The Prague Conservatory, the oldest in central Europe, which had been founded in 1808 and open to students since 1881, was nationalized following the creation of Czechoslovakia in 1918. Founded in 1948, the Academy of Music is more recent. Even though the standard of teaching is the same as that available at the Conservatory, the Academy appears to offer opportunities for more advanced study and research. Students wishing to transfer to the Academy from the Conservatory have to pass an entrance examination. The current director of the Academy is cellist Chuchro, while his opposite number at the Conservatory is composer Jaroslav Neumann. The roster of composers who have graced these institutions either as a students or as teachers is impressive. Since the days of Dvořák ● 46, composers who have taught at the Academy have included Suk, Hovák, Foerster and Hába, and the great historian Otakar Šin.

St Nicholas' Church ★ ● 72

In 1625, shortly after the Battle of White Mountain ● 34, the Jesuits received from Ferdinand II of Habsburg the Church of St Nicholas (Kostel sv. Mikuláše), a Gothic parish church founded in 1283. The followers of Saint Ignatius of Loyola maintained it in good condition and in 1653 commissioned Italian architects Giovanni Domenico Orsi, and then Carlo Lurago, to rebuild it. The east, north and east wings were completed at the end of the 17th century.
A FAMILY OF ARCHITECTS. Starting in 1704, three architects from the same family were involved in this major building

St Nicholas' Gate
The entrance is surmounted by the coat of arms of Count Kolowrat-Liebsteinský, the donor of the church. The second level is crowned by a cornice and, in the center, by a balustrade framed by Fathers of the Church. The attic is decorated with a statue of Saint Nicholas and the letters IHS, a monogram that spells *Jesus habemus socium* (We have Jesus as a companion).

project: Krištof Dientzenhofer, who did the nave, and probably the magnificent façade adorned with sculptures from the workshop of Hieronymus Kohl; Kilián Ignác Dientzenhofer, who succeeded his father in 1722 and was responsible for the choir and cupola; and Anselmo Lurago, Kilián's son-in-law, who added the clocktower in 1755 and took charge of the interior design.

INTERIOR. The interior of St Nicholas' emphasizes the dynamism of the exterior; this is largely due to the oblique positioning of the pillars. The ceiling is decorated with an *Apotheosis of St Nicholas* and scenes from his life by Austrian artist Johann Lucas Kracker (1717–79). Covering almost 1,800 square yards, it is not only the largest painting in Prague but also one of the most interesting of the whole period: Kracker's skill at achieving detail in the plaster enabled him to give his characters a sharpness and plastic freshness that were most unusual in the 18th century.

FRESCO OF ST CECILIA. The organ case is surmounted by a trompe l'oeil fresco that seems to add an extra level to the church. The main scene depicts an *Apotheosis of St Cecilia* by Silesian artist, Franz Xaver Palko (1724–67). Palko, who had studied in Italy, initially had difficulty in making a name for himself as Bohemian painters distrusted foreign ideas; however, they were eventually obliged to give way to this artist who brought the Viennese style to Prague, and who

CUPOLA OVER THE CHOIR
According to legend, while Franz Xaver Palko was painting his *Glory of the Holy Trinity*, he demanded that no one should see his work until it was finished. A Jesuit ignored this request, and when the painter caught him, he promised that his curiosity would be punished. When the painting was unveiled, the priest saw, to his considerable embarrassment, that his face had been given to a fisherman, one of the characters in the fresco, for all posterity to see.

ST NICHOLAS' CHURCH, THE APOGEE OF BAROQUE ✪
Seen from the Castle, the verdigris dome of St Nicholas' Church resembles a clover leaf floating on a sea of red roofs. The interior is stunning; let the eye be taken in by the vertiginous detail of the trompe l'œil statues, the Rococo angels and the paintings that cover the ceiling. The summer concerts (of music by Mozart, who performed there to great acclaim) are unforgettable.

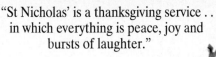

> "St Nicholas' is a thanksgiving service . . .
> in which everything is peace, joy and
> bursts of laughter."
>
> Paul Claudel

even rivaled the great Reiner.
Nonetheless, when he collaborated with
sculptor Ignác Platzer, he opted for a more
restrained approach to art that pervades all the
works he executed for St Nicholas' Church. Palko
also did a *Death of Saint Francis Xavier* for one of the
chapels: on this occasion, there are no little angels,
celestial clouds or dazzling flashes of lightning. The
walls of the main nave present a glorification of the life
of Saint Nicholas. They were painted between 1761 and
1770 by Johann Lucas Kracker.

CHOIR. The choir is of a more restrained, more classical,
appearance. Built by Kilián Ignác Dientzenhofer, it is topped
by a cupola decorated with a fresco by Palko, the *Glory of
the Holy Trinity* (1752). The four sculptures of the Fathers
of the Church (1768–9) by Ignác Platzer are in a
neoclassical style and are the best of the statues
decorating the choir. The pulpit, made in 1765 by
Richard Georg Prachner, is adorned with elegant
motifs and small angels; the absence of a staircase
underlines the sense of lightness.

SIDE CHAPELS. Most of the sculptures are by Platzer,
while the frescos are by J. Hager, Johann Lucas
Kracker and Josef Kramolin. Each of the paintings in
the chapels relates to an aspect of the Counter-
Reformation: they include a scene of charity (*Saint
Thomas of Villeneuve Giving to Charity*) in the first
chapel on the left after entering the church,
and a Crucifixion by Karel Škréta.

MOZART. Wolfgang Amadeus Mozart played
on the organ of this church when he was staying
in Prague in 1787 ▲ *322*. His death in extreme

▲ *322*

**STATUES IN THE
CHOIR**
The four statues
made by Platzer
represent four
Fathers of the Church
whose names appear
clearly on each
pedestal: they are
Saint Basil, Saint
Cyril, Saint John
Chrysostom and Saint
Gregory of
Nazianzus. All of
them were Greek
Fathers who left the
Eastern Church
before the Great
Schism.

Interior of St Nicolas'
Church in Malá
Strana.

253

Commemorative plaque of Jan Neruda.

JAN NERUDA (1834–91)
Jan Neruda, the author of *Tales of the Malá Strana*, was born in this quarter of Prague and lived in the house "Of the Two Suns". He published numerous collections of poems and short stories, and was a masterful journalist. It was out of admiration for his work that Pablo Neruda, winner of the 1971 Nobel Prize for Literature, chose his name as his pseudonym.

penury in Vienna is well documented, but his passing was greatly lamented in Prague: a few days after his death, over four thousand people gathered at St Nicholas' Church in Malá Strana, and his friend Josefina Duškova sang a Requiem in his memory. Another fifty years were to pass before Vienna accorded Mozart similar honors.

NERUDOVA STREET ★

Nerudova Street, which starts in Malá Strana Square, is one of the most famous in Prague. It also contains a marvelous group of Baroque houses.The house at no. 2 "Of the Tomcat" (*U kocoura*) has Renaissance doors and stucco decoration; the brewery sells a beer of which writer Bohumil Hrabal and film director Miloš Forman have sung its praises. At no. 4, the house "Of the Golden Anchor" (*U zlaté kotvy*) has an 18th-century façade adorned with a bust of Saint John Nepomuk, while no. 10, known as Švab, belonged to Bartholomew Spranger, one of the most important Mannerist painters in the Court of Rudolph II ● *31*. The house at no. 12 "Of the Three Little Fiddles" (*U tří housliček*) is one of the best known: according to Angelo Ripellino in his *Magic Prague*, "The charming sign of the Three Violins in Nerudova Street could easily stand as a symbol for the doleful music-making of Malá Strana". It was originally in the Gothic style, but was then rebuilt in the Renaissance manner and renovated in the 18th century. The sign of the three violins is a reminder that, between 1667 and 1748, the house was inhabited by the Edlinger family of instrument makers. Valkoun House at no. 14 was built by Krištof Dientzenhofer, and then by Jan Blažis Santini-Aichl, who renovated it in the early 18th century; the same architect also worked on the neighboring house "Of the Golden Goblet" (*U zlaté číše*). The house "Of St John Nepomuk" (*U svatého Jana Nepomuckého*), at no. 18 was built in 1556 and still bears the original sgraffito.

MORZIN PALACE. This palace stands next to the House "At the sign of the Golden Goblet" and today houses the Romanian Embassy. Architect Santini-Aichl, one of the greatest in Prague's Baroque period ● *80*, made the plans and built the façade. The palace combined four separate houses, and work began in 1713–14; the balcony is supported by two Moorish atlantes carved by Ferdinand Maxmilián Brokoff, the doors depict Day and Night and the roof statuary represents allegories of the four corners of the world.

THUN-HOHENSTEIN-KOLOVRAT PALACE. Thun-Hohenstein-Kolovrat Palace is at no. 20 and stands opposite Morzin Palace. It is decorated with a range of sculptures made by Santini-Aichl who, at the time, lived at no. 14. The House "Of the Golden Crown" (*U zlaté koruny*) has a Renaissance façade that was altered during the Empire Period.

CHURCH OF OUR LADY OF PERPETUAL SUCCOR OF THE GAETANI. (*Kostel Panny Marie ustavičné pomoci u Kajetanů*) This church, also known as the Church of the Theatines, a religious order that settled in Prague in 1665, is also the work of Santini-Aichl; it was originally entrusted to the Italian Guarino Guarini and then to J. B. Mathey, but it finally fell to Santini-Aichl in 1797. He was also responsible for the exterior decorations. The church was consecrated in 1717, and contains a painting by Jacques Callot depicting a Virgin with

Saint Gaetano. THE FORMER MONASTERY OF THE THEATINES stands at no. 24. Following secularization under Joseph II, it was bought in 1793 by Count Morzin, who opened up a passageway that connected to steps leading up to the Castle; the passageway can still be seen to this day. Between 1835 and 1837, the refectory was used as a Czech Theater under Josef Kajetán Tyl. A number of writers including Mácha and Sabira acted here in an amateur capacity.

FROM NO. 27 TO NO. 47. The House "Of the Golden Key" (*U zlatého klíče*) is at no. 27, while the House "Of the Golden Wheel" (*U zlatého kola*) at no. 28 boasts a rich façade in the Baroque style. Former Bretfeld Palace at no. 33 is attributed to Jan Josef Wirch (1765): during the 18th century, it was a very fashionable place and the cream of Prague society, including Casanova and Mozart, were invited to balls held there. The sign of Wenceslas on horseback at no. 34 identifies a former pharmacy that may have been the first in Malá Strana. The House "Of the White Beetroot" (*U bílé repý*) at no. 39 was originally Gothic, but has been altered since. Its name derives from an owner who cultivated the market

THUN-HOHENSTEIN-KOLOVRAT PALACE
This building, which now houses the Italian Embassy, dates back to the period 1715–25. The entrance is adorned with two eagles holding the Thun-Hohenstein coat of arms. These sculptures are by Matthias B. Braun.

". . . of the palaces on sloping Neruda Street, the one belonging to Count Morzin stands out with its two thick-lipped, frizzy-haired atlantes. Two black men, or perhaps two Moors."
Dominique Fernandez
Le Banquet des anges

ENTRANCE TO ST THOMAS'
The most magnificent part of the façade consists of the elements framing the main entrance, which itself dates from the Renaissance (1617); the broken pediment resembles a pair of pincers. The dynamism of the curved lines are sufficient to save the monumentalism of the doorway from a complete lack of expression. Another feature is the elegant embrasures.

INTERIOR DESIGN
The numerous altars in the nave and aisles are decorated by different artists. Karel Škrěta ▲ *164, 220* painted the reredoses of the Holy Trinity and the Assumption (in the choir, 1644), and a portrait of Saint Thomas on the right of the nave.

gardens on Strahov ▲ *237*. Sculptor Johann Anton Quitainer lived here for many years before he died in 1765. The next two houses, no. 41 "Of the Red Lion" (*U červeného lva*) and "Of the Green Lobster" (*U zeleného raka*), were rebuilt in the early 18th century and combined in 1968. Over the House "Of the Black Lion" (*U černéo lva*) at no. 45, is a representation of a lion gripping a tankard between its paws; this is an amusing way of indicating a tavern. The House "Of the Two Suns" (*U dvou sluncū*) ● *80,* at no. 47 has one of the most appealing façades in the whole street; it dates from 1673–90.

ST THOMAS' CHURCH ★

HISTORY. St Thomas' Church (Kostel sv. Tomáše) belongs to the Augustinian Hermits who were brought to Prague by Wenceslas II in 1285. The Augustinians were adversaries of the Hussites, and their monastery was burned down in 1420. It was rebuilt at the end of the 15th century but was destroyed again in the fire of 1541. The present church is in the Baroque style and was built by Kilián Ignác Dientzenhofer (1723–1731). In the monastery (*U sv. Tomáše*, 12 Letenská Street) beer was first brewed in 1358; today, in the old monastery vault, a famous dark beer is still sold.

FAÇADE. St Thomas' Church has one of the most spectacular façades in the whole of Prague. It overlooks a narrow, one-way street, and has an extremely powerful, sculptural appearance, in every way worthy of Kilián Ignác Dientzenhofer, on whose plans it was based. The statue of Saint Augustine over the entrance (1684) and the statue of Saint Thomas over the south door are both by Kohl.

INTERIOR. Like the interior, the exterior lies halfway between the monumental and the elegant. The archways in the nave and the pilasters articulate the space with authority, but in the galleries Dientzenhofer introduced gold Corinthian capitals, cartouches, delicate stucco work and richly molded pediments. The vaults are decorated with paintings by Václav Reiner and his workshop (1728–30) depicting the life of Saint Augustine. The sculptures include works by Quintainer, father and son: the father, Andreas Philipp (1679–1729), was responsible for a sculpture of Saint Vitus over one of the altars in the left-hand aisle that incorporates a cock as an emblem. On the same altar, there are representations of Saint Augustine, Saint Adalbert and St Wenceslas, all dating from 1720–1. The statues are made of limewood and are models of the silver statues that once adorned the high altar; they were melted down in 1729 to pay for alterations to the church, and the wooden models have stood on the altar ever since. At the entrance to the nave, there are two glass coffins containing the remains of Saint Just and Saint Boniface; such representations of death exemplify the sensitivity characteristic of the Counter-Reformation.

HIGH ALTAR. The overall design of the high altar is by Kilián Ignác Dientzenhofer. The *Martyrdom of St Thomas and St Augustine and the Child* by Rubens are copies; the originals (1638–40) are kept in Sternberk Palace ▲ *229*. Johann Anton Quitainer, the son, was responsible for the two angels that flank the main reredos. The patron saints are from the workshop of Brokoff and were completed by his collaborator, Ignác Müller. *St Augustine and the Child* is a comment on the inadequacies of scholarship; it represents one of the most common legendary iconographies applied to this saint from the Renaissance onward. In this painting, he is seen walking along the seashore, and meeting a child who with the help of a shellfish is pouring seawater into a hole hollowed out of the sand. The saint seems surprised but the child, who is in fact an angel, replies: "It would be easier for me to pour all the water into this hole than for you to explain the tiniest part of the mystery of the Trinity."

ST THOMAS' CLOISTER. The entrance to the cloister is on the left of the main entrance of the church. This tranquil spot contrasts with the hubbub of nearby Malá Strana Square. The Monastery's ancient buildings once incorporated a retreat house. A halt on one of the benches placed in the middle of the cloister provides an opportunity to admire the pure lines of this white building; it is possibly most restful place to be found anywhere in this increasingly busy city. Architecture enthusiasts may manage to get inside St Barbara's Chapel; the entrances, identifiable by Renaissance doors made by Bernardo de Alberto in 1596, are situated in the middle of the cloister's east wing. The chapel escaped renovation in the Baroque manner, and the original Gothic style has survived. The beautiful reredos by Josef Heintz the Elder (c. 1600) depicts the Virgin with Saint Barbara, Saint Catherine and some angels.

BAROQUE ORGAN
The organ case in St Thomas', dated 1751, is by Friedrich Fassmann.

"U KRALE BRABANTSÉHO"
Over the entrance, this Renaissance bar ("Of the King of Brabant") pays homage to Jan Primus, King of Flanders and Brabant. According to legend, he worked here secretly on a treatise on the manufacture of beer ● *60*, the celebrated Gambrinus. According to an inscription,

Wenceslas IV is also said to have enjoyed coming here. None of this is historically attested, but staff are always happy to indicate his seat inside the tavern.

THE LION OF BOHEMIA. The lion, the emblem of Bohemia, appears in the Vyšehrad Codex ● 43 as early as 1085. Prince Wenceslas is seated on a curule chair decorated with the head and paws of a lion.

SNĚMOVNÍ ULICE
In this part of Malá Strana, the narrow streets are beautifully laid out, and peace and tranquility prevail. Sněmovní Street has some superb Baroque façades. Part of the street is in the form of a small square called "Fünfkirchen Square" until the 19th century. At the time, the population of Prague was mixed, with Germans and Czechs living side by side.

HOUSE "AT THE SIGN OF THE GOLDEN STAG"

Near St Thomas' Church, standing on the corner of Letenská Street and Tomášská Street, is Schnell House (*U Schnellů*), a well-known restaurant and tavern at one time frequented by many famous people including Tsar Peter the Great of Russia. Next to it is the House "Of the Golden Stag" (*U zlatého jelena*), which was designed by Kilián Ignác Dientzenhofer in 1725–6. The 18th century was a time when the bourgeoisie acquired confidence in architectural matters, and took over from the aristocracy and the clergy the task of reconstructing old buildings. The House "Of the Golden Stag" is one of the more successful examples from this period.

ST JOSEPH'S CHURCH

Only a few steps from St Thomas' Church in Josefská Street stands a Carmelite church, whose curious façade and simple, serene interior the busy tourist could easily miss.
BAROQUE RUBENS-STYLE. The façade of this Baroque church, which was built between 1683 and 1693, was more influenced by Flemish models than by Romanesque buildings. Most unusually, the building is constructed on a central plan with a cupola, and there is altogether little subtlety of balance with the double columns overwhelming the chapels, and the obelisk-shaped pilasters in opposition to the feeling of space in the cupola. It is nonetheless a captivating church with an inconspicuous pulpit, but a complete absence of sculptures, frescos and any other dramatic decoration. The high altar

"The inexhaustible charm of Malá Strana, hanging on to the side of the Castle. This totally Baroque quarter is as big as a Parisian arrondissement."

Dominique Fernandez

is decorated with a painting of the *Holy Family* (1702) by Petr Brandl; another, also by Brandl, showing a vision of St Theresa is to the right of the pulpit. The importance in Baroque art of pictorial and plastic representations of ecstasy is well established, and it is easy to agree with Émile Mâle that, from the 17th century onward, they became the "seal of holiness". One of the altars on the left is decorated with limewood statues by Matěj Václav Jäckel (1696). They include a beautifully crafted Saint Ludmila on the right, holding a crown of martyrdom in one hand and her sash in the other; the movement of the drapes and the saint's swaying gait and proud air make for a wonderful combination of elegance and large scale. The other statue is of Saint Wenceslas.

THUN PALACE

A short journey from St Joseph's Church takes the visitor to this palace; it involves walking in the direction of St Thomas', then going to the end of Tomášská Street, turning left into Thunovská Street, and then right into Sněmovní Street (Diet Street). Thun Palace occupies the whole length of the righthand side of this street. It was built by Santini-Aichl between 1696 and 1720 and, from 1861 onward, housed the provincial Diet; it was also here that the deposition of the Habsburgs from the Bohemian throne was announced on November 14, 1918, the date that also marks the creation of the Czechoslovak Republic and the election of Masaryk as President. The Senate sat in the palace from 1918 to 1940, and was followed by the Czech National Council from 1968. It now houses the British Embassy. The main decoration on the façade is a lion, the symbol of Bohemia.

THOMÁŠ GARRIGUE MASARYK ● *36.* Masaryk was born into a very humble family, but became Professor of Philosophy and Sociology at the Czech University in Prague in 1882. As a member of the Sokols and a Slavist, he founded the *Athenaeum* review, and his political career was established when he was elected to the Reichsrat in 1891. He soon set up the Realist Party and, in his writings, synthesized and proposed a model of Czech identity that turned Czechs into democratic humanists, and heirs to the traditions of Hus, Kmujkés and the Enlightenment. From 1915, in France, and later on in the United States, he was among those putting forward the idea of a Czechoslovak state. He became the first President in October 1918.

AROUND THUN PALACE. At no. 5 Sněmovní ul. is LAZANSKÝ PALACE, built by Francesco Caratti in 1670 and then renovated by F. M. Kaňka in 1712. Next is the House "Of the Golden Swan" (*U zlaté labutě*) at no. 6. At

ST JOSEPH'S CHURCH
The three statues decorating the façade are the work of Matěj Václav Jäckel: they represent Saint Joseph, Saint Theresa and Saint John of the Cross.

THOMÁŠ G. MASARYK
Masaryk (1850–1937) devoted much of his energy to a number of major works, including *The Czech Question* (1895) and *The Social Question* (1898), in which he rejected Marxism and the theory of class struggle. His originality lies in his scientific analysis of Czech society.

no. 13 is BYLANDT-RHEIDT PALACE, designed by J.-B. Mathey: while it was under construction, the Romanesque Church of St Michael had to be pulled down to make way for it. Sněmovní Street terminates at the blind alley "Of the Golden Well" (*U zlaté studně*): the façade of the "Painters' House" (U malířů) house at no. 3 has a mural by Karel Klusáček (1897), and at no. 4 is the House "Of the Golden Well".

WALLENSTEIN PALACE

Several palaces line Wallenstein Square (Valdštejnské náměstí). AUERSPERK PALACE, at no. 1, is in the Baroque style going back to 1751; LEDEBOUR-TRAUTTMANSDORFF PALACE, at no. 3, was built by Palliardi in 1787.

WALLENSTEIN DEIFIED
The large banqueting-room is two stories high, and because of the way the mirrors are placed appears to be even larger. The ceiling was decorated by Baccio del Bianco with a representation of Wallenstein, Duke of Friedland, as Mars, God of War in Roman mythology.

THE BIGGEST PALACE IN PRAGUE. The square is closed off by the façade of Wallenstein Palace (Valdštejnsky palác), the entrance to which is through the gardens in Letenská Street. It was built between 1623 and 1629, and covers a site once occupied by twenty-six houses. Wallenstein entrusted the project to Italian architect Andrea Spezza (died 1628), who had been very active in Cracow; he was succeeded by Niccolo Sebregondi, but it was Giovanni Pieroni who designed the huge *sala terrena* of the grounds. The interior of the palace, generously endowed with marble, stucco and frescos, is in keeping with the first owner's ambitions, and the palace's chapel by Ernst Heidelberger (c. 1630) contains one of the best Baroque altars in Prague.

DUKE OF FRIEDLAND. Albrecht Václav Eusebius was born in Bohemia in 1583; his mother was from the Smiřický family, an old Czech aristocratic family. He was brought up according to the teaching of the Union of Czech Brethren, and studied in Prague and Germany before fighting for the Imperial Army against the Turks. After converting to Catholicism, he returned to Prague and in 1608 married a rich widow, the owner of huge estates in Moravia. About the same time, a Prague banker, Hans de Witte, became his administrator. Wallenstein was then widowed in 1614 and he was sole heir to his deceased wife's fortune. His second marriage introduced him to the corridors of power, his father-in-law, Count Karl von Harrach, being an influential member of the Viennese Catholic Party and a future Private Councillor to Ferdinand II. Wallenstein was ambitious and in 1617 put together an armed force, which he put at the service of Ferdinand, then at war with Venice. His valor earned the future Emperor's gratitude. On his return, he was not directly involved in the Battle of White Mountain although his private regiment took part. His wealth continued to grow as he appropriated the estates abandoned by Albrecht Smiřický, who had no heir. By dint of skilful acquisitions, Wallenstein increased his lands around Jičín, the fief of the Smiřický family: these included mines. Within a few years, his property became the most prosperous in all Bohemia, and also the best administered. As master of a quarter of the land in Bohemia, and in his capacity as Duke of Friedland and Prince of Sagan, he ruled what was virtually a principality of over three hundred subjects. He also became one of the Emperor's biggest creditors; this was a relatively easy ambition to achieve as, with Hans de Witte, he was a member of the financial consortium charged with minting coins. The privilege lasted for no more than fourteen months, but it was quite sufficient to enable the two men to amass fortunes. At the height of his powers, Wallenstein was in a position to place a 24,000-strong army of well-paid, well-fed men, the only force worthy of the name of "army", at the disposition of an Empire devastated by the Thirty Years' War. However, the story had a sad ending. Too much power all too easily leads to trouble, and the Emperor began to fear his subject; matters came to a head when Ferdinand learnt that Wallenstein was negotiating secretly with the Saxons and the Swedes, and demanding absolute loyalty from his officers. The Emperor had him assassinated in his bed at Cheb in 1634.

THE GARDENS ★. A visit to the gardens is a must; the grotto, the *sala terrena* (1623–7) and the statues bring an element of animation to the otherwise static setting. The SALA TERRENA is the most beautiful part of the palace. It is an immense loggia inspired by Italian models like the Loggia dei Lanzi in Florence and is the finest architectural achievement of the

LEDEBOUR AND PALLFY PALACE GARDENS. The Baroque terraced gardens of the Ledebour-Trauttmansdorff and Pallfy palaces, with their loggia, *sala terrena* and statuary, are carved into the southeastern slopes of Prague Castle where once grew vineyards but are now derelict. They are being restored by the Prague Heritage Fund set up by President Václav Havel and the Prince of Wales. Above, left to right: Ledebour-Trauttmansdorff Palace, the *sala terrena*, the fountain in the grounds of Wallenstein Palace; the statue of Hercules fighting the dragon (above) is by Adriaen de Vries, sculptor to Rudolph II.

View of the lake in Wallenstein Palace.

KOMENSKÝ OR COMENIUS
Jan Ámos Komenský was a Humanist and cultural pioneer, and a contemporary of René Descartes.

period. The paintings and stucco work by Baccio del Bianco recall the Trojan War and the *Aeneid*.

PALACES IN VALDŠTEJNSKÉ SQUARE

KOMENSKÝ MUSEUM. No. 20 Wallenstein Square houses the fascinating Komenský Pedagogical Museum. JAN ÁMOS KOMENSKÝ, or Comenius (1592–1670) ● *43*, maintained the momentum of Czech reform and humanist thought, and proposed the idea of nursery schools, insisting on the importance of play in education. After becoming a Bishop in the Union of Czech Brethren at the age of twenty-six – he was to be the last – Komenský became one of the great Czech writers of the 17th century; he wrote in both Czech and Latin. On being exiled in 1624, he threw his inexhaustible energies into "federating" the dispersed communities, and emphasized pre-school education: as he said later, "It is easier to educate than to re-educate". In *Didactia Magna* (1632) particularly, he urged the use of music at school, together with experience and images. His manuals, *Orbis Pictus* and *Janua linguarum reserata*, were used in Jesuit education in the country of his birth. Even today, a number of private schools in Prague that have been opened since 1900 have adopted some of the teaching principles set out in his pedagogical texts.

LEDEBOURG AND PALFFY GARDENS. (no. 3) These elegant terrace gardens, designed in the 18th century and recently restored, lead directly to the castle's gardens in the summer, enabling the visitor to avoid the busy Nerudova Street. Concerts and plays are put on in these enchanting surroundings.

PALFFY PALACE. This palace at no. 14, built in the early 18th century on the ruins of two old houses, now contains the CONSERVATORY OF MUSIC. The Conservatory was founded in 1811 on the initiative of the Association for the Encouragement (or the Renaissance) of Music in Bohemia, and initially it was based in the Dominican Monastery near St Giles' Church ▲ *285*: instrumental lessons were given with a view to turning out orchestral players. In the late 19th century, the Conservatory merged with the Academy of Music, which was housed in Liechtenstein Palace ▲ *250*. Antonin Dvořák ● *46* was Director at the end of the 19th century. Upstairs there is a pleasant restaurant, and the terrace commands a lovely view over the gardens of the SMALL CZERNIN PALACE at no. 12.

KOLOWRAT PALACE
This palace was the residence of the Presidents of the Czechoslovak Republic from 1918 to 1940.

KOLOWRAT-CZERNIN PALACE. Like its neighbors, this house at no. 10 was built on land previously covered by gardens. Ignaz Johann Palliardi, who laid out these gardens in the Late Baroque style in 1784, had also designed the remarkable gardens on the terrace ▲ *274*.

> "You gagged me and bound my eyes in vain.
> I trust in God that you will not
> bind my reason and my thought."
>
> Jan Ámos Komenský

FÜRSTENBERG PALACE. Fürstenberg Palace at no. 8 was built in 1743–7 in a style that has survived to the present day; it also has some beautiful Baroque gardens. The palace now houses the Polish Embassy.

KLÁROV

Valdštejnská Street runs into the Klárov crossroads, which are lined with several Empire-style buildings.

KLÁR INSTITUTE. The Klár Institute at no. 6 was designed by Alois Klár (1763–1833) and built by his brother between 1836 and 1844. This two-story building once gave shelter to blind people; a relief shows Tobias giving sight to a sick man.

RICHTER HOUSE. Karel Emanuel Richter had this house at no. 3 rebuilt in 1832. An inscription on the façade recalls that the actor E. Vojan died here in 1920.

LETENSKÁ STREET. VRTBA PALACE at no. 5 was built between 1707 and 1725 for František Vrtba. It was built in the High Baroque style, and today houses the Union of Architects.

GROTTO IN VOJAN PARK
The main building in this garden is the curious St Elias Chapel, which resembles a grotto. It is formed of numerous stalactites and stalagmites. The paintings on the ceiling relate the legend of the prophet Elijah.

LUSACE SEMINARY STREET

VOJAN PARK. In the 17th and 18th centuries, Lusace Seminary accepted Catholic students from Protestant Germany, and particularly from Lausitz (Lusace); U lužického semináře Street passes through a more popular quarter of Prague. To the right behind a high wall is Vojan Park (Vojanovy sady) where the Archbishop's Palace was built. The garden, dating from the late 1800's belongs to the Discalced Carmelites.

PROLETARIAN MILITANTS. Several houses once belonged to individuals prominent in working-class movements and strikes of the late 19th century ● 28. The HOUSE "OF THE THREE GREEN CROSSES" (U tří zelených křížků) at no. 16 was the headquarters of the trade union magazine Dělnici (The Workers), while no. 12 housed the offices of another magazine, Budoucnost (The Future) founded by Ladislav Zápotocký (1852–1916) and Josef Boleslav Pecka (1849–97), the two founders of the Czechoslovak Workers' Social Democratic Party. The party adopted the ideas of Karl Marx, and in 1889 joined the Second International.

"VENICE IN PRAGUE". This is the name given to a district overlooking a stretch of the Vltava called Čertovka ▲ 266. Several houses were built on the remains of the former Judith Bridge; the last house, near Charles Bridge, is the House "Of the Three Ostriches" (U tří pštrosů), now a restaurant.

View from the Castle over the tile roofs of Malá Strana and Charles Bridge.

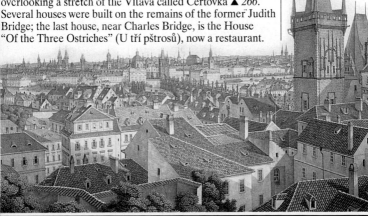

House signs are now ornamental, but in the Middle Ages they indicated which house was which. In those days, houses were not numbered.

Malá Strana 2:
da Kampa a Petřín

▲ Malá Strana 2:
da Kampa a Petřín

1. Sv. Mikuláš ★ 2. Kaunický palác 3. Maltézské náměstí 4. Turbovský palác 5. Panna Maria Vítězná 6. Panna Maria pod Řetězem

⏱ **1/2 giornata**

◆ **A** C5-C6-D3-D4-D5-E4-E5-E6

PAUSA DI DISTENSIONE SULL'ISOLA DI KAMPA ★
Separata da Malá Strana dal "canale del diavolo", l'isola dei mulini, con il suo parco e i suoi spazi erbosi, in estate affollati di studenti, invita a una passeggiata. Anche il suo nuovo museo merita una visita. Lasciando Kampa, percorrete il most Legií per raggiungere la Střelecký Ostrov.

Kampa

L'isola si estende tra la Moldava e la Čertovka ("canale del diavolo"), il braccio del fiume che un tempo serviva da gora per numerosi mulini ad acqua. Nel 1169 Ladislao II concesse un vasto territorio, tra cui Kampa, ai Cavalieri di San Giovanni di Gerusalemme, che vi edificarono il primo monastero di Malá Strana e diverse case borghesi: il territorio autonomo di Malá Strana era allora noto come Giurisdizione di Malta.

Na Kampě. Attorno a Na Kampě, la piazza dove ogni anno si tiene il mercato della ceramiche, s'innalzano abitazioni molto belle. Al n. 9, la dům U obrazu Panny Marie (casa "Al quadro della Vergine") dà sul ponte Carlo: secondo la leggenda, il dipinto della facciata raggiunse la casa, trasportato dalla corrente, durante un'inondazione; qui visse Adolf Kaspar (1877-1934), pittore e illustratore rinomato. Al n. 7 si trova la dům U zlatého lva (casa "Al leone d'oro"), costruita nel 1732 da Giuseppe Bartolomeo Scotti (1685-1737); al n. 13, la dům U

7. VELKOPŘEVORSKÝ PALÁC ★ 8. BUQUOYSKÝ PALÁC ★ 9. KARLŮV MOST ★ 10. ISOLA DI KAMPA 11. SV. JAN NA PRÁDLE 12. ŘÍČNÍ 13. MICHŮV PALÁC 14. KARMELITSKÁ 15. PETŘÍN 16. SV. MICHAL 17. SV. VAVŘINEC 18. PETŘÍNSKÁ ROZHLEDNA

BÍLE BOTY (casa "Allo stivale bianco"), dalla facciata rococò, è attribuita a Franz Josef Jäger (1731-1793); al n. 1, la DŮM U MODRÉ LIŠKY (casa "Alla volpe blu"), originariamente chiamata "Alle tre coppe d'oro", fu costruita nel 1605 per il fiammingo L. Stewardt, gioielliere alla corte di Rodolfo II. Come mostra la sua insegna (a lato), fu ricostruita nel 1664: il rilievo con la volpe risale alla stessa epoca.

CASA DI MARTINŮ. Al n. 11 visse Bohuslav Martinů (1890-1959) ● *47*, quando studiava al conservatorio (1906-1910). Ben presto il musicista decise di trasferirsi in Francia. Secondo violino dell'orchestra della Filarmonica ceca dal 1913, scoprì le opere di Debussy, di Ravel, di Dukas e soprattutto di Roussel. Di quest'ultimo suonò il *Poema della foresta* e, nel 1923, divenne suo allievo a Parigi, dove entrò a far parte della scuola di Parigi, nella quale moltissimi membri provenivano dall'Europa centrale. Braccato dai nazisti, lasciò la Francia per gli Stati Uniti, dove il grande direttore d'orchestra Serge Koussevitsky gli fece assegnare una cattedra a Princeton. Il compositore non ritornò più a Praga, ma non abbandonò mai l'ispirazione ceco-morava e *Giulietta* o *La passione greca* sono altrettanti omaggi al suo paese.

MUZEUM KAMPA. Na Kampě sbocca nella U Sovových mlýnů. Una galleria d'arte moderna, aperta da poco per iniziativa della Fondazione Mládek, occupa il n. 2. Le sue collezioni comprendono opere dei grandi artisti cechi del XX secolo, tra i quali Kolář ● *102*, Guttfreund ● *107* e Kupka. Al n. 4, l'ex palazzo Liechtenstein fu costruito in stile barocco da G.B. Alliprandi, poi rimaneggiato in stile tardo Impero, pur conservando intatto il portale barocco. Di fronte,

JOSEF DOBROVSKÝ (1753-1829)
Questo filosofo di tendenza critico-razionalista fu anche storico della letteratura ceca, filologo e iniziatore degli studi di slavistica. Fu una delle principali figure della rinascita nazionale ● *28*. A differenza di un altro "ridestatore", Josef Jungmann ▲ *290*, che fonda il suo concetto di nazione sull'identità linguistica, Dobrovský pubblicò in latino e in tedesco, per dare maggiore risonanza ai suoi studi.

al n. 7, s'innalza una villa (1798), all'epoca di proprietà del conte Nostitz, nella quale vissero Josef Dobrovský – il suo busto è eretto a due passi dalla villa –, nonché, nel XX secolo, il poeta Vladimír Holan ● *119* e l'attore Jan Werich. Da questa abitazione ha inizio uno dei parchi più apprezzati dai praghesi.

ŘÍČNÍ

Proprio alla fine della U Sovových mlýnů, la piccola Říční permette di lasciare l'isola di Kampa. Ai nn. 1 e 3 di Malostranské nábřeží si noterà un fastoso

IL MURO DELLA FAME
Carlo IV l'avrebbe fatto edificare per procurare lavoro ai poveri di Praga, che durante la carestia del 1360, per assoluta indigenza, erano costretti a rubare. Lo si chiama anche Chlebova zeď (il muro del Pane) e i suoi merli appuntiti servirebbero a ricordare che i denti della povera gente devono avere di che masticare.

edificio neorinascimentale, palazzo JECHENTHAL, costruito da Josef Schulz, l'architetto che operò anche al Rudolfinum ▲ *194* e al Teatro nazionale ▲ *294*: questo edificio fu per lungo tempo uno dei più monumentali della città.
SV. JAN NA PRÁDLE. All'angolo tra la Říční e la Všehrdova si innalza una delle antiche fondazioni di Malá Strana, la chiesa di San Giovanni del Lavatoio. Rimaneggiata nel XIII secolo, e durante il Rinascimento nel coro, venne secolarizzata nel 1784 e trasformata in lavatoio. Nel Medioevo era la chiesa parrocchiale del borgo di Újezd, che nel 1360 fu in parte annesso a Malá Strana e in parte rimase sobborgo. Dal 1935 è di nuovo un luogo di culto (della Chiesa hussita ceca). A ovest della chiesa, al n. 6 della Říční, si trova l'antico ospedale di Malá Strana, fondato nel 1620, ricostruito nel 1662 da G. di Capauli e soppresso nel 1784.

MICHNŮV PALÁC

Československo

Michnovský palá: Praha, Malá Strana

30h PRAGA

PRIMO BAROCCO. Si accede a palazzo Michna, chiamato anche Tyršův dům (casa Tyrš), risalendo la Všehrdova; molto esteso, si trova al confine tra la Újezd e la Karmelitská. L'ala più antica del palazzo, con la sua facciata a graffiti ● *78*, dà sulla Všehrdova e risale al 1580. In seguito l'edificio venne ingrandito da Francesco Caratti (1631-1644); il corpo della costruzione si apre sulla grande corte che, nel XVIII secolo, comprendeva ampi giardini. Caratti lavorò durante la guerra dei Trent'Anni per Pavel Michna di Vacínov, uno dei membri,

PALAZZO MICHNA
Lo stile di questo palazzo sviluppa il primo barocco praghese ● *80*, ispirato al possente barocco romano: la facciata è scandita da lesene e ornata da tutto il repertorio di frontoni, di oculi e di balconi a loggia.

Passeggiata a Petřín.

con Wallenstein, de Witte, Liechtenstein e il cardinale
Dietrichstein, del consorzio monetario ▲ *260* creato nel
febbraio 1622 che causò in soli quattordici mesi la bancarotta
del paese. La sala di rappresentanza è decorata con stucchi
di Domenico Galli autore anche degli stucchi esterni. Alla
fine del XVIII secolo, non ancora portato a termine, palazzo
Michna fu trasformato in caserma e in arsenale; nel 1921
fu finalmente acquistato e restaurato dall'associazione dei
Sokol, che vi organizzarono una palestra. Oggi è sede della
facoltà di educazione fisica dell'università Carlo ▲ *278*
e di un Museo di cultura fisica e sport.

I "SOKOLNIKI". La vita associativa della seconda metà
del XIX secolo offriva molte occasioni per militare per
la causa nazionale ceca. L'associazione di ginnastica
del Sokol ("falco"), fondata nel 1882 da Miroslav Tyrš
e da Jindřich Fügner, diventa un vero e proprio
movimento di massa: esaltando i valori di uguaglianza
e di fraternità molto vicini all'ideale dei Fratelli boemi
● *43*, i circoli si moltiplicarono non solo in Boemia e in
Moravia, ma anche in altri paesi slavi. I raduni dei *sokolniki*
mobilitavano migliaia di partecipanti: nel 1914 si contarono
128.000 membri; nel 1947 erano più di un milione, cioè un
ceco su quattordici! "Con l'educazione del corpo e dello
spirito, con l'energia fisica, con l'arte e la scienza, con tutti
i mezzi morali, risollevare la patria": questa era la parola
d'ordine dei Sokol. Dal 1990 l'associazione è in via di
ricostituzione e dovrebbe ora recuperare numerosi beni
immobiliari confiscati nel 1948: dopo i nazisti, i comunisti

vietarono i Sokol e ne imprigionarono
i principali responsabili.

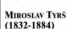

**MIROSLAV TYRŠ
(1832-1884)**
Il filosofo e storico
dell'arte ceca è
conosciuto in
particolare per le sue
opere *Laocoonte,
opera dell'epoca
romana* (1872)
e *Dello stile gotico*
(1881).

Sotto, torre di Petřín,
o belvedere.

PETŘÍN

In origine una vasta foresta
si estendeva dalla collina di Petřín
sino alla Montagna Bianca ▲ *321*.
Dal XII secolo l'area venne trasformata
in giardini e vigneti, per poi divenire
un bel parco dove passeggiare,
arricchito anche da alcuni interessanti
monumenti.

PETŘÍNSKÉ SADY. Per raggiungere
la collina di Petřín, basta prendere
la funicolare alla stazione Na Újezdě
(dal palazzo Michna, attraversate

la Újezd e prendete la U lanové dráhy, quasi di fronte).

Rozhledna. Il belvedere di Petřín è una copia in miniatura della torre Eiffel, innalzata per l'esposizione giubilare del 1891. Divenuta torre panoramica, offre possibilità uniche di osservazione sulla città, su Malá Strana in particolare.

Sv. Vavřinec. La barocca chiesa di San Lorenzo, progettata da Ignaz Palliardi e costruita fra il 1735 e il 1770, s'innalza sulle vestigia di un edificio romanico già citato nel 1135: qualche traccia della costruzione più antica è ancora visibile nell'ala sud dell'edificio attuale. La chiesa è addossata al Hladová zeď (muro della Fame) ▲ 268. Accanto a San Lorenzo si innalza la cappella del Calvario, costruita nel 1735. I graffiti della facciata, eseguiti nel 1936 su cartoni di Mikoláš Aleš, raffigurano la Resurrezione di Cristo.

La chiesa di San Lorenzo, a Petřín.

Kinského zahrada. Più a sud, in direzione della Holečkova, si trovano la villa e i giardini Kinský. L'edificio in stile Impero è opera di Jindřich Koch (1827-1831); vi si trova una statua di Psiche di Antonio Canova (1757-1822). Affittata nel XIX secolo agli arciduchi eredi Rodolfo e Francesco Ferdinando d'Asburgo ● 31, oggi è sede della sezione etnografica del Museo nazionale ▲ 175 (attualmente chiusa). Più esotica è la chiesa carpatica di **Sv. Michal** (San Michele; a lato). Questo antico santuario ortodosso degli Alti Tatra, nella catena dei Carpazi, interamente in legno, risale al XVIII secolo.

Madonna della Vittoria
Gli altari della chiesa sono incorniciati da una decorazione molto sobria e ornati da combinazioni di colore oro e nero. L'altare maggiore (sopra) è opera di J.F. Schor e possiede una statua della Vergine eseguita da J. Čapek.

In base al Trattato del Trianon (4 giugno 1920), insieme
alla Slovacchia l'Ungheria cedette al neonato Stato ceco
la Russia Subcarpatica; la chiesa venne trasferita
da un villaggio di questa regione a Praga nel 1929, affinché
la cultura e la tradizione di questa minoranza fossero
rappresentate anche nella capitale.

MONUMENTO A KAREL HYNEK MÁCHA. Si giunge a questo
monumento, punto di riferimento della coscienza nazionale
ceca, seguendo le mura delle antiche fortificazioni. Mácha
(1810-1836) è il più grande e il più autentico poeta del
romanticismo rivoluzionario ceco: si può ben affermare che
tutti, nel suo paese, sanno a memoria il suo più celebre
poema, *Máj* (Maggio), vero e proprio inno alla terra
natale. La tradizione vuole che, ogni primo maggio,
i giovani innamorati depongano fiori ai piedi della statua
e, calata la sera, si bacino.

PANNA MARIA VÍTĚZNÁ

Scesi da Petřín in direzione di Malá Strana, raggiungete
palazzo Michna e risalite la Karmelitská: al n. 9 si erge la
chiesa della Madonna della Vittoria. Originariamente tempio
luterano tedesco consacrato alla Trinità, nel 1624 l'edificio
verrà consegnato all'ordine dei Carmelitani scalzi spagnoli,
appena giunti in Boemia. La chiesa fu così chiamata in
memoria della battaglia della Montagna Bianca ● *34*:
la leggenda attribuisce la vittoria dei cattolici
all'azione e alle preghiere dell'abate superiore
dei Carmelitani, Domenico di Santa Maria.
Il portale della chiesa venne finanziato da uno
dei capi dell'armata imperiale, don Baltazar
de Marroas. L'edificio, costruito nel 1611
su progetto di Giuseppe Maria Filippi,
e totalmente rimaneggiato fra il 1636
e il 1644, ha fama di essere la prima
chiesa barocca ● *70* di Praga: è qui,
per esempio, che appare per la
prima volta la facciata tripartita a
lesene e volute. Dell'edificio
protestante non rimane che la
parte destra della facciata
e il fonte battesimale in
marmo. I quadri che,
sul terzo altare
laterale,

PRAŽSKÉ JEZULÁTKO
Si può forse dire che
la principale
attrazione della
chiesa della Madonna
della Vittoria sia il
*Bambin Gesù di
Praga*. Nel 1628 la
principessa Polyxena
Lobkowitz, moglie
del gran cancelliere
del regno, offrì
alla chiesa questa
statuetta di cera
che la madre, Maria
Manrique de Lara,
aveva portato in dote
venendo dalla Spagna
per sposare, nel 1555,
Vratislav di Pernštejn.
La statua del *Bambin
Gesù di Praga*,
ritenuta miracolosa
sin dal XVII secolo,
attira ancora
numerosi pellegrini.
Questa statuetta
possiede un
guardaroba molto
ricco e le si cambia
l'abito ogni
capodanno. Nel 1742,
dopo la partenza dei
francesi, la regina
Maria Teresa ● *31*
fece confezionare
una serie di abiti
in broccato d'oro
per ringraziare
il Bambin Gesù di
avere protetto la città
dal saccheggio.

PALAZZO NOSTITZ
Il manifesto con la facciata di palazzo Nostitz ricorda che vi si tengono concerti d'eccezione durante il festival musicale della "Primavera di Praga" ● *48*.

**MADONNA SOTTO
LA CATENA**
Il nome della chiesa deriva da una leggenda secondo la quale il ponte Giuditta sarebbe stato chiuso da una catena d'oro. La missione di proteggere il ponte Giuditta fu affidata ai Cavalieri dell'ordine degli Ospedalieri di San Giovanni di Gerusalemme, poi Cavalieri di Malta. Nel 1253, all'epoca dell'edificazione delle fortificazioni di Malá Strana, la testa del ponte fu unita al monastero con dei bastioni.

raffigurano san Giuseppe, san Gioacchino e sant'Anna, come anche il san Simone, sulla sinistra, sono di Peter Brandl e risalgono all'inizio del XVIII secolo. La visita alla cripta permette di vedere alcuni sepolcri aperti in cui riposano i corpi, eccezionalmente conservati, dei Carmelitani eminenti e dei loro benefattori. Di fronte alla chiesa della Madonna della Vittoria s'innalza, al n. 8, all'angolo con la Harantova, il ROHANSKÝ PALÁC (palazzo Rohan): costruito da Josef Zobel nel 1796, è ora sede del ministero della Pubblica Istruzione.

KLÁŠTER SV. MAŘÍ MAGDALÉNY

Ai nn. 2, 4 e 6 della Karmelitská si trovava il monastero di Santa Maria Maddalena. Le guerre hussite ● *32* distrussero il primo edificio dell'inizio del XIV secolo, appartenente all'ordine dei Maddaleniti; un complesso conventuale venne allora ricostruito fra il 1656 e il 1677 con il sostegno dei Domenicani e, in parte, grazie ai finanziamenti di Václav Michna di Vacínov ▲ *268*. Il progetto della chiesa è di Francesco Caratti e di Christoph Dientzenhofer, che si dice vi sia seppellito con il figlio Kilian Ignaz. La soppressione degli ordini nel 1783 costrinse il monastero a diverse funzioni: dal 1791 al 1849 fu adibito a ufficio postale, poi a caserma della gendarmeria, quando fu ristrutturato in stile Impero. Dal 1945 ospita gli archivi di Stato, accessibili a ricercatori e studiosi cechi e stranieri.

MALTÉZSKÉ NÁMĚSTÍ

Per raggiungere Maltézské náměstí, lasciate la Karmelitská e prendete la Prokopská o la Harantova.
STRAKOVSKÝ PALÁC. Posto al n. 14, palazzo Straka sarebbe stato disegnato da Jean-Baptiste Mathey verso il 1690.
TURBOVSKÝ PALÁC. Palazzo Turba, costruito da Franz Josef Jäger nel 1767-1768, presenta una facciata strutturata da una trama serrata di lesene e solo i frontoni sono segnati dalla fantasia del rococò. Ristrutturato nel 1990, l'edificio è uno dei più raffinati della città e ospita l'ambasciata del Giappone.
NOSTICKÝ PALÁC. La parte nord della piazza è fiancheggiata sul lato destro da palazzo Nostitz (al n. 1), attribuito a Francesco Caratti: l'architetto l'avrebbe eretto negli anni 1660-1670 in uno stile che viene di solito indicato come "primo barocco", qui segnato dall'ordine gigante. La facciata, però, venne rimaneggiata durante il XVIII secolo: la balaustrata e le torrette d'angolo del tetto, come il portale d'accesso (A. Haffenecker) e gli stucchi, in stile rococò, hanno ingentilito l'insieme. In restauro, dovrebbe ospitare il ministero dei Beni Culturali.

Panna Maria pod Řetězem

Da Maltézské náměstí raggiungete la Lázeňská, dove si trova la chiesa della Madonna sotto la catena.

Antico cuore della commenda. Questa chiesa è la più antica fondazione di Malá Strana: il santuario romanico sorse infatti tra il 1169 e il 1182. Il re Ladislao II ● *30* la fece costruire per l'ordine dei Cavalieri di San Giovanni di Gerusalemme, poi di Malta. Nel corso del XIV secolo l'edificio romanico doveva essere abbattuto e sostituito da una nuova chiesa, ma il progetto fu abbandonato. La costruzione attuale conserva quindi, fra le due torri del 1385, belle vestigia romaniche. La nuova chiesa è dei primi anni del XVII secolo, tranne il coro, rifatto da Carlo Lurago nel 1640-1660. L'altare maggiore è ornato da un trittico di Karel Škréta, *La Vergine, san Battista e la battaglia di Lepanto*; il pulpito è attribuito a Johann Georg Bendl, che ha invece sicuramente realizzato le statue di san Gerardo e di santa Ubaldeska. La grande statua in marmo della navata centrale (E. Max, metà del XIX secolo) ha i tratti di Rodolfo Colloredo-Waldsee, Gran Maestro dell'ordine, che difese Praga contro gli svedesi nel 1648.

Difendere il ponte. Il ponte Giuditta ▲ *154*, costruito nel XII secolo, era sorvegliato alle due estremità da chiese fortificate: dalla parte di Staré Město dall'allora chiesa di San Clemente ▲ *152*, e dalla parte di Malá Strana dalla chiesa della Madonna sotto la catena.

FRANÇOIS RENE DE CHATEAUBRIAND BYDLIL V TOMTO DOMĚ V HOSTINCI NAZVANÉM V LÁZNÍCH 24.-30. KVĚTNA 1833

Velkopřevorský palác

Addossato al lato destro della chiesa, il palazzo del Gran Maestro fu costruito da G.B. Scotti tra il 1724 e il 1728. Sino al 1990 era sede del Museo della musica ceca ● *48*. La modesta facciata presenta tre occhi di bue sormontati da maschere di pietra, il più alto si inscrive nella campata del portale, dove si concentra tutta la ricchezza decorativa. A sinistra della chiesa si trova un'altra proprietà dell'ordine di Malta: l'antico monastero, ricostruito da Thomas Haffenecker fra il 1728 e il 1731. Di fronte, al n. 11, si erge la DŮM U ZLATÉHO JEDNOROŽCE (casa "All'unicorno d'oro"), antica locanda frequentata anche da Mozart e Beethoven.

Maltézské náměstí
La monumentalità degli edifici e l'aspetto immutato nel tempo hanno fatto della piazza la scena ideale per il film *Amadeus* di Miloš Forman.

Dům v lázních
La casa era la locanda "Ai bagni", dove sostarono Pietro il Grande e, nel 1833, Chateaubriand, durante la sua missione presso Carlo X, allora in esilio a Praga ● *114*.

Dům u malířů
Questo edificio, al n. 11 di Maltézské náměstí, è del 1531. Il suo nome ("Ai pittori") e la sua insegna, sotto, ricordano che, nella seconda metà del XVI secolo, vi abitò il pittore Jiří Šic. Oggi ospita un ristorante di lusso.

Durante il XVII secolo e nella prima parte del XVIII lo spirito barocco trionfa a Praga: le arti fioriscono in una sintesi architettonica e decorativa la cui quintessenza si manifesta nella pianificazione dei giardini. Sui terreni lasciati liberi dall'incendio di Malá Strana del 1541 i nobili poterono creare, nelle vicinanze del castello e di Petřín, sui pendii delle colline, palazzi barocchi circondati da giardini a terrazze. Da questa natura tormentata nascerà così una complessa composizione propria del "genius loci", meravigliosamente servita dai giochi di proporzioni e di prospettive. Il fascino intimo e segreto di questi "teatri verdi", organizzati attorno a un asse centrale, invita chi passeggia a fantasticare. A lungo dimenticati, sono oggi in restauro.

Statue di Adriaen de Vries, palazzo Wallenstein ▲ 261.

Castello di Troja ▲ 318, incisione del XVIII secolo.

«E POI IMPROVVISA, LA MERAVIGLIA: UNA SORTA DI TEATRO ALL'APERTO, SCAVATO NEL FIANCO DELLA COLLINA, A TERRAZZE ARROTONDATE, ORNATO DI STATUE BELLISSIME...»

DOMINIQUE FERNANDEZ

GIARDINI DEI SENSI
Sale terrene, grotte decorate, gloriette (sopra)...
L'architettura dei giardini di Praga avvicenda a piacimento rilassanti viali a scalinate, a volte estremamente ripide, che sboccano su portici, passaggi insoliti o terrazze a balaustrate.

Intrecci di piante e di fogliame, aperture inattese sul paesaggio, aiuole profumate dai sapienti arabeschi e festonate dall'arte topiaria, vasche dove gorgheggiano giochi d'acqua musicali... Sensazioni ed emozioni si liberano variando continuamente sotto lo sguardo delle statue dei più grandi artisti barocchi.

OMAGGIO A LENNON
Per i praghesi questo fu uno dei modi per dimostrare la propria dissidenza.

KAUNICKÝ PALÁC
Palazzo Kaunitz è tra i più belli di quelli che fiancheggiano la Mostecká. Costruito da Anton Schmidt (1730-1775) è oggi sede dell'ambasciata

della Jugoslavia (n. 15). Le statue dell'attico provengono dalla bottega di Ignaz Platzer (1717-1787).

Veduta della Mostecká con, sullo sfondo, la chiesa di San Nicola di Malá Strana ▲ 251.

VELKOPŘEVORSKÉ NÁMĚSTÍ

BUQUOYSKÝ PALÁC. Il più bel palazzo di Velkopřevorské náměstí è senza dubbio palazzo Buquoy, già dei Wallenstein, edificato verso il 1682 da Jean-Baptiste Mathey. Nel 1719 la facciata venne rimaneggiata da F.M. Kaňka. Gli stucchi provengono dalla bottega di Matthias Bernhard Braun, che divenne collaboratore fisso di Kaňka. Oggi palazzo Buquoy è sede dell'ambasciata di Francia.

PALÁC METTYCHŮ Z ČEČOVA O HRZÁNŮ. Situato al n. 1, palazzo Mettych di Čečov o Harzan, dal nome dei vari proprietari, ha conservato il portale e i frontoni rinascimentali. Ľala sinistra, barrocchizzata nel 1760, dà sulla Čertovka. Qui nacque il compositore Josef Bohuslav Foerster (1859-1951) ● 47, ▲ 306.

JOHN LENNON A PRAGA. Di fronte, il muro del giardino del palazzo del Gran Maestro è coperto di omaggi a John Lennon: durante la normalizzazione i giovani si riunivano davanti al "muro di John Lennon" la sera dell'anniversario della sua morte e attendevano, seduti in silenzio, che la polizia venisse a sloggiarli con la forza. Arrivavano molte lettere, indirizzate semplicemente al "Monumento John Lennon – Praga", che i postini attaccavano a un chiodo sul muro. Ma la normalizzazione si è compiuta e il ritratto del cantante, che mostra i segni del tempo, ormai attira solo i turisti.

MOSTECKÁ

Risalite la Lázeňská per sbucare sulla Mostecká, una delle vie più animate del quartiere. Il cortile del n. 16 conserva le vestigia del palazzo episcopale gotico, distrutto dagli hussiti appena iniziata la loro rivolta ● 32; al n. 3 sorge la SASKÝ DŮM ("casa sassone"), antica residenza gotica, la cui facciata è stata rifatta alla fine del XVI secolo. La via è chiusa dalle torri del ponte Carlo e dalla MALOSTRANSKÁ BRÁNA (porta di Malá Strana). La più piccola delle torri risale al 1166 e apparteneva alle fortificazioni dell'antico ponte Giuditta ▲ 154; la più alta risale alla fine del XV secolo.

DAL KAROLINUM
AL NÁRODNÍ DIVADLO

1. KARLŮV MOST ★
2. BETLÉMSKÁ KAPLE
3. SV. JILÍ
4. SV. HAVEL
5. KAROLINUM
6. STAVOVSKÉ DIVADLO

⌚ **1 giornata**

◆ **B** A4-A5-A6-B4-B5-B6-C4-C5-C6

Sotto, arazzo nell'aula magna del Karolinum, raffigurante Carlo IV e san Venceslao.

KAROLINUM ❤

FONDAZIONE DI CARLO IV.
Dopo il fallito tentativo di Venceslao II (1278-1305) di creare nella sua capitale uno *studium generale*, Carlo IV fonda nel 1348, sul modello dell'università di Bologna e della Sorbona di Parigi, l'università di Praga, la prima in Europa centrale (quelle di Cracovia e di Vienna seguirono rispettivamente nel 1364 e nel 1365). A partire da questo momento la formazione delle *élites* del regno e dei paesi vicini non dipende più unicamente dalle università italiane e francesi, ma viene assicurata anche a Praga dalle quattro facoltà delle università medievali: arte (filosofia), diritto, medicina e teologia.
GLI EDIFICI. Il cuore del Karolinum era la casa gotica del finanziere Rotlev, che la donò all'istituto. Gli elementi barocchi risalgono ai rimaneggiamenti del 1718 operati da F.M. Kaňka.
Il Karolinum oggi rimane un edificio universitario, riservato soprattutto a cerimonie ufficiali; le belle sale a volta del pianterreno, a destra entrando,

Università.

accolgono invece esposizioni di arte contemporanea.

CENTRO INTELLETTUALE EUROPEO. Carlo IV aveva fondato l'università prima di tutto per i bisogni del regno di Boemia, poi per quelli dell'Impero. Nel 1363, e fino al 1470, l'istituzione fu organizzata in quattro "nazioni", ciascuna delle quali esprimeva un voto nelle deliberazioni universitarie e i cui rappresentanti si avvicendavano nelle cariche di rettore e di cancelliere: la ceca (comprendente i moravi, gli ungheresi e gli slavi del Sud), la polacca (con gli slesiani e i loro vicini tedeschi), la bavarese e la sassone (svedesi, norvegesi e danesi). Sin dall'inizio, tuttavia, la fondamentale suddivisione degli studenti e dei docenti era tra cechi e tedeschi. L'università intrattenne fruttuose relazioni con le università di Parigi e di Oxford e tra le sue file annoverò teologi di grande fama, come Mattia di Cracovia.

JAN HUS, RETTORE DELL'UNIVERSITÀ. Dall'inizio del XV secolo, Jan Hus insegnò il pensiero del teologo John Wycliffe, come d'altronde la gran parte dei suoi colleghi cechi, partigiani del realismo. La predicazione di Wycliffe si rifaceva a un'eresia del IV secolo, combattuta da sant'Agostino, il pelagianesimo. I docenti tedeschi, nominalisti, criticavano questa dottrina; ma la loro autorità venne annullata quando Venceslao IV, il 18 gennaio 1409, riformò lo statuto universitario: da allora, infatti, durante le elezioni universitarie, i docenti della "nazione" ceca ebbero diritto a tre voti, mentre i docenti delle altre tre "nazioni" potevano esprimere un voto solo. "Le leggi umane, la legge divina, l'istinto naturale, tutto ordina che siano i cechi ad avere la priorità in Boemia", scriveva Hus, che divenne rettore nel 1409. Il 16 maggio 1409 studenti e docenti tedeschi lasciarono allora Praga e costituirono una nuova università a Lipsia. Jan Hus, invece,

Del primo Karolinum non restano che le arcate del pianterreno e il bovindo della cappella che dà su Ovocný trh.

SIGILLO DI CARLO IV Alla fine del XIV secolo era l'università più importante dell'Europa centrale.

279

"Tractatus de pestilentia"
Pagina estratta da un codice del XV secolo della biblioteca del Karolinum.

Josef Kajetán Tyl (1808-1856)
Il Teatro degli Stati generali una volta portava il nome di Tyl, uno dei più fecondi autori drammatici popolari del suo tempo. Da una delle sue commedie, *Fidlovačka* (1834), verrà tratto l'inno nazionale ceco: *Dov'è la mia patria?* Tyl fu anche tra gli organizzatori dei balli pubblici ● 52, detti "balli cechi".

venne arso sul rogo nel 1415. Dopo diverse esitazioni, nel 1417, i docenti dell'università dichiararono la comunione sotto le due specie necessaria alla salvezza. Da allora l'università svolse un ruolo decisivo nella formazione del programma hussita conservatore: verso il 1419 vennero qui redatti i "Quattro articoli di Praga", versione moderata di questo programma. Nel 1420 l'università sostenne la legittimità della rivolta contro il re per difendere la causa di Dio. Verso il 1430 l'insegnamento di fatto cessò. Sotto Giorgio di Poděbrady ● 30 l'università rimase utraquista e tale restò sino alla battaglia della Montagna Bianca ● 34. I docenti giurarono fedeltà al re e al calice: da allora, gli studenti stranieri cattolici non frequentarono più l'università di Praga, che venne quindi esclusa dal circuito culturale dell'Europa del tempo. Nel XVI secolo la riforma luterana permise il ristabilirsi dei contatti con i paesi divenuti protestanti. Gli studenti di Praga andavano a perfezionare la loro formazione a Wittenberg, poi a Basilea e a Ginevra. Sino alla Montagna Bianca l'università fu un'istituzione molto importante in Boemia: nel XVI secolo le scuole urbane e provinciali, tranne quella dell'Unione dei Fratelli boemi, erano sotto il suo controllo. Dopo il fallimento degli Stati protestanti di Boemia, l'università venne chiusa e, nel 1622, fu affidata ai Gesuiti. Le facoltà di diritto e di medicina cessarono la loro attività sino al 1654, data in cui l'università prese il nome di Carlo-Ferdinando (da Ferdinando III), che mantenne fino al 1918. Diritto e medicina vennero allora messe alle dipendenze dello Stato, arte (filosofia)

e teologia dei Gesuiti. A partire dal 1747 vennero introdotte nuove riforme che condussero, alla fine del XVIII secolo, alla sottomissione totale allo Stato. Così nel 1748 il tedesco sostituì il latino come lingua d'insegnamento. Malgrado tutto, ben prima del 1848, la facoltà di filosofia fu uno dei luoghi in cui prese forma la rinascita nazionale ceca. Dopo le riforme del 1848-1850 l'università si scisse finalmente, nel febbraio 1882, in un'università tedesca e in un'università ceca, frequentata anche dagli sloveni, dai serbi e dai croati. Nel 1918, a partire dalla creazione della Cecoslovacchia, riprese il nome di università Carlo (Karlova univerzita), che conserva tuttora.

TRADIZIONE MUSICALE ● *46.* All'epoca di Carlo IV la musica della corte, dell'università e della chiesa venne a trovarsi alla confluenza dell'*Ars Nova* e del canto gregoriano, senza contare l'affermazione di particolarismi locali e il risorgere delle tradizioni della liturgia slava. L'università doveva formare i cantori per il capitolo della cattedrale di San Vito ▲ *214.* Le cerimonie religiose e la musica di corte trassero nuovo impulso dall'uso della polifonia e dalla fioritura strumentale di cui invece Jan Hus denunciò la ricchezza inutile e perversa, condannando l'uso degli strumenti musicali nel rituale liturgico.

STAVOVSKÉ DIVADLO

I progetti del Teatro degli Stati generali sono dell'architetto Anton Haffenecker (1781). L'edificio in seguito venne rimaneggiato: nel 1859 gli si aggiunse un piano, e nel 1881 al salone fu aggiunta una struttura metallica e una decorazione in stile neorinascimentale ● *84.* In restauro a partire dal 1983, il teatro ha riaperto i battenti nel 1992.

SENTIMENTO NAZIONALE. La costruzione del

TEATRO DEGLI STATI GENERALI
La sala, tra le più celebri di Praga, accolse nel 1787 la prima del *Don Giovanni* di Mozart e, nel 1791, quella della *Clemenza di Tito.* Nel 1984 Miloš Forman vi ha girato le scene d'opera del film *Amadeus.*

FRANTIŠEK ŠKROUP (1801-1862)
Il compositore partecipò attivamente alla rinascita nazionale, senza mai chiudersi nel settarismo: direttore dell'opera tedesca e del Teatro degli Stati generali, fece scoprire ai praghesi Liszt, Wagner e Berlioz.

Proprio accanto al Karolinum s'innalza il Teatro degli Stati generali – a seconda delle epoche, Teatro Nostitz, Teatro nazionale, Teatro tedesco e Teatro Tyl – voluto alla fine del XVIII secolo da un mecenate, il conte Franz Anton Nostitz-Rienek, grande burgravio del regno di Boemia.

**IL MERCATO
DI SAN GALLO**
San Gallo è oggi uno
dei più animati
quartieri di Praga:
ogni giorno vi si tiene
un colorato e
simpatico mercato.

UHELNÝ TRH
La parte sud-
occidentale della città
di San Gallo ha
conservato qualche
casa rinascimentale
con arcate. Fino al
1807 esisteva qui una
fucina dove si
vendeva anche il
carbone. Chiamata
mercato del carbone,
questa piccola piazza
prese più tardi il
nome di mercato
verde, poi di mercato
della verdura. Fra le
antiche case della
piazza, la dům U tří
zlatých lvů (casa
"Ai tre leoni d'oro")
è d'epoca gotica
e fu rimaneggiata
nel XVII secolo
in stile barocco.
Alla fine del XVIII
secolo apparteneva
al compositore
F.X. Dušek e
W.A. Mozart, suo
amico, vi soggiornò
nel 1787 ▲ *323.*

teatro del conte Nostitz segna anche una data nella rinascita
nazionale ceca ● *28.* Nonostante vi fossero rappresentate
soprattutto opere tedesche, dal 1785 il pubblico poté assistere
anche a spettacoli in ceco quali *Il cappello miracoloso*, *Adrian z
Řimsu* di V.K. Klicpera, e anche la prima opera ceca moderna,
Lo stagnino di František Škroup (1826). Nel 1786 un gruppo di
attori ottenne dall'imperatore il permesso di fondare un teatro
in legno, chiamato Bouda ("baracca"), situato vicino al teatro
Nostitz, in Václavské náměstí ▲ *172,* già Koňský trh ("mercato
dei cavalli"), per rappresentarvi soprattutto opere ceche.
Nel 1789 il teatro Bouda cessò la sua attività. Nel 1799 il conte
Nostitz vendette il suo teatro alla Dieta (o Stati) di Boemia
per 60.000 fiorini: da allora assunse il nome che a lungo
ha mantenuto e che gli è stato ridato nel 1991.

HAVELSKÉ MĚSTO

PRIVILEGIO REALE. Non lontano dal Teatro degli Stati
generali, i tracciati delle attuali Havelská, V kotcích
e Rytířská delimitavano l'antica città di San Gallo.
Il borgo primitivo si era sviluppato in epoca romanica, col
prolungamento della Città Vecchia. All'epoca occupava
lo spazio compreso fra Ovocný trh ("mercato della frutta"),

«Mozart guardava questo amabile spiazzo dalla finestra di una delle case, la sera, dopo […] aver deposto la pesante parrucca.»

Jaroslav Seifert

e Uhelný trh ("mercato del carbone"); nel 1232 Venceslao I accordò al borgo lo statuto di città e, inoltre, fece erigere a Praga la prima cinta di bastioni, che racchiudeva circa 40 ettari: le fortificazioni incoraggiarono il sorgere di nuovi quartieri. Fu proprio in questo contesto che si sviluppò la neonata città di San Gallo, principale punto di riferimento dei mercanti tedeschi. Molto attiva, fece presto concorrenza a Staroměstské náměstí ▲ 146.

Sv. Havel

La chiesa di San Gallo, fondata insieme alla città omonima nel 1232, venne ricostruita verso il 1330. In seguito, fra il 1671 e il 1680, fu profondamente rimaneggiata da Carlo Lurago e Domenico Orsi. La facciata venne innalzata solo nel 1723-1738, su progetto di Johann Blasius Santini Aichel (1677-1723). L'opera più preziosa conservata nella chiesa è una Crocifissione con i quattro evangelisti di F.M. Brokoff.

Nell'ottobre 1414 in San Martino sul muro, Jakoubek di Stříbro officiò, per la prima volta, l'eucarestia sotto le due specie.

Gli edifici conventuali annessi alla chiesa, una volta occupati da Carmelitani scalzi, dopo la secolarizzazione degli ordini religiosi voluta da Giuseppe II, furono rilevati da privati. Né il chiostro né il refettorio hanno subìto gli oltraggi del tempo.

Discorso riformatore. È nella chiesa di San Gallo che predicava Konrad Waldhauser (1326 ca-1369), precursore del movimento hussita ● 34 in Boemia. Questi giunse a Praga nel 1363, dopo essersi dedicato per più di dieci anni alla predicazione itinerante, denunciando i costumi corrotti e la simonia del clero. Anche Jan Hus vi predicò nel 1404.

Sv. Martin ve zdi

Dalla chiesa di San Gallo la Havelská conduce al mercato e Uhelný trh la congiunge alla Martinská, dove si trova l'antica chiesa gotica di San Martino sul muro, probabilmente fondata nel XII secolo. L'edificio venne ricostruito durante il XIV e il XV secolo. Il soffitto a cassettoni è del 1610 e il portale del 1779. Gli scultori Brokoff, padre e figli, sono sepolti nel cimitero di San Martino, come indica una targa sul muro della chiesa. Vi si può accedere solo in occasione di concerti.

SAN MARTINO SUL MURO
Nel XIII secolo il muro sud della chiesa venne incorporato nella cinta della Città Vecchia: ciò spiega il nome "sul muro". In basso, l'interno dell'edificio gotico.

Utraquismo. Discepolo di Matěj di Janov, Jakoubek di Stříbro (1373 ca-1429) è l'autore di una voluminosa opera teologica, paragonabile a quella di Jan Hus. Secondo Jan Lavička, "egli fra tutti i maestri cechi è quello che, per la sua dedizione e le sue innovazioni in materia di culto, più di tutti si avvicina ai protestanti. Ma l'austerità scolastica dei suoi scritti latini e la fama di cui Jan Hus godette dopo la morte l'hanno fatto cadere nell'oblio". Il principio della comunione vuole che ogni fedele possa comunicarsi sotto le due specie (*sub utraque specie*). Da qui ha origine la scelta del calice come simbolo della Riforma, nonché i termini "calicista" e "utraquista", che indicano i riformati di Boemia.

Fratelli boemi. La chiesa di San Martino sul muro appartiene ormai all'Unione dei Fratelli boemi. Questa comunità nacque nel 1457 da una scissione in seno agli hussiti radicali. Molti dei Fratelli emigrarono dopo il 1620 ● *32*. L'Unione si ricostituì all'inizio del XVIII secolo a Herrnhut, in Sassonia, sotto il nuovo nome di Fratelli moravi e con statuti e dottrina molto differenti dall'originaria Chiesa dei Fratelli boemi. I Fratelli di Herrnhut, missionari, si diffusero in tutto il mondo e soprattutto negli Stati Uniti, dove ancora possiedono un'università a Baltimora. Fra quelli rimasti in Boemia e in Moravia una parte nascose la propria fede sino al 1781 e nel 1918 scelse di riprendere il nome di Chiesa di Comenio e dei loro antenati, ribattezzandosi "Chiesa evangelica dei Fratelli boemi".

Vratislavský dům

Da Uhelný trh la Skořepka permette di raggiungere la Jilská. Fra il 1813 e il 1817, Karl Maria von Weber alloggiò al n. 16, nella casa Vratislav, dal nome del proprietario del XVIII secolo, il conte Vratislav. Quando il Teatro Nostitz ▲ *281* passò alla Dieta di Boemia e l'egemonia del teatro italiano cominciò a svanire, Weber venne nominato direttore di questo teatro, divenuto Teatro degli Stati generali, al posto di Wenzel Müller (1807-1813). Weber ebbe l'incarico di riorganizzare l'opera con il favore degli aristocratici melomani, tra cui i membri delle famiglie Nostitz, Pachta o Lobkowitz. Malgrado il suo successo e la volontà di migliorare il livello artistico e di ampliare il repertorio, sino ad allora dominato dagli italiani, il nuovo direttore, di salute precaria, sopportò difficilmente le ostilità dei praghesi: questi infatti guardavano con poca simpatia all'ennesimo direttore tedesco alla guida del teatro. È questa un'evidente dimostrazione sia del mutamento degli spiriti sia dell'influenza dei Ridestatori ● *28* e del pubblico.

Dům na rybárně
Questa statua orna la facciata della casa "Al mercato del pesce", situata al n. 10 di Betlémské náměstí. Verosimilmente fu l'architetto Alliprandi che ricostruì l'edificio in stile barocco verso il 1704.
La costruzione ospita oggi una taverna (U plebána) rinomata per i suoi vini, conosciuti sotto il nome di "vini dei re di Boemia".

A fronte, in alto: particolari del complesso della Cassa di Risparmio di Boemia di A. Wiehl (1891-1895), al n. 29 della Rytířská.

Betlémské náměstí
In questa immagine della piazza d'inizio secolo si può riconoscere, in secondo piano, il Museo Náprstek.

Sv. Jiljí

Influenze cistercensi. L'entrata della chiesa di Sant'Egidio si trova nella Husova, su cui si affacciano anche diverse gallerie d'arte contemporanea. Jan Milíč di Kroměříž, antesignano di Hus, vi predicò a partire dal 1365. Sant'Egidio è l'unica chiesa di Staré Město ad avere conservato l'aspetto esterno gotico. Fu iniziata nel 1330 sotto l'ultimo vescovo di Praga, Jan di Dražice. Questo prelato aveva soggiornato dal 1318 al 1329 alla corte papale di Avignone e aveva potuto apprezzare l'architettura gotica francese, della quale divenne il precursore in Boemia. Il gotico boemo quindi affonda le proprie radici nel gotico cistercense borgognone; si spiegano così la sobrietà della facciata, la scelta di un protiro e quella di un capocroce piatto.

Decoro interno. L'aspetto dell'interno della chiesa è frutto di una barocchizzazione intrapresa da František Špaček nel 1733. Wenzel Lorenz Reiner (1689-1743) è l'autore degli affreschi delle volte, la cui parte meglio riuscita, il *Trionfo dei Domenicani sull'eresia*, si trova nella navata centrale (1733-1734). Questo praghese permise alla pittura murale boema di raggiungere i vertici da tempo già toccati dalla scultura. Egli seppe comporre mirabilmente dipinti di grande respiro mantenendo intatta la tensione drammatica.

Chiesa di Sant'Egidio
La più bella decorazione della chiesa è costituita dalle volte ricoperte di affreschi illusionistici. L'altare maggiore (1734-1738) è ornato da sculture lignee di Franz Ignaz Weiss.

Betlémské náměstí

Da Sant'Egidio riprendete la Husova sulla sinistra; la prima via a destra sbocca su Betlémské náměstí. La piazza prende nome dalla cappella omonima, detta anche cappella dei Santi Innocenti. Secondo una tradizione praghese qui esisteva una fontana dove le ragazze madri avrebbero gettato i figli indesiderati. Al n. 10 una casa barocca, dove nacque il pittore

JAN HUS
L'impegno universitario al Karolinum ▲ *279* e quello di predicatore nella cappella di Betlemme, dove operò dal 1402 sino al 1414, costituirono le due priorità della vita di Jan Hus.

Jaroslav Čermák (1830-1878), presenta sul frontone un busto dell'imperatore Giuseppe I. Qui, nel 1848, ebbe luogo la prima riunione del gruppo di democratici radicali cechi conosciuto con il nome di Lípa slovanská ("tiglio slavo"). Oggi su questa piazza sorgono negozi d'antiquariato, venditori di libri usati e accoglienti ristoranti.

BETLÉMSKÁ KAPLE

COSTRUZIONE. Fondata da Hanuš di Milheim (Mühlheim), amico e consigliere di Venceslao IV, la cappella di Betlemme venne costruita dal 1391 al 1394. È di uno stile molto sobrio, sul modello di una *Hallenkirche* (chiesa "a sala", in cui le navate laterali sono di altezza pari a quella centrale), e sin dall'inizio venne consacrata alla predicazione in lingua ceca. All'epoca il quartiere in cui era edificata era popolare e di continuo sottoposto a inondazioni. Di grandi proporzioni – poteva contenere 3000 persone – è il primo edificio la cui disposizione corrisponde alla sensibilità della Riforma. Distrutta alla fine del XVIII secolo, fu ricostruita nel 1950-1952 dalle autorità comuniste, in memoria delle rivendicazioni egualitarie della Riforma ceca. La ricostruzione sembra molto fedele – come testimonia la mostra permanente al primo piano dell'edificio – e si è articolata intorno ai tre muri esterni preservati e integrati ad abitazioni vicine. A destra della cappella esiste ancora la casa di Jan Hus, oggi chiamata CASA DEL PREDICATORE.

SERMONI HUSSITI. Dal 1402 al 1414 Jan Hus predicò ogni giorno nella cappella davanti a più di 3000 persone, artigiani, operai, piccoli commercianti, chierici senza impiego... che egli incitava al ritorno alle pratiche evangeliche. Non si lasciò mai intimorire dai divieti dell'arcivescovo. Il suo pensiero poté facilmente diffondersi poiché il clero povero costituiva una parte importante della popolazione praghese: circa 1200 individui su 50.000 abitanti.

CANTI HUSSITI. Pregare nella lingua locale corrispondeva a uno dei principi fondamentali della Riforma hussita. La rivoluzione linguistica andava di pari passo con la composizione di canti popolari in lingua ceca dei cui testi Hus stesso a volte fu autore o adattatore. A partire dallo

JAN HUS SUL ROGO
Arrestato e poi condannato al Concilio di Costanza, il predicatore fu arso vivo il 6 luglio 1415 ● *32*.

hussitismo, nacque in Boemia una grande tradizione di canti, che influenzerà per sempre la musica ceca. I soldati hussiti, guidati da Jan Žižka, innalzarono questi canti durante i combattimenti contro le truppe papali e imperiali. Fra le composizioni hussite, si ricorda più spesso *Coloro che sono i combattenti di Dio*, frequentemente utilizzato dai compositori,

principalmente da Smetana ● 47 nell'opera *Libuše*
▲ 296 e nel ciclo sinfonico *La mia patria*, e da
Janáček ▲ 296, nel secondo movimento del *Viaggio
del signor Brouček nel XV secolo*. Gran parte dei canti
hussiti è stata raggruppata nel *Canzoniere* di Jistebnice
(1436), villaggio nei pressi di Tábor.

NÁPRSTKOVO MUZEUM

All'angolo tra la Náprstkova e la Betlémská si trova
il Museo etnografico Náprstek, ospitato nella dům
U Halánků (casa "Dagli Halánek"), che venne
ricostruita alla fine del XVIII secolo.
NASCITA DI UN MUSEO. Vojtěch Fingerhut-
Náprstek (1826-1894) era un patriota: discepolo
di Josef Jungmann ▲ 290, molto attivo
nell'organizzazione dei balli di Josef Kajetán
Tyl ▲ 280, partecipò alla rivoluzione del 1848
● 20, prima di andare in esilio negli Stati
Uniti. Nel 1858, di ritorno a Praga, Náprstek
portò con sé molti souvenir, tra cui i primi
esemplari etnografici e tecnologici della
sua collezione. Nel 1863 organizzò un

vero e proprio museo industriale, con la collaborazione molto devota di numerosi praghesi in vista, tra i quali la principessa Taxis. Le collezioni del suo museo industriale sono state integrate nei fondi del Museo tecnico nazionale ▲ *316*. Oltre al gusto per la tecnologia, Náprstek si impegnò anche in favore del diritto di voto per le donne e per il loro diritto al lavoro. L'ultima passione di Náprstek, l'etnologia, rende illustre il museo della casa "Dagli Halánek". Diversi amici esploratori (Holub, Hloucha, Kořenský, Frič, Vraz...) gli offrirono le collezioni degli oggetti che costituiscono oggi il fondo dell'attuale Museo etnografico Náprstek: maschere, armi ecc.

Ex Dům odborů

Da Betlémské náměstí prendete la Průchodní, che sbocca sulla Bartolomějská. Realizzata dall'architetto Alois Dryák (1871-1932) nel 1925, l'ex casa dei sindacati è stata la sede delle riunioni dei comunisti cechi a partire dal 1945. Klement Gottwald ● *39* vi preparò la sua scalata al potere, nel 1948; in seguito l'edificio divenne la sede della pubblica sicurezza e numerosi oppositori del regime vi subirono severi interrogatori.

Jezuitský konvikt

Collezioni
Il Museo Náprstek raccoglie numerosi pezzi provenienti dall'Africa: sopra, una maschera della Nuova Guinea e, in alto, tamburi della stessa origine.

"Questa vecchia Praga con i suoi passaggi, dalle case che sbucano su due o tre strade, dai passaggi coperti che

si collegano così bene l'uno all'altro che si possono attraversare quartieri interi senza mai uscire all'aperto.**"**
Roger Grenier

Al n. 11, di fronte all'ex casa dei sindacati, s'innalza un antico collegio gesuitico che fa angolo con la Průchodní. Nel Medioevo tutta l'area era assai povera e infestata dalla prostituzione; i Cistercensi vi edificarono un monastero, il Convitto, che i Gesuiti acquistarono nel 1660.
Ex sala da concerto. Il complesso conventuale è ora in restauro. Negli anni Venti del XX secolo fu adibito a cinema. Tra le sue pareti consumate dal salnitro risuonava ancora l'eco di melodie musicali: a metà del XIX secolo, il Convitto ospitava infatti la migliore sala da concerto di Praga. Nel 1798 vi si poté ascoltare Beethoven (Tomášek ne raccontò poi il successo), che suonò il suo *Concerto, Opera 15 in do maggiore*, "l'adagio e il rondò grazioso in la maggiore, Opera 2" e improvvisò sul duetto tra Annio e Servilia nella *Clemenza di Tito* di Mozart: "*Ah tu fosti il primo oggetto*". Replicò il suo concerto e "fondò un'accademia". Nel 1836 la sala perse il suo primato a vantaggio di quella dell'isola Slava ▲ *302*, ma restò comunque in funzione sino all'inizio del XX secolo e ancora vi si poterono ascoltare Hans von Bülow, Rubinstein, Veniawski e molti altri, fra i quali i celebri violinisti cechi Ondříček e Laub. Josef Suk vi rappresentò il proprio ciclo per piano, *Fra la vita e la morte*. Il 5 febbraio 1840 fu proprio al Convitto che si svolse il primo ballo "patriottico" ceco ● *53*, organizzato da J.K. Tyl ▲ *280*. Nel 1859 vi si tenne il primo concerto dell'associazione Männergesangverein che nel 1861, poiché la maggioranza

first concert given by the Männergesangverein; in 1861, this group was renamed the Česká beseda as most of its members were Czechs. The concert hall was housed in the former refectory of an establishment with another claim to fame. It was once the famous Organ School which replaced the School of Composition, as the Music Conservatoire founded in 1811 was devoted exclusively to instrumental playing. The majority of Czech composers from the time of Smetana onward worked here.

ROTUNDA OF THE HOLY CROSS ★

Bartolomějská Street runs into Karoliny Street, a road that takes its name from the writer Karolina Světlá who was born in the House "Of the Three Kings"(U tří králů) (no. 3) in 1830. She was a great admirer of George Sand, and was influenced by the city of Prague, and later by northern Bohemia. The Rotunda of the Holy Cross is also in this street. This 12th-century church, one of the few Romanesque buildings left in Prague ● 68, was saved from demolition and was restored between 1864 and 1876 to plans by Vojtěch Ignác Ullmann ▲ 184; the interior was decorated around the same time by Waschmann, and contains vestiges of Gothic mural paintings.

FORMER TRADE UNION BUILDING
The bas-reliefs on this building recall the inspiration of Proletarian Realism that was fashionable around 1920.

ST BARTHOLOMEW'S CHURCH
This church is attached to the former Jesuit College, and was built by Kilián Ignác Dientzenhofer between 1725 and 1731. It is currently being restored. The lavishly decorated main façade overlooks the College courtyard. The church was pulled down after 1773, but was restored in 1854 on the instructions of the Grey Sisters. The paintings on the vaults are by Václav Vavřinec Reiner.

Jungmann Square

Church of Our-Lady-of-the-Snows. This church where Jan Želivský ▲ 308 once preached was one of Charles IV's foundations. It is also the tallest building in the city, and yet is no more than the choir of a building constructed between 1379 and 1397 specifically to be the venue of Charles IV's coronation. Religious wars delayed the construction of both the nave and the façade, which were never ultimately built, although the vault of the choir was redone in the 16th century. The south face of the convent is marked by a very pleasant garden which belongs to the Franciscan monastery to which the church is attached.

Monument to Josef Jungmann. Jungmann Square (Jungmannovo náměstí) This square contains not only a remarkable Cubist street lamp (opposite) but also a monument to the memory of Josef Jungmann. This sculpture, executed in 1878 by Ludvik Šimek, commemorates one of the major figures of the National Awakening Movement ● 28. Jungmann was convinced that Czech could establish itself as a language for poets and intellectuals, just like French and German, and in 1835 published a five-volume *Czech-German Dictionary* which was to become an essential tool for anyone seeking to understand and use the Czech language. For each word, Jungmann and his team produced a literary history which referred to medieval and Baroque usage, and when there was no word to express an idea, they looked for one in Polish or Russian or in other Slav languages. Similar linguistic research was also adopted by many mathematicians, philosophers and physicians.

Above: Mosaic on the door to the Church of Our-Lady-of-the-Snows, and an interior view of the church which contains the biggest high altar in Prague.

Josef Jungmann (1773–1847) Jungmann believed that the great expressive powers of the Czech language placed it on a par with the monuments of world literature. Accordingly, he translated Shakespeare, Molière, Voltaire, Schiller and Goethe, in addition to his greatest successes, Chateaubriand's *Atala* and Milton's *Paradise Lost*.

Urbánek House

This building at no. 30 Jungmannova ul. belonging to the Urbánek publishing house used to be called the "Mozarteum"; it was constructed by Jan Kotěra between 1911 and 1913. Although the architect only used quite modest bricks, he managed to bring the façade to life by means of a number of subtle decorative touches. In the 1920's, the large concert hall was used for conferences that were addressed by specialists in Functionalist architecture including Oud, Gropius, Le Corbusier, Ozenfant and Loos, and by Jan Kotěra, the leading representative of this trend in Prague.

Adria Palace

This building by Joseph Zasche ▲ 170 and Pavel Janák (1923–5) ▲ 197, 223 is a fine example of the inventiveness of Prague's architects at the beginning of

> "I am sitting in the café next to the window; outside the snow is falling. Národní Avenue is decorated with swastikas, . . . the police are there, and in the street the German motorized army parades past."
>
> Jiří Mucha

the 20th century. They took their inspiration directly from the Venetian palazzi of the Italian Renaissance. It was commissioned by an Italian insurance company, the Riunione Adriatica di Sicurtà.

SECESSION GALLERY ★ ● 82. The Adria Palace's Secession gallery is lit up at night, and is probably one of the most beautiful in Prague. The mosaics on the floor are in the three colors of Czechoslovakia: red, blue and white.

ZA BRANOU II THEATER. Nowadays, the Adria Palace hosts a wide range of activities, including a terrace café and the ZA BRANOU II THEATER. The owner and director, Otomar Krejča, has been a prominent figure in Prague theater life since the 1950's. The theater was closed down by the authorities in 1972, but it resumed business with the return of democracy and, by way of celebration, was renamed Za Branou II.

HLÁVKOVY DOMY
The backs of the neo-Renaissance houses in Vodičkova Street are adorned with sgraffito ● 79. The drawings (above), on a black background, depict allegorical themes of work.

NÁRODNÍ AVENUE

For many years, Národní Avenue (Národní třída), or National Avenue, was known as "Ferdinandstrasse". Since 1781, it has marked the boundary between Staré Město and Nové Město, and it follows the route of one of the town's former defensive moats.

MAJ STORE. The building occupied by the Maj Store was designed in 1970 by Miroslav Masák, Johnny Eisler and Martin Rajniš, a group of architects working under the name "Sial 02". Since the Velvet Revolution, Maj has belonged to the American chain, K-mart.

ALBATROS PUBLISHING HOUSE. Albatros, a publisher of children's books, is opposite the Maj Store. This building has replaced a neoclassical structure which once housed the CAFÉ UNION ● 59 on the

ZA BRANOU THEATER
The entrance to the Za Branou Theater in the gallery of Adria Palace has adopted the forms and decorative devices of the Secession ● 88.

second floor. Albatros was very well known at the beginning of the 20th century, and attracted many writers, artists and scientists. In particular, members of the "Devětsil" Group used to go there. As the writer Jaroslav Seifert has so aptly put it, "We spent hours on end in cafés that overlooked the street, and we neglected neither circuses nor panoptics. It was all in line with our new artistic program – when art had ceased to be art, when Malevich brought figurative art to an end with his square abstract paintings."

PRAHA INSURANCE COMPANY
Of all the commissions given to the architect Osvald Polívka ▲ *176* by the city of Prague, the Praha Insurance Company building is the most successful. With a skilful use of symmetry, Polívka articulates the façade with windows and balconies, and the colored decoration of the surface is adorned with masterful attic sculptures by Ladislav Šaloun. Above: architect's plan (1903).

KAŇKA HOUSE

This small building at 16 Národní Avenue is without question one of the oldest in the road. Kaňka House – it takes its name from the architect who designed it – dates from 1730 and boasts a Baroque façade lavishly adorned with stucco decoration. Beneath the recently restored arches (opposite, right) is a plaque commemorating the great demonstration of November 17, 1989 which, in the course of the few days that followed, led to the Velvet Revolution ● *29* ▲ *173*.

ST URSULA'S CHURCH

URSULINE CONVENT. St Ursula's Church, which was built by Marcantonio Canevale (1652–1711) between 1702 and 1704, once belonged to an Ursuline convent built thirty years earlier to plans by the same architect.
INTERIOR. Before the Dientzenhofers ▲ *251* carried out their great

works, the nave of St Ursula's was the first example of the type of nave with pilasters that was to become extremely popular in Prague's High Baroque period ● *70*. A number of statues, particular those of Saint Jude Thaddeus and Saint Philip and the statues on the high altar (1709–10), are by FRANTIŠEK PREISS. Preiss (c. 1660–1712) ▲ *163*, a pupil of Jan Kohl, was among the first to welcome Roman art when it was brought to Prague by Ottavio Mosto. To the left of the high altar, there is an *Assumption of the Virgin* by Petr Brandl (1668–1739), the painter who conclusively represented the high point of Baroque painting in Bohemia.

FORMER PRAHA INSURANCE COMPANY BUILDING

This building at 7 Národní Avenue was designed by Osvald

Polívka for the Praha Insurance Company. The façade is, for once, significantly influenced by the Viennese Secession, and is decorated with complex figurative motifs and sculptures by Ladislav Šaloun. Šaloun (1870–1946) was a member of the Mánes Society ▲ *303* and one of the most active representatives of the Secession Movement ● *86* in Prague. He executed the decoration depicting the three stages of life on the façade of the Praha Insurance Company building, but he was also responsible for the monument to John Huss ▲ *146* and the reliefs framing the entrance to the new Town Hall in Old Town ▲ *149*.

TOPÍČ HOUSE

Topíč House, at 9 Národní Avenue, is also the work of Osvald Polívka (1910). These two buildings, which stand side by side, express two contrasting visions of the Secession, with Topíč House presenting a more geometrical, more Germanic, version. Between the two world wars, it was owned by Borový, a celebrated publisher who specialized in French literature and who brought out editions of the work of all the great writers from the first few decades of the 20th century.

JOSEF ZÍTEK (1832–1909)
Josef Zítek was a celebrated exponent of neo-Renaissance style and, in his day, was one of the most highly regarded architects in Prague. The Rudolfinum is one of his greatest achievements ▲ *194*.

"The passengers ended up by getting off the trams which had come to a halt, and rejoining the procession which turned off at the corner by the National Theater. On the different floors of the Theater, and framed from head to foot in the golden light of the glass bays, the usherettes in their black dresses . . . waved their hands as a sign of their complicity."
Sylvie Germain

NATIONAL THEATER ★

This deeply symbolic building both represented and crowned the struggles of the Czech people to have their national culture recognized. Any music lover with a sense of Czech history will be as keen to see the National Theater as the Vltava.

PAID FOR BY THE PEOPLE. Theaters had been presenting shows in Czech since the end of the 17th century, but they had been few and far between. It followed that Czech people felt a profound need to have a theater they could call their own. In 1849, a decision was taken to build a National Theater, and donations came in from both Prague and the provinces – and, what is more, from all social classes. The German-dominated Estates of Bohemia refused to fund the project.

FOUNDATION STONE. In 1868, the "Committee for the Construction of the National Theater", the body charged with managing the money collected, felt that work could begin on the plans provided by Josef Zítek. The preparations aroused extraordinary collective enthusiasm and, on May 16, 1868, 50,000 people formed the procession that marched before the foundation stones brought from all the historic sites of Bohemia and Moravia. The first stone, which was laid by František Palacký ● *28*, came from Říp Hill where Čech, the Czech people's legendary ancestor, is said to paused in his travels. Jan Masaryk, the son of President Masaryk, once said of Čech, "That fool! Why did he have to set us down between the Germans and the Russians?"

A FIRE. However, the theater had hardly been completed when it burned down in July 1881 after only a dozen performances. The Czech people once again mobilized and, within two months, a subscription campaign collected enough money to rebuild the theater in two years. This time, the design was by one of Zítek's collaborators, Josef Schulz (1840–1917), architect of the National Museum ▲ *175* and the Museum of Decorative Arts ▲ *195*. Schulz's masterpiece combines monumentalism and a range of other effects, the first level being decorated with bosses, while the remainder are punctuated with Corinthian pilasters and crowned with a dome. Each façade is designed with the setting and the angles in mind: for instance, the loggia overlooking Národní Avenue is decorated with statues of Apollo and the nine Muses by Bohuslav Schnirch.

THE "NATIONAL THEATER GENERATION". The job of decorating the interior of the National Theater enthused Prague's artists to such an extent that they came to be known as the "National Theater Generation". They included MIKOLÁŠ ALEŠ (1852–1913), the most celebrated of the group, who executed the scenes inspired by Smetana's *Má vlast* on the fourteen lunettes in the Grand Foyer. He was held in contempt by official institutions run by the Germans and, in a bid to stir up a polemic, was elected President of the Mánes Society ▲ *303*. His interest in popular art gained him much credibility among the younger artists of the Secession. VOJTĚCH HYNAIS (1854–1925) was greatly inspired by French Symbolism – he studied at the School of Fine Arts in Paris from 1878 to 1880 – and went on to enjoy an international career; he also taught

MAGIC LANTERN
In this production at the National Theater, the lively performance given by actors, singers and dancers is accompanied by music, kinetic scenes and projections, including film. The result is a unique spectacle.

National Theater poster advertising Dvořák's *Rusalka* ● *46*.

"LIBUŠE"
Poster for Bedřich Smetana's famous opera.

many Secession artists. For the National Theater, he painted the four allegories of the Seasons in the ladies' restroom and the décor on the main curtain ● 55. Other members of the "Generation" were less well known; they included Václav Brožík, another artist trained in Paris, who executed the historic compositions in the men's restroom, and Julius Mařák, who did the paintings of towns that adorn the corridors. The sculptures are by Myslbeck, Antonín Wagner ▲ 175 and Bohuslav Schnirch.

BEDŘICH SMETANA AND THE NATIONAL THEATER.
Smetana's life was intimately linked to that of the National Theater. On his return from Sweden in 1861, Smetana ● 47 threw himself into the political and musical struggle surrounding it. When the foundation stone was laid on May 16, 1868, the very date on which his national opera *Dalibor* was first performed, Smetana announced that "the future of the Czech people is in music. . ." and "Father of the Fatherland" historian František Palacký ● 28 declared that, with its National Theater, the nation truly existed and would never die. Work was started on the site of a former saltworks where the Provisional Theater (1862) had already been built. The two buildings merged in 1883 and they were officially opened on November 18. For the foundation stone ceremony, Smetana composed a solemn *Prelude* and a chorus dedicated to the Czech peasantry as a tribute to the villagers who, in the darkest hours for the Czech language and music, had put up most of the money for the theater and its maintenance. The National Theater was reopened on November 18, 1983 and, just as a century earlier, the occasion was marked by a performance of Smetana's historical-cum-mythological opera *Libuše*.

LEOŠ JANÁČEK. The National Theater's repertoire permitted the great Czech composers to give full voice to their lyric inspiration. One of these, Leoš Janáček (1854–1928), was not a citizen of Prague, but he was nonetheless recognized as a great Czech musician. While in the capital during 1874–5, he spent all his time at the School of Organists, but otherwise lived most of his life in Brno. However, it was at the National Theater that his opera *Jenufa*, written in 1903 and poorly received in Brno, was first performed in

Above: the small sitting room of the Presidential Box at the National Theater.

"Prague's National Theater has a history of long struggles, untiring perseverance, and the final triumph of a nation for which it symbolizes art and literature."
Louis Léger

NÁRODNÍ DIVADLO
Today, Prague boasts over twenty theaters, but the National Theater is still without question the best in the country. The repertoire includes operas and plays as well as ballet and concerts.

> "The theater . . . must be the spiritual home of the period."
>
> Václav Havel

1916. Having finally achieved recognition at the age of sixty, Janáček now worked without pause and, in the space of a dozen years, produced some of the most important works in the Czech canon. They include *Taras Bulba* (1915–18), the *Sinfonietta* (1926), the *Glagolithic Mass* (1926), and his operas *Kat'a Kabanova* (1919–21), *The Makropulos Affair* (1923–5) and *From the House of the Dead* (1927–8) after Dostoievsky. Janáček's music struggles relentlessly to express emotions as directly as possible, a risky strategy as the libretti are often extremely dramatic. His orchestration demands from musicians the suppleness and veracity in which the orchestras of Prague are unrivaled.

DÉCOR AT THE NATIONAL THEATER
As a member of the "National Theater Generation", František Ženíček decorated the auditorium and the main foyer with allegories of the arts; the exceptions were the lunettes. Above: The ceiling of the theater.

MAGIC LANTERN. For its centenary, the National Theater was completely restored and modernized, and it was also provided with a new stage called the "New Stage". It houses the famous Magic Lantern where musical performances are occasionally given. The Magic Lantern is very well known abroad, and enjoyed considerable success at the Universal Exhibition in Brussels in 1958, and then in Montreal. Its performances are based on a wide range of artistic genres, and it makes use of all the technical possibilities offered by drama and cinematography. Magic Lantern programs are devised in such a way as to appeal to, and be comprehensible to, foreign audiences.

OPERA TO THE FORE. As the National Theater concentrates on the Czech repertoire, the practise is for the company to alternate with a resident company. Famous names from the world of opera to have performed here include Ema Destinnová, Karel Burián, O. Mařak, Antonín Vávra, Josef Lev and Karel Strakatý, and directors and conductors such as Karel Kovařovic, Otakar Ostřcil and, in particular, Václav Talich, who conducted triumphant performances of Bohuslav Martinů's *Julietta* ▲ 267 in 1938. Star performers since World War Two have included Ivo Žídek, Karel Bermann, Karel Pruša, Vilém Přybil, Beno Blachut, Věra Soukupová, Gabriela Beňáčhová and Peter Dvorský, and the conductors Břetislav Bakala, Jaroslav Krumholc, Bohumil Gregor, Zdeněk Košler and František Jílek. The Estates Theater is administratively and artistically linked to the National Theater and, for the most part, concentrates on a theatrical repertoire.

BEDŘICH SMETANA
Smetana's name is more closely associated with the National Theater.

Center: costume for Smetana's opera, *The Devil's Wall*.

THE PERENNIAL CAFÉ SLAVIA ✪
On the corner of Národní Street and Smetana Quay, opposite the National Theater, is the Café Slavia. Once the favorite haunt of the intelligentsia and of artists, it has seen the passing of many years, the very air imbued with memories of the past. Its newly restored Art Deco interior is an attraction in itself (the toilets are especially worth seeing). The green lighting and the painting on the far wall pay tribute to all the absinthe that is consumed there. Meals are served at all hours, although the simple pleasure of enjoying a pastry is as you watch the river flow by is equally attractive.

Right: the Café Slavia, the 1992 student stronghold, and below: decoration detail.

LAŽANSKÝ PALACE ★

At no. 3 Národní třída is the Czechoslovak Academy of Sciences, a neo-Renaissance building by Vojtěch Ullmann (1858–61) ▲ *184, 289*, who was also responsible for the Lažanský Palace at no. 1. This neo-Renaissance palace in the French style was built between 1861 and 1863 for Count Prokop Lažanský to plans by Ullmann on land occupied by baths in the 14th century and then by a hospital belonging to the Brothers of the Cross. Between 1863 and 1869 it was the home of Bedřich Smetana ● *47*, and it was here that he composed two of his most famous operas, *The Bartered Bride* (1866) and *Dalibor* (1868). The building now houses the Academy of Fine Arts, and for many years the famous Café Slavia was on the first floor.

CAFÉ SLAVIA. Prague has innumerable cafés ● *58* and, in 1910, around the time of the National Awakening, it is estimated that there were as many 1,500. During that period all polemical texts, manifestos and speeches were written in cafés. From the 1930's onward, the Café Slavia became the favorite haunt of the progressive intelligentsia, and later of the dissidents. Closed for a long time, it was restored at great expense and reopened in 1997. Its décor has not been altered much and is still a favorite with the people of Prague.

Around
Charles Square

1. CHARLES SQUARE 2. TOWN HALL 3. TRINITY CHURCH 4. DIAMOND HOUSE

🕐 **One day**
◆ **D** B2-B3-C2-C3-C4-D4

Masaryk Quay at the beginning of the 20th century.

MASARYK QUAY ★

Masaryk Quay (Masarykovo nábřeží) is breathtaking, particularly when the sun is setting over Petřín Hill and the evening light lingers on the façades of the houses along the quay. It was entirely rebuilt in the early years of the 20th century by the greatest architects of the day. Until 1990, it was called Gottwaldovo nábřeží after the first Communist President of the Czechoslovakian Council. From the offices of the Goethe Institute at no. 32 as far as the neo-Baroque building on the corner of the quay and Jiráskovo náměstí, there is not a single façade that is not outstanding in one way or another, despite the profusion of styles ranging from neo-Renaissance and neo-Baroque to Art Nouveau. Strictly speaking, these are not historic houses as such; the Quay is simply a magnificent architectural complex overlooking the Vltava.

No. 32. This fine structure, built for a bank by Jiří Stribal in 1905, marries Secession and neo-Baroque styles and is adorned with external

The façade of the Goethe Institute.

decorations by Ladislav Šaloun. It was the site of the East German Embassy until 1990, and has since been turned into the Goethe Institute.

Nos. 30, 28, 26 and 22. No. 30 is another neo-Baroque building dating from 1905 but, with its strange pediment, is not entirely lacking in Baroque elements. The figurative panels depict modern scenes. The unusually elegant house at no. 28 is by Matěj Blecha (1904–5) ▲ *175, 192, 310*; no. 26, by Kamil Hilbert, has a fine entrance with stained-glass windows; and no. 22 recalls the Renaissance with two distinct kinds of windows: Czech designs on the fourth and fifth floors, and Italian for the sixth floor with arches resting on small columns.

No. 16. A plaque states that the building was constructed on plans by Josef Fanta for Hlahol, a celebrated Czech singing club that played a key role in the nationalist politics of the late 19th century. The club's conductors included Smetana in 1863, Bendl from 1865 to 1877, and Knittl from 1877 to 1903. The mosaics and the entrances are very elegantly worked. Hlalol soon merged with the Circle of Artists (Umělecká beseda), a body founded in 1863 to represent Czech music and to counter the Deutsches Casino (1862).

MASARYK QUAY, AN ARCHITECTURAL DELIGHT ✪
This quay is named in honor of the first President of the Czech Republic. The extraordinary diversity of the façades and the contrasting colors of the houses that line it do not detract from the striking harmony of the whole, so that a walk along the quay is a visual treat. On Slav Island, a little way off the center of the quay, is the renowned Mánes Gallery, specializing in modern art. For a rest after visiting the gallery, there are benches along the Vltava or the pleasure of a peaceful boat ride on the river.

Façades on Masaryk Quay.

General view of Slav Island.

SLAV ISLAND (SLOVANSKÝ OSTROV, ŽOFÍN)

A MUSICAL ISLAND. Originally known as Sophia Island, after the Archduchess Sophia, the mother of Franz Joseph, Slav Island has always been famous for the society balls and the concerts that were held in its 400-seater hall after 1840. Many great soloists and composers have performed there, including Berlioz in 1846, and later Liszt. An Academy of Music founded here in 1840 by Alois Jelen was inaugurated by a rendering of Václav Tomášek's *Coronation Mass* and, on his return from Sweden, Smetana conducted a performance of his three symphonic poems, *Richard III*, *Wallensteins Lager* and *Hakon Jarl*. The city of Prague purchased Sophia Island in 1884, and since then it has been used for dances and sporting and folk events. It declined in importance after the opening of the Rudolfinum ▲ *194* in 1885 and even more so after the Town Hall ▲ *164* was built.

SLAV CONGRESS. The hall is currently being restored. The island's modern name is a reminder that this was the venue of the pan-Slav Congress of June 1848 ● *28*; the meeting was cut short by an uprising in the city that was brutally put down by the Austrian General Windischgrätz.

ZDENĚK FIBICH. It was here, in the late 19th century, that the composer Zdeněk Fibich ● *47* met Anežka Schulzová, a woman of letters who became his pupil and librettist. The famous *Poems of Fibich* is a testament to their love affair.

RODIN EXHIBITION
The ´Mánes Gallery organized an important Rodin retrospective in 1902. The exhibition was to have a remarkable impact, if only because it established Rodin as a major figure in Prague, and opened up a new world for Czech artists ▲ *304*. It was most enthusiastically received. Rodin exhibited ninety-eight sculptures, including his superb *Balzac*, and seventy-five drawings. Above: the gallery's former home, and Auguste Rodin surrounded by Czech artists, including Alfons Mucha standing to his right.

MÁNES GALLERY

The design of this Functionalist building seems slightly anachronistic in a locality abundant with the splendors of so many neo-styles and the Secession; the explanation is that it was built very late. The Mánes Gallery was constructed in 1923–32 by Otakar Novotný ▲ *185*, an adherent of Rigorist Modernism. The first gallery was situated in the Kinský Gardens at the foot of Petřín Hill, but was pulled down shortly before World War One and replaced by the present building. The tower has nothing to do with the gallery: it is part of the Šítkovsky Water Tower (opposite). The building is now the premises of the Union of Artists, and a café and a restaurant on the side facing the river offer lovely views.

MÁNES SOCIETY. This society was founded in 1887, and brought together those teachers and students from Prague's Academy of Fine Arts and School of Applied Arts who yearned to disturb the slumber into which official art had fallen. The society's organ was a monthly review called *Volné Směry* (*Free Trends*) that first appeared in 1896; it was an important forum for ideas and became very well known. The Mánes Society also played a key role in the opening up of Czech art to modernist thinking and to cosmopolitan currents, and its major exhibitions ▲ *304* were very important events.

ST ADALBERT'S CHURCH

St Adalbert's stands in Vojtěšská Street, and was built in the 13th century; it was given two naves in 1370, renovated in the Baroque manner in 1720–30, and then restored in 1885–91. The church is of little interest except for the fact that it is dedicated to one of Bohemia's most important patron saints and, in the 19th century, was the scene of great music-making.

SAINT ADALBERT. Adalbert (Vojtěch) was born into the Slavník family, one of the most powerful in eastern Bohemia. He became Prague's first bishop in 973, but was forced into exile in Rome after his entire family was murdered. He was

A SECOND MAJOR EXHIBITION
The Edvard Munch exhibition of 1905 was also held at the Mánes Gallery. It was the occasion of another "esthetic" revolution ▲ *304* which produced an entire generation of Czech Expressionists.

ŠÍTKOVSKY WATER TOWER
This is one of four water towers which supply Nové Město's public fountains and taverns with water. This Gothic construction was redesigned in the Renaissance style; the onion dome was added only at the end of the 18th century.

SOPHIA PAVILION
The Sophia (Žofín) Pavilion, a dance and concert hall, was built on Sophia Island in 1837. It became an important center of the city's social and cultural life and, from 1841 onward, was the venue for the most celebrated of the Czech patriotic balls ● *52*.

At the beginning of the 19th century, Prague was in rebellious mood under the influence of the Viennese Secession. At the same time the city was straining to adapt Secession to its own traditions and myths. Furthermore, Prague was trying to thwart Austria's cultural domination by seeking models elsewhere in Europe, particularly in France. After the Great War, German Dadaism and Italian Futurism had a certain impact on the formation of an emerging Czech artistic consciousness. However, Paris remained th source of all innovation; only Moscow, the symbol of the October Revolution and of bold experimentation in all the arts, represented any form of counterweight to the influence wielded by Paris.

PARIS: THE SOURCE OF ARTISTIC REVOLUTION

Auguste Rodin's major retrospective organized by the Mánes Society in 1902 was the first of a series of events establishing the predominance of French creativity. Czech Cubism was born in 1910, and the "Plasticians", a group that included artists and architects, launched their *Art Monthly* around the same time. The "Plasticians" included Picasso, Friesz,

Derain, Braque and Gris in their 1912 exhibitions, and the Paris School in their 1914 exhibition.

THE EMERGENCE OF SURREALISM

The arrival of Josef Šima in Paris in 1921, and of other Czech artists shortly afterward, strengthened links with André Breton's group and with circles that grew out of Surrealism. The Czech Surrealist group was formed in May 1934 even before translations of Breton's books went on sale in Prague.

THE AVANT GARDE

Both the tragedy of war and national independence brought about huge changes in the artistic and literary life of Prague's intelligentsia. The Tvrdošijní (Obstinate) group came out boldly against established values; the "Devětsil" Group was founded in 1920 ● 59.

EDVARD MUNCH

Prague's more creative artists were never going to be satisfied with an influence as exclusive as that of the French. They were overwhelmed with enthusiasm for Edvard Munch's paintings in 1905, and later on observed the developments of Expressionism in Germany with passionate interest. Czech Cubism owes its originality to its Expressionist past which counterbalanced Cézanne's formalism.

BOHUMIL KUBIŠTA
Self-portrait March 17 1910 by the best-known exponent of Czech Cubism.

Poster for an exhibition of the Independents in Prague in 1910.

MOSCOW: THE OTHER SOURCE OF INSPIRATION

When Roman Jakobson was sent to Prague with the Soviet Legation as Press Attaché, he sought to build bridges between the Czech capital and the capital of the fledgling USSR. He became the propagandist of Russian Futurism. In 1921, he published *New Russian Poetry. First Sketch* in Prague, although not in Moscow, and introduced the works of Mayakovsky and Khlebnikov. He was close to the group of Poetists and, in Karel Teige, the instigator of the Czech Surrealist Group, he found a fervent supporter of Constructivism. Teige tried hard, but with little success, to convince his painter, sculptor and architect friends to follow the path of Malevich and Rodchenko.

ST ADALBERT'S CHURCH
Views of the interior and exterior. The vaulting is Gothic.

martyred while on a journey to convert Prussians in 997. Saint Adalbert is also the patron saint of Poland and Hungary.

A MUSICAL CHURCH. St Adalbert's Church is well known to musicians for its associations with the composers Josef Foerster and Antonín Dvořák. In the 19th century Foerster (1833–1907), the church's choirmaster and organist, introduced Gregorian chant and the music of Palestrina in the 19th century, and foreign musicians, including Saint-Saëns, never failed to come and listen when they were passing through. Dvořák, too, worked here: between 1874 and 1877, while still poor and little known, he earned small sums playing the organ. Josef Bohuslav Foerster (1859–1951), ● 47, ▲ 276, also a composer, succeeded his father from 1882 to 1888.

FOERSTER MUSEUM. The presbytery at 17 Pětrošsová Street is a fine Baroque building, and the staircase is worth a visit for the trompe l'oeil painted by Johann Hoffmann in 1778. The building now houses the Foerster Museum. Josef Bohuslav Foerster was a very active man: he was a composer, a noted critic and the organist at St Adalbert's and choirmaster at Our-Lady-of-the-Snows. After teaching for a few years in Vienna, he returned to Prague where, from 1919 onward, he taught at the Conservatory. He wrote a large number of symphonies and concertos, but his greatest skill lay in choral compositions and in operas, the best remembered of which is *Eva*.

Late 15th-century Gothic statue of the Virgin of Zderaz on an altar in St Adalbert's Church.

U FLEKŮ TAVERN ★

Of Prague's innumerable taverns, the U Fleků (Křemencova 11) is undoubtedly the most famous. Its reputation also extends far beyond the boundaries of the Czech Republic. Since 1499, the U Fleků has dispensed a famous dark beer called *flekovský ležák* ● 61.

CHURCH OF ST CYRIL AND ST METHODIUS

This Baroque church (Kostel sv Cyrila a Metoděje), initially dedicated to Saint Carlo Borromeo, was built by Kilián Ignác Dientzenhofer (1730–6). Pavel Ignác Bayer painted the ceiling fresco depicting the life of Carlo Borromeo. The church served as a place of worship for those who lived in the adjoining house, a group of old priests who had retired from diocesan work in Bohemia. This had been founded in 1681, but it was pulled down by Joseph II in 1783. The church was not used during the first Republic until 1935, when it was handed over to the Czech Orthodox Church and rededicated to Cyril and Methodius. These two holy men first came to Grand Moravia from Thessalonika in 863, translated liturgical books into Old Slav and developed a Glagolithic alphabet.

ASSASSINATION OF HEYDRICH. This church has the unhappy distinction of being the last hiding place of the members of the Resistance who killed Reichsprotektor Reinhard Heydrich

> "The great brewer handed me a pint of orange beer,
> a pint overflowing with a rush of steam bubbles."
>
> Bohumil Hrabal

U FLEKŮ
All the buildings that make up the tavern, together with the dining rooms and the garden lined with arches, are carefully looked after. The rooms are decorated with frescos and carved wood, and each one has a different name.

(below) on May 26, 1942 ● *39*. This led to violent reprisals, including the seizure of 10,000 hostages and the annihilation of the inhabitants of the village of Lidice and the tiny hamlet of Ležáky (all the men were murdered and the women and children were deported). Heydrich's assassination had been ordered by the government-in-exile in London as a way of establishing the Czech Resistance's identity; the Nazis threatened to murder one Czech in ten and promised to reward anyone who would denounce Heydrich's killers. The parachutists responsible for the assassination took refuge in the crypt, and eventually died there. The Czech orthodox Bishop Gorazo, who had given them shelter, was also executed by the Germans.

St Wenceslas' Church

St Wenceslas' (sv. Václav na Zderaze) is close to the Church of St Cyril and St Methodius, but the main door opens onto Dittrichova Street. It is extremely old, founded before 1180, and was a parish church by the late 13th century. In the nave and tower are Romanesque remains. Mělnický's 16th-century vault and the choir were redone in the 17th century by the Augustinians.

MEMORIES OF THE RESISTANCE
A commemorative plaque and innumerable bullet marks on the façade

of the Church of St Cyril and St Methodius recall the tragic events of 1942.

● *26.* When the sermon was over, the crowd marched behind the preacher to Nové Město Town Hall to call for the release of citizens imprisoned for their Hussite sympathies. When they were refused, three councillors and seven members of the Prague bourgeoisie were thrown from the windows by the people of Nové Město.

CHARLES SQUARE (KARLOVO NÁMĚSTÍ)

THE CENTER OF NOVÉ MĚSTO.

This square, the largest in Prague, is 1,700 feet long and 490 feet wide. When it was opened in 1348, it was effectively the center of New Town (Nové Město), which had been founded by Charles IV, and it was the site of the livestock market, one of three markets in the town. In May of each year, Charles had the Crown Jewels displayed in the middle of the Square, and then, after 1382, in the Corpus Christi Chapel, a church modeled on the Palatine in Aix-la-Chapelle, which was destroyed in 1791.

LAID OUT AS A GARDEN.

Between 1843 and 1863, the Square was turned into a public park divided into two sections by Ječná Street, a wide thoroughfare served by trams. It was dotted with statues of famous people, including V. Strunc, a scientist who discovered the uniqueness of fingerprints, the poet Vítězslav Hálek, Karolina Světlá and Eliška Krasnohorská, both women of letters, the naturalist Jan Evangelista Purk, and the botanist B. Roezl; lastly, there is the statue of the revolutionary Hussite priest, Jan Želivský, which dates from 1960.

At the top of the page, a relief frieze with inscriptions:

ZDE ŽIL A ZEMŘEL JAN EV· PVRKYNĚ

VĚNOVÁNO SP·Č·LÉKAŘŮ A VM·BESEDOV·

NOVÉ MĚSTO TOWN HALL

This building occupies the entire north side of the square, but a distinction needs to be drawn between the east section (the old part of the Town Hall) and the west section (today the Law Courts). New Town's Town Hall (Novoměstská radnice) was founded before 1367 and built in 1377, and it was then rebuilt and enlarged between 1411 and 1418 under the supervision of Martin Friček and Master Kříž. The hall, on the first floor, with columns and two naves, dates from this period; it was turned into a marriage parlor in 1957. The tower was erected in 1452–6 and bears the Gothic emblems of Nové Město. After being frequently damaged by fire, the Town Hall was renovated in the 16th century when three pediments in the Renaissance style were added. After 1784, the year in which the towns of Prague were united in a single city, it was used as the Law Courts, offices and a prison. In 1905–6, Antonín Wiehl and Kamil Hilbert tried to restore the building's original appearance.

FOUNDING OF NOVÉ MĚSTO
The founding of New Town (Nové Město) was a key element in Charles IV's intention to develop the city. His plan was quite unique for the time, and is admirable even by today's standards. It is encircled by ramparts 2½ miles long and covers 890 acres, three times the size of Old Town, and for five hundred years, it was deemed large enough to contain the town's population. The old roads were retained, but new ones between 60 feet and 85 feet wide were constructed, forming crossroads at the huge market places. These were the livestock market and the horse market, both in Charles Square, and the hay market in Senovážné náměstí.

ST IGNATIUS' CHURCH (KOSTEL SV. IGNÁCE)

In 1623 Ferdinand II gave the Jesuits the Gothic Church of Corpus Christi in the center of Charles Square, along with the neighboring houses and land, on which they were to build a seminary. This Baroque building was constructed by Carlo Lurago from 1665 to 1670, then by Pavel Ignác Bayer to plans by Giovanni Domenico Orsi and modeled on the Gesù in Rome. The protruding, monumental façade is adorned with stucco decoration on the surfaces and various figures in the portico, and crowned with a radiant statue of Saint Ignatius, the founder of the Jesuit Order.

JESUIT COLLEGE

This college (Jezuitská kolej) was the third building that the Jesuits had constructed in Prague. A Baroque structure, and older than the church, it was built between 1658 and 1667 on the site of twenty-three houses and thirteen gardens. The restrained façade punctuated by pilasters is most impressive, and the two doors, which date from the 1760's, were designed by Jan Josef Wirch ▲ 226. In 1773, when the Order was abolished on the Pope's instructions, the College was closed and turned into a hospital. It was partly destroyed in an air raid in 1945, but was later meticulously reconstructed.

A FINE INTERIOR
Jan Jiří Heinsch's painting over the high altar is a glorification of Saint Ignatius; the vaulting of the first side chapel is frescoed with themes of the Last Judgement.

SPÁLENÁ STREET

DIAMOND HOUSE. Just before the other side of the square is Spálená ulice; a few yards along, on the corner with Lazarská Street, stands Diamond House, a Cubist building designed by Ladislav Sřívánek, Matěj Blecha and Antonín Pfeiffer in 1910–12. The monumental proportions and the stylization of the carved figures on the fourth floor recall the Babylonian elements that Blecha ▲ *175* used to such brilliant effect. The entrance is framed by two massive pilasters (above). Diamond House is connected to the Baroque Church of the Holy Trinity by a strange Cubist arch beneath which stands a statue of Saint John Nepomuk.

OLYMPIC BUILDING. This building, dating from 1923–7, was the first Functionalist construction to be seen in Prague. It brought its architect Jaromir Krejcar (1895–1949) immediate fame. Krejcar had started his career as a builder and site foreman, before studying under Kotěra ▲ *174*; he then worked for the Gocá agency until 1923 before launching his own business. As a member of the "Devětsil" Group ● *59*,

CUBIST ARCHITECTURE
"Blecha's little summer house – possibly designed together with Pfeiffer – contains an 18th-century statue of Saint John Nepomuk, just next to Diamond House. The symbiosis between the Cubist summer house and the Baroque sculpture is so subtle, so happy, that it proves that the relationship claimed by Cubists with the *genius loci* is sincere and viable."
Luca Quattrochi
The Secession

RUDOLPH II, A TORMENTED SOUL
Certain aspects of the King's behavior, which involved magic, were so extreme that many believed he was possessed by the devil. It was said that the very sight of the Cross provoked him to fits of hysteria.

he played an important role in the diffusion of Purist and Constructivist theories around Czechoslovakia.

U Nováků House

Vodičkova Street is on this side of the square and leads directly to U Nováků House. This neoclassical building was entirely renovated in the Art Nouveau style by Polívka ▲ *176* between 1902 and 1904. It was originally a large shop, but now contains a restaurant.

Faustus House

This house (Faustův dům) was renovated for the Mladotat ze Solopysk family in 1740–70 and is not unrelated to the mysterious Renaissance residence which, according to legend, was inhabited by no less a person than Dr Faustus (opposite). It is more than likely that the Devil would have come to look for him here, and there are even claims that it is still possible to see the hole in the roof through which he carried off one of his disciples. There are several Faustus Houses in Prague. On a more everyday level, the house was inhabited by several alchemists including the celebrated English adventurer, Edward Kelley. While in the employ of Rudolph II, he undertook to discover the philosopher's stone but, although the Emperor made him a "Knight of Imana", he nonetheless suffered a sorry fate. The King grew tired of waiting and threw him into prison (Kelley had already had his ears cut off in England after being found guilty of forgery). On his release, he died of poisoning.

PRAGUE, A CITY OF FANTASIES. Prague is enormously popular with writers of fantastic stories, both Czech and foreign. Many factors have contributed to the development of this trend over the centuries. The reign of Rudolph II (1576–1611) particularly enhanced the magic reputation of the city. The Emperor was prey to profound melancholia and even fits of madness, and sometimes actually figured in fantastic stories: an example is Mikhail Bulgakov's *The Master and Margarita* in which Rudolph is among the guests invited to Satan's Ball. A society as strange as that which surrounded Rudolph II, one in which astrologers, witches and alchemists mingled with truly learned men and practical jokers, was bound to have its Dr Faustus. Although he had lived in Germany in the late 15th and early 16th centuries, legend allows its hero to move freely in both time (by permitting him to live in two centuries) and space.

Mosaic in the insurance company Česka Pojistovna in Spálená Street.

U Nováků House
The façade is adorned with stucco, a profusion of wrought iron, and an immense mosaic representing an allegory of commerce and industry made after cartoons by Jan Preisler ● *87*. The first floor still has its glass canopies and splendid stained-glass windows. Apart from Novak establishments on two of the floors, this house was the home of the Liberated Theater ● *54* from 1924 to 1938. The U Nováků gallery links with the Lucerna and Rokoko galleries, and together they form one of the most important passageway complexes ● *82* in Prague.

EMMAUS MONASTERY (KLÁŠTER NA SLOVANECH) ★

SLAVONIAN LITURGY. This monastery was founded in 1348 by Charles IV who, with the support of Pope Clement VI, wanted to bring the Eastern and Western Churches closer together. Croatian Benedictines came to settle here as soon as the new monastery was completed in 1353; their job was to recopy the old Slav manuscripts and to perpetuate the memory of Slavonian, a language that they alone were authorized to use although they followed the Latin rite. In 1419, the Benedictines of Emmaus began to accept Hussitism and their monastery was saved; in 1445, they were allowed to renew the rules of their Order, and the monastery became the only one run by the Hussites. During the 16th century, the monastery was used by the sub-Utraquist Consistory, the Utraquists' highest council. After White Mountain ● 34, the monastery was passed over to Spanish Benedictines and then, in the 20th century, to another group from Beuron. The church was renovated in the Baroque manner in 1712, and in 1880 it was restored in an Early Gothic style. The roof was destroyed by bombing in 1945, but replaced in 1965–8 by modernistic spires. The building is now occupied by a number of Czech and European scientific institutes.

REGISTRUM SLAVORUM. The monastery rapidly became one of the most important cultural centers in Bohemia. In particular, it housed an outstanding scriptorium which produced a large number of works including the *Registrum Slavorum* in 1395. This register, which is also known as the "Slavonic Lectionary" and the "Coronation Service" of the Kings of France, consists of two separate books, the first in Cyrillic, the second in Glagolithic.

FRESCOS. The cloister frescos are rare vestiges of Prague's Gothic mural paintings because, during the Hussite Wars, and between 1419 and 1421 in particular, many churches were badly damaged and works of art destroyed. The cloister in Emmaüs Monastery was built in 1360. It is now in a poor state of repair, but iconographical evidence coincides with representations on numerous stained-glass windows: on the upper level is a scene from the New Testament; on the lower level, one from the Old Testament. The message is clear: the Old Testament is a

"REGISTRUM SLAVORUM"
This is the most valuable manuscript held in the Municipal Library of Rheims. The manuscript was brought here in the 16th century by the Cardinal of Lorraine, Archbishop and Duke of Rheims, and he offered it to the Treasury of Rheims Cathedral. From the time of Henry III onward, the kings of France took their vows on this lectionary.

prefiguration of the New Testament, and a number of stories from it anticipate various episodes from the life of Christ. The cycle is attributed to three artists, two of whom have been identified: Nikolaus Wurmser, a painter from Strasbourg, and Master Oswald, a painter at the Court of Charles IV. The third artist, who was responsible for the west and north wings, has still not been identified.

Above: external view of Emmaus Monastery; detail of a fresco; the interior of the Church of St-John-on-the-Rock.

CHURCH OF ST-JOHN-ON-THE-ROCK ★

This fine Baroque church (Kostel sv. Jana na Skalce) with its two steeples over the west façade was built in 1730 by Kilián Ignác Dientzenhofer. The beautiful, monumental, external staircase was executed by Schmidt in 1776–8 for a brotherhood of artisans in New Town. The statues on the façade are by Seeling and date from 1880, while Brokoff's statue of Saint John Nepomuk ▲ 233 on the high altar served as a model for the statue he made for Charles Bridge.

Manuscript in Cyrillic script.

NA SLUPI STREET

CHURCH OF OUR LADY OF THE ELIZABETHINES. Kilián Ignác Dientzenhofer built this church on the site of the summer palace of the Auxiliary Bishop J. Dlouhoveský z Dlouhé Vsi in 1724–5. The ST TEKLA CHAPEL next door boasts wonderful stucco decorations and a mural by Kracker depicting the life of Saint Tekla (1726).
CHURCH OF THE ANNUNCIATION. This church was built between 1360 and 1365, at the same time as the Servite

"St John Nepomuk keeps his right hand over us! May God grant us what he has given you, and may our language never rot in the grave!" These lines by the 19th-century writer Karel Havlíček-Borovský are known to every Czech.

BOTANICAL GARDEN
The Botanical Garden dates from 1845; it is really the university park, but is nonetheless open to the public. Although the Garden is quite small, there are delightful walks round the flowerbeds and greenhouses.

313

DVOŘÁK MUSEUM
Although Bedřich Smetana was the founder and standard bearer of the Czech School, Antonín Dvořák (1841–1904) is seen as the Czech composer par excellence. Better than any other, he expressed the relationship in the Czech Baroque tradition between the original characteristics of a form of music that was both national and universal. He was a brilliant composer of symphonies and chamber works, and in his oratorios he created a new tradition that has survived to this day.

Magnificent decoration in the Karlov Church.

Monastery. It was founded by Charles IV, and is an interesting example of the restrained Gothic churches of the second half of the 14th century. It has a tower and a square nave with a vault supported by a single pillar. This former convent, which was rebuilt in the neo-Gothic style by Grueber in 1858, now houses a medical research institute.

VILLA AMERIKA ★

This house, best known as the "Villa Amerika", was originally a very beautiful summer pavilion which Kilián Ignác Dientzenhofer built for Count Michna of Vacinov on his return from Vienna in 1717. The interior design is particularly interesting for Johann Ferdinand Schor's frescos of 1720; the sculptures in the garden come from Braun's workshop. The villa is now the Dvořák Museum and recounts the composer's life through a range of personal belongings, including his viola and piano, as well as photographs of his public and private life and his works. Concerts are sometimes given here.

OUR-LADY-OF-THE-ASSUMPTION-AND-THE-EMPEROR-CHARLEMAGNE (KARLOV)

This building has a most unusual appearance with its red roof and huge surbased cupola. After being founded by Charles IV in 1350, it was dedicated to Charlemagne and was intended to be an imitation of the Imperial Chapel in Aix-la-Chapelle. Only the masonry from this period survives. In 1575, Bonifác Wohlmut surmounted the church with a cupola 80 feet in diameter and in the form of an eight-pointed star. Like most churches in Prague, it was restored in the Baroque manner, and then renovated mainly by Kaňka in 1733–8.

SCALA SANTA. Only a few years earlier in 1798, Santini-Aichl constructed the *Scala Santa*, a series of steps which pilgrims had to climb on their knees. The interior decoration is a perfect example of Baroque theatricality, with the balconies adorned with lifelike pictures and polychrome statues depicting the life of Christ.

The outskirts

TROJA CASTLE

✈ AIRPORT

STROMOVKA PARK

LETNÁ

BŘEVNOV ABBEY

←WHITE MOUNTAIN

VILLA BERTRAMKA

Vynohrady

VYŠEHRAD CONVENT

ZBRASLAV

LETNÁ

From the vast Letná plateau, which is best approached along Paris Avenue ▲ *190* and Svatopluk Bridge, there are fine views out over Prague and the Vltava. The very edge of Letná overhangs the river, and from 1858 this part was laid out as a park. More remote sections were used for military maneuvers until the end of the 19th century. During the last century, sports facilities were also added, and after 1948 Letná was used for Spartakiads and other official celebrations. On May 1, 1955, a monumental statue of Stalin was erected on the slope overlooking the Vltava; Otakar Švec, the sculptor responsible for the statue, committed suicide the day after the unveiling. In 1991, the statue was pulled down but the plinth remains and on it now stands a gigantic metronome symbolizing time.

HANAVSKÝ PAVILION. This pavilion in the west of the park was built by Otto Hieser for the Jubilee Exhibition of 1891, and then transferred to Letná in 1898. Here, the neo-Baroque style is not so far removed from Art Nouveau. The pavilion was a gift from the Prince of Hanau to the city of Prague; it was designed to promote Hanau's steel products in Bohemia although, in the words of Petr Wittlich, a writer based in Prague, the Hanavský was more of an "amalgam of decorative moldings". The pavilion today contains a restaurant. In the east of the park, there is the fascinating NATIONAL TECHNICAL MUSEUM and, not far away, along Dr-Milady-Horakove Street, is a block of rented accommodation for teachers at 35 Kamenická ulice; it was designed by Otakar Novotný ▲ *185, 303* in 1923, and there are elements of Cubism ● *89* in both its structure and decoration.

HANAVSKÝ PAVILION
The first municipal swimming pool was opened next to this pavilion.

THE "BELVEDERE"
In the 18th century, Letná was called the "Belvedere" because of the magnificent views it afforded over Prague.

STROMOVKA PARK ● 20

This is one of the most beautiful parks in Prague, and was once a hunting ground for the Kings of Bohemia. John of Luxemburg made this lovely park a royal hunting reserve in 1319. In 1569 the lake was created, and in 1584 Rudolph II then linked the lake to the Vltava by a canal system that is still in operation. In 1804, the Governor of Prague, Jan Rudolph Chotek, opened the park to the public and the architect Georg Fischer designed the small neo-Gothic summer palace on the site of the building by Vladislav Jagiello.

EXHIBITION CENTER. In 1888, it was decided to commemorate the centenary of the first Prague Universal Exhibition of 1791. It was an opportunity to promote the new styles of architecture, emphasizing the use of glass and iron, as well as to herald recent industrial advances under the Dual Monarchy. The 1891 Exhibition consisted of 140 pavilions in the new "Exhibition Park" (now Výstaviště), east of Stromovka, and received almost two million visitors.

MUSEUM OF MODERN ART. The museum is installed in the former Palace of Exhibitions, on Veletržní Street. The building is an emblem of the functionalist style of architecture and was built between 1925 and 1929 to the designs of Oldrich Tyl and Josef Fuchs. It was partly destroyed by fire in 1974, and was then completely renovated in 1995 to become one of the exhibition halls of the National Gallery ▲ 227. The museum provides an exhaustive coverage of all the great European artistic movements of the 19th and 20th centuries. The collection of French painting is particularly splendid.

MUSEUM OF MODERN ART ✪
Over four floors the museum explores several artistic styles (including Symbolism, Expressionism, Cubism, Surrealism and Abstract Art) and disciplines (such as architecture, design and photography). The collection of French painting and art is exceptional, and includes works by such masters as Courbet, Delacroix, Rodin, Braque, Van Gogh, Cézanne, Gauguin, Matisse, Léger and Picasso.

VINEYARDS
From the reign of
Charles IV to the
11th century, the
rural properties and
domains surrounding
the four historic
towns of Prague
included large
numbers of vineyards
owned by the King,
the city of Prague, the
clergy, the nobility
and the bourgeoisie.
During the 17th and
18th centuries, many
winegrowers' cabins
and houses were
converted into smart
residences. There are
still a few acres of
vines here and there,
just below the
picturesque chapel on
the hill overlooking
Troja Castle. The
capital's other
Botanical Garden
is also here.

PALACE OF INDUSTRY. The Palace of Industry, now the Czech
Congress Building, is a masterpiece of the glass and iron
architecture that anticipated Art Nouveau. It was the
centerpiece of the 1891 Exhibition, being 680 feet long and
covering 15,548 square yards. The architect Bedřich
Münzberger was assisted by František Prášil, an engineer
from the steel factory in Prague, who built the central
part of the pavilion. The immense glass arcade which
links the two towers consists of eight arches 70ft high, and
weighs 500 tonnes. In Výstaviště it is still possible to visit
the LAPIDARIUM from the National Museum's Department of
Sculpture. A swimming-pool, an art movie theater and finally
a lunapark complete the attractions.

TROJA CASTLE ★

It is thanks both to Count Václav Vojtěch Šternberk
(c. 1640–1708) and to the origins of the palace of the same
name at Hradčany ▲ *227* that this splendid castle on the
banks of the Vltava was built at the end of the 17th century.
Troja Castle was built between 1679 and 1691 as a summer
pavilion for the Šternberk family, and was one of the first
villas of any significance outside the city. What attracted
the Count to the area was the proximity of the newly
completed Royal Enclosure at Stromovka: this gave him
the opportunity to offer hospitality to the King
and his companions when they were out hunting
and thus demonstrate his loyalty. In the
late 17th century, the Domain of Zádní
Ovenec – only the castle was called Troja –
occupied the entire area, and incorporated
all the Count's lands and vineyards. A boat
departs daily for Troja from Rašin Quay, a
short distance down river from Palacký
Bridge. Alternatively, to take the one-mile
walk from Stromovka Park, follow signs
to the zoo and cross Cisářský Ostrov Island.
FRENCH INFLUENCES. Present-day Troja
Castle, the work of the Dijon architect
Jean-Baptiste Mathey, is a far cry from
the original building designed by the
Italian, Giovanni Domenico Orsi.
Mathey seems to have worked here
from 1685 onward. The first castle was
flanked by two wings terminating in
pavilions, a device that doubled the
current width. However, the
disappearance of these two blocks
did little to affect the balance of the
overall construction. J.-B.Mathey was
greatly influenced by Roman classicism and
the castles of the French Renaissance with
their articulated pavilions, a design quite
new to Prague. All the castle's architectural
elements are painted red, while the walls
are whitewashed. The garden, also in the
French style, was laid out by Georg Seemann
after 1698. It consists of various terraces
in a star-shaped plan defined by

narrow paths. The supreme harmony of the garden is most fully appreciated by entering it, not through the side gate, but through the old, stately gateway whose Baroque ironwork has now been restored.

By taking this route, the visitor then approaches the magnificent monumental steps directly, and can simultaneously marvel at the castle's refined elegance.

MONUMENTAL STEPS. The double flight of steps, richly decorated with sculpture, is by Johann Georg Heermann (c. 1650–after 1700), a Dresden sculptor strongly influenced by the work of the Mannerist sculptor Bernini. Heermann was assisted by his nephew, Paul (1673–1732), and the decoration was completed in 1703. The scheme depicts a struggle between gods and giants; the defeated sons of Gaia support the head of the stairs. The subject matter is replete with political significance, and prepares the visitor for the story told in the paintings in the main hall – a metaphor for the Emperor's victory over the Turks at Kahlenberg (1683) and in Hungary (1686). The terrace is lined with a remarkable collection of decorated terracotta pots. The pots are adorned with festoons, little angels, heraldic motifs and busts of emperors. The artist responsible for them was a mysterious craftsman named Bombelli, of whom nothing is known except his work here and at Slavkov u Brna Castle.

PAINTED DECORATION. The monumental steps lead directly to the Imperial Banqueting Room, which is decorated with the same theme. The murals were painted by the brothers Abraham and Isaac Godyn, who came to the castle from Antwerp in 1690. Abraham began by painting the trompe l'oeil decorations in the corridors, and the Count then set him to work in the large reception room on the second floor. He worked here for six years on the paintings, which are devoted to a glorification of the Habsburgs. The guidebook to the castle explains the cycle of paintings to the visitor. The paintings in the other rooms are earlier, and of lesser quality; they are by Francesco Marchetti (before 1640– before 1707) and his son Giovanni, both from Trentino. The chapel, which they decorated in 1690, has a ceiling representing the apotheosis of the Count and his wife.

19TH–CENTURY CZECH PAINTING. Once in a poor state of repair, Troja Castle and its gardens have been restored on a number of occasions since they were purchased by the state in 1922. After 1976 it was decided to display here part of the collection from the National Gallery in the city of Prague. This led to further restoration work, and since 1989 the castle has housed Czech art from the 19th century – the second half in particular – and the early 20th century. Artists whose work has been exhibited here include Josef Čermák, Václav Brožík ▲ *319*, Julius Mařák, Antonín Chitussi ▲ *182*, Maxmilián Pirner, Jan Preisler ▲ *165* and Mikoláš Aleš ▲ *175*. A visit to this collection complements that in the Museum of Modern Art ▲ *317*.

THE IMPERIAL BANQUETING HALL
The decoration of this hall highlights the Habsburgs' principal virtues: moderation, clemency, and fear of God as manifested by piety. The Habsburgs' devotion to the Eucharist is the dominant theme of this décor, and it is illustrated on the wall by the legend of Rudolph I. The west wall celebrates Leopold I's triumph over the Turks.

The original Břevnov coat of arms included a branch (*břevno*) with three knots on a red background. The coat of arms opposite is a variant with a lion, the emblem of Bohemia, on a red background, and three branches with three knots on a blue background.

ST MARGARET'S CHURCH
"Its single nave, a version of the Germanic model of barn-like church, contains oval bays which weave in and out of one another, and whose arches rest on diagonal pilasters, The pilasters punctuate the white surface of the walls, which is itself embellished with secondary altars with painted trompe l'oeil decorations that are full of fantastic illusions."
Léon and Xavier de Coster

BŘEVNOV ABBEY

The foundation of this Benedictine abbey (Klášter sv. Markéty), the first religious houses for men in Bohemia, goes back to 993 and was jointly conceived by Duke Boleslav II and Saint Adalbert, Bishop of Prague. It was rebuilt on many occasions; the oldest parts date from the 10th century and only came to light during archeological excavations in 1964. The period between the 15th century, the era of Hussite reforms ● *32*, and the 18th century was a difficult time for the monastery, and it fell into serious decay; however, the monastery buildings, a garden, a church and a chapel were rebuilt in the Baroque style under the direction of Krištof Dientzenhofer between 1708 and 1745. The buildings that can still be seen today date from this period. The entrance to the monastery is through a door dating from 1740 ● *70* that was executed by Kilián Ignác Dientzenhofer. In 1990, Břevnov was returned to the Benedictines, and on February 13, 1991, it was declared a historic monument. The previous administration had only used it for storage.

ST MARGARET'S CHURCH. This church, which was built by Dientzenhofer between 1708 and 1714, is one of the most remarkable Baroque constructions in Bohemia. The powerful sweep of the walls, the generous undulations and the enormous skylights with carved pediments also make it one of the most typical. The ceiling frescos of the interior, dating from before 1721, are the work of Johann Jakob Steinfels and depict the legend of Saint Adalbert, to whom the church was originally dedicated. The church was only rededicated to Saint Margaret in the 14th century. The reredos on the high altar was made by Petr Brandl around 1720, and the whole church was restored between 1980 and 1983.

THERESA HALL. The Abbey's ceremonial hall is decorated with a fine fresco, *The Miracle of Saint Gunther* by Cosmas Asam (1686–1739), a Bavarian painter and architect, and one of the greatest German fresco artists and decorators of the 18th century.

CHURCH OF OUR-LADY-OF-THE-VICTORY AT WHITE MOUNTAIN

A chapel dedicated to Saint Wenceslas, patron saint of Bohemia, was first built on the site of White Mountain (Bilá Hora) ● *34* shortly after the battle in 1620. However, Ferdinand II founded a Servite monastery there in 1628 and ordered the construction of a Chapel of Our-Lady-of-the-Victory to replace the earlier church. In 1704–30, it was turned into a place of pilgrimage. The architects may have been Alliprandi or Santini-Aichl. The church contains a copy of the painting of the Virgin which a Carmelite, the Venerable Dominic of Jesus-Maria, carried up to the front line. The victory at White Mountain has often been attributed to the miraculous intercession of the Virgin Mary. Although the monastery planned for this site was never completed, the interior was decorated by the greatest artists of the time: Reiner was responsible for the ceiling fresco above the altar of Saint Rosalind, and Asam painted the Assumption over the high altar. Other decoration was carried out by Schöpf.

HVĚZDA SUMMER PALACE

This country residence dates from 1555–6, and its name (Letohrádek Hvězda or Star Summer Palace) explains its original conception. Archduke Ferdinand of Tyrol had it built according to his own design, that of a six-pointed star, inside the royal game reserve that had been selected by his father, Emperor Ferdinand I. The pavilion was built by Aostalli and Lucchese under the direction of the architects Hans Tirol and Bonifác Wohlmut, and decorated by Italian stucco artists, probably including Brocco. The ceilings on the first floor have splendid stucco decoration depicting subjects from mythology and ancient history. The basement houses an exhibition that recounts the story of the Battle of White Mountain in 1620; elsewhere the castle has exhibitions of the work of the painter Mikoláš Alcš (1852–1913) and the writer Jiří Jirásek (1851–1930), both of them major figures in the Czech National Movement.

In the 16th century Hvězda Summer Palace was topped by a steeple, but this was replaced by a cupola in the 17th century. The present roof dates from the 18th century.

MOZART'S BERTRAMKA
MOZARTSBERTRAMKA
BERTRAMKA DE MOZART
60,- Kč

A COUNTRY HOUSE
Villa Bertramka takes its name from its first owner, František Bertram. It was an affluent country residence built in an opulent, bourgeois style, and situated in the middle of one of the many vineyards that surrounded Prague at the time.

Detail of the score of Mozart's concert aria, *Bella mia fiamma* (right).

Interior of the villa: the drawing-room with the harpsichord used by Mozart.

VILLA BERTRAMKA ★

In the midst of the dilapidated Smichov quarter, Villa Bertramka is an oasis of greenery and tranquility. At one time, the area was covered with vineyards, and access to the house was down a long avenue of chestnut trees. On April 23, 1784, the house was sold to Josefina Dušková, a celebrated singer married to the well-known pianist, teacher and composer, František Dušek (1731–99) ▲ *282*. Dušek was a key figure in the early days of Czech piano music, and he wrote many works for piano as well as a number of chamber pieces. He also taught several composers, including Leopold Koželuh, who succeeded Mozart as court composer to the Emperor. Indeed, the villa would have remained unknown if the couple had not invited Mozart there on several occasions. The Dušeks had met him while Josefina was on tour in Vienna and Germany, mainly Dresden, and later in Salzburg in 1777. Then, in 1787, they collaborated with other admirers, including Count Thun, to invite Mozart to Prague where his *Seraglio* and *The Marriage of Figaro*, the previous year (1786) had been well received.

MOZART'S FIRST STAY. On his first visit to Prague in January 1787, Mozart did not stay at Villa Bertramka but with Count Thun ▲ *259*. On January 19, he conducted a concert of his music and, on the following day, a performance of *The Marriage of Figaro*. On that occasion, with the applause still ringing in his ears, he is said to have made his famous remark to Bondini, the theater manager, "My Praguers understand me!" Bondini promptly commissioned an opera specially for

Prague in return for the (usual) fee of 100 ducats and free accommodation for Mozart and his librettist, Lorenzo da Ponte. In early October 1787, while still working on *Don Giovanni*, the composer returned to Prague, accompanied by his wife, Constanze. He first lodged at the House "At the sign of the Three Small Golden Lions", which also belonged to the Dušeks, and then at Villa Bertramka. It was probably there, on the evening preceding the première on October 29, 1787, at the Estates Theater ▲ *281*, that he composed the overture to *Don Giovanni*.

K 528. Josefina Dušková is said to have locked the composer in the summer pavilion until he finished the concert aria, *Bella mia fiamma*. It was not commonly known at the time that Mozart had composed the aria, *Ah, lo previdi*, K 272, for her ten years earlier. Mozart was also a guest at Bertramka when he visited Prague in 1789; on that occasion, he went to see František Němeček, his first biographer, at Sadská.

"LA CLEMENZA DI TITO". Mozart's last official visit to Prague was during the summer of 1791 and on that occasion he was commissioned to write a new opera for the coronation of Leopold II as King of Bohemia in September 1791. *La Clemenza di Tito* was composed at Villa Bertramka in just eighteen days. It was an uncomfortable stay, and Mozart, who was ill, had to leave for Vienna as soon as he had completed the opera. It was a failure, although his bitterness was slightly assuaged by the success of *The Magic Flute* while he continued to work on his *Requiem*. He died on December 5, 1791, and the Czechs were the only people to honor his memory at the time ▲ *254*.

MEMORIAL TO MOZART. The Villa Bertramka was bought by the Popelka family in 1838 and in 1876, on the occasion of the centenary of Mozart's birth, they turned it into a memorial. The centenary of *Don Giovanni* was also celebrated there in 1887. In 1925, the last private owner, Matylda Slivenská, presented Villa Bertramka to the Salzburg Mozarteum and, in the late 1920's, part of the house was converted into a museum. After World War Two, the state took over responsibility for restoration and upkeep of the house, and founded a Museum that opened in time for the bicentenary of Mozart's birth in 1956. Further restoration took place in 1973 in anticipation of the bicentenary of *Don Giovanni* in 1987, and this phase of refurbishment gave the museum the appearance it has today.

Like the Smetana and Dvořák Museums, Villa Bertramka forms part of the

Praga Mozarteana

musical department of the National Museum. Concerts are given in the terrace garden and in the main sitting room.

Don Giovanni and Zerlina, characters in Mozart's *Don Giovanni*.

VYŠEHRAD

A LEGENDARY FOUNDATION. Kosmas, writing in the 11th century, and later Václav Hájek z Libočan in his *Kronika Česka* (*Czech Chronicle*) ▲ *233* of 1541, state that Libussa was the founder of Vyšehrad. According to Hájek, after the death of Čech, Krok was elected Duke (or Prince) of the Czechs. He had three daughters, of whom Libussa was the youngest, and they were all magicians and prophetesses; Libussa was the wisest and the most enlightened. After Krok's death, she was elected to succeed her father in 710, and founded Psáry Castle, as Vyšehrad was first known, where she lived and which she embellished and enlarged. She founded Prague Castle in 717. All this is legend, of course. In fact, Vyšehrad Castle was founded in the first half of the 10th century and was known as Chrasten and, from the end of the century, it belonged to the Přemyslids, who struck denarius coins there. It joined forces with the Castle to defend the town of Prague. After that, Vyšehrad was more or less abandoned until Charles IV gave it a new lease of life. It was felt that Nové Město had adequate defenses to the south by the rock, but it was not until the 17th century that Vyšehrad was properly restored, and a fortified and buttressed curtain wall was erected in 1654–80.

LIBUSSA. Krok's youngest daughter, the legendary founder of Prague, is also the legendary founder of the first royal dynasty of Bohemia. Realizing that the men did not like being governed by a woman, Libussa agreed to take a husband, and she nominated one in a prophecy. She indicated a field near the village of Stadice where a man would be working with two oxen. The man was called Přemysl (the Thinker), she said. Messengers were taken by Libussa's white horse to find him. Later, Přemysl Oráč (Přemysl the Ploughman) came to Vyšehrad, bringing with him his shoes made of the bark of the lime tree and his bag by which he wanted to record for posterity his peasant origins. At Vyšehrad, he married the princess and became the legendary founder of the Kingdom of Bohemia.

THE SITE AT VYŠEHRAD. The few ancient remains at Vyšehrad include the old Rotunda of St Martin (left), the fortifications and Ferdinand I's monumental gates. Between the first gate, the Tábor Gate (1655), and the Leopold I Gate (1678), there are vestiges

THE STORY OF PRAGUE: LIBUSSA'S PROPHECY
"I see a great fortress whose glory reaches up to the sky; I see a place in a forest thirty cubits from our castle [i.e. Vyšehrad] and on the edge of the Vltava . . . When you arrive there, you will find a man carving a threshold in the middle of the forest. As even great lords have to stoop before a low threshold, you shall name the castle that you shall construct on your journey 'Prague' (*Praha*), the Threshold (*Prah*)."

Vyšehrad coat of arms.

of the fortifications that Charles IV had ordered to be built. To the right is one of the oldest Romanesque rotundas in Prague and Vyšehrad's oldest building, the ROTUNDA OF ST MARTIN; the entire structure dates from 1050–1100, except for the south gate, which was rebuilt as part of a restoration program in 1878–9. The other medieval religious buildings have disappeared, and only the scantiest vestiges of the Romanesque BASILICA OF ST LAWRENCE remain. Major archeological excavations are now taking place.

The tomb of the composer Antonín Dvořák by the sculptor Ladislav Šaloun and, to the right, the arches of the cemetery. Vyšehrad Rock, overlooking the Vltava (below).

CHURCH OF ST PETER AND ST PAUL. Of the Romanesque Church of St Peter and St Paul (Kostel sv. Petra a Pavla), which was founded by Vratislav II, nothing remains except for the foundations, which are now covered by a neo-Gothic church of little architectural interest. The church dates back to the reign of Charles IV, who had it built from 1369. It has been much altered: during the 19th century, Josek Mocker ▲ *167, 190* attempted to give it a Gothic appearance and even the clocks (1902–3) are modern. It nonetheless has some interesting features, including a 14th-century Madonna of Humility showing the Virgin seated, and statues by Myslbek depicting characters from Czech mythology and including Přemysl the Ploughman. At one time, all of these groups decorated Palacký Bridge. There is also a rather unusual group of megaliths in the grounds.

CEMETERY. The small cemetery built in 1660 took on a new importance with the addition of a portico with neo-Renaissance arches and painted vaults in 1875. Most of the country's leading citizens are buried here, including the painters Václav Spála and Alfons Mucha and the writers Vítězslav Nevzal and Mácha, and many musicians, including Bedřich Smetana and Antonín Dvořák. The cemetery is dominated by a monument erected in honor of the country's founder guardian spirit and called *Slavín* (Place of Glory).

VYŠEHRAD, LEGENDARY CRADLE OF THE PRINCES OF BOHEMIA ✪

Vyšehrad is reached by walking up Vratislava Street as far as Prague Gate. A small museum set into the curtain wall, to the left, explains the history of the site. In the park stands the ancient Rotunda of St Martin, vestiges of the Gothic Spicka Gate, the Devil's Pillars and the Plague Column. The little candles that flicker after dark on the tombs of the illustrious dead give Vyšehrad's old cemetery, next to the the Church of St Peter and St Paul, a magical atmosphere.

VINOHRADY THEATER
This neo-Baroque building ● *82* by Alois J. Censký has Art Nouveau ornamentation (below).

CHURCH OF THE SACRED HEART
Below: the façade and interior of the Church of the Sacred Heart, a magnificent example of modern religious architecture (exterior and interior).

CHOCHOL HOUSE
A striking feature of this house in Libušina Street is the pentagonal projection of the façade looking onto the garden.

CUBIST HOUSES IN VYŠEHRAD AND PODSKÁLI ● *89*

At the foot of Vyšehrad rock are three examples of Cubist architecture by Josef Chochol (1880–1956), all of them built between 1911 and 1913. After studying in Prague, Chochol trained in Vienna in 1908 under Otto Wagner, like so many of his generation, including Engel, Roith, Janák, Kotěra and Plečnik. After a period as one of the better exponents of Rondo-Cubist architecture, Chochol opted for Russian Constructivism and then became attracted to Functionalism.

THREE-FAMILY HOUSE. The house at 6–10 Rašínovo nábreži gets its name from the fact that it consists of three totally independent dwellings in one building.

ONE-FAMILY HOUSE. This house, which is considered to be Otakar Novotný's greatest achievement, is in Libušina Street next door to SEQUENS HOUSE (1912), also by Novotný. The two façades, which overlook the street and the garden, are finely distinguished.

APARTMENT BLOCK. This recently restored building at the end of Neklánova Street (no. 30) is an outstanding example of Cubist architecture. The decorative device over the first-floor windows is reflected in the cornice. Not a single detail has been neglected – neither the door and window handles, nor the form of the entrances, nor the ceramic tiles arranged diagonally on the staircase.

VINOHRADY

The royal vineyards planted by Charles IV in the 14th century – he also introduced seedlings and vine stock from Burgundy – extended throughout this quarter. Until the 19th century, it was called Královsky vinohrady, and it is

> "The moment war broke out, I could not
> stop thinking of Žižka's drum."
>
> Gustav Meyrink

now known simply as Vinohrady. The vineyards were abandoned in the late 18th century and partly replaced by rows of trees. Then, in 1875, the district began to be developed, with members of the Czech bourgeoisie, officials and civil servants settling here, as well as businessmen and people of independent means. In 1843, there were

only 169 inhabitants; by 1869, the population had risen to 5318, then 14,831 by 1880 and to 52,483 by 1900. Vinohrady formally became a town in 1879 and was integrated into Greater Prague in 1922; it straddles three districts and contains a number of Secession and Art Nouveau buildings. A walk through Rieger Gardens (Riegrovy sady) toward Jiříz Poděbrad náměstí (George Poděbrady Square) takes in several streets well worth visiting, including Polská and Kroknošská.

MUNICIPAL THEATER (DIVADLO NA VINOHRADECH) ● *54*. Between 1913 and 1920, the Municipal Theater's repertoire moved dynamically in the direction of Expressionism. From November 18, 1989, it became a meeting place of the Civic Forum ● *38*, the actors being among the leading lights.

CHURCH OF THE SACRED HEART. This brick-built church in Jiříz Poděbrad Square was built between 1927 and 1933 by the Slovenian Josip Plečnik (1927–57) ▲ *211, 213*, and is the most important building by this architect in Prague. After the war he was put in charge of restoring the Castle ▲ *211*.

Villa Gröbe in Havlíček Gardens was built between 1871 and 1888 in Italian Renaissance style for a businessman named Gröbe. Since 1953, it has been the House of Youth.

NATIONAL MEMORIAL
To the north of Vinohrady, on Žižkov Hill, is the National Memorial, erected between 1925 and 1932. The interior has mosaics depicting great moments in the nation's history; opposite the memorial is the equestrian statue of Jan Žižka (opposite) by Bohumil Kafka. Žižka, who died in 1424, was a brilliant horseman in Wenceslas I's retinue; he led the Taborite troops (Hussite radicals from the south of Bohemia) and defeated the Emperor Sigismond at the Battle of Vitkov (modern Žižkov) in 1420.

The convent buildings opening onto the main courtyard.

Statue in the grounds of the Zbraslav Convent.

ZBRASLAV CONVENT ★

Zbraslav Convent occupies a marvelous rural setting 8 miles south of Prague, on the banks of the River Berounka a short distance before it flows into the Vltava.

A CISTERCIAN CONVENT. In 1292, on the site of a royal hunting pavilion, Wenceslas II founded a convent which he later gave to the Cistercians. The convent was finished in 1333, and the church, since destroyed, became a mausoleum for the last of Přemyslids. Wenceslas donated large tracts of land to the convent and it soon

prospered but, having suffered the ravages of the Hussite Wars and the Thirty Years' War ● *32*, the buildings were restored in the early 18th century. The architect in charge of the restoration was Santini-Aichl (1677–1723), and the work was spread over the period 1709–27, with Kaňka taking responsibility for the last part. There are no traces of medieval design about this monastery; in fact, it is an excellent example of the Baroque-Gothic style for which Santini-Aichl ▲ *243, 254, 283* was famous. The convent was closed down in 1781.

U-SHAPED PLAN. The U-shaped buildings surround a main courtyard which acts as a cloister; a very low porch giving access to the courtyard was added later. The façade facing the river corresponds to the main hall, and is rounded. At the two ends of the "U" there are two pavilions and, on the south side, there is a small aedicule which breaks up the overall symmetrical design. Other pavilions punctuate the center of each of the wings, and they are topped with pointed roofs, including pagodas. The large windows on the first floor are underlined by a cornice supported by consoles.

A CLOISTER DIVIDED IN TWO. The ambulatory within the cloister is, unusually, divided in two. The first corridor, each bay of which is covered by a vault with a pendentive, is broken up with huge windows. The second corridor, which is behind the first, is covered with barrel vaulting punctuated at regular intervals by windows in the separating wall. This second ambulatory is adorned with mezzanine windows, bays and gaps which allow plays of light and shade. In the corners of the cloister, there are two staircases, each of two flights, with the middle floor forming a balcony.

MURALS. Some of the rooms are decorated with paintings; the fresco in the refectory painted by Franz Xaver Palko in about 1770 is the most beautiful.

Practical information

by Robert Anderson

els – selected by Robert Anderson

WEBSITES

www.visitczech.cz
Site of the national Czech Tourist Office.
www.pis.cz
Prague Information service.
www.travelguide.cz
Hotels, restaurants, camp sites. Online reservations.
www.heartofeurope.cz
Guide to museums, galleries and exhibitions.

ADDRESSES

→ EMBASSY OF THE CZECH REPUBLIC

United Kingdom
28 Kensington
Palace Gardens
London W88 4QY
Tel. (020) 7243 7942/3
United States
3900 Spring of
Freedom St. NW
Washington DC 20008
Tel. (202) 274 9123
www.mzv.cz. washington
Consulate General
1109 Madison
Avenue
New York, NY 10028
Tel. (212) 717 5643
Fax (212) 717 5064
www.mzv.cz.newyork

→ CZECH TOURIST AUTHORITY

United Kingdom
95 Great Portland St
London W1N 5RA
Tel. (020) 7291 9925
www.tourist-offices. org.uk
www.visitczech.cz
United States
1109 Madison Ave
New York, NY 10028
Tel. (212) 288 0830
www.czechcenter. com

BY AIR

→ FROM THE US

There are direct flights from New York to Prague with ČSA Czech Airlines and Delta Airlines, with connecting flights from other US destinations. The average travel time New York to Prague non-stop is 8 hours.
Delta Airlines
Tel. 800 241 41 41
www.delta.com

ČSA
Tel. (212) 765 6022
www.csa.cz
Continental Airlines
Tel. 800 231 0856
www.continental.com
British Airways
Tel. 800 247 9297
www.britishairways. com

→ FROM THE UK

There are daily direct flights London to Prague. Average travel time is 2 hours.
British Airways
Tel. 0345 222 111
www.britishairways. com
ČSA
Tel. (020) 7255 1898
www.csa.cz
Go!
Tel. 0845 605 43 21
www.go-fly.com
The low-cost airline.
■ Also check out
www.cheapflights. com
www.expedia.co.uk

BY COACH FROM THE UK

Bohemian Express International
Tel. (020) 7794 3264
Capital Express
Tel. (020) 7243 0488
Eurolines
Tel. (01582) 404 7500
www.eurolines.com
Kingscourt Express
Tel. (020) 8673 7500

BY ROAD

→ DOCUMENTS

A valid driving license, car registration papers and insurance documents.

→ ROAD TAX

Short-term permits for mortorway driving can be bought at the border or at gas stations.
Family car
(under 3.5 ton):
800 Kč
Coaches
(under 12 ton):
2,000 Kč

BY TRAIN FROM THE UK

– Via Paris: Eurostar to Paris Gare-du-

Nord, transfer to Gare de l'Est for the Paris–Prague Express
– Via Berlin: from London-Victoria, traveling via Ostend and Cologne.
Rail Europe Direct:
179 Piccadilly
London W1
Tel. 08705 848 848
www.raileurope.co.uk
Information for US residents:
www.raileurope. com.us
EuropeOnRail:
www.europeonrail. com
Eurostar
Tel. 0870 160 6600
www.eurostar.com
French railways
www.sncf.fr

CLIMATE

→ SPRING

min/max:
March: 32/45° F
April: 37/55°F
May: 48/64°F

→ SUMMER

June: 52/72°F
July: 55/75°F
August: 55/74°F

→ FALL

September: 50/66°F
October: 41/54°F
November: 36/43°F

→ WINTER

December: 28/34°F
January: 24/32°F
February: 28/34°F

COST OF LIVING

■ A mug of beer:
25 Kč
■ 1 ticket to a concert: 360 Kč
■ 1 dish in an average restaurant:
200 Kč
■ 1 entrance ticket to a museum:
70 Kč–100 Kč
■ 1 night in a centrally located hotel: 4,500 Kč
■ 1 entrance ticket to a jazz club:
130 Kč
■ 1 CD: 360 Kč

DON'T FORGET

■ Travel insurance valid throughout the Czech Republic.
■ Student card,

giving discounts (transport, concerts, museums).
■ Credit card numbers and emergency telephone numbers in case of loss or theft.

FORMALITIES

US and UK visitors: no visa necessary for stays of up to 90 days. Make sure your passport is valid for at least six months from date of entry. No vaccinations are needed. Other nationalities: contact the Czech embassy for any visa requirements.

→ CUSTOMS

1 liter of spirits or liqueur or 2 liters of wines. 200 cigarettes or 50 cigars. Pets must have a valid certificate of vaccination against rabies and proof of a recent health check.

LANGUAGES

Czech is the national language. English and German are widely spoken.

MONEY

The unit of currency is the Koruna (Kč), which is made up of 100 hellers (halér). Notes come in 20, 50, 100, 200, 500, 1000, 2000 and 5000 Kč denominations.

→ EXCHANGE RATES

£1 = around 50 Kč
$1 = around 32 Kč
(at the time of printing)

TELEPHONE

To call Prague from the UK or US, dial the international code (011 from US, 00 from UK), 420 for the Czech Republic, then the number beginning with 2.

TIME DIFFERENCE

Prague is one hour ahead of London, and six hours ahead of New York.

ACCOMMODATION

→ ACCOMMODATION IN PRIVATE HOMES

Many residents make available rooms in their homes to paying guests. It is best to book through an agency. However, there are many bed-and-breakfast signs in the streets of Prague, and you may decide to make your own arrangements. Prices vary according to the location and the season.

Ave
– Wilsonova 8
Tel. 224 22 35 21
Open daily 6am–10.30pm.
– Na Příkopě 18
Tel. 224 19 71 11
Open Mon.–Fri.
9am–7pm;
Sat. 9am–3pm.
Rates
500–1,500 Kč per person per night, according to the season and location. Payment is made in Koruna or German Marks. Breakfast is usually included in the room rate, but it is advisable to check.

→ CAMPSITES

PIS and Čedok offices (see under "Tourist information" p. 336) have a list of campsites in Prague and its surrounding area.
Categories
From 0 to 3 stars. Sites labeled 0 or * have a cold water only. Those campsites in the ** and *** categories should provide electricity, hot water, eating facilities and a television room. Caravans and camping-cars are welcome, and individual bungalows or chalets are also available. All have communal bathrooms and cooking areas, as well as children's playgrounds. Located outside Prague, they can be reached by urban transport.
Rates
From 100 to 240 Kč a night, according to the category.

→ HOTELS

Early bookings are recommended for the summer holidays.
Categories
Hotel ratings are based on a star system comparable to that used in Western Europe, determining prices and facilities. You may still encounter the older alphabet-based system:
A* (deluxe)
A, B*, B and C (in decreasing order).
Rates
Allow about £180/$270 for a 5-star hotel, and about £20/$30 for a one-star hotel situated outside the city center. A room in a two-star hotel costs around £40/$60. A double room in a centrally located hotel costs at least £65/$97.

→ YOUTH HOSTELS

CKM Travel
Manesova 77
Tel. 22 72 15 95
Around 3,000 beds are provided by this organization, who will take the reservation and tell you where beds are available.
Prices
Prices vary according to the season. Allow 200 Kč (£4/$6.25) a night in a dormitory, 350 Kč (£7/$11) for a double room. A membership card entitles the holder to discounts.

AIRPORT

→ RUZYNĚ AIRPORT

Located 12½ miles northwest of the city center.
Tel. 220 113 314

→ AIRPORT TRANSFER

■ **Shuttle**
The best value option to get to the city center. Both Cedaz and Welcome Touristic Praha run shuttle vans between the airport and the city center (6am–9pm for Cedaz, 8.30am–7pm for Welcome). Departures every 30 minutes, journey time around 30 minutes. Tickets are available on board: 90/95 Kč. However you have to wait until the shuttle is full and it may go all over Prague before it gets to your hotel or its terminus, Náměstí Republiky.
■ **Buses 119 and 179**
The cheapest way to get from the airport to Dejvická subway station (line A) or Nové Butovice Metro Station (Line B). Departs every 10 mins, journey time 30/40 mins. Cost: around 12 Kč
■ **Taxis**
One taxi firm has the monopoly on airport transfers. It charges a steep 600 Kč but check before you get in. A cheaper option is to phone one of the taxi firms listed in the Urban Transport section once you have collected your luggage. To reach the taxi meeting point,

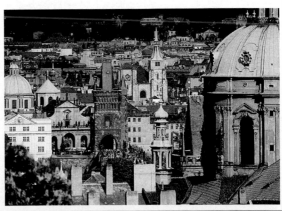

take a right out of the arrivals terminal. And check that the price list, registration number and company name are displayed in the taxi before entering.

BEER HALLS, BARS AND CAFÉS
→ "PIVNICE", OR "HOSPODA"

A *pivnice* or *hospoda* is a Czech pub or beer hall. Bills are scribbled on the table. One mark means one beer (from about 10 Kč to 40 Kč, depending on the beer). When your glass is empty, the waiter will automatically bring a new beer unless asked not to.

An extensive choice of beers

Each brewery produces its own beer from varieties of barley and hops grown in Bohemia. Among the hundreds of brands, the most famous are the golden and creamy-headed beers from České Budějovice and Plžen, such as *Pilsner, Pilsen Urquell* and *Budvar*. The quality of Plžen beer is the fruit of a long and respected tradition. Some beers, such as *Staropramen* are brewed in Prague.

Warning:
"Don't drink and drive" isn't just an empty slogan in the Czech Republic. Fines are high for anyone breaking the "zero blood-alcohol" rule. Drivers may like to try one of the alcohol-free beers. The dark special beers (Ležák) have a very high alcoholic content.

→ "VINÁRNA"

Vinárna are wine bars that also function as restaurants, and sometimes even as nightclubs. Wine is served by the bottle, the jug or the glass, with or without food. Some of the *vinárna* belong to wine-makers' cooperatives and sell only the wines made by these organizations. But most offer offer a varied list of local, national and foreign wines.

Vintage wine

The Czech Republic is a big producer of wine. The best are the dry or medium-dry white wines (*bílé víno*) from Bohemia, (*Bílá Ludmila* and *Mělník*), and the wines of southern Moravia (*Mikulov, Znojmo* and *Bzenec*). Slovakia also produces good wine. Don't forget to sample or even bring home some Czech specialties, *Slivovice* (plum spirit) *Becherovka* apéritif, and absinthe.

→ "KAVÁRNA"

These cafés, with their convivial and literary atmosphere, are the place to eat a plate of ham or cheese with a glass of beer, or nibble at pastries while sipping an expresso or Viennese or Turkish coffee (*káva*). Russian coffee comes with vodka. Tea is also served.

→ "CUKRÁRNA"

These are tearooms catering to the Czech sweet tooth. Waffles, cakes, pancakes (*palačinky*), fruit tarts (*koláče*), delicious donuts (*vdolky*), strudels, and poppy-seed cakes abound.

CELEBRATIONS AND FESTIVALS

January 14–21
International dance week
Mid May
Book Fair

Mid May–beginning of June
Prague International Spring Music Festival
June
Concertino di Praga (Young Musicians' Master Classes); Contemporary Dance and Mime Festival
July–August
Culture in the Prague summer (concerts, opera, theater, etc.)
August
Čedok Open (international tennis tournament)
September 28
St Wenceslas' Day
September–October
Fall musical events
October
International Jazz Festival
November 17
Anniversary of the Velvet Revolution: demonstrations around Wenceslas Square
December 26
Swimming competition in the Vltava, with water at 37° F!

DRIVING
Warning:
As said above, Czech law prohibits driving with any alcohol in the bloodstream, and seatbelts are compulsory.
The speed limit is 70 mph/130km on freeways, 55mph/90kmh on main roads, and 35mph/50kmh in towns.

→ CAR RENTAL
Information
Rental agencies are located in the city center or at the airport. Addresses are available from tourist offices (see p. 336).

Rates
Czech agencies offer very good rates. Typical prices for A-category cars and gasoline:
1–3 days: 990 Kč per day.
1 week: 850 Kč per day.

→ PARKING
Rules
Parking spaces are scarce. If you park illegally, you may be fined or the car may be impounded. The city center is divided into 3 zones:
– Orange zone limited to 2 hours
10 Kč: 15 mins
40 Kč: 1 hour
Free between 6pm and 8am and on Sundays.
– Green zone limited to 6 hours. Zone for vehicles carrying tourists
30 Kč: 1 hour
120 Kč: 6 hours
– Blue zone reserved for Prague residents.

Main parking lots
The central train station, the National Theater and the Kotva store all have parking lots.

Park and Ride
There is also a "Park and Ride" system enabling visitors to park near one of the following subway stations and take trains into the city center (parking lots are guarded).
– Tariff:
Unlimited parking time: 10 Kč.
– Locations:
V Rybnickach (Line A, Skalka station)
Bucharova (Line B, Nové Butovice)
Radlická (Line B, Radlická station)
Zličín (Line B, Zličín station).
Hrnciska (Line C, Opatov station)
Holešovice Railway Station (C-line, Nádraží Holešovice station)
Palmovka (B-line, Palmovka station)

→ TRAFFIC
The roads that have priority are signed with a yellow square.

Warning:
Beware of tramway cars and buses leaving their stops.

→ EMERGENCY NUMBER
ABA (Autoklub Bohemia Assistance)
Tel. 1240

EATING OUT
→ BRASSERIES AND WINE BARS
Good food is cheaper than in the traditional restaurants (a good meal rarely exceeds 150 Kč). The surroundings are attractive and the service tends to be faster.
Knedlíky, goulasch, roast pork with cabbage, potato cakes, chicken, soup, apfelstrudel, cold meats and cheese are served with wine and beer.

→ RESTAURANTS
A great number of restaurants have opened since the Velvet Revolution. Most are very good value for money. The most expensive menu will cost you around 1,500 Kč for delicious dishes served in exquisite surroundings. For 350 Kč you can enjoy a hearty lunch or dinner with a glass of wine or beer.

→ SELF-SERVICE BUFFETS
These self-service establishments (called *Automat*, or *samoobsluha*) offer cheap lunches. They are often full and customers tend to eat quickly, without sitting down. Five thick slices of bread (with surimi, celery, scrambled eggs, etc.) and tea cost around 50 Kč. Roast chicken, pork fritters and potato cakes, sandwiches, salads, *knedlíky* (sliced balls made of potato or flour), and toasts are also

served with beer, wine, tea or coffee.

→ STALLS
The cheapest and fastest way of eating. Food stalls offer various types of sausages and regional hot dishes for about 100 Kč (£2/$3). Salami and ham sandwiches, hamburgers (13 Kč), potato cakes (*bramboraky*), hot dogs (25 Kč), grilled sausages with mustard, waffles, beer and mulled wine are also on offer.

→ TIPPING
In pubs and cheaper restaurants it is normal to round up the bill in front of the waiter to the nearest 10 Kč. In smarter places it is usual to leave 10% of the bill. Some places add a cover charge or bill for bread.

FINDING YOUR WAY
→ ADDRESSES
The name of the street precedes the number. In the historic center the buildings have a double numbering system:
Blue plaque
Indicates the number.
Red plaque
This shows the property registration number, that is, the building's number in the neighborhood (never used in this guide).

→ DISTRICTS
The city of Prague (*Praha*) is divided into ten districts. The number of the district (1–10) appears as the second figure in the postal code.

→ HISTORIC CENTER
The historic heart of the city is made up of four different areas:
■ Staré Město (Old Town),

■ Nové Město (New Town),
■ Hradčany (the Castle)
■ Malá Strana (Little City).

HEALTH
Health centers are open from 7.30am to 5.30pm. Pharmacies are open longer (until around 6.30pm). Details of night and weekend services are posted on the doors.
First aid
Palackého 5
Praha 1
Tel. 224 94 91 81 (emergencies)
Tel. 224 94 69 81 (dental emergency)
Open Mon.–Fri. 7pm–7am;
Sat.–Sun. 24 hours
Central pharmacy
Belgická 37
Praha 2
Tel. 222 51 97 31 or 222 51 33 96
Open 24 hours
Emergency medical service
Nemocnice na Homolce Hospital (Foreign Pavilion)
Roentgenova 2
Praha 5
Tel. 257 27 21 44 or 257 27 21 46
24-hour service
American Medical Center
Na Homolce Hospital
Janovskeho 48
Tel. 220 80 77 56

MAIL
Central post office
Jindřišská 14
Praha 1
Tel. 221 13 14 45
Open daily 7am–8pm
24-hour post office
Hybernská 13
Praha 1
Tel. 224 22 58 45
Open 24 hours.
■ Other offices are open Mon.–Fri. 8am–6pm;
Sat. 8am–noon

MONEY
→ ATM
There are many ATMs throughout the city center for

holders of Visa, MasterCard or American Express cards.

→ BANKS
Banks are open Mon.–Fri. 9am–5pm. Exchange rates are favorable (and commission does not exceed 2%).
American Express
Václavské náměstí 56
Tel. 224 21 99 78
Open Tue.–Sat. 9am–7pm
Chequepoint
Staroměstské náměstí 21 and 28 října 13
Komerčni Banka
Ná Příkopě 33 (Můstek subway station)
Tel. 222 43 21 11
Open Mon.–Fri. 8am–5pm
Zivnostenska Banka
Ná Příkopě 20
Tel. 224 12 11 11
Open Mon.–Fri. 8.30am–5pm

→ BUREAUX DE CHANGE
Located in tourist areas. Most are 0pen daily 9am–11pm

→ EXCHANGE RATES
£1 = around 50 Kč
$1 = around 32 Kč
(at the time of printing)

→ LOSS OR THEFT
Notify your embassy or consulate (see p. 336) and the nearest police station as soon as possible. Report all stolen bank cards and checkbooks and have them stopped.
American Express
Tel. 222 80 01 11
Diners Club
Tel. 267 19 74 50
Mastercard/ Eurocard
Tel. 261 35 46 49
Visa
Tel. 224 12 53 53

NEWSPAPERS
There are many newsstands, offering a good selection of international

newspapers, especially daily, weekly and monthly English-language publications.
The Prague Pill
This trendier-than-thou free magazine can be found in many bars. It is particularly strong on music and club listings.
www.prague.tv/pill
The Prague Post
Weekly newspaper published every Wednesday in English, listing cultural and other events in Prague.
www.praguepost.com
Prehled Kulturnich Poradu V Praze
Monthly listing of cultural events in Prague. Available in the Information Offices in English or German.

NIGHTLIFE
→ CLASSICAL MUSIC
Orchestras and choirs hold performances in the streets of the Old Town, in churches, cloisters, former palaces and cultural centers. In summer they perform on bandstands, café terraces, in public parks and in the gardens of the Castle.

→ JAZZ
The International Jazz Festival takes place in October every year. Performances in jazz clubs start at 9pm. The best ones are:
Jazz Club zelezna
Zelezna 16
Tel. 224 23 96 97
www.jazzclub.cz
Open daily 3pm–1am; concerts at 9pm.
Reduta
Národní 20
Tel. 224 91 22 46
Open Mon.–Sat. 9pm–2am
Tickets can be bought from 5pm on weekdays, and from

6pm on Saturdays.
Agharta Jazz Centrum
Krakovská 5
Tel. 222 21 12 75
Open daily 5pm–1am.

→ NIGHTCLUBS
Casual dress is tolerated in most places but is not always accepted. Many brasseries also operate as nightclubs and have their own dance floors.
Rock Café
Národní tř. 22
Praha 1
Tel. 224 91 44 16
Open until 3am
Radost
Bělehradská 120
Praha 2
Tel. 224 25 47 76
Roxy
Dlouhá 33
Tel. 224 82 63 90

→ ROCK
Rock is the favorite music of young people, of Václav Havel, and former opponents of the Communist regime, who took major figures of rock counter-culture such as Bob Dylan or the Velvet Underground, as models and ideological reference points. The most popular Czech groups are Krystof, Lucie, Cechomor, Monkey Business, J.A.R and Chinaskt.

→ THEATERS
Prices
A ticket costs from 45 to 800 Kč.
National Theater (Národní divadlo)
Národní tř. 2
Tel. 224 91 34 37
Wide-ranging program of plays, concerts and opera. Performances begin at 7pm on weekdays and 2pm on Sundays.
Estates Theater (Stavoské divadlo)
Ovocný trh 1

Tel. 224 90 14 48
This is one of the most important centers for theatrical activity.
Laterna Magika
Národní tř. 4
Tel. 224 91 41 29
Booking office open Mon.–Fri 10am–8pm; Sat.–Sun. 3–8pm
Part of the National Theater, the Laterna Magika combines ballet, mime and theater performances with film showings.
■ **National Puppet Theater**
Žatecká 1
Tel. 224 81 93 22

→ TICKETS AND PROGRAMS
A monthly list of concerts, plays and films is available from the Prague Information Service, Prague Tourist Center (see under "Tourist Information" page 336 for both) and in hotels. Cultural events are also listed in the Prague Post and the Prague Pill. Tickets can also be bought at the door of the theaters, at some hotels, and at Čedok and BTI offices. Famous opera houses and theaters are often fully booked months in advance, but you may be able to get tickets from last-minute cancellations.
Ticketpro
– Reservations by telephone:
Tel. 296 32 99 99
– Reservations via Internet:
www.ticketpro.cz
– Reservations by mail:
Salvátorská 10
110 00 Praha 1
Tel. 24 81 40 20
or 24 81 80 80
Fax 296 32 88 88
Open Mon.–Fri. 8.30am–8.30pm; Sat.–Sun. 2.30–8.30pm
BTI (Bohemia Ticket International)
– Malé nám. 13

Tel. 24 22 78 32
Open Mon.–Fri. 9am–5pm; Sat. 9am–2pm
– Na Příkopě 16
Tel. 24 21 50 31
Open Mon.–Fri. 10am–7pm; Sat. 10am–5pm; Sun. 10am–3pm
www.ticketsbti.cz

PARKS AND GARDENS
Petřín Park
East of Malá Strana (funicular or streetcars nos. 12 and 22).
Letná Park
Situated between the Holesovice and Hradčany districts.
Vojan Park
In Malá Strana.
Stromovka Park
The largest in Prague.
Vrtba Gardens
in Malá Strana, Karmelitská.
Open 8am–7pm
Hvězda Park
Final stop of streetcar no. 22.

PUBLIC HOLIDAYS
January 1
New Year's Day, 'Day of Renovation of the Independent Czech State'
Easter Monday
May 1
Labor Day
May 8
Liberation Day (1945)
July 5
St Cyril and St Methodius Day
July 6
Anniversary of the death of John Huss
September 28
'Czech Statehood Day'
October 28
Independence Day (1918)
November 17
Anniversary of the Velvet Revolution.
December 24
Christmas Eve
December 25–26
Christmas

SHOPPING
→ OPENING TIMES
Most shops open at 9am and close at

6pm, Monday to Saturday. Department stores close at 8pm. In general, big city center stores, souvenir shops and some bookshops are open in the evening, Sundays and even on public holidays.

→ **PAYMENT**
Most shops accept credit cards.
Tax-free shopping for foreign visitors
If you purchase goods costing more than 1000 Kč in one transaction, you can get them free of (sales tax), providing you have a certificate from customs.

→ **BOHEMIAN GLASSWARE**
There are several varieties of Czech glassware, the most beautiful being "Bohemia" (made with lead to strengthen the glass), and the fine-cut, fragile "Moser".
Moser
Na Příkopě 12
Tel. 224 21 12 93
Open Mon.–Fri. 9am–8pm; Sat.–Sun. 10am–
Sklo Bohemia
Na Příkopě 17
Tel. 224 21 05 74
Open daily 10am–7pm
Celetná crystal
Celetná 15
Tel. 222 32 40 22
Open daily 10am–7pm
Magasin Kotva
Náměstí Republiky 18
Open Mon.–Fri. 9am–8pm; Sat.–Sun. 10am–6pm
Rott Crystal
Malé Náměstí 3 Praha 1
Open Mon–Fri. 9am–8pm; Sat.–Sun. 10am–6pm

→ **BOOKS**
Books are inexpensive and you will find in Prague

wonderful antiquarian bookstores. Štěpánská and Karlova streets are good places to browse, and you never know what treasured rarity you might find there.

→ **COMPACT DISCS, VINYL RECORDS AND CASSETTES**
High in quality and low in price, these are widely available in the streets and in specialist stores:
Knihkupectuí Kafka
Staroměstské náměstí 12
Tel. 223 21 14 34
Open daily 10am–6pm
Bontonland (Palais Koruna)
Václavské náměstí 1
Tel. 224 23 53 56
Open Mon.–Sat. 9am–8pm; Sun. 10am–6pm

→ **CRAFTS**
Česká Lidová řemesla
Melantrichova 17 (in the Old Town)
Mostecká 17 (in Malá Strana)
Both branches of this shop specialize in local crafts.
Thun
Pařižská 2, Praha 1
China
Botanicus
Ungelt, Praha 1
(Plus many other branches). Think Body Shop but cheaper.

→ **SECOND-HAND SHOPS**
For old bobbin-lace, embroidered tablecloths, books, engravings and so on.
U Prazskeho Jezulatka
Karmelitska 16
Tel. 257 53 24 41
Open daily 10am–noon, 1–6pm.
U Zlate Cise
Nerudova 16/212
Tel. 257 53 13 93
Open Mon.–Fri. 10am–6pm; Sat.–Sun. 10am–5pm

→ MUSICAL INSTRUMENTS AND SHEET MUSIC
In order to export old instruments you will need to obtain a license from the Museum of Decorative Arts and pay a tax of 20%. In general, instruments more than a hundred years old are difficult to acquire, and they can only be bought through specialized channels.
Amati Kraslice
U Obecního domu
(behind the Town Hall)
Tel. 222 00 23 46
Open Mon.–Fri. 9.30am–6pm
Wind instruments specialists.
U Zlatého Kohouta
Michalská 3
Tel. 224 21 28 74
Open Mon.–Fri. 10am–6pm
Violin specialists.
Music Goca
V Kolkovně 6
Open Mon.–Fri. 10am–6pm
String instrument specialists.

→ OBJETS D'ART
A number of art galleries (which are listed in weekly and monthly programs) present paintings, drawings, prints and ceramics. Prints and engravings are sold in the streets.
Warning:
Don't forget to check customs requirements with vendors.

→ TOYS
Puppets, wooden toys and traditional dolls hang in clusters in specialist stores.
Firma Ami
Nerudova 47
Tel. 257 53 27 35
Open daily 10am–6pm
Fantazie Kubenovci
Rytířská 19, Praha 1

→ ANTIQUES
Prague is not the best place to pick up antiques – small towns outside the city are – but you can still find some bargains here. Good places to search include:
Vetešnictví
Vitězná 16, Praha 1
Art Deco Galerie
Michalská 21, Praha 1

→ GARNETS
The Bohemian home-grown gem. Try:
Granat Turnov
Dlouhá 30, Praha1

TAXIS
Prague taxi drivers are notorious. In theory, fares are fixed at 22 Kč a kilometer, with a 30 Kč pick-up charge, and drivers are obliged to give a signed receipt from the meter. In practice taxi drivers often do not turn the meter on and simply demand whatever they feel they can get away with at the end of the journey. Or they have the meter rigged with so-called "turbo" devices which exaggerate the kilometers traveled. The worst offenders are the organized gangs which control the stands at the main railway stations and tourist zones. These drivers can demand 10 times the official fare or more and threaten violence

if the tourist objects. We recommend you always telephone for a taxi. The following companies have the best reputation and most of their operators speak English:
■ Profitaxi
Tel 14035 or 261 31 41 51
■ AAA Taxi
Tel. 233 11 33 11

TELEPHONE
→ FROM THE POST OFFICE
Calling from the post office is a lengthy process. You must pay a deposit, then the operator will dial the number for you; at the end the operator gives you the change.

→ FROM TELEPHONE BOOTHS
Public telephones in the center of the city are usually in good order, but not those outside. Some take telephone cards (from 100 Kč to 280 Kč), available from post offices, Čedok offices, tobacconists and subway stations.

→ NEW TELEPHONE NUMBERS
Following an update of the telephone system almost all Prague telephone numbers now have 9 digits, starting with 2. A local call is very cheap.

→ ENQUIRIES
National
Tel. 1180
International
Tel. 1181

→ EMERGENCIES
Police
Tel. 158
Emergencies (medical help)
Tel. 155
Fire department
Tel. 150
Car breakdown services
Tel. 1230 or 1240

→ TO CALL THE UK
To call the UK from Prague dial 00 44 + the number you require, omitting the initial zero.

→ TO CALL THE US
To call the US from Prague dial 00 1 + area code and the number you require.

TOURIST INFORMATION
→ INFORMATION CENTERS
Czech Tourist Authority
Staroměstské nám. 6
Tel. 224 82 69 84/5
Vonihradska 46
Tel. 221 58 06 11
Open summer daily 9am–6pm; winter Mon.–Fri. 8.30am–5pm.
www.visitczech.cz
Prague Information Service (PIS)
Staroměstská radnice (Old Town Hall), or Na Příkopě 20
Tel. (420) 12444 for both addresses
tourinfo@pis.cz
www.pis.cz
Open summer Mon.–Fri. 9am–7pm; Sat.-Sun. 9am–5pm; winter Mon.–Fri. 9am–6pm; Sat. 9am–3pm
www.pis.cz
Prague Tourist Center
Rytířská 12
Tel. 224 21 22 09 and 224 23 60 47
Open daily 9am–8pm
www.ptc.cz

→ TOURS
Pragotour
Staroměstské
náměstí, Praha 1
Tel. 224 48 25 62
Guided tours of the
main sights (in
several languages).
Prague Walks
Nezamyslova 7
Praha 2
Tel. 261 21 46 03
Walking tours with a
theme: 'Old Prague
pubs', 'The Velvet
Revolution',
'Prague's ghosts' etc.
*www.pha.comp.cz/
pwalks/*

→ EMBASSIES
UK Embassy
Thun Palace
Thunovská 14
11800 Praha 1
Tel. 257 53 02 78
www.britain.cz
US Embassy
Tržiště 15
11801 Praha 1
Tel. 257 53 06 63
www.usic.cz
Canadian Embassy
Mickiewiczova 6,
12533 Praha 6
Tel. 272 101 800

→ LOST PROPERTY
Karoliny Světlé 5
Praha 1
Tel. 224 23 50 85
For loss or theft of
credit cards, see
under "Money".

TRAINS
Hlavní nádraží
The Central Station
is located at
Wilsonova třída
(Hlavní nádraží
station, line C).with
several tourist
information points.
Purchase tickets at
the ticket offices or
from automatic
machines.
■ Information
Tel. 224 22 42 00

**URBAN
TRANSPORT**
Prague's transport
system is very
practical and
inexpensive.

See map ◆ 384

**→ INFORMATION
DESKS**
There is an
information desk in
five subway stations:
Muzeum (lines A, C)
Můstek (line B)
Andel (line B)
Nádraží Holešovice
(line C)
Cerny Most (line B)
See also the website
www.dp-praha.cz

**→ BUSES
AND TRAMWAYS**
Both tram and bus
routes are shown
at stops and on
the city maps.
While you are
traveling, a recorded
announcement
indicates each
stop as it arrives
and the next one
to come.
Day services
Between 4.30am
and midnight
Night services
Between midnight
and 4.30am

Buses
Lines nos. 501 to 512
Tramways
Lines nos. 51 to 58

**→ FUNICULAR
RAILWAY**
Toward Petřín Hill
It follows the
direction Újezd-
Nebozízek-Petřín.
Open daily
9.15am–8.45pm.
Every ten or fifteen
minutes.

→ SUBWAY
The network consists
of three lines
indicated by different
colors and letters:
Line A: green
(Salka–Dejvická),
Line B: yellow
(Černy most–Zličín),
Line C: red
(Nádraží
Holešovice–Háje)
Times
Daily between 5am
and midnight.

→ TICKETS
Buy tickets at the
subway station,

newsstands,
tobacconists,
tourist offices
and hotels.
Free
Children under
6 years of age and
disabled people.
Concessions
50% reduction for
children 6–15 years.

→ TARIFFS
No line change
Basic tickets cost
8 Kč (concessions
4 Kč). These are
valid for 15 mins
from the time you
stamp your ticket
on buses and
trams, or for four
subway stops.
Several changes
12 Kč ticket
(concessions
6 Kč), valid 60 mins
(90 mins at night
and weekends)
**Tourist period
tickets**
1 day: 70 Kč
3 days: 200 Kč
7 days: 250 Kč
15 days: 280 Kč

◆ GLOSSARY

ACCOMMODATION

Bathroom: *koupelna*
Bill: *účet*
Camping: *kemping*
Do you have rooms?:
máte volné pokoje ?
Full board:
plná penze
Room in a private
home:
pokoj v soukromí
Single / Double room:
*jednolůžkový /
dvoulůžkový pokoj*
Key: *klíč*
Night: *noc*
Reserve: *rezervovat*
Toilets: *záchod / toaleta*
Youth hostels:
mládežnická ubytovna

CALENDAR

January: *leden*
February: *únor*
March: *březen*
April: *duben*
May: *květen*
June: *červen*
July: *červenec*
August: *srpen*
September: *září*
October: *říjen*
November: *listopad*
December: *prosinec*
Monday: *pondělí*
Tuesday: *úterý*
Wednesday: *středa*
Thursday: *čtvrtek*
Friday: *pátek*
Saturday: *sobota*
Sunday: *neděle*

COUNTING

One: *jeden / jedna /
jedno*
Two: *dva /dvě*
Three: *tři*
Four: *čtyři*
Five: *pět*
Six: *šest*
Seven: *sedm*
Eight: *osm*
Nine: *devět*
Ten: *deset*
Fifty: *padesát*
One hundred: *sto*
Five hundred:
pět set
One thousand: *tisíc*
Million: *milión*

CULTURE

Booking office:
předprodej vstupenek
Change in a program:
změna programu
Chamber music:
komorní hudba
Concert: *koncert*
Dance: *tanec*
Fully booked:
vyprodáno

Jazz: *džez*
Movies: *kino*
Musical (a):
hudební komedie
Original version:
původní znění
Theater: *divadlo*
Ticket: *vstupenka /
lístek*

IN THE CAR

Beware of the train /
tramway:
pozor vlak / tramvaj
Breakdown: *porucha*
Car rental:
půjčovna automobilů
Customs: *celnice*
Driving license:
řidičský průkaz
Gasoil: *nafta*
Gasoline: *benzín*
Leadfree gas:
bezolovnatý benzín
Oil: *olej*
To fill up: *natankovat
plnou nádrž*

EATING

Beef: *hovězí*
Beer: *pivo*
Bon appétit!:
dobrou chuť'!
Bread: *chléb*
Cabbage: *zelí*
Cheese: *sýr*
Cold dishes:
studené jídlo
Fish: *ryby*
Fork: *vidlička*
Game: *zvěřina*
Glass: *sklenice*
Ham: *šunka*
Hot dishes:
teplé jídlo
Ice cream: *zmrzlina*
Knife: *nůž*
Lamb: *jehněčí*
Mutton: *skopové
červené víno*
Pâtisserie:
zákusky-moučníky
Pork roast:
vepřová pečeně
Potato cakes:
bramborák
Poultry: *drůbež*
Soup: *polévka*
Spoon: *lžíce*
Sugar: *sladký*
The bill, please:
u čet, prosim
The menu, please:
*jídelní lístek,
prosim*
To your health!:
nazdraví!
Waffles: *vafle*
Water: *voda*
White / rosé /
red wine: *bílé / růžové /
červené víno*

FINDING YOUR WAY

Avenue: *třída*
Bridge: *most*
Cemetary: *hřbitov*
Church: *kostel*
Crossroads: *křižovatka*
Garden: *sad*
House: *dům*
Island: *ostrov*
Left: *nalevo / vlevo /
doleva*
Place: *náměstí*
Platform: *nábřeží*
Right: *napravo / vpravo /
doprava*
Street: *ulice*

HEALTH

Aspirin: *acylpyrin /
aspirin*
Blood group:
krevní skupina
Cold (a): *rýma*
Dentist: *zubní lékař /
zubař*
Clinic (dispensary):
zdravotní středisko
Doctor: *lékař*
Hospital: *nemocnice*
I'm not feeling well:
je mi špatně
Pharmacy: *lékárna*
Surgery hours:
ordinační hodiny

MAIL

Address: *adresa*
Money order: *poštovní
poukázka*
Parcel: *balíček / balík*
Post office:
poštovní úřad
Postcard: *pohlednice*
Registered letter:
doporučený dopis
Stamp: *známka*
Telegram: *telegram*
Telephone: *telefon*
Telephone card:
telefonní karta
Telephone directory:
telefonní seznam

MONEY

Auto-teller: *peněžní
automat / bankomat*
Bank: *banka*
Bureau de change
směnárna
Cash: *hotovost*
Change: *směna peněz*
Commission: *poplatek*
Credit card: *úvěrová
karta / kreditní karta*
Crown: *Koruna*
How long does it take
to change...?:
jaký je kurs ?
Money: *peníze*
Traveler's cheque:
cestovní šek

STORES

Antique store:
stardžitnosti
Baker's: *pekárna*
Bohemian glassware:
český křišťál
Bookstore (second-
hand books):
antikvariát
Butcher's: *řeznictví*
CD: *kompaktní deska*
Closed: *zavřeno*
Cut / blown glass:
broušené / foukané sklo
Department stores:
obchodní dům
Doll: *panenka*
Embroidery: *výšivka*
Entrance: *vchod*
Exit: *východ*
How much is...?:
kolik to stojí?
Lace: *krajka*
Open: *otevřeno*
Puppet: *loutka*
Sweets: *cukrovinky /
cukrárna*
What is it?: *co je to?*

TRANSPORT

Avenue: *třída*
Book of tickets:
soubor jízdenek
Discount: *sleva*
Transfer: *přestup*
Central railway station:
hlavní nádráží
Exit: *výstup*
Funicular train: *lanová
dráha / lanovka*
Next station:
příští stanice
Stop: *zastávka*
Subway line: *trasa*
Terminal: *konečná
stanice*
Traffic: *doprava*
Train: *vlak*
Validate: *označit*

COMMON EXPRESSIONS

Excuse me: *pardon*
Good morning:
dobré ráno
Goodbye:
na shledanou
Hello/Good day:
dobrý den
Help!: *pomoc !*
How much?: *kolik ?*
I don't understand:
nerozumím
No: *ne*
Please: *prosim*
Thank you: *děkuji*
What?: *jak ?*
What's your telephone
number?: *jaké máte
číslo telefonu?*
When? *kdy?*
Yes: *ano*

HOTELS ◆

Selected by Robert Anderson

The ▲ symbol refers to the Itineraries section. The ◆ symbol refers to the map section. The key to the other symbols is given on page 329.

Abri
(off map C)
Jana Masaryka 36
Praha 2
Tel. 222 51 51 24
Fax: 224 25 42 40
www.abri.cz
Vinohrady (◆ **C** B6) sometimes called the Kensington of Prague, is a good hotel hunting ground for visitors who don't want or cannot afford to be right in the tourist vortex. This leafy 19th-century suburb is also full of restaurants and bars and it's only 15 minutes walk from Wenceslas Square. The Abri is a comfortable hotel with a restaurant and a charming terrace over the courtyard. Some of the rooms are small, but they are bright and have modern bathrooms. 26 rooms.
⊡ P ⬆

Anna
◆ **C** C6
Budečská 17
Praha 2
Tel. 222 51 31 11
Fax 222 51 51 58
www.hotelanna.cz
If you're prepared to be just outside the center this Vinohrady hotel is a bargain. It even has a smart pink neo-classical façade and the inside sports Art Nouveau flourishes. The rooms are not so extravagant but they are still comfortable and are equipped with modern bathrooms. Twelve of the 36 rooms are in a cheaper annexe.

The National Museum is only a few minutes' walk down Vinohradská Street. Children's rates.
⊡ ⬆ ☒

Betlem Club
◆ **B** B5
Betlémské náměstí 9
Praha 1
Tel. 222 22 15 75
Fax 222 22 05 08
www.betlemclub.cz

Betlem Club has a great location in a quiet square in the heart of the Old Town, two hundred yards from Charles Bridge, and opposite the chapel where Czech hero John Huss used to preach, denouncing the wealth of the Church and the trade in indulgences. The two-storey hotel is a bit kitsch but this is easily forgivable at this price. The rooms are comfortable, though a little retro in furnishing. Breakfast is served in a rough stone cellar with medieval

weapons hanging on the wall. 21 rooms.
⊡

Casa Marcello
◆ **B** D2
Řásnovka 783
Praha 1
Tel. 23 10 260
Fax 23 13 323
www.casamarcello.cz
Situated in a quiet area near St Agnes Convent, Casa Marcello is full of character. It is a beautiful long building that follows the curve of a small alley, with an inner courtyard used in the summer. The bedrooms are all tastefully arranged, with well-equipped bathrooms. There is some beautiful furniture in the reception areas. 27 double rooms and 5 apartments. Access available for disabled people.
⊡ ♿ P

Charles
◆ **A** E3
Josefská 1
Praha 1
Tel. 257 53 29 13

Fax 257 53 29 10
The Charles is very popular with tourists, and for good reason. Set in a beautiful Renaissance gabled building, and freshly painted in green and white, this hotel is only 150 yards from Charles Bridge. Spacious rooms and beds. 20 rooms.
⊡ ⬤

Dientzenhofer
◆ **A** E4
Nosticova 2
Praha 1
Tel. and Fax
257 31 13 19
Set in an 18th-century villa behind Kampa Park, along the Vltava, this boarding house is a haven of peace. It is a hidden address in a quiet little street outside the usual tourist routes. In summer, breakfast is served on a terrace looking out onto the park. Access available for disabled people. Friendly atmosphere. 4 double rooms and 2 suites.
⊡ P ♿ ⬆

Dum U Krále Jiřího
◆ **B** B5
Liliová 10
Praha 1
Tel. 224 24 87 97
Fax 224 24 87 97
www.kinggeorge.cz
Close to Charles Bridge, Liliová Street is one of the most picturesque and tranquil streets in the Old Town. Fine old houses with red-tile roofs, interior gardens, and porches that open onto the grounds of a 17th-century convent or a seemingly abandoned garden. 14 comfortable rooms.
⊡

◆ HOTELS

Selected by Robert Anderson

Dům U Velké Boty
◆ **A** C3
Vlašská 30
Praha 1
Tel. and Fax
257 53 20 88
www.volweb.cz/rippl
A quiet family boarding house situated opposite the Embassy of the United States, in a very tranquil area. It offers a warm, friendly welcome and spacious rooms with showers or baths, and looks out over a quiet little square. In summer, fireworks from the American Embassy light up Prague's night sky. 8 rooms.
🔲

Elite
◆ **B** A6-B6
Ostrovní 32
Praha 1
Tel. 224 93 22 50
Fax 224 93 0787
www.hotelelite.cz
The Elite is a stylish luxury hotel on the edge of the trendy bar district that extends from the National Theater toward Spálená. The rooms are a bit small and the elegant modern furnishings clash with the original Renaissance ceilings. Most look on to the hotel's pretty courtyard. Rather incongruously, breakfast is served in the Ultramarin bar which becomes a happening place at night with a nightclub in the cellar. 79 rooms.
🔲🍴🅿

Esplanade
◆ **B** E6
Washingtonova 19
Praha 1
Tel. 224 50 11 72
Fax 224 22 93 06
www.esplanade.cz
Prague central railway station,

an authentic Art-Nouveau building, is literally opposite the Esplanade, a stone's throw from Wenceslas Square. Owned by a foreign chain, this beautiful hotel enjoys a high reputation thanks to its luxurious décor and comfortable salons. The quality of the rooms varies, but you can view them before making a decision. Rooms 711 and 712 have a magnificent view. Excellent restaurant. 74 rooms.
🔲❌🅿

ESPLANADE/DR

Evropa
◆ **B** D6 ▲ *174*
Václavské náměstí 25
Praha 1
Tel. 224 22 81 17
Fax 224 22 45 44
www.evropahotel.cz
Despite its slightly run-down appearance, the Evropa still has great charm. A symbol of Art Nouveau, its façade has floral motifs and wrought-iron and ceramic balconies. Built in 1889 by the architect Bělský, it was rebuilt in the Art Nouveau style in 1903. Once you get past the heavy revolving door, you are transported into the enchanting atmosphere of the early 20th century. Carry on past the reception area

and enter the restaurant, which has a sumptuous décor of caryatids and stained glass. The old wooden elevator creaks a bit as it takes you to the upper floors, but the wrought-iron staircase is stunningly elegant. However, the bedrooms are of uneven quality so it is perhaps best to take a look at several of them before deciding whether to stay on. The bathrooms may not offer all modern amenities, but the

Louis-XVI-style furniture and décor are unique and may compensate. You can enjoy breakfast in the gallery leading to the café of the hotel. This café is also open to non-residents (see p. 346). 90 rooms and 2 apartments.
🔲🅿❌

Four Seasons
◆ **B** B4
Veleslavínova 2a, (not marked on map, next to František u Křižovníků)
Praha 1
Tel. 221 42 70 00
Fax 221 42 60 00
www.fourseasons.com/prague
The new Four Seasons hotel has raised the standard that Prague's other luxury five-star hotels must try to reach. The hotel is

right on the Vltava River, just on the edge of the Old Town, and has sweeping views of the Charles Bridge nearby and across to Prague Castle on the other bank. Because its site is so central the $60m-development provoked a huge controversy which dragged in even President Václav Havel, the Castle's occupant. But the sceptics have been proved wrong and the four interconnected old and new buildings blend in both with each other and the surroundings. From the river the new modern block is shielded from view by the neoclassical house and the fantastic 18th-century Baroque villa, all finished in yellow sandstone or plaster. On the Old Town side, the hotel is fronted by the richly detailed neo-Renaissance house with its domes and buttresses. Guests can specify which building they would prefer, but inside the maze of passages it is sometimes difficult to tell which century one is in. Even the rooms look similar – each of the 142 rooms is large, at around 430 sq ft – though the ones in the neo-Renaissance House are easily distinguishable by their tall 12-ft ceilings. There are also 20 suites, including several on two levels with separate living and sleeping areas. For visitors to Mr Havel, the four-bedroom, 2,500-sq ft presidential suite – which takes up the whole first

◉ *< 3,000 Kč*
◉ *3,000 to 4,500 Kč*
◉ *> 4,500 Kč*

floor of the Baroque villa – should be the natural choice. Only around 45 of the units have full river views but the superb Italian restaurant Allegro has a terrace facing onto the embankment.
142 rooms
◉⬆♒Ⓟ♿

Grand Hôtel Bohemia
◆ **B** D4
Králodvorská 4
Praha 1
Tel. 224 80 41 11
Fax 222 32 95 45
www.grandhotel bohemia.cz
Perfectly situated behind the Municipal House, this hotel belongs to the Austrian chain "Austria Hotels". The rooms are comfortable and the service of high quality. The halls are large and pleasant and the restaurant has a huge sitting capacity. With its balconies, stuccos and gorgeous ceilings, the neo-Baroque ballroom, called "Boccacio", is sometimes used for receptions and important dinner parties.
78 rooms.
◉ⓍⓅ♿

Hoffmeister
◆ **A** F1
Pod Bruskou 9
Praha 1
Tel. 251 01 71 11
Fax 251 01 71 20
www.hoffmeister.cz
The Hoffmeister, which belongs to the French "Relais & Châteaux" luxury chain of hotels, has an uncomfortable location, at the busy intersection outside Malostranská subway station, but it is a surprising oasis of calm away from the Malá Strana tourist

tempest. In the 1920's it was one of the places to be seen and it is full of caricatures of the period, sketched by the current owner's father, Adolf Hoffmeister. Today it is more peaceful but it still has a restaurant famed for its wine cellar.
38 rooms.
◉Ⓟ♿

Josef
◆ **B** D3
Rybná 20
Praha 1
Tel. 221 70 01 11

PALACE/DR

Fax: 221 70 09 99
www.hoteljosef.com
The Josef is a new modern hotel in the Old Town for the style-conscious business traveler. The rooms are furnished with simple but luxurious modern furniture and the superior ones have bathrooms with glass and metal walls. The hotel also has a top floor fitness center with its own terrace, a ground floor breakfast room looking out onto

the hotel's own courtyard, and a trendy lobby bar.
110 rooms.
◉ⓍⓅ♿

Palace
◆ **B** D5
Panská 12
Praha 1
Tel. 224 09 31 11
Fax 224 22 12 40
www.hotelpalace.cz
The Palace opened just before World War I and entered its heyday in the 1920's and 1930's when it entertained an international artistic cast including

Josephine Baker and Enrico Caruso. It began its slow decline during the World War II, when it was frequented by the Gestapo, and was then left to moulder quietly by 40 years of Communist neglect. What you see today is the result of a massive reconstruction completed – with exquisite timing – just before the Velvet Revolution. The façade was left intact, with its beautiful Art

Nouveau details around the windows, and the grand entrance, with its flanking statues holding glass lanterns, gives an idea of what it must once have been like. However, the inside, with its grand staircases and reading salons, was ripped out. In its place a modern hotel with 114 rooms and 10 suites was constructed. It could have been a disaster but care was taken to give a nod to the past by including Art Nouveau flourishes such as colored glass, mirrors and chandeliers, together with vaguely fin-de-siècle paintings and statues. There are places, such as the new American-style bar, where the influence of the 1920's is rather less obvious, but going into the dark paneled (and award winning) Gourmet Club Restaurant is like entering a time capsule. A word of warning: the Palace is located outside the old town (opposite the new Mucha Museum), in the busy, main commercial district. 124 rooms. Book well ahead for both hotel and restaurant.
◉♿

Paříž
◆ **B** D4 ▲ *162*
U Obecního domu 1
Praha 1
Tel. 222 19 51 95
Fax 224 22 54 75
www.hotel-pariz.cz
The elegant canopy at the entrance, in authentic Secession style, is in itself a work of art. Art-Nouveau enthusiasts (with the necessary means) usually elect to stay at the

Paříž, which was fashionable at the start of the 20th century, when it was built. Other visitors may find the décor, immortalized by the Czech writer Bohumil Hrabal in "I Served the King of England", a little cold. In 1991 this stunning hotel, located next to the Town Hall, was returned to its former owners, the Brandejs, who restored it beautifully. It must be said that the rooms are a little small, but they are comfortable and well-equipped. The restaurant, with its Art Nouveau decorations, is truly magnificent. The service, however, lacks warmth. 94 rooms.
🅿️❎🅿️

Pod Věží
◆ **A** E3
Mostecká 2, Praha 1
Tel. 257 53 20 41
Fax 257 53 20 69
www.podvezi.com
This boutique hotel is, as its name suggests, just under the tower on the Malá Strana end of Charles Bridge. The view naturally is superb, though it is really a bit too close to the constant stream of tourists crossing the bridge. The 12 rooms are classically elegant and there is also a restaurant facing the bridge.
🅿️🅿️🈂️

Radisson SAS Alcron
◆ **B** D6, **D** D1-D2
Štěpánská 40, Praha 1
Tel. 222 82 00 00
Fax 222 82 01 00
www.radissonsas.com
The Alcron, like the Palace, was in

its heyday in the 1930's when it hosted celebrated figures from around the world. During the World War II the hotel provided accommodation first for high ranking German officers and then at the end of the war for their Red Army conquerors. Under the Communist

era it fell into steep decline, being famous more for prostitutes and secret policemen. The Radisson SAS group has now lovingly restored the hotel's stunning Art Deco interior and furnished the rooms up to luxury five star standard. The Alcron restaurant is regarded as one of Prague's finest, The La Rotonde is

almost as good. The Alcron is just off Wenceslas Square in the business district. 211 rooms.
🅿️♿🅿️

Résidence Nosticova
◆ **A** E4
Nosticova 1
Praha 1
Tel. 257 31 25 13
Fax 257 31 25 17
www.nosticova.com

A fine establishment off the usual tourist routes. This fairly new hotel, housed in a 17th-century building, has been tastefully decorated by its Italian owners. A rough stone staircase leads to the bedrooms and apartments. Inside the rooms, fireplaces, canopied four-poster beds, mahogany furniture and tapestries make this hotel an ideal

place for a romantic week end. 10 rooms (7 apartments and 3 bedrooms) – the bigger ones have a modern kitchenette.
🅿️🅿️

Savoy
◆ **A** A2
Keplerova 6, Praha 1
Tel. 224 30 24 30
Fax 224 30 21 28
www.hotel-savoy.cz
This is Prague's luxury hotel par excellence. Top-class service and spacious rooms with terraces looking out over the Church of Loreto. Also available are a fitness center with sauna, a jacuzzi, a hairdressing salon, 24-hour room service and a beautiful library. Impeccable restaurant. 61 rooms and 5 apartments.
🅿️♿❎🅿️🈂️

Sax
◆ **A** C3
Jánský Vršek 328/3
Praha 1
Tel. 257 53 12 68
Fax 257 53 41 01
www.sax.cz
Superb environment in a very quiet area at the heart of Malá Strana. Set in an Empire-style building, this modern hotel is built around a three-storey atrium. The rooms are spacious and well furnished. The windows look out over the rooftops of Malá Strana, Strahov and the Castle. Very romantic.19 rooms and 3 suites.
🅿️🈂️

U Krále Karla
◆ **A** C3
Úvoz 4, Praha 1
Tel. 257 53 12 11
Fax 257 53 10 49
www.romantichotels.cz
The King Charles, which lies just off the steep tourist

◘ < 3,000 Kč
◙ 3,000 to 4,500 Kč
▣ > 4,500 Kč

climb up to the Castle, must be probably the most beautiful hotel in Prague. It's such a riot of stained glass and patterned ceilings that it's almost garish. It has a fantastic baroque façade and one's first view of the stained-glass skylight over the narrow central atrium is breathtaking. The rooms have antique furniture, fireplaces, and wooden-beamed ceilings. There is also a restaurant. 19 rooms.
▣

U Kříže
◆ A E5-E6
Újezd 20
Praha 1
Tel. 257 31 32 72
Fax 257 31 25 42
www.ukrize.com
Hotel-restaurant in a renovated 16th century building, with a view over Petřín Hill, five minutes from St Nicholas Cathedral. Good value for money. 22 rooms.
◘ P ⬆

U Medvídků
◆ B B5
Na Perštýně 7
Praha 1
Tel. 224 21 19 16
Fax 224 22 09 30
www.umedvidku.cz
This boarding house, run by young people, is one of the cheapest in the city center, considering its convenient location between Bethlehem Square and the National Theater. The house may not look like anything special, but the rooms are comfortable. Excellent value for money. 31 rooms.
◘ ✕

Unitas
Bartolomějská 9,
Praha 1
Tel. 224 21 10 20
Fax 224 21 08 00
www.unitas.cz
This Old Town pension was until the Velvet Revolution a prison and once entertained future President Václav Havel. The cellar rooms are bare cells

U TŘÍ PŠTROSŮ/DR

with metal doors, while the upstairs rooms boast carpets, some furniture and bright colored walls. The shared showers are a long walk down the corridor in your towel. Smoking, drinking and staying out late are banned. 27 rooms.
◘ P

U Pava
◆ A F3
U Lužického Semináře 32
Praha 1
Tel. 257 53 35 73
Fax 257 53 09 19
www.romantichotels.cz
The Peacock is located in one of the most beautiful squares of Malá Strana, very close to

Charles Bridge. In 1991 the house was saved from imminent destruction, renovated and turned into a hotel that managed to keep an old charm atmosphere. In 2000 the interior of the hotel itself was completely refurbished in the style of an English stately home, with slightly garish results. There is also a cellar restaurant, and a sauna with a whirlpool. Very comfortable. 27 rooms.
▣ P ♿ ♨

U Staré Paní
◆ B B5
Michalská 9
Praha 1
Tel. 224 22 80 90
Fax 224 21 21 72
www.ustarepani.cz
The Old Lady is a good mid-range choice in the heart of the Old Town. The rooms are nothing special but the hotel has charm, plus a good restaurant, and a well-known jazz club. 18 rooms.
◙

U Tří Pštrosů
◆ A F3
Dražického nám. 12
Praha 1
Tel. 257 53 24 10
Fax 257 53 32 17
www.upstrosu.cz
This is one of the oldest houses in Prague, at the end of Charles Bridge. Legend has it that a foreign delegation came to meet Emperor Charles IV and had to spend the night in the company of three ostriches that were intended as a present. The birds became the symbol of the house, as illustrated in a fresco on the façade. The rooms are spacious and comfortable, with beams on the ceilings decorated with rural motifs. Very good restaurant. 18 rooms.
▣ P ♨

U Zlaté Studně
◆ A E2
U Zlaté Studně 3
(not marked on map; hotel is next to Starý Královský Palác)
Praha 1
Tel. 257 01 12 13
Fax 257 53 33 20
www.zlatastudna.cz
Not to be mixed with U Zlaté studny below. This hotel is housed in a 16th-century Renaissance building, that once belonged to Rudolf II and later to the famous astronomer Tycho Brahe. Nestling just below the Castle walls it has some of the best views in Prague. All rooms have views and are stylishly furnished with replica antiques. The restaurant is also one of the best in Prague (see p. 349). 17 rooms and 3 suites.
◙

U Zlaté studny

◆ **B** A4-B4

Karlova 3

Praha 1

Tel. and fax

222 22 11 13

This Old Town hotel has a marvelous façade, decorated with six statues, including one of St John Nepomuk, and looks out onto a small square at the entrance of the Clementinum. It is a prestigious address though, with only 4 spacious suites 2 double rooms. The suites have original vaulted ceilings, parquet floors and antique furniture.

A note of warning: The 16th-century house is on Karlova street which can be crowded day and night.

🔳🅿

U Zlatého Stromu

◆ **B** A4-B4

Karlova 6

Tel. and fax

222 22 04 41

www.zlatystrom.cz

A handsome three-story house with a gabled front locateed only 50 yards from Charles Bridge, this hotel-restaurant has recently been thoroughly restored. The beamed ceilings are quite low, as in most of the houses found in the Old Town. Public spaces and bedrooms contain some genuine Austrian antiques, such as trunks and painted wardrobes. The suites are tucked away under the eaves. There is a restaurant serving Czech cuisine, as well as a very discreet nightclub in the cellars.

23 rooms.

🔳

U Žlute Boty

Jánský vršek 11,

Praha 1

Tel. 257 53 22 69

Fax 257 53 41 34

www.zlutabota.cz

The Yellow Shoe is a pink Renaissance house in a quiet narrow street in one of the most beautiful parts of Malá Strana. Inside, the hotel is simple but cosy with wooden floors and ceilings. Many of the rooms have painted decorations but can be a little dark. There is also a small courtyard. The hotel is great value for this part of the city.

8 rooms.

🔳🖿

Waldstein

Valdštejnské

náměstí 6

Praha 1

Tel. 257 53 39 38

Fax 257 53 11 43

www.avetravel.cz

The Waldstein is located in a quiet corner of Malá Strana next to the Senate, which was the palace of General Albrecht von Waldstein (Wallenstein) of Thirty Year's War notoriety. This Renaissance building has a small courtyard and a barrel-vaulted cellar breakfast room with its own well. The rooms have low timber-framed ceilings and are equipped with rather heavy antique furniture but modern bathrooms. There is no lift and half of the rooms are in nearby annexes. 24 rooms.

🔳

PUBS, BEER HALLS ◆

Selected by Robert Anderson

■ < 220 Kč
■ 220 to 550 Kč
■ > 550 Kč

The ▲ symbol refers to the Itineraries section. The ◆ symbol refers to the map section. The key to the other symbols is given on page 329.

PUBS, BEER HALLS

Báračnická Rychta
◆ **A** D3
Tržiště 23
Praha 1
Tel. 257 53 24 61
Open Mon–Sat. noon–midnight; Sun. noon–9pm
A genuine old-style Czech pub with wood-paneled booths just off the tourist track among the alleys of Malá Strana. Solid food, good beer, outdoor tables in the summer, and a bewildering variety of live music in the evening.
■🍴🎵

Kolkovna
◆ **B** C3
V. Kolkovně 8
Praha 1
Tel. 224 81 97 01
Open daily 11am–midnight
Kolkovna is a fake – it's a new branch of the Pilsner Urquell chain – but it's great for all that. The Czech food is better than most, the pilsner is beautifully poured, and unlike many pubs it is bright and airy and not too smoky. Consequently it gets packed and service can be very slow.
■

U Černého Vola
◆ **A** B3
Loretánské náměstí 1
Praha 1
Tel. 220 51 34 81
Open daily 10am–10pm
A real Czech pub in the Bohemian Disneyland around the Castle! Although
it's on the main tourist thoroughfare, the Black Bull thankfully keeps a low profile and requires determination to find. Once you've spotted the sign, stride confidently past the regulars blocking the doorway and try to find a spare part of a bench to squat on. You haven't come here to eat, but the bar snacks here are the real thing too.
■

U Fleků
◆ **D** B1 ▲ *307*
Křemencova 11
Praha 1
Tel. 224 93 40 19
Open daily 10am–11pm
www.ufleku.cz
U fleků is probably the most famous pub in Prague but it's not quite clear why. Yes, it has a gorgeous Gothic room and it brews its own beer but it is also overpriced and full of tourist groups and oom-pah bands. No self-respecting Czech would ever step through the door. Watch the extras here as well – the nibbles on the table and the proffered Becherovka apéritif are neither complementary nor cheap.
■◻🍴♨🎵

U Medvídků
◆ **B** B6
Na Perštýně 7
Praha 1
Tel. 224 21 19 16
Open daily 11.30am–11pm
The Bear Cubs is a big beer hall just off Národní, worth checking out for its Budvar beer and wide range of traditional Czech dishes. It is slightly ersatz but mercifully low on
tour groups or smoke.
■

U Zlatého Tygra
◆ **B** B4-B5
Husova 17, Praha 1
Tel. 222 22 11 11
Open daily 3pm–11pm
The Golden Tiger is a great Old Town pub that has been saved from the tour groups. Bohumil Hrabal used to be a regular here and a few tables are still reserved for local diehards to preserve the pub's character. It is reputed to serve the best Pilsner Urquell in Prague. If you have to eat with your beer, it provides some Czech favorites, as well as bar snacks. The pub is tiny so come early to have any chance of finding a bench.
■

RESTAURANTS AND CAFÉS

Amici miei
◆ **B** C3
Vězeňska 5
Praha 1
Tel. 224 81 66 88
Open daily 11am–4pm, 6.30pm–midnight
Elegant Italian restaurant close to the Spanish synagogue in the Jewish quarter. In the summer you can eat outside on the pavement. Enjoy the great fish dishes, excellent wine list, and the smooth service.
■■🎵

Arzenal
◆ **B** B4
Valentinská 11
Praha 1
Tel. 224 81 40 99
Open daily 10am–midnight
Prague's best Thai restaurant by a mile is hidden at
the back of a fancy glass store near Staroměstská subway station. The few diners that find their way here use beautiful plates, cutlery and glasses from the store. Some of the dishes are truly fiery, as Thai food should be.
■

Bakeshop Praha
◆ **B** C2-C3
Kozí 1, Praha 1
Tel. 222 31 68 23
Open daily 7am–7pm
Bakeshop Praha is a great place to grab a sandwich or quiche as it is just a stone's throw from the Old Town Square. The bakery now offers coffee to go with its mouthwatering array of American cakes and muffins.
■

Bellevue
◆ **B** A4
Smetanovo nábřeží 18
Praha 1
Tel. 222 22 14 38
Open Mon.–Sat. noon–3pm, 5.30–11pm; Sun. 11am–3.30pm, 7–11pm
In the past the Bellevue suffered from indifferent service, basic furnishings and an unimaginative cuisine, but its location on the banks of the Vltava made up for these negative attributes by offering a superb view of Malá Strana and of the Castle opposite. Today, however, both the high-quality décor and the cuisine make this restaurant one of the best in Prague. The Sunday brunch is a must. Piano music on weekday evenings and a jazz ensemble at the weekend.
■♨🎵

345

◆ RESTAURANTS, CAFÉS

Selected by Robert Anderson

Bistrot de Marlène
◆ **D** B4
Plavecká 4
Praha 2
Tel. 224 92 18 53
Open
Mon.–Fri. noon–
2.30pm, 7–10.30pm;
Sat. 7–10.30pm
*Owner and chef
Marlène Salomon
first opened her
bistrot in 1995.
The 15 years she
spent in Provence
seem to have
influenced the
bright, sunny décor
of her restaurant.
The menu is often
amended according
to the produce
available. Specialties
include duck cutlet
in bilberry sauce,
pheasant terrine
and foie gras.*
■■■

**Café at the
Evropa Hotel**
◆ **B** D6
Václavské
náměstí 25
Praha 1
*This grand café, on
Wenceslas Square,
is well worth a visit
for its remarkable Art
Nouveau décor.
(See the hotel's
description p. 340.)*
■

Le Café Colonial
◆ **B** B3
Široká 6, Praha 1
Tel. 224 81 83 22
Open daily
10am–1am
*Part café, part
brasserie, the
Jewish district's
Le Café Colonial
does everything
from a coffee to a
full dinner. Some
dishes don't work
and the tables are
a little too close
together but it's
always a cool and
relaxed standby.*
■

Café Milena
◆ **B** C4
Staroměstské
náměstí 22
Praha 1
Tel. 221 63 26 02

Open 10am–8pm
*Located on the Old
Town Square, it
offers a good view
of the astronomical
clock, as well as
some delicious
cakes.*
■

BISTROT DE MARLÈNE/OR

Café Montmartre
◆ **B** B5
Řetězova 7
Praha 1
Tel. 222 22 12 44
Open Mon.-Frid.
9am–11pm; Sat-
Sund noon–11pm
*Between the wars
this Old Town bar
used to be the place
to catch up with
Franz Kafka, Max
Brod, Gustav
Meyrink, or Jaroslav
Hašek. Now it's an
airy, quiet place to
get away from the
tourist throng and
recharge your
batteries before
making the final
assault on Charles
Bridge.*
■

Café Slavia
◆ **B** A6 ▲ *298*
Smetanovo
Nábřeží 1
Praha 1
Tel. 224 21 84 93
Open 9am–11pm
*Built for Count
Lazansky, this was
the last palace to be

constructed for an
aristocrat. Opened
in 1863, it became
a favorite meeting
place for students
and intellectuals.
Smetana, the
composer, and the
writers Neruda and
Hašek were often
seen here. A symbol
of Czech dissidence,
the legendary café
was closed for a
long time, but was
completely
renovated and
reopened in 1997,
to the delight of the
people of Prague.
The décor has been
preserved, but there
is a new addition:
a very modern
restaurant with a
wonderful
view over the Vltava
and the Castle.*
■■■

Circle Line
◆ **A** D3
Malostranské
náměstí 12, Praha 1
Tel. 257 53 00 21
Open Mon–Fri.
noon–11pm;
Sat.–Sun.
11am–11pm
*Extremely popular
with food lovers, this
new restaurant tops
the recommended
list in some gourmet
guides. The large,*

vaulted room has
a sober décor and
the menu is quite
impressive: try the
fried veal liver or the
roasted chicken in
hot sauce.*
■

Dahab
◆ **B** C3-D3
Dlouhá 33
(entrance in Rybna)
Praha 1
Tel. 224 82 73 75
Open daily
noon–1am
*Bizarre thousand-
and-one-nights'
décor bar in the
Jewish quarter
serving passable
couscous and a
huge variety of Arab-
style coffees, teas,
and cakes. For the
full experience, sit
on the carpets in
the back room and
order a hookah pipe.*
■

Dobrá Šajovna
◆ **B** C5-D6
Václavské
náměstí 14
Praha 1
Tel. 224 23 14 80
Open Mon.-Sat.
10am–11pm,
Sun. 2–11pm
*Cukrárna (tearoom)
with a great choice
of teas.*
■

Flambée
◆ **B** B5
Husova 5
Praha 1
Tel. 224 24 85 12
Open daily
noon–1am
*You will find the
Flambée under a
porch in the narrow
Husova Street,
almost opposite
St Giles' Church.
It is set in rough-
stone, vaulted
cellars, reached
via a rather steep
staircase. The tables
are pleasantly
decked with flowers,
and the lighting is
rather subdued but
adequate. Paintings
and 17th-century
mirrors decorate the*

🔲 *< 220 Kč*
🔲 *220 to 550 Kč*
🔲 *> 550 Kč*

---

walls. Specialties:
roasted partridge,
loin of stag.
🔲

Kampa Park
◆ **A** E3-F3
Na Kampě 8
Praha 1
Tel. 257 53 26 85
Open daily
11.30am–1am
*Kampa Park is
famous for its
summer terrace
perched on the
MaláStrana riverfront
just next to Charles
Bridge but it has a
cosy back parlour
and a bright airy
front room with
a view of the
kitchen too. The
international-style
food, especially the
fish, is pretty good
too.*
🔲 ⛆ 🔼

Kinský Palac
◆ **B** C3
Týnská ulička 3
Praha 1
Tel. 224 81 07 50
Open Mon.-Sat.
noon–3pm, 6–11pm
*This cellar restaurant
just round the corner
from the Old Town
Square offers
excellent Continental
and Czech cuisine
in elegant
surroundings. The
service is particularly
attentive. But it can
be a bit quiet for
those not particularly
wishing to hear the
sound of their own
voice.*
🔲

Kogo
◆ **B** C4
Havelská 27
Praha 1
Tel. 224 21 45 43
Open daily
8am–11pm
*Kogo's is the best
mid-priced Italian
restaurant in the
centre. The pastas
and desserts are
superb and it can
often be hard to get
a seat. There is also
a bigger flashier
branch in the*

Slovanský Dům
complex on *Na
Příkopě* which has
a courtyard for
summer dining but
more variable
cooking.
🔲

Lotos
◆ **B** B4
Platnéřská 13
Praha 1
Tel. 222 32 23 90
Open daily
11am–10pm
*Lotos is a serious
vegetarian restaurant
where you can atone
for your pork and
beer excesses of
the night before.
The décor is a little
clinical and the
mood subdued if
not dead, but the
food is imaginative
and delicious. Go
for lunch rather than
dinner.*
🔲 ▭

Mlýnec
◆ **B** 4B
Novotneho lávka 9
(not marked on map,
but situated above
the Smetana
Museum), Praha 1
Tel. 221 08 22 08
Open daily
noon–3pm, 5–11pm
*Mlýnec offers an
eclectic range of
dishes to suit every
palate and wallet.
For those lucky
enough to grab one
of the few tables on
the terrace, It also
provides a great
view of the Old Town
end of the Charles
Bridge. Have an
aperatif in one of the
snugs while you wait
for your table to be
prepared.*
🔲 ⛆

Nebozizek
◆ **A** D5
Petřínské sady 411
Praha 1
Tel. 257 31 53 29
Open daily
11am–11pm
*For one of the best
views in Prague
reserve a window
table here and catch*

the furnicular railway
from Úzejd, getting
off half way up Petřín
Hill. The Czech
cuisine is indifferent
but for a romantic
dinner it's hard to
beat. And you've still
got the walk down
through Prague's
most romantic park.
🔲 ⛆

Obecní Dům
Kavárna
◆ **B** D4
Námesti Republiky 5
Praha 1
Tel. 222 00 27 63
Open daily
7.30am–11pm
*The Municipal House
café is worth visiting
just for its Art
Nouveau décor.
The service can be
indifferent and the
prices are steep but
it's still one of the
classiest places for
a coffee. You can
sit outdoors in the
summer but stay
inside for the best
view.*
🔲 ⛆

Odkolek
◆ **B** C5
Rytířská 12
Praha 1
Mon.–Fri. 7am–8pm,
Sat. 8am–8pm,
Sun. 10am–8pm
*Cukrárna (tearoom)
where the bread and
sweets can also be
purchased to take
away.*
🔲

Palffy Palác
◆ **A** E2 ▲ 262
Valdštejnská 14
Tel. 257 53 05 22
Praha 1
Open daily
10am–1am
*Palffy Gardens have
just been restored,
providing an
additional reason
for reserving a table
at the restaurant on
the second floor of
the 18th-century
palace. As you go
under the porch, you
will more than likely
hear musical scales
being practised. Do*

not be surprised as
Prague's Music
Academy is just
above. The
restaurant has high
ceilings, with
stuccos and wooden
floors, green plants
and 15 tables. On
the walls hang prints
of famous musicians.
Specialties: scallops
and duck in orange
sauce.
🔲 🔼 ⛆

Parnas
◆ **B** A5-A6
Smetanovo
nábřezí 2
Praha 1
Tel. 224 23 96 04
Open daily
noon–11pm
*Parnas, like Bellevue,
provides polished
service, elegant
surroundings, classic
continental cuisine
and a stunning view
over the river.
However, the
consensus among
the cognoscenti is
that it has fallen
behind its neighbor.
See if they're right,
go and do your own
compare and
contrast if you can
afford it.*
🔲 ⛆

Perle de Prague
◆ **D** B2-B3
Rašínovo
nábřezí 80
Tel. 221 98 41 60
Open Tue-Sat. noon–
2pm, 7–10.30pm;
Mon. 7–10.30pm
*Situated on the river
banks, above the
National Theater,
the "Dancing House"
(Tančící dům)
resembles a
concrete building
folded with grace
and care. You will
find the restaurant
on the 8th floor of
this unusual
building; it has a
bright dining room
and large bay
windows giving a
exceptional view
over the Castle. The
ceilings are high and
the tables are well*

◆ RESTAURANTS CAFÉS

Selected by Robert Anderson

spaced out. French cuisine: foie gras in puff pastry, roasted lobster and grilled turbot.

♣ ✦

Pravda
◆ **B** B2-B3
Pařížská 17
Praha 1
Tel. 222 32 62 03
Open daily
noon–1am
A relatively new hip addition to the Prague restaurant scene, Pravda has swiftly become the place to see and be seen. The restaurant is full of the beautiful people, and has big windows on to Pařížská, the most expensive street in Prague where they all do their shopping. However, the jack of all cuisines approach to the menu does not always work.
♣

La Provence
◆ **B** C4
Stupartská 9
Praha 1
Tel. 257 53 50 50
Open daily
noon–1am
La Provence was one of the first western-style restaurants to open in Prague's Old Town after 1989 and its relaxed style and competent provençal cuisine has kept it popular. Ignore the tacky go-go bar upstairs and head down to the cellar for good fish, a long wine list, and almost too comfortable seats. Early reservations essential.
♣

Radegast
◆ **B** D4
Templová ulica 2
Praha 1
Tel. 222 32 82 37
Open daily 11am-midnight
In summer, beer-

drinking competitions are organized outside the restaurant. Two teams made up of thirty men and women compete

U MODRÉ KACHNIČKY/DR

U FLEKŮ/DR

U CISAŘU/DR

to down as much beer as possible in the shortest time possible. Tucked away next to Celetná Street, this is a favorite place for the people of Prague, who can relax and enjoy the hearty food on offer here,

especially during the winter months. Good value for money. Specialties: oven-baked duck or knuckle of ham.
♣

U Cisaŗu
◆ **A** B3
Lorentánská 5
Praha 1
Tel. 220 51 84 84
Open
10am–11.30pm
www.ucisaru.cz
On your way up to Strahov Monastery, book a table at

The Emperors. The windows look down onto the Malá Strana gardens, and in summer you can enjoy the coolness of the cellars, and admire the interesting medieval weapons that decorate the rough stone walls. Lively Czech folk music is played at lunchtime, quieter piano music in the evening. The vast choice of wines is impressive. Czech cuisine features game specialties.
♣ ⌂ ♫

U Modré Kachničky
◆ **A** E4
Nebovidská 6
Praha 1
Tel. 257 320 308
Open noon–4pm,
6.30–11.30pm
www.umodrekachnicky.cz
One of the best restaurants in Prague. The emblem of this establishment is a "blue duck". Discreet colors, tinted windows, and prints and small pictures depicting hunting scenes displayed on the walls. Specialties are duck in orange sauce, rabbit old Bohemia style, and carp with cumin. Good wine list. Reservations are a must.
♣ ♫

U Patrona
◆ **A** F3
Dražického
náměstí 4
(not marked on map, on the western edge of Charles' Bridge),
Praha 1
Tel. 257 53 07 25
Open Mon-Sat
6–11.30pm
This tiny Malá Strana restaurant offers beautifully prepared continental dishes in an intimate and relaxed setting. The standard of

■ < 220 Kč
■ 220 to 550 Kč
■ > 550 Kč

the cuisine may not quite be up with the very best Prague can offer, but it makes up for it in atmosphere. In summer ask for one of the balcony tables with a view. Garden open from April 1.
■■■

U Zlaté Studně
◆ **A** E2
U Zlaté Studně 4 (not marked on map; hotel is next to Starý Královský Palác)
Praha 1
Tel. 257 53 33 22
Open daily
11am–11pm
This hotel-restaurant perched under the Castle is another strong contender for the best view in Prague but it also serves superb continental cuisine, particularly fish, and mouthwatering desserts. Go in the summer for the terrace. See p.343 for the hotel's description.
■ ■

Universal
◆ **B** B6
V Jirchářích 6
Praha 1

Tel. 224 93 44 16
Open daily
11.30am–1am
Universal has long been the leader among the pack of restaurants in the trendy area behind the National Theater (Národní Divadlo). The food is the Czech idea of French, with good salads thrown in, and the prices are very reasonable. A reliable choice before hitting the district's bars but very popular in the evenings.
■

Vinarna v Zátíší
◆ **B** B4-B5
Liliová 1
Praha 1
Tel. 222 22 11 55
Open daily noon–3pm, 5.30–11pm
The flagship of the Zátíší group – which also includes Circle Line, Mlýnec and Bellevue – tends to be overlooked among its newer and flashier peers but it's still worth visiting for its old world elegance and classic continental cuisine.
■

Zahrada v Opeře
◆ **D** E1-E4
Legerova 75
Praha 1
Tel. 224 23 96 85
Open daily
11.30am–1am
This relatively new restaurant in the back of the old Czechoslovak Federal Parliament has quickly become a favorite, despite its unpromising location on the highway at the top of Wenceslas Square. The international cuisine is very good value and the restaurant space is airy and modern. Perfect for a bite after catching a performance at the State Opera.
■

◆ PLACES TO VISIT

The ▲ symbol refers to the "Itineraries" section.
The ◆ refers to the map section.

PRAGUE

BERTRAMKA MUZEUM **W. A. MOZARTA** Villa Bertramka – Mozart Museum Mozartova 169, Praha 5, Subway B Tel. 257 31 74 65 / 257 31 84 61 Fax 257 31 67 53	*Open daily, Apr.–Oct. 9.30am–6pm,* *Nov.–Mar. 9.30am–5pm.* *Admission: 90 Kč.*	▲ 322
CAROLINUM Ovocný trh. and Železná	*University building. Also used for exhibitions.* *Open daily 10am–5pm.*	▲ 278 ◆ B C4
FORMER TOWN HALL Staroměstská Radnice Staroměstské nám. 1 Praha 1 Tel. 224 48 22 02	*Open Apr.–Oct. Mon. 11am–6pm, Tue.–Sun. 9am–6pm;* *Nov.–Mar. Mon. 11am–5pm, Tue.–Sun. 9am–5pm.* *Admission: 30 Kč. Guided tour of the Town Hall* *Meeting Room every hour.* *One of the most efficient tourist offices is located on* *the first floor and organizes guided visits to UN-listed* *Czech towns and cities (see p. 336).* *The Town Hall also holds exhibitions on the history of* *the city of Prague and the Czech Republic.*	▲ 146 ◆ B C3
STRAHOV MONASTERY Klášter premonstrátů na Strahově Strahovské nádvoří 1 Praha 1/132 Tel. 220 51 66 71	*The monastery is open to the public daily for the* *6pm service. It houses the Museum of Czech* *Literature, including the Theology and Philosophy* *Rooms: open daily 9am–noon and 1–5pm* *(admission: 50 Kč).* *For a guided tour of these rooms, contact the* *Museum four days before your intended date of visit* *to book the two-hour guided tour (400 Kč).* *The monastery also houses the Strahov Gallery:* *open daily except Mon. 9am–noon and 12.30–5pm.*	▲ 237 ◆ A A3

THE CASTLE   ◆ A C2-D1-D2-E1

CASTLE Hradčanské nám. Praha 1 Tel. 224 37 33 68 *www.hrad.cz*	*Castle area open daily, Apr.–Oct. 5am–midnight.* *Nov.–Mar. 5am–11pm.* *Castle information center (3rd courtyard) open daily,* *Apr.–Oct. 9am–5pm, Nov.–Mar. 9am–4pm.* *Admission: 120 Kč (3-day pass, giving admission to* *Old Royal Palace, St Vitus' Cathedral, Powder Tower* *and St George's Basilica).* *Guided tours Tue.–Sat. 400 Kč for groups of 5 people.*	▲ 200
FORMER PALACE OF THE **BURGRAVES (TOY MUSEUM)** Jiřská ulice, Praha 1	*Also called the 'House of Czechoslovak Children'* *Open daily 9.30am–5.30pm.* *Admission: 40 Kč.*	▲ 223
HOLY CROSS CHAPEL Second courtyard Praha 1	*Open daily 10am–6pm.* *Classical music concerts.*	▲ 213
LOBKOWICZ PALACE NATIONAL **MUSEUM OF CZECH HISTORY** Jiřská ulice 1/3, Praha 1	*Open Tue.–Sat. 9am–6pm.*	▲ 223
OLD ROYAL PALACE Starý královský palác Third courtyard	*Open daily, Apr.–Oct. 9am–5pm, Nov.–Mar. 9am–4pm.* *Admission: 120 Kč (see Castle above).*	▲ 218
PRAGUE CASTLE **PICTURE GALLERY** Obrazárna pražského hradu Left under the porch leading to Powder Tower (Prašný most) Praha 1	*Open daily 10am–6pm.* *Admission: 100 Kč.*	▲ 212
ROYAL GARDENS Královská Zahrada Beyond Powder Bridge (Prašný most) Praha 1	*Open daily, Apr.–Sep. 10am–6pm.*	▲ 224

RIDING SCHOOL Praha 1	Open during exhibitions Tue.–Sun. 10am–6pm.	▲ 224
ROYAL SUMMER PALACE Castle gardens Praha 1	Open during exhibitions Tue.–Sun. 10am–6pm. Used for National Gallery exhibitions.	▲ 224
ST GEORGE'S BASILICA Fourth courtyard Praha 1	Open daily, Apr.–Oct. 9am–5pm, Nov.–Mar. 9am–4pm. Admission: 120 Kč (see Castle above). Admission free first Wed. of the month.	▲ 220
ST GEORGE'S CONVENT (NATIONAL GALLERY) To the left of St George's Basilica Klášter sv. Jiří, Praha 1	Open Tue.–Sun. 10am–6pm. Admission: 45 Kč.	▲ 220
ST VITUS' CATHEDRAL Third courtyard Praha 1	Open daily, Apr.–Oct. 9am–5pm, Nov.–Mar. 9am–4pm. Adults 120 Kč, children and students 60 Kč.	▲ 214
SPANISH HALL Second courtyard, above the Picture Gallery Praha 1	Visits by appointment.	▲ 213
TENNIS COURT Mičovna Castle gardens Praha 1	Open daily during exhibitions 10am–6pm. Concerts, dance performances and plays.	▲ 224
WHITE TOWER At the end of Golden Lane (Zlatá ulička) Praha 1	Open daily 10am–5pm. Admission free.	▲ 223

OTHER SITES IN PRAGUE

ARCHBISHOP'S PALACE Hradčanské nám. 16 Praha 1	Not open to the public.	▲ 226 ◆ A C2
BETHLEHEM CHAPEL Betlemské nám Praha 1	Open daily, Apr.–Oct. 9am–6pm, Nov.–Mar. 9am–5pm. Adults 30 Kč, children 20 Kč. Classical music concerts.	▲ 286 ◆ B B5
BOTANICAL GARDEN Botanická Zahrada Na Slupi 16–18 Praha 2 Tel. 224 91 89 70	Open daily, summer 10am–5pm, winter 10am–4pm. Free admission to gardens. Admission to greenhouses: 15 Kč.	▲ 313 ◆ D C3- C4
ČERNÍN PALACE Loretanské nám Praha 1	Not open to the public. Houses the Ministry of Foreign Affairs.	▲ 234 ● 80 ◆ A A2
CHAPEL OF MIRRORS Zrcadlová Kaple Křížovnické nám., Praha 1	Open for concerts.	▲ 151 ◆ B A4- B4
CHURCH OF OUR LADY OF LORETO Loretánské nám. 7/100 Praha 1 Tel. 220 51 67 40	Open Tue.–Sun 9am–12.15pm, 1–4.30pm. Services Sat. at 7.30am and Sun. at 6pm.	▲ 235 ◆ A B2
CHURCH OF OUR LADY OF PERPETUAL SUCCOR OF THE GAETANI Kostel panny Marie Ústavíčné pomoci a sv. Kajetána Nerudova 22, Praha 1 Tel. 257 53 26 75	Visits Tue. and Fri. 5.30pm, Sun. 2pm, 3pm.	▲ 255 ◆ A C2
CHURCH OF OUR LADY OF THE ELIZABETHINES Kostel panny Marie Na Slupi and Apolinářská Praha 2 Tel. 224 92 05 98	Services Wed. and Fri. at 5pm, and Sun. at 9am.	▲ 313 ◆ D C4
CHURCH OF OUR-LADY-OF- THE-SNOWS Kostel panny Marie sněžné Jungmannovo nám. Praha 1 Tel. 222 24 62 43	Open Mon.–Fri. 6.30am–7pm, Sat. 7am–7pm, Sun. 8am–7pm.	▲ 290 ◆ B C5

CHURCH OF OUR LADY OF THE VICTORY Karmelitská 9 Praha 1 Tel. 257 53 36 46	*Open Mon.–Sat. 8.30am–6.30pm, Sun. 9am–7pm.* *Small museum and souvenir shop inside the church* *open Mon.–Sat.*	▲ 271 ◆ A D4
CHURCH OF OUR LADY OF TÝN Staroměstské nám. Praha 1	*Open for services Sat. at noon and 2pm,* *Sun. at 11.40am, 5pm and 9pm. Open by request* *Mon.-Fri. 3.30pm–5.30pm.*	▲ 147 ◆ B C4
CHURCH OF OUR LADY UNDER THE CHAIN Kostel panny Marie pod retězem Lázeňská, Praha 1 Tel. 257 53 08 76	*Church built for the Order of the Knights of Malta.* *Open for services Mon.–Sat. at 5pm,* *Sun. at 9.30am, 11am (Latin mass) and 5pm.*	▲ 273 ◆ A E3
CHURCH OF ST CLEMENT Karlova Praha 1 Tel. 222 22 03 64 or 221 66 31 11	*Open for services Mon.–Sat. at 5pm,* *Sun. at 7.30am, 8.30am, 10am and 11.30am.*	▲ 152 ◆ B A4
CHURCH OF ST CYRIL AND ST METHODIUS Kostel sv. Cyrila a Metoděje Resslova 9 Praha 2 Tel. 224 92 06 86	*Services Tue., Thur. and Sat. at 8am, and Sun. at 9am.* *Memorial to the Czech resistance in the crypt: open* *Tue.–Sun., summer 10am–5pm, winter 10am–4pm.* *Admission: 30 Kč.*	▲ 306 ◆ D B2
CHURCH OF ST FRANCIS SERAPHIM sv. Františka Serafiského Krisovnické nám. Praha 1 Tel. 221 10 82 66	*Open Tue.–Sat. 4–8pm.* *Services daily at 7am.* *Concerts daily Apr.–Oct. at 9pm.*	▲ 153 ◆ B A4
CHURCH OF ST JOHN OF NEPOMUK Kostel sv. Jana-Nepomuckého U kasáren Praha 1	*Open for services.*	▲ 233 ◆ A B2
CHURCH OF ST JOHN-ON-THE-ROCK Kostel sv. Jana Nepomuckého na skalce Vyšehradská 49 Praha 2 Tel. 224 91 53 71	*Service Sun. at 6pm.*	▲ 313 ◆ D C3
CHURCH OF ST JOHN OF THE WASH HOUSE Kostel sv. Jan Křtitelle Říční and Všehrdova Praha 1	*Open for services.*	▲ 268 ◆ A E5
CHURCH OF ST LAWRENCE on Petřin Hill	*Open summer Mon.–Fri. 10am–4pm,* *in winter by request.* *Services Sun. at 11am and 5pm, and Tue. at 5pm.* *Open for concerts.*	▲ 270 ◆ A C5
CHURCH OF ST MARTIN-IN-THE WALLS Kostel sv. Martina Martinská 8, Praha 1 Tel. 06 03 42 06 05		▲ 283 ◆ B B5
CHURCH OF ST PETER AND ST PAUL Vyšehradské sady Praha 4 Tel. 224 91 86 37	*Open summer Mon., Wed.–Thur. and Sat. 9am–noon,* *1–5pm, Fri. 9am–noon, Sun. 11am–noon, 1–5pm;* *winter Wed.–Sun. 10am–noon, 1–4pm.*	▲ 325 ◆ D B6
CHURCH OF ST SIMON AND ST JUDE Kostel sv. Šimona a Judy Dušni Praha 1 Tel. 222 32 10 68	*Open for classical music concerts.*	▲ 184 ◆ B C2

CLAM-GALLAS PALACE Clam-Gallasův palác Husova 20 Praha 1 Tel. 224 22 24 96	Used for exhibitions. Open daily 10am–5.30pm. Admission: 60 Kč.	▲ 140 ◆ B B4
CLEMENTINUM Křížovnické nám., Karlova or Mariánské nám. Praha 1 Tel. 221 66 32 77	Tower open Apr.–Oct. Mon.–Fri. 2–9pm, Sat.–Sun. 10am–9pm; Nov.–Dec. Sat.–Sun. 10am–8pm. Library open Mon.–Fri. 9am–5pm, Sat.–Sun. 8am– 7pm. Admission: 100 Kč. Houses the Chapel of Mirrors, also known as the Chapel of the Annunciation (open only for concerts).	▲ 150 ◆ D B6
DIAMOND HOUSE Spálená 4 Praha 1	Not open to the public.	▲ 310 ◆ D C1
FAUSTUS HOUSE Faustův dům Karlovo nám. 40 Praha 2	Not open to the public.	▲ 311 ◆ D C3
FOERSTER MUSEUM Pštrossova 17	Open for concerts.	▲ 306 ◆ D B1
GOETHE INSTITUTE Masarykovo nábř. 32 Praha 1 Tel. 224 91 57 25 Fax 229 94 21	Open Mon.–Fri. 9am–6pm. Movies screened. Library: open Mon., Wed. 2–7pm, Tue. 10am–1pm, 2–5pm, Thur. 2–5pm, Fri. 10am–1pm.	◆ B A6 D B1
GOLTZ–KINSKÝ PALACE **(NATIONAL GALLERY)** U Radnice 5	Open for exhibitions Tue.–Sun. 10am–6pm. Adults 110 Kč, children and students 50 Kč.	▲ 143 ◆ B C4
HIGH SYNAGOGUE Červená 2 Praha 1 Tel. 224 81 07 58	See Jewish Museum.	▲ 193 ◆ B B3
HVĚZDA SUMMER PALACE Pavillion Liboc (obora Hvězda) Praha 6 Tel. 235 35 79 38	Open Apr.–Oct. Tue.–Sun. 10am–5pm (closes at 4pm in Apr. and Oct.).Admission: 30 Kč Subway A (Hradčanska), trams 8, 22 (to Vypich), 1, 18 (terminus).	▲ 321
JAROSLAV JEŽEK MEMORIAL – **BLUE ROOM** Památník Jaroslava Ježka Kaprova 10 Praha 1	Open Tue. 1–6pm.	◆ C F4
JEWISH MUSEUM Jáchymova 3 Praha 1 Tel. 224 81 94 56 or 224 81 00 99 www.jewishmuseum.cz	The museum is made up of several different sites (see individual listings): – The Maisel Synagogue which houses the Museum of the History of Bohemian and Moravian Jews from the 10th to the 18th century (until the Emancipation). – The Spanish Synagogue which houses the Museum of the History of Bohemian and Moravian Jews from the Emancipation until today. – The Pinkas Synagogue which includes the Memorial to the Victims of Nazism. – The Old–New Synagogue. – The former Jewish cemetery. – The Klaus Synagogue and the Burial Guild Ceremonial Hall house the Museum of Jewish Traditions. All these sites are open Mon.–Sat., Nov.–Mar. 9am– 4.30pm. Apr.–Oct. 9am–6pm; closed Sun., Jewish holidays. Admission to the Jewish Museum only: 300 Kč. Combined ticket for the Jewish Museum and the Old–New Synagogue: adults 490 Kč, children under 6 years free.	▲ 184- 193 ◆ B B3 C3
JEWISH TOWN HALL Židovská radnice Maiselova 18 Praha 1	Not open to the public.	▲ 193 ◆ B B3

KLAUS SYNAGOGUE U Starého Hřbitova Praha 1	*See Jewish Museum.*	▲ *191* ◆ B B3
KORUNA PALACE Václavské nám. 1 Praha 1 Tel. 224 21 95 26	*Open Mon.–Sat. 9am–8pm, Sun. 10am–6pm.* *Boutiques and offices.*	▲ *174* ◆ B C5
LICHTENSTEIN PALACE Lichten Štejnský palác Malostranské nám. 13 Praha 1 Tel. 257 53 42 05	*Houses the Music Academy.* *Open-air concerts held in the courtyard (Apr.–Sep.).*	▲ *250* ◆ A D3
MAISEL SYNAGOGUE Maislova 10 Praha 1	*See Jewish Museum.*	▲ *193* ◆ B B3
MÁNÉS GALLERY Masarykovo nábř. Praha 1	*Open Tue.–Sun. 10am–6pm.* *Admission: 30 Kč.*	▲ *303* ◆ B A6
MUCHA'S HOUSE Kaunický Palác Panská 7 Tel. 221 45 13 33 *www.mucha.cz*	*Open daily, summer 10am–6pm, winter 11am–6pm.* *Admission: 120 Kč.*	▲ *232* ◆ B D5
MUSEUM OF **CZECH LITERATURE** Památnlk národního písemnictví	*Located in one of the Strahov Monastery's buildings* *(see Strahov Monastery).*	▲ *242* ◆ A A3
MUSEUM OF DECORATIVE ARTS Ul. 17. listopadu 2 Praha 1 Tel. 251 09 31 11	*Open Tue.–Sun. 10am–6pm. .* *Admission: 80 Kč.*	▲ *195* ◆ B B3
MUSEUM OF MODERN ART **(NATIONAL GALLERY)** Veletržní Palace Exhibition Hall Dukelských hrdinú 47 Praha 7–Holešovice Tel. 224 30 11 11	*Open Tue.–Sun. 10am–6pm.* *Admission free first Wed. of the month.* *Visit of one floor: 80 Kč.* *Visit of two floors: 130 Kč.* *Visit of three floors: 180 Kč.*	▲ *317*
MUSEUM OF THE CZECH **RESISTANCE AND MILITARY MUSEUM** Muzeum Odboje a dejin armády U Památníku 2 Praha 3 Tel. 220 20 49 24	*Open Tue.–Thur., Sat.–Sun., May–Oct. 10am–6pm,* *Nov.–Apr. 9am–5pm.* *Admission: 30 Kč (free on Tue.)*	◆ C D1
NA SLOVANECH MONASTERY **"EMMAUS"** Kiášter na slovanech Vyšehradská 49 Praha 1 Tel. 224 91 53 71	*Open Mon.–Fri. 7am–7pm.* *Admission 10 Kč.*	▲ *312* ◆ D B3
NÁPRSTEK **ETHNOGRAPHICAL** **MUSEUM** Náprstkovo muzeum Betlémské nám. 1 Tel. 224 49 75 00	*Open Tue.–Sun. 9am–5.30pm.* *Admission: 40 Kč.*	▲ *287* ◆ B B5
NATIONAL MUSEUM Národní muzeum Václavské nám. 68 Praha 1 Tel. 224 49 71 11 or 224 49 72 12 *www.nm.cz*	*Open daily, May–Sep. 10am–6pm,* *Oct.–Apr. 9am–5pm.* *Closed first Tue. of the month.* *Admission free first Mon. of the month.* *Library open Mon.–Fri. 9am–7pm.*	▲ *175* ◆ B E6
NATIONAL THEATER Narodni Divadlo Narodni třida 2 Praha 1 Tel. 224 90 14 4 8 *www.narodni-divadlo.cz*	*Open Mon.–Fri. 10am–6pm,* *Sat. 10am–12.30pm, 3–6pm.* *Guided tours available.*	▲ *294* ◆ B A6

NOSTITZ PALACE Nostický palác Maltézské nám. 1 Praha 1	Classical music concerts.	▲ 272 ◆ A E4
NOVÉ MĚSTO TOWN HALL Novoměstska radnice North of Karlovo nám. Praha 2	Open for exhibitions Tue.–Sun. 10am–6pm. Visits to the tower: May–Sep. Tue.–Sun. 10am–6pm.	▲ 309 ◆ D C1
OLD-NEW SYNAGOGUE Červená ulice Praha 1	See Jewish Museum.	▲ 190 ◆ B B3
OLD TOWN'S NEW TOWN HALL Nová radnice Mariánské nám. 2, Praha 1 Tel. 224 48 11 11	Open Mon.–Fri. 9am–6pm.	▲ 149 ◆ B B4
OUR-LADY-OF-THE-ASSUMPTION-AND-THE EMPEROR-CHARLEMAGNE Kostel panny Marie a sv. Karla Velikého Ke Karlovu 1, Praha 1 Tel. 224 92 21 78	Open Sun. 7am–5pm.	314 ◆ D E4
PETŘÍN HILL FUNICULAR RAILWAY Station na Újezde, Újezd Praha 1	Open daily 9.15am–8.45pm. Tickets: 12 Kč.	▲ 270 ◆ A C5
PETŘÍN PARK Malá Strana Praha 1 and 5	Open all year round.	▲ 269 ◆ A C5
PETŘÍN BELVEDERE Petřín Park Praha 1	Open daily 10am–6pm. Adults 30 Kč, children 20 Kč.	▲ 270 ◆ A C5
PETŘÍN VILLA AND GARDENS Holečkova parc Petřín Praha 1	Open Tue, Sun 9am–5pm. Ethnographical Museum.	◆ A D6
PLANETARIUM Kralovska obora 233 Praha 7 Tel. 233 37 64 52	Open Sat.–Thur. 8am–8pm.	
POWDER TOWER Prašná Bráná Na Příkopě 1 Praha 1	Open Mar.–Oct. daily 10am–6pm. Admission: 30 Kč.	▲ 167 ◆ B D4
PRAGUE CITY MUSEUM Muzeum hlm. Prahy Na Poříčí 52, Praha 1 Tel. 224 81 67 72 www.muzeumprahy.cz	Open Tue.–Sun 10am–6pm. Admission: 30 Kč. Admission free first Thur. of the month.	▲ 169 ◆ B F3
ROTT HOUSE 3 Malé nám. Praha 1	Open daily 10am–10pm. Houses a fine jewelry and Bohemian glassware store.	▲ 148 ◆ B B4
ROTUNDA OF THE HOLY CROSS Konviktská and Karoliny Světlé Praha 1 Tel. 233 35 35 47	Services Tue. and Sun. at 5pm.	▲ 289 ◆ B A4
RUDOLFINUM **(HOUSE OF ARTISTS)** Nám. Jana Palacha 2 Tel. 224 89 31 11	Houses the House of Artists and the Czech Philharmonic Orchestra. Open for concerts.	▲ 194 ◆ B A3
ST ADALBERT'S CHURCH Kostel sv. Vojtěcha Vojtěšská 10, Praha 1 Tel. 224 93 05 77	Services Mon.–Sat. at 9.15am, Sun. at 9am and 5.30pm.	▲ 303 ◆ D B1
ST AGNES CONVENT **(NATIONAL GALLERY)** Kiášter sv. Anežky České U Milosrdných 17, Praha 1 Tel. 224 81 06 28	Houses the National Gallery's collections of ancient Central European art. Open Tue.–Sun. noon–6pm. Admission: 100 Kč. Admission free first Wed. of the month.	▲ 182 ◆ B C2

◆ PLACES TO VISIT

ST BARTHOLOMEW'S CHURCH Kostel sv. Bartoloměje Bartolonějská Praha 1 Tel. 222 32 13 30	*Open for services at 11.30am.*	▲ 289 ◆ B B5
ST HAVEL'S (ST GALL'S) CHURCH Kostel sv. Havla Havelská Praha 1	*Open for services Mon.–Fri at 12.15pm and Sun. at 7.30am.*	▲ 283 ◆ B C4
ST GILES' CHURCH Kostel sv. Jiljí Husova 8 Praha 1 Tel. 224 22 02 35	*Services Mon.–Fri. at 7am and 6.30pm, Sat. at 6.30pm. and Sun. at 8.30am, 10.30am, noon and 6.30pm.*	▲ 285 ◆ B B5
ST IGNATIUS' CHURCH Kostel sv. Ignáce Ječná 2 and Karlovo nám. Praha 2 Tel. 224 92 12 54	*Services Mon.–Fri. at 6.15am, 7.30am and 5.30pm, Sat. at 6.30am, 7.30am and 5.30pm, and Sun. at 7am, 9am, 11am and 5.30pm.*	▲ 309 ◆ D C2
ST JAMES' CHURCH Malá Štupartská and Jakubská Praha 1	*Open Mon.–Sat. 9.30am–noon, 2–4pm, Sun. 7.30am–noon, 2–4pm.*	▲ 160 ◆ B C3
ST JOSEPH'S CHURCH Kostel sv. Josefa Nám. Republiky 2 Praha 1 Tel. 222 31 45 72	*Open Mon.–Fri. 6.30am–5.50pm, Sat. 6.30–8am, Sun. 7.30am–7.50pm. Services Mon.–Sat. 7am and 6pm; Sun. 7.30am and 9pm.*	▲ 163 ◆ B D3
ST JOSEPH'S CHURCH Kostel sv. Josefa Josefská 8 Praha 1 Tel. 257 31 52 42	*Open 12.30–2.30pm.*	▲ 258 ◆ A E3
ST NICHOLAS' CHURCH Staroměstské nám. Praha 1 Tel. 223 225 89	*Open Mon. 10.30am–4pm, Tue.–Sat. 10am–4pm.*	▲ 145 ◆ B B4
ST NICHOLAS' CHURCH Kostel sv. Mikuláš Malostranské nám. Praha 1	*Open daily, summer 9am–5.30pm, winter 9am–4pm. Tower open Mar.–Nov. Sat.–Sun. 10am–5pm. Admission: 45 Kč (church), 30 Kč (tower).*	▲ 251 ◆ A D3
ST SAVIOR'S CHURCH sv. Salvátora Křížovnické nám. Praha 1 Tel. 222 22 13 39	*Open for classical music concerts and for service on Sun. at 8am.*	▲ 153 ◆ B A4
ST SAVIOR'S CHURCH Kostel sv. Salvátora Salvátorská Praha 1	*Service Sun. at 9am. Classical music concerts.*	▲ 184 ◆ B C3
ST THOMAS' CHURCH Kostel sv. Tomáše Letenská Praha 1 Tel. 257 53 05 56	*Visits by request. Services in English and Portuguese.*	▲ 256 ◆ A E2
ST URSULA'S CHURCH Kostel sv. Voršily Národní třida 10 Praha 1	*Open for services Mon.–Fri. at 5pm in Czech, Sun. at 10am in Slovenian and 11am in Spanish.*	▲ 292 ◆ B A6
ST WENCESLAS' CHURCH Resslova 6 and Dittrichova Praha 2 Tel. 224 91 10 69	*Open for services Sun. at 10am (summer) and 9.30am (winter). Also used for exhibitions.*	▲ 307 ◆ D B2
SCHWARZENBERG-LOBKOWICZ PALACE AND MILITARY MUSEUM Hradčanské nám. Praha 1 Tel. 220 20 20 23	*Closed for renovation.*	▲ 230 ● 76 ◆ A C2

SMETANA MUSEUM Muzeum Bedřicha Smetany Novotného lávka 1 Praha 1 Tel. 222 22 00 82	*Open Mon., Wed.–Sun. 10am–5pm.* *Admission: 50 Kč.*	▲ *156* ◆ **B** A4
SPANISH SYNAGOGUE Dušni 12 Praha 1	*See Jewish Museum.*	▲ *184* ◆ **B** C3
STERNBERG PALACE **(NATIONAL GALLERY)** Hradčanské nám. 15 Praha 1 Tel. 220 51 46 34	*National Gallery's collections of European Art.* *Open Tue.–Sun. 10am–6pm.* *Admission: 180 Kč. Admission free first Wed. of the* *month.*	▲ *227* ◆ **A** C2
STROMOVKA PARK Bubeneč Praha 7	*Open summer 9am–5pm, winter 9am–4pm.*	▲ *317*
SWEERTS-SPORCK PALACE Hybernská 3–5 Praha 1	*Not open to the public. Houses the Philosophy* *Department of the University.*	▲ *168* ◆ **B** E4
SYLVIA-TAROUCCA PALACE Na Příkopě 10 Praha 1	*Not open to the public.* *Its three connecting courtyards house a casino,* *a theater and a Kosher restaurant.*	▲ *171* ◆ **D** D6
TOWN HALL Obecní dům Nám. Republiky 5 Praha 1 Tel. 222 00 21 00	*Cultural and information center open 10am–6pm.* *Offers guided tours of the city Sat. noon, 2pm, 4pm,* *Sun. 10am, noon, 2pm, 4pm, Mon. 10am, noon, 2pm.* *Price 160 Kč. Tours last 40 mins.*	▲ *164* ◆ **B** D3
TROJA CASTLE U Trojského Zámku 1 Praha 7 Tel. 274 00 81 11 www.citygalleryprague.cz	*Visits Nov.–Mar. Sat.–Sun. 10am 5pm. Apr.–Oct Tue.–* *Sun. 10am–5pm.* *Admission: 120 Kč.* *Admission free first Tue. of the month.* *Subway O (Nádraži Holešovice station), then Bus 112.*	▲ *318*
TÝN COURTYARD Týnský Dvůr, Malá Štupartská Access behind the Church of Our-Lady-of-Týn Praha 1	*Boutiques and restaurants.*	▲ *160* ◆ **B** C4
U HYBERNŮ CHURCH Nám. Republiky and Hybernská, Praha 1	*Not open to the public.*	▲ *167* ◆ **B** D4
URBÁNEK HOUSE Mozarteum Jungmannova 30 Praha 1 Tel. 296 24 50 24	*Open only for exhibitions and concerts* *Tue.–Fri. noon–6pm, Sat. 11am–6pm.* *Bookstore: same opening hours.*	▲ *290* ◆ **B** C6
VILLA AMERIKA Dvořák Museum Museum A. Dvořáka Ke Karlovu 20, Praha 1	*Open Tue.–Sun. daily 10am–5pm. Admission: 40 Kč.* *Classical music concerts Apr.–Oct. Tue. and Fri. at* *8pm (tickets approx. 500 Kč).*	▲ *314* ◆ **D** D2
VOJAN PARK Vojanovy sady U lužického semináře Praha 1	*Open daily, Apr.–Sep. 8am–7pm,* *Oct.–Mar. 8am– 4pm.*	▲ *263* ◆ **A** E2- F2
VRTBA GARDENS Karmelitská Praha 1	*Open Apr.–Oct. Mon.–Fri. 10am–6pm,* *Sat.–Sun. 10am–7pm.*	◆ **A** D3
VYŠEHRAD CEMETARY Vyšehradské sady, Praha 4 Tel. 224 91 99 39 or 224 92 07 35 www.praha-vysehrad.cz	*Open daily, Apr–Oct. 9.30am–6pm,* *Nov.–Mar. 9.30am–5pm.*	▲ *325* ◆ **D** B6- C6
VYŠEHRAD NATIONAL MEMORIAL on Vyšehrad Hill Tel. 224 91 99 39 www.praha-vysehrad.cz	*Open Apr–Oct. 9.30am–6pm,* *Nov.–Mar. 9.30am–5pm.* *Admission: 20 Kč.*	▲ *327* ◆ **D** B6
WALLENSTEIN PALACE Valdsteinke nám. 4 Praha 1	*Not open to the public. The entrance to the gardens* *of the Wallenstein Palace is in Letenska Street.* *Open daily, Mar. 21–April and Oct 10am–6pm;* *May 9am–6pm.*	▲ *260* ◆ **A** E2

ZBRASLAV CONVENT **(NATIONAL GALLERY)** Bartosova 2 156 00 Praha 5 Tel. 257 92 16 38/26 17	*Open Tue.–Sun. 10am–5pm* ▲ 328 *Admission: 70 Kč* *Admission free first Tue. of the month* *Bus 129, 241, 243 from Smichov Station (line B)*
ZOO U Trojského zámku 120 Troja Praha 7 Tel. 2688 04 80	*Open daily 9am–7pm in summer, 9am–4pm in winter* *Admission: 60 Kč* *Bus no. 112 from the Nadraži Holesovice subway* *station (line C), or from Trojska station (lines 5, 14, 17)* *then bus no. 12*

THE OUTSKIRTS

KARLŠTEJN *www.hradkarlstejn.cz* Reservations: SPUSC, Sabinova 5, Praha 3 Tel. (+420) 274 00 81 54 rezervace@spusc.cz (no bookings possible at the Castle) **By car:** take the D5, come off at Beroun east, then continue for 9 miles on the 116 **By train:** from Smichov Station in Prague or Hlavni nádraži	*Gothic castle built in 1348 by the emperor Charles IV to* *accommodate the royal treasure. It contains a gallery of* *portraits of Czech kings, a banqueting hall, royal chamber, St* *Catherine's chapel and the Holy Rood chapel.* *Guided tours of the castle (50 min.)* *Mar., Nov., Tue.–Sun. 9am–noon, 1–3pm;* *Apr., Oct., Tue.–Sun. 9am–noon, 1–4pm,* *May–June, Sep., Tue.–Sun. 9am–noon, 12.30–5pm, July–Aug.* *Tue.–Sun. 9am–noon, 12.30–6pm.* *Admission: 200 Kč. Guided tours of the castle and the Holy* *Rood chapel (70 mins): 300 Kč (July to Nov. only).*
KOLÍN Tourist office: Na Hradbach 157 Tel. 0321 712 021 *www.mukolin.cz* **By car:** road n° E67 (D11) then n° 38. **By train:** from Prague's Central Station	*A medieval town which has preserved its 13th-century town* *plan and interesting sites: the Gothic cathedral of St* *Bartholomew, the Baroque facades of Charles Square, and* *the old Jewish ghetto with its synagogue (1642) and 15th-* *century cemetery.* *Tourist Office open Tue.–Sun. 9am–5pm.*
KONOPIŠTE Tel. 0301 721 366 Reservations: Tel. 02 7400 8154 *www.zamek-konopiste.cz* **By car:** freeway n° E 55 in the direction of Brno then Benesov. **By train:** from Prague's Central Station	*A romantic manor house with rich Gothic, Renaissance and* *Baroque interiors. It contains the Archduke Ferdinand's* *arsenal, St George's museum, and luxurious rooms and* *apartments. Beautiful park and garden.* *Admission: 130 Kč.*
KŘIVOKLÁT Tel. 0313 558 120 or 0313 558 440 *www.krivoklat.cz* **By car:** road n° E50 (D5), in the direction of Beroun, then roads n° 116 and n° 236. **By train:** from Smichov Station	*Late-Gothic royal castle, among the oldest in Bohemia,* *housing Gothic art collections, a hunting museum, the* *Fürstenberks museum (19th–20th-century art) and a library.* *Walks on the ramparts provide panoramic views. Guided tours* *of the castle:* *Jan.–Feb., Mon.–Fri. 9am–noon, 1–3pm (reservation required);* *Mar., Tue.–Fri. 9am–noon, 1–3pm (reservation required), Sat.-* *Sun. 9am–noon, 1–3pm;* *Apr.–June, Tue.–Sun. 9am–-noon, 1–4pm;* *July–Aug., daily 9am–noon, 1–5pm;* *Sep.–Oct., Tue.–Sun. 9am–noon, 1–4pm;* *Nov.–Dec., Tue.–Fri. 9am–noon, 1–3pm (reservation required),* *Sat.–Sun. 9am–noon, 1–3pm.* *Admission: 120 Kč. Groups of 10 or more must book.*
KUTNÁ HORA Tourist office: Palackého námesti 377 Tel. 0327 515 556/124 *www.kutnohorsko.cz* **By car:** freeway D11 in the direction of Hradez Kralové, exit Nymburk-Kolin, then follow road n° 38 to Kolin and Kutná Hora. **By train:** from Masarykovo Station to Kutná Hora-mesto (central station) or Kutná Hora-Hlavní nádreži (main station, further out of town).	*A historic town which has been on UNESCO's world heritage* *list since 1995.* *Principal sites: the Gothic cathedral of St Barbara, the* *cathedral of the Virgin Mary, the Gothic palace (the silver* *museum), the Ursuline convent.* *The tourist ofice offers guided tours of the town costing from* *70 Kč to 210 Kč per person depending on the route.*

ESSENTIAL READING

◆ BROOK (S.): *Philip's Prague, Architecture, History, Art*, London, 1992
◆ NEUBERT (K.): *The Treasures from the Past, the Czechoslovak Cultural Heritage*, Prague, 1992

GENERAL BOOKS AND GUIDES

◆ ABEL SMITH (L.) and KOTALÍK (J.): *A Guide, Prague*, John Murray, 1991
◆ BATT (J.): *Czechoslovakia in transition, from federation to separation*, London, 1993
◆ BURIAN (J.) and HARTMANN (A.): *Prague Castle*, London, 1975
◆ CHOTĚBOR (P.): *Prague Castle*, Prague, 1991
◆ DENSTEIN (V.) and KOTALÍK (J.): *Prague*, London, 1979
◆ DUBČEK (A.): *Hope Dies Last, the Autobiography of Alexander Dubček*, London, 1993
◆ FLEGL (M.): *Prague*, Olympia Guides, Prague, 1989
◆ HUMPHREYS (R.): *Prague, the Rough Guide*, London, 1992
◆ KADRI (S.): *Prague*, Cadogan City Guides, London, 1993
◆ KOVTUN (G.) (ed.): *The Spirit of Tomáš G. Masaryk, an anthology*, Basingstoke, 1990
◆ MICHEL (P.): *Politics and religion in Eastern Europe: Catholicism in Hungary, Poland and Czechoslovakia*, Oxford, 1991
◆ PLICKA (K.) and POCHE (E.): *Walks Through Prague, a photographic guide*, Prague, 1984
◆ RIPELLINO (A.): *Magic Prague*, Basingstoke, 1994
◆ RYBÁR (C.): *Jewish Prague: A Guide to the Monuments*, Akropolis Publishers, 1991
◆ SADEK (V.): *The Old Jewish Cemetery and the Klausen Synagogue*, Prague, 1989
◆ SKILLING (H. G.) and WILSON (P.) (eds.): *Civic Freedom in Central Europe: Voices from Czechoslovakia*, Basingstoke, 1991

ART AND ARCHITECTURE

◆ BIALOSTOCKI (J.): *The Art of the Renaissance in Eastern Europe, Hungary, Bohemia, Poland*, Oxford, 1976
◆ *The Czech Avant-Garde of the 1920s and 1930s*, ex. cat., London, 1990
◆ DODWELL (C.): *Jewish Art Treasures from Prague, the State Jewish Museum in Prague and its collection*, London, 1980
◆ DRAHOTOVÁ (O.): *Bohemian Glass, Prague Museum of Decorative Arts*, 1992
◆ FAROVA (A.): *Josef Sudek, Poet of Prague*, London, 1990
◆ *Gypsies, photographs by Josef Koudelka*, London, 1975
◆ HASALOVA (V.) and VAJDIS (J.): *Folk Art of Czechoslovakia*, London, 1975
◆ HOOLE (J.) and SATO (T.): *Alphonse Mucha*, London, 1993
◆ LAMAROVA (M.): *Czechoslovakian Cubism, architecture, furniture and decorative arts 1910-1925*, New York, 1992
◆ MARGOLIUS (I.): *Cubism in architecture and the applied arts, Bohemia France, 1910-1914*, Woolwich, 1979
◆ *Pavel Rüchler, Untitled Portraits*, ex. cat., Glasgow, 1988
◆ *Rudolf Fila*, ex. cat., Glasgow and London, 1989
◆ SEIBT (F.): *Gothic Art in Bohemia: architecture, sculpture and painting*, Oxford, 1977
◆ ŠKVORECKÝ (J.): *All the Bright Young Men and Women, a Personal History of the Czech Cinema*, Toronto, 1975
◆ VANN (P.): *Three Contemporary Czechoslovakian Artists*, Great Britain, 1990
◆ VLČEK (T.) and SEKALOVÁ (H.): *Bohemian Glass of the Art Nouveau Period*, Prague, 1985

HISTORY

◆ CHROPOVSKY (B.): *The Slavs, their Significance, political and cultural history*, Prague, 1989
◆ DAWISHA (K.): *The Kremlin and the Prague Spring*, London, 1984
◆ KEJŘ (J.): *The Hussite Revolution*, Prague, 1988
◆ KIRCSHBAUM (S.) and ROMAN (A.) (eds.): *Reflections on Slovak History*, Toronto, 1987
◆ MASARYK (T.): *The Meaning of Czech History*, edited and with an introduction by René Wellek, Chapel Hill, 1974
◆ SKALNIK-LEFF (C.): *National Conflict in Czechoslovakia and the Remaking of a State 1918-1987*, Guildford, 1980
◆ SVITÁK (I.): *The Unbearable Burden of History, the Sovietization of Czechoslovakia*, Academia, 1990

MUSIC

◆ HOLZKNECHT (V.): *Antonín Dvořák*, Prague, 1977
◆ LARGE (M.): *Martinů*, London, 1975
◆ MIHULE (J.): *Bohuslav Martinů*, Prague, 1972
◆ MORIKE (E.): *Mozart's Journey to Prague*, London, 1976
◆ TAUSKY (V and M.): *Janáček, Leaves from his life*, London, 1982
◆ TYRRELL (J.): *Czech Opera*, Cambridge, 1988; *Intimate Letters, Leoš Janáček to Kamila Stösslová*, London, 1994

CZECH LITERATURE

◆ ČAPEK (K.): *R.U.R. and The Insect Play*, London, 1961; *Three Novels*, London, 1948
◆ HAŠEK (J.): *The Good Soldier Svejk*, tr. Cecil Parrott, Everyman's Library, 1993
◆ HAVEL (V.): *Disturbing the Peace, a conversation with Karel Hvížďala*, London, 1990; *Open letter, Selected Prose, 1965-1990*, London, 1990; *Summer Meditations, on politics and civility in a time of transition*, London, 1992
◆ HOLAN (V.): *A Night with Hamlet*, London, 1980
◆ HRABAL (B.): *I Served the King of England*, London, 1989
◆ KAFKA (F.): *Collected Stories*; tr. Willa and Edwin Muir, Everyman's Library, 1994. *The Trial*; tr. Willa and Edwin Muir, Everyman's Library, 1993. *The Castle*; tr. Willa and Edwin Muir, Everyman's Library, 1993. *The Diaries of Franz Kafka, 1910-1923*; edited by Max Brod, London, 1992
◆ KISCH (E.): *Tales from Seven Ghettos*, London, 1948
◆ KUNDERA (M.): *The Book of Laughter and Forgetting*, London, 1992; *The Farewell Party*, London, 1993; *Immortality*, London, 1991; *Jacques and his Master*, London, 1986; *The Joke*, London, 1992; *Laughable Loves*, London, 1988; *Life is Elsewhere*, London, 1986; *The Unbearable Lightness of Being*, London, 1984
◆ NERUDA (J.): *Selected Poems*, Prague, 1904
◆ *The Poets of Prague - Czech Poetry between the Wars*, London, 1969. *Malá Strana Tales*, London, 1957
◆ SEIFERT (J.): *An Umbrella from Piccadilly*, London, 1983
◆ *Three Czech Poets, Vítězslav Nezval, Antonín Bartušek, Josef Hanzlík, with an Introduction by Graham Martin*, Harmondsworth, 1971

LITERATURE

◆ APOLLINAIRE (G.): *The Wandering Jew*, London, 1967
◆ CAMUS (A.): *Selected Essays and Notebooks*, Harmondsworth, 1970
◆ CHATEAUBRIAND: *Memoirs of François René Vicomte de Chateaubriand, Vol. 5*, London, 1902
◆ FERMOR (P.L.): *A Time of Gifts - On Foot to Constantinople*, London, 1983
◆ ROTH (P.): *The Prague Orgy*, Jonathan Cape, 1985
◆ SYMONS (A.): *Cities*, London, 1903

◆ LIST OF ILLUSTRATIONS

Front cover (US):
Jewish Town Hall, litho 1898 © J.-L. Charmet / Bridgeman Art Library.

Back cover (US):
Panorama of Prague, Vincenc Morstadt, watercolor, Prague Museum © Dagli Orti.

Front endpaper:
Our Lady of Týn © S. Grandadam, Créteil. Statues on Charles Bridge, general view of Prague, ph. J. Sierpinski © Scope.
Interior of Veletžní Palace © V. Vasquez/Gallimard Guides
The Old Jewish Cemetery, ph. J. Sierpinski © Scope.
The Castle, National Museum, ph. S. Guilbert.
Reliquary book and polychrome sculpture, Theology Room, Strahov Monastery, ph. G. Roli, Milan. *Malá Strana Square, arcades*, ph. S. Guilbert.
From the nave toward the apse, St Nicholas, Malá Strana © Scala, Florence. *Kampa*, ph M. Frank. *Café Slavia*, ph. Anne Garde, Paris. *Masaryk Quay* © V. Vasquez/Gallimard Guides.
Vyžehrad Cemetery, ph. J. Sierpinski © Scope.
10-11 *The Frozen Vltava*, 1820, photo, all rights reserved.
12-13 *"Praha" bus in front of the Castle*, postcard, all rights reserved.
14 *Grocer's in the Old Town*, photo, all rights reserved.
17 *Charles Bridge and the Vltava*, ph. R.Holzbachová.
18 *Petřín Hill*, ph. Gallimard.
20 *Stromovka Park*, ph. Gallimard.
22 *Kestrels*, ph. Šťastný.
23 *Seal of Rudolph II of Habsburg*, 1603, Archives nationales, Paris © Lauros-Giraudon.
24 *Přemyšl the Ploughman*, illustration 1891, ph. S. Guilbert.
Vyšehrad Code, stamp, all rights reserved.
24-25 *Seal of Charles IV*, 1355, ph. J. Kašpar.
25 *Fresco of Charles IV, Chapel of Our Lady, Karlštejn* © Giraudon.
Vladislav II Jagiello, illumination, ph. S. Guilbert.
Crown of Bohemia, stamp, all rights reserved.
26 *Hussite charge*, M. Aleš, drawing, 1902, Orbis pub., ph. S. Guilbert.
Jan Hus at the stake, miniature, ph. S. Guilbert.
Louis Jagellon, Brožík, o/c 1909, ph. S. Guilbert.
27 *Rudolph II*, Flemish, late 16th c., Versailles © Lauros-Giraudon.
Behem, detail, map of Bohemia 1550, all rights reserved.

Joseph II, Austrian, 18th c., Versailles © Lauros-Giraudon.
28 *Frantíšek Palacký*, J. V. Hellich, o/c , Národní Muzeum, ph. S. Guilbert.
The Popular Guard and the students exercising in 1848, detail, M. A. Witka, litho © Roger-Violiet.
President Masaryk arrives in Prague, 1918, from a Hungarian newspaper of the time © J.-L. Charmet.
29 *Beneš and Churchill*, from *"La Vie tchécoslovaque"* 1939, Orbis, ph. S. Guilbert.
Demonstration in 1950 © Werner Bischof/Magnum.
Demonstration in November 1989 © D. Lefevre/VU.
Press conference by Václav Havel, November 1989 © idem.
30 *Royal crown* © Národní Muzeum.
Přemyšl Otakar II, illumination, 18th c., ph. S. Guilbert.
Saint Wenceslas, o/c, Saint Vitus' Cathedral, ph. S. Guilbert.
George Poděbrady, ph. J. Kašpar.
Vladislav II Jagellon, postcard, all rights reserved.
31 *Ferdinand I*, Kupelwieser, o/c © Art Museum, Vienna.
Equestrian statue of Rudolph II, National Gallery, ph. J. Kašpar.
Empress Maria-Theresa, o/c 1890, Václav Brožík, Town Hall, ph. S. Guilbert.
32 *Sigismund of Luxemburg*, A. Pisanello, oil on wood, Kunsthistorisches Museum, Vienna, ph. E. Lessing © Magnum.
Wenceslas IV, detail, votive panel by Jean Očko de Vlašim, distemper on wood, 14th c., National Gallery © Giraudon.
Portrait of Jan Hus, engraving © Bibl. nat., Paris.
32-33 *Jan Hus at the stake*, Ulrich Richenthal, wood-block, 1483, Polonaise library, Paris © J.-L. Charmet.
33 *Hussite Fighter*, Krumlov Codex, Prague Museum, ph. S. Guilbert.
Jan Hus, Ulrich Richenthal, watercolor © Giraudon.
34 *Ferdinand II of Habsburg*, Justus Sustermans, Pitti Palace, Florence © Giraudon.
Frederick V leaves for the hunt, detail, Anthonie Palamedes, priv. coll., Sussex © Giraudon.
Defenestration of Prague, 1618, A. Mucha, drawing © Roger-Violiet.
34-5 *Battle of the White Mountain, 1620*, litho, Bibl. nat., Paris © J.-L. Charmet.
35 *Execution in Prague,*

1621, engraving © Roger-Violiet.
Old Town Square, litho 1841, Prague Museum.
36 *President Masaryk*, V. Dlouhý, drawing, 1926, ph. S. Guilbert.
36-7 *President Masaryk arrives in Prague, January 1919*, photo © L. de Selva/Tapabor, Paris.
37 *Sudeten Germans welcome the German Army*, photo © AKG, Berlin.
Edouard Beneš, photo © Roger-Violiet.
E. Beneš' conference credentials, Versailles 1919, ph. S. Guilbert.
38 *Swastikas*, all rights reserved.
March 1939, The Germans enter Prague, photo © Keystone, Paris.
39 *1944, Soviet troops and units of the Czechoslovak Corps enter Prague*, photo © Édimédia, Paris.
Klement Gottwald, photo © Roger-Violiet.
R. Heydrich and A. Eichmann, photo © Roger-Violiet.
40 *Political poster against the occupation of Czechoslovakia*, Paris, October 1968 © Roger-Violiet.
Prague 1968, poster, all rights reserved.
Demonstrators in Wenceslas Square 1968, photo © J. Koudelka/Magnum.
Dubček, photo © D. Lefevre/VU.
Prague 1989, Aleš Najrt, poster, all rights reserved.
41 *Václav Havel on World Human Rights Day*, December 10, 1988, photo © Lobo/VU.
The Velvet Revolution, poster, all rights reserved.
42 *Kralice Bible*, Press of the Czech Brethren, 1593, ph. S. Guilbert.
Slavonic Gospel-book, detail of Cyrillic writing, Reims library.
Jan Hus, fresco, Bethlehem Chapel, ph. R. Holzbachová.
43 *Vyšehrad Codex*, Clementinum library © Giraudon.
Frontispiece of Complete Works of J. A. Komenský, © Bibl. nat. Paris.
44 *Hračky*, Toy-shop design, ph. S. Guilbert.
Na Baště, sign, 1757, ph. S. Guilbert.
Bilingual street name-plate, ph. D. Rolland.
Czech poster for the newspaper "Zlatá Práha", 1895, Museum of Decorative Arts, Paris, Maciet Collection © J. Vigne, Gennevilliers.
45 *Traditional costume of Bohemia*, Pilsen region, c. 1890, Museum of

Decorative Arts, Paris, Maciet Collection © J. Vigne, Gennevilliers.
46 *The Singing-Lesson*, wood-block, 1564, all rights reserved.
Signature of Antonín Dvořák, all rights reserved.
Antonín Dvořák conducting an orchestra, Antonín Dvořák Museum © Dagli Orti.
47 *Page of a gradual, telling of the day when Jan Hus was burnt at the stake*, 1569-1572, all rights reserved.
Bedřich Smetana, photo 1866 © Interfoto, Munich.
Portrait of Bohuslav Martinů, ph. S. Guilbert.
Portrait of Leoš Janáček, 1970 © CTK Pressfoto.
48 *Concert by Kubelík in Old Town Square* © Cedri, Paris.
Concert in Strahov Church, ph. G. Roli, Milan.
48-9 *Decorated violin*, Gasparo de Salo, Brescia, 1584, ph. M. Krob.
49 *Concert by the Philharmonia* © Cedri, Paris.
Massed choirs of the "Šedifony", J. Šedivá, 1901-1913, ph. M. Krob.
Giraffe piano, early 18th c., ph. M. Krob.
Hurdy-gurdy, with a relief of the Annunciation carved on the lid, probably Bohemian, 18th c., ph. M. Krob.
50 *The Drawing-Room Polka*, Thierry Frères, detail, litho 1844, Bibl. nat., Paris © Roger-Violiet.
Bedřich Smetana at the piano, litho from a painting, archives B. Smetana © Dagli Orti.
Škoda Lásky, polka by Jaromír Vejvoda and Vašek Zeman, record sleeve, all rights reserved.
51 *Musical score of the "Esmeralda" polka*, Frantíšek Matěj Hilmar, 1838, all rights reserved.
The Bartered Bride, Bedřich Smetana, title page 1872, all rights reserved.
The Drawing-Room polka, Thierry Frères, detail, litho 1844, Bibl. nat., Paris © Roger-Violiet.
52 *Stará pražská polka*, record sleeve, all rights reserved.
Coronation Ball of Leopold II, Frantíšek Heger, 1791, Prague Museum, ph. S. Guilbert.
Funfair in Hvězda park, Viktor Barvitius, o/c 1861, National Gallery, ph. S. Guilbert.
Czech ball in Pomněnka, 1848, City Archives, ph. S. Guilbert.
53 *Fan made for a student ball*, 1849 © Bibl. des Langues Orientales, Paris.
Dancing school © B.

360

◆ LIST OF ILLUSTRATIONS

LIST OF ILLUSTRATIONS ◆

363

◆ LIST OF ILLUSTRATIONS

LIST OF ILLUSTRATIONS ◆

ILLUSTRATORS
Cover:
Henri Galeron
Maurice Pommier
Contents:
10: Jean Chevallier, Philippe
Candé
Nature:
16–17: Jean Chevallier,
François Desbordes.
18–19: Catherine Lachaud,
Claire Felloni, François
Desbordes, Jean Chevallier
20–21: François Desbordes,
Jean Chevallier, Catherine
Lachaud
22: François Desbordes,
Jean Chevallier
History:
38–9: Philippe Candé
Architecture:
66–7: Bruno Lenormand
67: Philippe Candé
68–69: Maurice Pommier
70–1: Amato Sorro
72–3: François Pichon
74–5: Maurice Pommier
76–7: Jean-Marie Guillou
78–9: Bruno Lenormand
80–1: Claude Quioc
82–3: Jean-Marie Guillou
84–5: Jean-Claude Sené
86–8: Philippe Candé
89: Bruno Lenormand
90–1: Maurice Pommier
92: Bruno Lenormand
Itineraries:
Maurice Pommier, except
139: Philippe Candé
151: Lauro Massin
154–5: Jean-Michel
Kacédan
Practical information:
Maurice Pommier
Cartography:
Éric Gillion
Color: Isabelle-Anne
Chatellard
20: Patrick Merienne
Computer graphics:
Paul Coulbois,
Christophe Chemineau,
Antoine Fumet (mini-maps)

Where no town name is
shown above, the entry
refers to Prague, except for
ACR, J.-L. Charmet, E.
Chaspoul, Dagli-Orti,
Gallimard, Magnum, Scope
et VU in Paris, P. Jusseaux
at Savigny-le-Temple and
Giraudon à Vanves.

◆ LIST OF ILLUSTRATIONS

We would like to thank the following people for their help:

M. Petr Beránek
  (Dir. Art Gallery, Ostrava)
Mme Vlasta Cibulová
  (Villa Bertramka)
M. Guy Erismann
Mme Anna Fárová
  (Sudek Collection)
M. Nicolas Galaud
  (Municipal lib. Reims)
Mme Helena
  Koenigsmarková
  (Museum of Decorative
  Arts)
Mme Méguernes
  (Éditions Flammarion)
M. Zdeněk Mika
  (Dir. Prague Museum)
Mme Danièle Monmarte
M. Arnauld Pontier
  (Paris Museum)
Mme Hana Povolná
  (Dir. Jewish Museum)
Mme Joëlle Ribas
  (Bücher Publishers,
  Munich)
Mme Jitka Sedlářová
  (Moravská Galerie,
  Brno)
Mme Dagmar Šefčíková
  (Dir. National Gallery)
Mme Jana Vejdovská
  (Tourist Office)
Mme Nina Všetečková
  (Center for Musical
  Information)
M. Klaus Wagenbach
  (Archives Kafka)

Acknowledgements

Grateful acknowledgement is made to the following for permission to reprint previously published material.

◆ AYER COMPANY, PUBLISHERS, INC.: Excerpt from *Intimate Things* by Karel Čapek, translated by Dora Round. Reprinted by permission of Ayer Company, Publishers, Inc., N. Stratford, NH.
◆ ALFRED A. KNOPF INC.: Excerpt from *The Book of Laughter and Forgetting* by Milan Kundera, translated by Michael Henry Heim, English translation copyright © 1980 by Alfred A. Knopf, Inc. Reprinted by permission of Alfred A. Knopf, Inc.
◆ FARRAR, STRAUS & GIROUX, INC.: Excerpt from *The Prague Orgy*, by Philip Roth, copyright © 1985 by Philip Roth. Reprinted by permission of Farrar, Straus & Giroux, Inc.
◆ JONATHAN CAPE LIMITED and DEBORAH OWEN LITERARY AGENCY: Excerpt from *The Thirty Years War*, by C.V. Wedgwood (Jonathan Cape Limited, 1938). Reprinted by permission of Jonathan Cape Limited, a division of Random House UK Limited, and Deborah Owen Literary Agency, London.
◆ OXFORD UNIVERSITY PRESS: Excerpt from *Dr Burney's Musical Tours in Europe, Vol.*

II edited by Percy A. Scholes (Oxford University Press, Oxford, England, 1959). Reprinted by permission of Oxford University Press.
◆ RANDOM HOUSE, INC. and GRANTA/PENGUIN BOOKS LTD.: Excerpt from *The Magic Lantern* by Timothy Garton Ash, copyright © 1990 by Timothy Garton Ash. Rights outside the U.S. from *We The People* (Granta Books) administered by Granta/ Penguin Books Ltd., London. Reprinted by permission of Random House, Inc., and Granta/ Penguin Books Ltd.
◆ CHARLES SCRIBNER'S SONS and GRANTA BOOKS: Excerpt from *My Golden Trades*, by Ivan Klíma, translated by Paul Wilson, English translation copyright © 1992 by Paul Wilson. Rights outside the U.S. administered by Granta Books, London. Reprinted by permission of Charles Scribner's Sons, an imprint of Simon & Schuster, and Granta Books.
◆ SCHOCKEN BOOKS: Franz Kafka diary entries for November 18, 1911, and March 14, 1913, from *The Diaries of Franz Kafka, 1910–1913*, by Franz Kafka, edited by Max Brod, translated by Joseph Kresh, copyright © 1948, copyright renewed 1976 by Schocken Books, Inc. Reprinted by permission of Schocken Books, published by Pantheon Books, a division of Random House, Inc.
◆ VIKING PENGUIN and JOHN MURRAY (PUBLISHERS) LIMITED: Excerpt from *A Time of Gifts* by Patrick Leigh Fermor. Copyright © 1977 by Patrick Leigh Fermor. Rights outside the U.S. administered by John Murray (Publishers) Ltd., London. Reprinted by permission of Viking Penguin, a division of Penguin Books USA Inc., and John Murray (Publishers) Ltd.

◆ INDEX

◆ INDEX

◆ INDEX

Map section

◆ STREET INDEX

◆ HRADČANY, MALÁ STRANA, PETŘÍN

A

BUBENEČ - DEJVICE
BUBENEČ

CUKROVARNICKÁ

U PRAŠNÉHO MOSTU

JELENÍ

JÍZDÁRNA

PATOČKOVA

KEPLEROVA

KARLOVY - VARY

HRADČANY

MYSLBEKOVA

NOVÝ SVĚT

U BRUSNICE

OBRÁZÁRNA

ŠTERNBERSKÝ PALÁC
(NÁRODNÍ GALERIE)

KEPLEROVA

ČERNÍNSKÁ

KAPUCÍNSKÁ

KANOVNICKÁ

U KASÁREN

ARCIBISKUPSKÝ PALÁC

PANNA MARIA ANDĚLSKÁ

SV. JAN NEPOMUCKÝ

Hradčanské náměstí

LORETA

TOSKÁNSKÝ PALÁC

SCHWARZENBERSKÝ PALÁC

ČERNÍNSKÝ PALÁC

Loretánské náměstí

SV. KAJETÁN

NERUDOV

LORETÁNSKÁ

ÚVOZ

JÁNSKÝ VRŠEK

VL

PARLÉŘOVA

POHOŘELEC

NEMOCNICE MILOSRDNÝCH SESTER

KARLOVY - VARY

DLABAČOV

SV. ROCH

LOBKOVICKÝ PALÁC

STRAHOVSKÝ KLÁŠTER

SV. KAREL BOROMEJSKÝ

VLAŠSKÁ

STRAHOV

LOBKOVICKÁ ZAHRADA

VANÍČKOVA

STRAHOVSKÁ ZAHRADA

STRAHOVSKÁ

SV. VAVŘINEC

PETŘÍN

BŘEVNOV

OLYMPIJSKÁ

VANÍČKOVA

STRAHOVSKÝ STADIÓN

CHALOUPECKÉHO

6

JEZDECKÁ

JEZDECKÁ

ŠERMÍŘSKÁ

KINS

STRAHOVSKÝ TUNEL

KARLOVY - VARY - PLZEŇ

ATLETICKÁ

ŠERMÍŘSKÁ

SV. MICHAL

VILA KINSKÝCH

A **B** **C**

B

7

LETENSKÉ SADY

GOGOLOVA

HANAVSKÝ PAVILON

NÁBŘEŽÍ ÉDVARDA BENEŠE

ÉDVARDA BENEŠE

NÁBŘEŽÍ

KOSÁRKOVO NÁBŘEŽÍ

MÁNESŮV MOST

RUDOLFINUM

NÁBŘ.

17 LISTOPADU

DVOŘÁKOVO NÁBŘ.

BŘEHOVA

CECHŮV MOST

Náměstí Curieových

VLTAVA (MOLDAVA) →

NA FRANTIŠKU

NEMOCNICE NA FRANTIŠKU ✚

ANEŽSKÝ KLÁŠTER NÁR. GALERIE

SV. SALVÁT

SV. FRANTIŠ Z ASSISI

SV. HAŠT

KOZÍ

DUŠNÍ

U MILOSRDNÝCH

KOZÍ

OBECNÍHO DVORA

ELIŠKY KRÁSNOHORSKÉ

BÍLKOVA

PAŘÍZSKÁ

ŠPANĚLSKÁ SYNAGÓGA

STARONOVÁ SYNAGÓGA

UMĚLECKO PRŮM. MUZEUM

STARÝ ŽIDOVSKÝ HŘBITOV

VISOKA SYN.

SV. DUCH

VÉZEŇSKÁ

V KOLKOVNĚ

HAŠTALSK

KOZÍ

DLOUHÁ

STARÉ

 MĚSTO

MASN

PINKASOVA SYN.

ŠIROKÁ

ŽATECKÁ

MAISELOVA SYN.

PAŘÍZSKÁ

KOSTEČNÁ

SV. SALVÁTOR

DUŠNÍ

DLOUHÁ

TÝNSKÁ

MÁNESŮV MOST

Náměstí Jana Palacha

ALŠOVO

JOSEFOV

STARO-MĚSTSKÁ Ⓜ

KAPROVA

ŽATECKÁ

VALENTINSKÁ

KŘIŽOVNICKÁ

PLATNÉŘSKÁ

SV. MIKULÁŠ

PALÁC KINSKÝCH

Staroměstské náměstí

TÝNSKÝ CHRÁM

TÝNSKÁ ULIČKA

ŠTUPARTS

SV. JAK

CELETN

SV. FRANTIŠEK U KŘIŽOVNÍKŮ

KARLŮV MOST

KLEMENTINUM

SV. KLIMENT

LINHARTSKÁ

Mariánské náměstí

CLAM-GALLASŮV PAL.

Malé nám.

STAROMĚSTSKÁ RADNICE

MELANTRICHOVA

ŽELEZNÁ

KOZA

KAMZÍKOVA

Ovoc trh

KAROLINUM

STAVOVS DIVADL

SV. SALVÁTOR

KARLOVA

ANENSKÁ

NA ZÁBRADLÍ

 LILIOVÁ

RETĚZOVÁ

HUSOVÁ

JILSKÁ

MICHALSKÁ

SV. JILJÍ

HAVELSKÁ

SV. HAVEL

SPOŘITELNA

MUZEUM BEDŘICHA SMETANY

STŘÍBRNÁ

NÁPRSTKOVA

NÁPRSTKOVO MUZEUM

BETLÉMSKÁ KAPLE

Betlémské náměstí

JILSKÁ

V HAVELSKÁ

V KOTCÍCH

RYTÍŘSKÁ

MŽSTKU

NA

NÁBŘ.

BETLÉMSKÁ

SKOŘEPKA

VEJVODOVA

Uhelný trh

PERLOVA

28. ŘÍJNA

MŮSTE Ⓜ

Václavs náměs

KAROLINY SVĚTLÉ

KONVIKTSKÁ

BARTOLOMĚJSKÁ

NA PERŠTÝNĚ

MARTINSKÁ

SV. MARTIN VE ZDI

MŮSTEK Ⓜ

PANNA MARIA SNĚŽN

SMETANOVO

DIVADELNÍ

SV. KŘÍŽ

KROCÍNOVA

NÁRODNÍ

PALÁC ADRIA

CHARVÁTOVA

MOST LEGIÍ

MASARYKOVO

NÁRODNÍ DIVADLO

NOVÁ SCÉNA

KLÁŠTER VORŠILEK

VORŠILSKÁ

OSTROVNÍ

Mikulandská

NÁRODNÍ TŘÍDA Ⓜ

VLADISLAVOVA

JUNGMANNOVA

PALACKÉHO

OSTROVNÍ

VJIRCHÁŘÍCH

SV. MICHAL

SPÁLENÁ

VODIČKO

HRADČANY - MALÁ STRANA

BETŘÍN - MALÁ STRANA

C

A B   C

HOLEŠOVICE

KŘIŽÍKOVA

FLORENC

MALÉHO

TROCNOVSKÁ

NA FLORENCI

AUTOBUSOVÉ
NÁDRAŽÍ
PRAHA-FLORENC

PRAHA-
-MASARYKOVO NÁDRAŽÍ

HUSITSKÁ

HAVLÍČKOVA

STARÉ MĚSTO

DLÁŽDĚNÁ

HYBERNSKÁ

1

PŘÍBĚNICKÁ

ŘEHOŘOVA

OPLETALOVA

BOLZANOVA

WILSONOVA

ŘEHOŘOVA

STARÉ MĚSTO

Senovážné
náměstí

JUBILEJNÍ SYN.

VRCHLICKÉHO SADY

Náměstí
W. Churchilla

SEIFERTOVA

U RAJSKÉ

HAVELKOVA

2

HLAVNÍ NÁDRAŽÍ

WILSONOVA
HLAVNÍ NÁDRAŽÍ

PRAHA
HLAVNÍ NÁDRAŽÍ

ITALSKÁ

RAJSKÁ
ZAHRADA

ZAHRADY

OPLETALOVA

WILSONOVA

KUNĚTICKÁ

VOZOVÁ

3

LICHNICKÁ

ŠPANĚLSKÁ

ŽELEZNIČNÍ
NEMOCNICE

CHOPINOVA

U DIVADLA

STÁTNÍ
OPERA

HELÉNSKÁ

ITALSKÁ

RIEGROVY
SADY

NA SMETANCE

VINOHRADSKÁ

MÁNESOVA

POLSKÁ

VINOHRADY

4

RUBEŠOVA

ŘÍMSKÁ

BALBÍNOVA

VINOHRADSKÁ

LETENSKÉ

ANNY

BLANICKÁ

MÁNESOVA

BUDEČSKÁ

TŘEBÍZSKÉHO

VINOHRADSKÁ

NOVÉ MĚSTO

BĚLEHRADSKÁ

LONDÝNSKÁ

ITALSKÁ

ANGLICKÁ

ŘÍMSKÁ

DIVADLO
NA VINOHRADEC

ZÁVSKÁ

SÁ-

SLEZSKÁ

U TRŽNICE

ŠUMAVSKÁ

SADY

5

JUGOSLÁVSKÁ

Náměstí
Míru

SV. LUDMILA

NÁMĚSTÍ MIRU

BLANICKÁ

KORUNNÍ

BUDEČSKÁ

MORAVSKÁ

BĚLEHRADSKÁ

RUMUNSKÁ

LONDÝNSKÁ

BELGICKÁ

AMERICKÁ

FRANCOUZSKÁ

VARŠAVSKÁ

ŠUMAVSKÁ

LUŽICKÁ

NOVÉ MĚSTO

6

A B   C

BRNO - BENEŠOV

KUTNÁ HORA

◆ VYŠEHRAD, NOVÉ MĚSTO

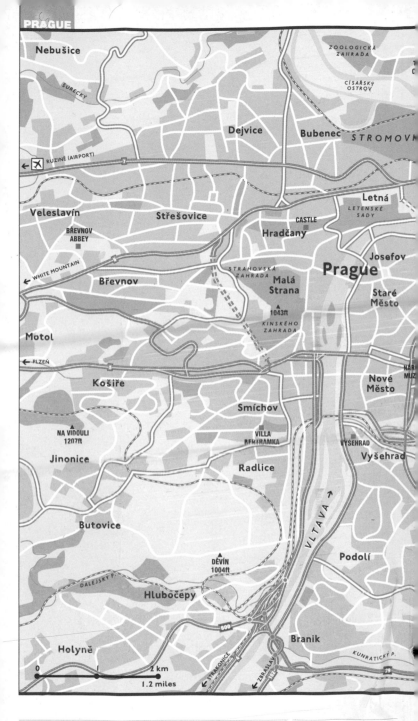

PRAGUE FACTS AND FIGURES

THE FIVE MAJOR DISTRICTS
Staré Město (Old Town); Josefov (former Jewish quarter); Nové Město (New Town); Malá Strana and Hradčany.

AREA
130 square miles
ENVIRONMENT
Green space: 2150 acres
TRANSPORT
Metro: 3 lines (A, B and C)
POPULATION
1.2 million.

ECONOMIC DATA
Economically active population by type of activity (in thousands of people) :
→ white collar: 3
→ blue collar: 134
→ service industries: 476
Unemployment: 3.5 %

TOURIST DATA
2.3 million visitors per year
HERITAGE
22 museums, over 100 art galleries. 5,000 theatrical and operatic performances a 200 concerts

◆ TRANSPORT PLAN